Contemporary Mis

C000062285

"We have good reason to be wary of mise en scène, but that is all the more reason to question this wariness ... it seems that images from a performance come back to haunt us, as if to prolong and transform our experience as spectators, as if to force us to rethink the event, to return to our pleasure or our terror." – Patrice Pavis, from the foreword

Contemporary Mise en Scène is Patrice Pavis's masterful analysis of the role that staging has played in the creation and practice of theatre throughout history. This stunningly ambitious study considers:

- the staged reading, at the frontiers of mise en scène
- scenography, which sometimes replaces staging
- the reinterpretation of classical and contemporary works
- the development of intercultural theatre and ritual
- new technologies and their usage live on the stage
- the postmodern practice of deconstruction.

But it also applies sustained critical attention to the challenges of defining mise en scène, of tracking its development, and of exploring its possible futures. Joel Anderson's powerful translation lucidly realises Pavis's investigation of the changing possibilities for stagecraft in the context of performance art, physical theatre and modern theory.

Patrice Pavis is Professor of Theatre Studies at the University of Kent. He was formerly Professor of Theatre Studies at Paris VIII University. His *Dictionary of the Theatre* has been published in 30 different languages.

Contemporary Mise en Scène
Staging theatre today

Patrice Pavis
Translated by Joel Anderson

LONDON AND NEW YORK

First published 2013
by Routledge
2 Park Square, Milton Park, Abingdon, Oxon OX14 4RN

Simultaneously published in the USA and Canada
by Routledge
711 Third Avenue, New York, NY 10017

Routledge is an imprint of the Taylor & Francis Group, an informa business

© 2007 Patrice Pavis

Translation © 2013 Routledge
Translator's note and editorial matter © 2013 Joel Anderson

The right of Patrice Pavis to be identified as author of this work has
been asserted by him in accordance with sections 77 and 78 of the
Copyright, Designs and Patents Act 1988.

British Library Cataloguing in Publication Data
A catalogue record for this book is available from the British Library

Library of Congress Cataloging-in-Publication Data
Pavis, Patrice, 1947-
[Mise en scène contemporaine. English]
Contemporary mise en scène : staging theatre today / by Patrice Pavis ; translated by Joel
Anderson.
p. cm.
Includes bibliographical references and index.
1. Theater–History–20th century. 2. Theater–History–21st century. 3. Theater–Production
and direction. 4. Theaters–Stage-setting and scenery. I. Title.
PN2189.P3813 2012
792.0973'09041–dc23
2012018569

ISBN: 978-0-415-55343-8 (hbk)
ISBN: 978-0-415-55344-5 (pbk)
ISBN: 978-0-203-12513-7 (ebk)

Typeset in Baskerville
by Saxon Graphics Ltd, Derby

MIX
Paper from
responsible sources
FSC
www.fsc.org   FSC® C004839

Printed and bound in Great Britain by
TJ International Ltd, Padstow, Cornwall

In memory of Laurent Proteau
For Marie-Christine Pavis

Contents

**12   Staging calamity: mise en scène and performance
at Avignon 2005**   242

13   Conclusions: Where is mise en scène going?   270

Illustrations

Acknowledgements

How can I begin to thank all the people who have helped me over the years of preparing this book? There are more than can possibly be thanked on an individual basis. They are in my thoughts, however, and I gratefully thank them from the bottom of my heart. I do not wish to forget those who work in the theatre, either in front of and behind the performance. The often precarious status of such people makes the task arduous and always risky. The world of performance and of art might well be going through a chronic crisis, but it is also expanding and constantly searching: it is one of the few areas where there remains any cause for hope.

This study of mise en scène since the 1990s does not claim to offer a complete panorama, a measured history of a period in which we are still immersed. More modestly, it endeavours to take note of a few trends, to map out a few genres of performance by way of specific examples. I imposed on myself the rule of only discussing productions that I had myself seen. This is obviously no mark of objectivity – far from it, in fact! Indeed, if my conscious goal is not a critical evaluation, a parade of my tastes and convictions, but rather a theoretical and historical undertaking, I know very well that theory is not above the subjective laws of critique, that it cannot eliminate all value judgements. It is in my opinion neither possible nor desirable to separate arbitrarily theoretical reflection and critical appreciation. In taking stock of a performance several hours, several days or several years later, even from notes taken at the time, memory is not only a victim of forgetting, but is also a magnifying glass, operating upon some aspects that are striking but isolated, accentuating certain high points, changing the proportions, and fixing something that was conceived as ephemeral.

No neutral or universal point of view should be expected (or feared) in such an enterprise. Mirroring theatre which, from Chaillot to the

Cartoucherie, from Bobigny to Berlin, from Lorient to Seoul, joyously scatters its missions and its illusions. Where in times gone by it was chained to the ground, theatre, having become postmodern, disappears in mid-air. How could we not wish to follow it? Do we know yet what we think, when we recall past theatrical illusions? With France under our feet and in our soul, Germany in our spirit, the Anglo-American world in the head, Korea in the heart, it is hard to follow the movement, to distinguish – somewhere between Faust and Mephisto, like the flying carpet in Murnau's film – the places where we have been, physically or virtually.

I thus thank all those who have brought me back down to earth. Marie-Christine Pavis and Jean-Marie Thomasseau were my first readers, and were merciless as well as kind. Sophie Proust, Cathy Rapin and Dina Mantcheva were the last to spot a few oversights and other omissions. Jérôme Cailleux rescued me at the eleventh hour, digitising the manuscript and photographs. I am very grateful to all the photographers who granted permission for me to use their images.

Most of the chapters were written between 2002 and 2007, following a series of lectures at the University of Kent at Canterbury, organised by Paul Allain and with the support of the Leverhulme Foundation. The questions and comments of my colleagues and my students, the distance of language and of cultural climate helped me to put together my ideas about mise en scène, a notion that remains untranslatable in their language. From that point, my life consisted of seeking out the difference between the terms and concepts 'mise en scène' and 'performance'.

In inviting me for the last ten years to give a report on the Avignon festival, Alain Girault, editor of the journal *Théâtre/Public*, has encouraged me to keep up with current work and to sift through the enormous range of theatre productions there.

Thanks are also due to those who checked the English version of the text. In particular, I am grateful to my colleagues from the University of Kent: Paul Allain, Melissa Trimingham and Ken Pickering. Thanks to their comments, I was able to clarify my '*pensée anglaise*'. And thanks finally to my translator, Joel Anderson, for his patient and thankless toil. Thanks to Maria Delgado's invitation to come to Queen Mary University of London, there I was able to work on the second edition of the French version of the book, upon which this translation is based.

This was a voyage through a turbulent landscape, where, as for Orpheus, to turn back would be perilous; it is a marvellous and painful voyage which today leads the spectator, in spite of everything, to bear witness to something barely seen from a world that is gone forever, a world that ceaselessly haunts the spectator.

Foreword

We believe we know what mise en scène is and what purpose it serves: surely, mise en scène is the visible part of theatre, that which the actors and their director have prepared for us? Surely it is what is kindly offered up to us when – traumatised by our memories of school theatre trips, half-forced and half-delighted – we return 'to the theatre', surprised that everything we learned now seems of little use. And surely it is a done deal: theatre likes the sound of its own voice when we read it and what we see of it on the stage is only any good for the purpose of impressing us, confusing our minds – and our bodies!

We have good reason to be wary of mise en scène, but that is all the more reason to question this wariness. Already, on the way home, it seems that images from a performance come back to haunt us, as if to prolong and transform our experience as spectators, as if to force us to rethink the event, to return to our pleasure or our terror. Mise en scène, in its familiar form, has existed for over one hundred years, and yet we must always remember that it has changed our ways of conceiving of theatre, and beyond that, our relationship with literature and the arts. This is stated, and quite rightly, in Pascal Charvet's preface to an excellent set of studies on *L'Ère de la mise en scène:*

> Mise en scène is thus not a random life supplement, a notebook full of pictures to give the characters a face or brighten up a book, but a way towards understanding, an integral part of the history of the play and its meaning. It is a complete *mise en jeu* (setting in play) of literature, as a reading and as writing.[1]

Mise en scène sets literature into play, without any doubt, but it also sets every artistic activity into play, every event and every experience into which mise en scène might take us. Such will be, in any case, the hypothesis of this study: mise en scène is a concept essential in judging how the theatre is set into play, and to some extent in judging how its very existence plays out.

Here, mise en scène is the culmination of theatrical creation, its completion. In this personal journey, it could come at the end, as the last part of a trilogy, following the analysis of performance[2] and the interpretation of contemporary plays.[3]

One single person, however, cannot hope to write a universal history of mise en scène in the twentieth century. The geographical, cultural and institutional contexts are too diverse and large in number. And the diversity of the genres and works demands skills beyond the competence of one individual. There is also another unexpected difficulty: any overall history of mise en scène presupposes theoretical reflection on this notion. And if the term 'mise en scène' is already confused, the notion and the reality of stage practice and types of performance are strictly intractable. Thus, here we will deal only with a 'sample' of mise en scène judged to be characteristic of stage practice from the last fifteen or twenty years. We will address the following areas:

- the staged reading, which challenges the stage by proposing ways of putting the work into the space or readings at the frontiers of mise en scène
- scenography, which sometimes replaces staging
- classical or contemporary works, which require stage practices that are sometimes different and sometimes similar
- the extension of intercultural theatre and ritual, with the example of Gómez-Peña and that of current stage productions in Korea
- new technologies and their live usage on the stage
- the challenge of the theatre of gesture and the dramaturgy of the actor
- the postmodern practice of deconstruction.

These chapters are all footholds serving to enter isolated and experimental areas, to test the relevance of the tool 'mise en scène' when applied to very divergent genres and practices.

The choice of examples, despite efforts towards maximum openness, is inevitably limited and arbitrary, in terms of the extent of scope and geographical boundaries. Thus the areas covered are Paris and the surrounding area, the showcase that is Avignon, and the results of a few excursions to the United Kingdom and Germany, and two seasons in Korea. Luckily, as will be evident, theatre itself has become internationalised.

Being 'globalised', theatre is no longer bound to any single territory, or even one culture: it travels in space and in its practices. It is up to us to follow its movement, not to seek to control it.

Where does mise en scène come from, and where is it heading? You might as well ask the same question about humanity itself, so vast is the subject!

A more modest proposition might be to observe where the term and the notion came from, to examine what purpose they had and still have.

Why did mise en scène take on a new dimension in around 1880, in the period described by Peter Szondi as that of 'the Modern Drama' (1880–1950)?* Things have always been put (*mise*) on stage (*scène*) according to some kind of system, but it was only with the arrival of naturalism, and then of symbolism, that mise en scène established itself as more than a technique: it became an art in itself, sometimes even detaching itself from the text – a stage practice in search of its own laws.

But let us merrily skip forward a century. Where are we now, at the beginning of the third millennium?

Such is the somewhat overambitious project of this book.

While it might be relatively easy to reconstruct the history of modern theatre from its key dramatic works, it is far trickier to follow the evolution of mise en scène over the century. And this is even more problematic since mise en scène, at the turn of the millennium, lends itself to a multitude of practices, to the point that one is not sure if it even remains the same thing.

To understand the present, we should study the past, and specifically the very rich history of the stage practices of the last century. In the beginning, mise en scène had to assert its legitimacy, and prove that it was neither superfluous decoration nor a derivative and arbitrary discourse. It had to prove that it was an art in itself and not the servant of literature. But today we witness its fragmentation into numerous practices. Mise en scène seems to have definitively left stage dramatisation and literature behind, in order to make alliances with other artistic practices. But is this actually the case? Where, then, has mise en scène ended up? Has it really changed? Has it changed to the point of becoming unrecognisable? A quick survey of the history of mise en scène in the twentieth century should remind us that the past well and truly paved the way for contemporary work.

---

* See Peter Szondi, *Theory of the Modern Drama*, Cambridge, Polity Press, 1987.

1 Where did mise en scène come from?

Origins and theory

Must we, once again and almost obsessively, return to the origins of mise en scène? Its appearance and the circumstances of its development were masterfully described by Bernard Dort forty years ago in a well-known article on the 'Sociological condition of theatrical mise en scène'.[1] A shift in the constitution of the audience or audiences obliged the theatrical establishment to call on the director to adapt work for the new needs of the stage. According to Dort:

> it was only in around 1820 that we started to talk about mise en scène, at least in today's usage of the term. Previously, to direct (*mettre en scène*) meant to adapt a literary text with a view to theatrical performance: the mise en scène of a novel, for example, was the stage adaptation of that novel.[2]

From 1828, the art of mise en scène, for example at the Théâtre de l'Ambigu, had its own muse, Sénéis, establishing it as an art in its own right.[3] But such dating is itself a subject of debate. According to recent research by Roxane Martin, the term was already in use at the time of the French Revolution.[4] Nevertheless, it is only in the 1880s, with Zola and Antoine (although they were following in the footsteps of the Meiningers from as early as 1868) that the director became the uncontested master of the meaning that emanates from the stage.

These disagreements around precise dates only confirm the problem of situating in time what is, in a strict sense, a new function, but one which is old in the sense that there was always, from the Greeks onwards, somebody charged with looking after the material aspects of the performance. Aeschylus himself thus wrote for specific acting conditions, composed the music, led the chorus, and took care of the costumes. In the middle ages, the 'maître du jeu' coordinated the elements of liturgical drama. The *capocomico* of the *commedia dell'arte* would decide the order of sequences and the general conduct of the performance. Molière was an actor and, as seen in the no doubt somewhat romanticised account of *L'Impromptu de Versailles*, was also in charge of interpretation – the director of actors, as we might put it today.

Despite these historical precedents, linked to the very practice of staging, we should reserve the term mise en scène and especially that of director (metteur en scène) for stage practices from the 1880s onwards, since the era of directors did not start before Zola and Antoine's radical critique of theatre or before the counterpoint provided by symbolism (at least in the context of France). This is why it will be useful to return for a moment to these early years. We will do this more from the perspective of a theorist preoccupied by current stage production that that of a theatre historian, even if the two functions can be difficult to separate.

In French theatre criticism, we note a general increase in the use of the term 'mise en scène', which has ended up referring to 'theatre' in general, or to a specific production on a stage or elsewhere. We will try to reserve this term for a system based on theatre performance, or the way in which theatre is put into practice according to a definite aesthetic and political plan.[5] It is one thing to recognise that staging Aristotle's opsis, or 'representation', plays a role at every point in theatre's history. It is another, however, to grasp the epistemological break of the 1880s and 1890s, which gave mise en scène its new status, beyond the idea of mere stage representation that is as opsis or mimesis.

Before undertaking a brief overview of a few different phases of mise en scène, we should carefully make the following distinctions between terms that are often used interchangeably.

- The *représentation* (the stage performance or production) is the concrete, physical and empirical object produced by the actors, the director and the creative team. *Représentation* also contains the idea that the stage re-presents, meaning it presents for a second time and renders present what was absent. Theatre is conceived as the repetition of an idea or of a pre-existing reality. Here one can observe a huge difference between this term and the English term 'performance': 'performance' suggests that the action is accomplished by way of the stage, and the stage cannot automatically, as is the case with the French term, be reduced to a question of the imitation of the real.
- *Spectacle* is the representation of different kinds of practices (which are sometimes called 'cultural performances' in English). The performing arts only make up a small fraction of all these

cultural performances. Theatre is no longer merely, as Richard Schechner suggests, the string quartet of the twentieth century.

- *Mise en scène* is thus a performance considered as a system of meaning controlled by a director or a collective. It is an abstract, theoretical notion, not a concrete and empirical one. It is the tuning of theatre for the needs of stage and audience. Mise en scène puts theatre into practice, but does so according to an implicit system of organisation of meaning.
- *Performance*, in the French use of the term (which translates roughly as 'performance art'), is often an autobiographical genre where the artist attempts to deny the idea of 're-presentation', enacting real, rather than fictional, actions, presented only once.
- *La direction d'acteurs* (the directing of actors) is a more recent term: it is the working relationship during rehearsals between the director and the actors (or other artists).[6]

The tendency among historians (such as Jean-Marie Thomasseau or Roxane Martin) is to go back to the start of the nineteenth century, or even the eighteenth century, to locate within the working methods some embryo of mise en scène. The acting was already to a great extent determined by the actors, and not according to any fixed tradition.[7] Our thesis here, however, will remain that mise en scène experienced an epistemological break around 1880 and that it thus took on its modern meaning, still signifying the passage from the text to the stage it is true, but increasingly doing so while enjoying the status of an autonomous art.

These details of terminology in place, we must again momentarily become historians, if only the better to understand current practices in theatre arts, practices that, as we will see, owe a great deal to the beginnings of mise en scène, to the moment where the modern world and its theatre were invented. This phenomenon is located in history at a given moment, and should not be reduced to mere performance or to the simple coordination of materials.

Mise en scène is a new notion, even if we could study in any period the specific way in which the different elements of performance are combined and interpreted:

> There was of course theatre before what we today call 'mise en scène', but something new – noticeable, sketched out, and sometimes required, in previous centuries – was institutionalised at the end of the nineteenth century: the art of mise en scène practiced by directors. Whatever one thinks of its genesis, of its nature, and of its virtues, the art of mise en scène constitutes

today the horizon of the art of theatre, just as geometrical perspective constituted that of Western painting, from the renaissance to the nineteenth century.[8]

It is a good idea to check continually, within each linguistic and cultural area, the meaning of all these terms, since they vary a great deal from one language to the next. 'Performance', in the French sense, has little to do with the usual meaning of the word in English, which is precisely untranslatable into French. As for mise en scène, which in French designates the totality and the functioning of the performance, it is usually limited in English to the visual environment of the scenography and the objects: 'This term is used to describe the director's role as visual story teller; how they choose to arrange the objects and scenery that the designer has supplied in order to create the desired environment.'[9] UK or US encyclopaedias nonetheless point to a recent extension of the notion beyond spatial arrangement:

> Strictly speaking, when applied to the techniques of stage representation the term refers to painted scenery, scenic effects, stage pieces, and properties. But it has a more expansive meaning, signifying not only the stage setting but also lighting, costuming, and all other related aspects of the spatial and temporal order of a theatrical performance. In this more comprehensive meaning, mise en scène refers to what happens in the spatial-temporal continuum, including the actions and movements of all the performers (actors, singers, or dancers) who provide the dynamic rhythm of the production. In the modern period, the role of the director is to organise all of these elements into a unified art-work.[10]
>
> In this sense mise en scène and Wagner's concept of the *Gesamtkunstwerk* are related, both evoking all the features and principles of a theatre presentation, from language, speaking, and music, to gesture, movement, and design.

A brief survey of the origins of mise en scène should assist us in understanding the provenance of contemporary mise en scène practices.

The origins of mise en scène: historical landmarks

Emile Zola

The 'invention' of mise en scène clearly did not happen overnight. It came in the wake of a long and severe critique of the state of the theatre.

Throughout the reviews, later collected in *Le Naturalisme au théâtre*, Zola becomes the mouthpiece of a profound dissatisfaction at the lack of new authors and the mediocrity of the condition of the stage. He is one of the first theatre reformers. Paradoxically, the crisis of authors, and their inability to show the world in its brutal detail, attracted and formed the basis, almost accidentally, of the naturalistic mise en scène of the future. Zola's critique begins with the actors, who he sees as slaves to ridiculous conventions, such as 'overly formal and grotesque entrances and exits, characters that always speak facing the audience.'[11] The actors 'play to the audience', 'as if on a pedestal .... If they lived the plays instead of playing them, things would change',[12] but 'the actors do not live the play; they declaim it'; 'they strive for personal success without any interest in the rest of the cast.'[13] Not only are they not directed as a group, as a director would like, but they are also not integrated into a 'detailed set [which] emerges as the necessary milieu of the work'.[14] The stage will thus have to reconstitute this milieu that determines human action, taking the risk of making scenography the 'spillway' of the text, the place where all the details of the milieu must be made visible. Such is nonetheless the function of naturalist sets: 'They took on in the theatre the importance that description took on in the novel.'[15] The use of gas from 1820 and electricity from 1880 led to the ability of light to sculpt an entire stage universe that appeared autonomous and coherent. Everything is therefore put in place to insist that theatre be reborn according to the new directives of mise en scène.

André Antoine

In the spirit of Zola, Antoine, considered France's first director, identified the same 'causes of the current crisis' (1890): the authors were mediocre and repetitive; their work performed in uncomfortable theatres where the prices were too high, they were betrayed by stars, ham-acting while surrounded by poorly trained actors, in companies lacking any cohesion. Having observed since 1874 the historical precision of the naturalist and authentic work of the Duke of Meiningen's Meininger troupe, Antoine retained that group's precise sense of detail, but also the unity of the acting and the integration of the actor within the set.

In 'Causerie sur la mise en scène' (1903),[16] Antoine gives one of the first systematic demonstrations of the mise en scène of his dreams. We find in this reflection on mise en scène a range of questions applicable to the brand new notion of mise en scène, questions that have not lost any of their significance today, so that we might still draw up a systematic list. Let us choose a few of these then new, and still relevant, points. Historical perspective should help us to follow the evolution of forms across the century, and notably the current mixture of aesthetic principles and styles.

Antoine distinguishes the role of the director of the theatre and that of the theatre director. In the old role of a 'hired hand', paid by the directors to 'sort out the play, do the preliminary work that they no doubt consider to be of little interest',[17] he sees a vital task, but one that is still barely understood – that of giving the work its first, decisive interpretation, 'the overview'.[18] But it is very difficult 'to find theatre artists who compel themselves to this fascinating but obscure task'.[19] In the early days of this new science, the director thus faced a task that was both obscure and thankless, since he still felt a responsibility towards concerned authors and famous actors. Antoine gives a few rules for directing actors, and then describes the stages of work. He cleanly divides the task into two distinct parts: 'the first is entirely material: that is the constitution of the set serving as a milieu for the action, the design and the blocking of the characters; the other is immaterial, that is the interpretation and movement of the dialogue'.[20] Good naturalist that he is, Antoine begins by setting up the stage milieu, before bringing in the actors and the second, interpretative phase of the process. But this interpretation does not deal with the reading of the story; it only targets the actual performance of the actors. The actors are asked not only to express themselves with the face and the voice, but to use their entire bodies, to live their part, without shouting or directly speaking to the assembly, to give to 'each scene of a play its own movement, subordinated to the general movement of the work'.[21] For Antoine, the milieu determines the identity and the movement of the actor, and not vice versa. The materiality of the performance is thus subject to the interpretation of the work by the director. With naturalism, mise en scène invents a setup that gives theatre its meaning back and regulates the performance. It is actually from a milieu, from a collection of details and signs, from exterior shackles, that the meaning of human actions is constituted, that the idea of mise en scène takes shape: to produce meaning from the invention of a particular setup. Thus, framed within a constraining milieu, naturalistic mise en scène is invented, and is immediately countered and contradicted by symbolist mise en scène. Symbolist mise en scène introduces the idea at the very heart of the performance, which becomes the focus of the entire performance, dematerialising it by the same token.

Beyond mimetic aesthetics and the famous 'bleeding slices of life' placed on the stage, what is important in Antoine's revolution is the material intelligence of all the operations of interpretation, his understanding of mise en scène as the production of meaning. Nevertheless, it seems that it is as the inventor of a closed milieu, complete with a fourth wall, that Antoine is remembered. Jean Vilar saw him as the one who had broken with the ancestral traditions of French theatre:

> Antoine, for his part, shut the lid. And that's what naturalist theatre is. The actor, in order to seem true, turns his back on the audience. The bleeding slice of meat. It's raw reality. ... Antoine's perspective, which was scrupulous to the point of absurdity, denied seven-and-a-half centuries of French tréteaux theatre.[22]

Vilar would have to wait for Copeau and his *tréteau nu* (bare boards, bare stage), less than ten years later, for the link with this French tradition to be re-established; at the time, the immediate counter-attack came from symbolism, which is the second source of mise en scène: an attack that was much more frontal and fierce, coming out of an entire symbolist current going back to Wagner and to Mallarmé and expressing itself best in the styles of Paul Fort (1872–1960) and Aurélien Lugné-Poe (1869–1940).

The symbolist movement

The symbolist movement was suspicious of the naturalistic stage, which it conceived as an accumulation of materials and signs. It would gladly replace it with an empty space, a pictorial sensation, or a book conceived by Mallarmé: 'A book, in our hands, if it sets forth any noble idea, replaces all theatres, not by way of the forgetting which it causes but on the contrary by imperiously reminding.'[23] Any physical presence on stage is thus troubling: 'Theatre takes place, no need to add to it.' The – never entirely controllable – presence of the actor would prevent the symbol, the idea, and the group harmony from appearing. This is what led authors such as Maeterlinck and directors like Craig to seek to replace the actor with a marionette. According to Maeterlinck, 'the representation of a masterpiece with the help of accidental and human elements is a contradiction in terms. Every masterpiece is a symbol and symbols cannot bear the active presence of man. ... The absence of man seems to me to be indispensable.'[24]

In this aesthetic, in this anxiety of dissemination, we reach the paradox of a mise en scène that refuses all materiality and seeks the single organising principle, which Lugné-Poe, without any humour whatsoever, resumes thus: 'Our desire is and will remain to make works known ... wherein the idea alone will dominate and we will attach only the merest importance to the material aspect known as theatre.'[25]

In order fully to understand the entrenched positions of symbolism and naturalism, we should juxtapose Antoine's reflections with the theatre manifesto of Pierre Quillard, 'On the absolute uselessness of detailed mise en scène'. Quillard rejects all raw reality onstage, since 'naturalism, that is the realisation of the particular fact, of the minimal and accidental document, is the very opposite of theatre'.[26] He conceives of the dramatic work as a synthesis whose characters 'are beings of general humanity' created by speech, which itself creates and replaces 'the decor along with everything else'. Are we then still talking about mise en scène, if 'the poet, mistrusting any foreign means, requires only the word and the human voice'?[27] That is the extreme position of idealistic mise en scène, brought back to the intangible idea of the author. It is as much about negating mise en scène, with its 'absolute uselessness', as it is about reducing it to a schematic view, to an idea, to a synthesis that is supposed to gather together, like the Wagnerian *Gesamtkunstwerk*, all the arts in all their perfection. But, unlike the Wagnerian total artwork, symbolist mise en scène denies its own materiality and ends up focusing on the void and on silence, evoking the world as allusive, concentrated, and poetic. As such it participates in an atemporal aesthetic that we find today in the work of Robert Wilson and Claude Régy.

This historical reminder at least reveals the double origin of mise en scène, and its contradictory nature. On the one hand, naturalistic staging attempts to imitate the world of objects and the social milieu, but it manages this only by finding other stage conventions, other types of codification, semiological mechanisms that are better hidden, which organise the real into networks of signs behind the spectator's back. On the other hand, symbolistic staging might well only make distant references to reality, but cannot entirely isolate itself from the world: living and uncontrollable bodies, and the reality effect, always find their way back to the stage, no matter how isolated it may be. This dialectic of opening and closing on the world is constitutive of every mise en scène. The works of Chekhov, which Meyerhold showed to be a fragile equilibrium between naturalist imitation and theatrical convention, best embody this double origin and this foundation of modern practice.

The foundation of the modern theatre has precise dates of birth: 1887 for Antoine's Théâtre-Libre, and 1891 for Paul Fort's Théâtre d'Art. This is also the point at which mise en scène no longer simply describes the passage of a text to the stage, but rather encompasses the autonomous organisation of the theatre work, the 'synthetic' vision of theatre and of mise en scène which is the subject of an accomplished study by Guido Hiss.[28] This autonomy would take different forms over the course of history. Here, we can only provide an outline, in order to suggest a possible periodisation of the changing conception of the art of mise en scène. Far from seeking to be exhaustive, the point here is to recognise the epistemological breaks, moments where the function of mise en scène changed radically. Of course, several models can coexist, and might even interact.

Steps in the evolution of mise en scène

In the name of pedagogical simplicity, we will sketch a portrait of a century of theatre conceived under the auspices of mise en scène. These are not schools with clearly defined programmes, but rather tendencies, or even temptations, which accompany the whole of the history of theatre. We will note for each of these phases the theory or the philosophy that best suits. We should also compare this evolution of mise en scène viewed from and taking place in France to those taking place in other European countries during the same period, study parallel developments in other countries, and attempt a history of mutual influence.

From 1887 to 1914

The double origin, naturalist and symbolist, of mise en scène only partially coincides with the polarity between *Théâtre Populaire* (Antoine, Gémier, Dullin) and *Théâtre d'Art* (Fort, Lugné-Poe). This polarity is maintained for the entire history of mise en scène until the 1960s.

Whatever the style, the director seeks to challenge the author, by helping the spectator better understand the play that is presented, proposing the director's own interpretation of the play.

1900 to 1930

The anti-naturalist backlash and research into space: Adolphe Appia and Edward Gordon Craig. Convinced of the aesthetic autonomy of the stage, these two artists and theorists seek the essential element of the performance: the actor lit in the space. The space carries the meaning, since, as Appia notes, 'the mise en scène is the art of projecting into space that which the playwright could only project into Time'.[29]

For Craig, one of the first to use the term 'stage director',[30] the 'art of the theatre' can only equal what we understand since the start of the twentieth century to be mise en scène – the use of the fundamental elements of performance, movement, set and voice.

> And when I say *action*, I mean both gesture and dancing, the prose and poetry of action.
>
> When I say *scene*, I mean all which comes before the eye, such as the lighting, costume, as well as the scenery.
>
> When I say *voice*, I mean the spoken word or the word that is sung, in contradiction to the word that is read, for the word written to be spoken and the word written to be read are two entirely different things.[31]

Craig is the originator of another conception of mise en scène: not the passage from the text to the stage (as is the case with Antoine), but the autonomy of a stage practice that emancipates itself from literature and from the author to the point of wanting to eliminate the author in favour of the actor and the director.[32] The confusion of mise en scène as the passage of the text to the stage with mise en scène as an autonomous art continues today.

1910 to 1930

The Russian avant-garde, with Stanislavski, Vakhtangov and (Michael) Chekhov in particular, is more interested in the systematic training of the actor, in the actor's interior technique, than it is with mise en scène in its visual and spatial dimension. But other artists, such as Meyerhold or Taïrov, in the spirit of the German avant-garde of the same period, conducted numerous spatial and constructivist experiments, and promoted the 'retheatricalisation' of the theatre.

1920 to 1940

The classical era of mise en scène, in France at least, is that of Copeau and of Cartel (Pitoëff, Dullin, Jouvet, Baty), which represents the apex of reflection on the reading of texts as well as the beginnings of the 'scenocratic' era, where the director controls the signs in the most rigorous way possible.

The definition of mise en scène thus becomes almost tautological: 'the activity that consists of assembling, in a particular time and a particular playing space, different elements of the stage interpretation of a dramatic work'.[33] Copeau gives the classical definition of mise en scène: 'the drawing of a dramatic action. It is the complex of movements, gestures, and attitudes, the coordination of physiognomies, voices and silences; it is the totality of the stage spectacle, emanating from a single thought which conceives, regulates, and harmonises it.'[34]

1930 to 1940

The era of rupture arrives with Artaud and Brecht. The author of *Theatre and its Double* demands an autonomous stage that is not interested in the passage from text to performance, because the performance is a unique event and 'all creation comes from the stage'.[35] This simple idea continues into the performance art of the 1960s. Artaud has an ambivalent attitude to mise en scène: he is seeking in no way to update its techniques, but rather to create a metaphysics of theatre, since 'the theatre, an independent and autonomous art, must, in order to revive or simply to live, realize what differentiates it from text, pure speech, literature, and all other fixed and written means'.[36] Artaud rejects the notion of spectacle and 'everything pejorative, accessory, ephemeral, and external that that term carries'.[37] He knows that mise en scène can most of the time be reduced to the transferring of a text to a performance, which explains his ambivalent attitude towards it. On the one hand, mise en scène is 'the truly and specifically theatrical part of the spectacle', but on the other, 'if the term *mise en scène* has taken on, through usage, this deprecatory sense, it is the result of our European conception of the theatre which gives precedence to spoken language over all other means of expression'.[38] With Artaud, we reach the point where the conception of mise en scène changes radically. No longer the stage realisation of a text, it becomes an autonomous practice: 'the mise en scène must be considered, not as the reflection of a written text, the mere projection of physical doubles that is derived from the written work, but as the burning projection of all the objective consequences of a gesture, word, sound, music, and their combinations'.[39] Dismissing Western mise en scène, Artaud opens new paths for the theatre, but neglects to show the way in practical and personal terms. Nevertheless, a new era begins for stage practice: a practice no longer centred on the text to be performed, or on the autonomous world that it ushers onto the stage; it is a practice that demands an analysis of the world and, if possible, the critical transformation of that world.

The same is true of Brecht, but for different reasons. For him, mise en scène has no inherent value, but is merely the battlefield for a confrontation between stage practice and textual material (the critical reading of a text); mise en scène takes on meaning only as a historical and political weapon. Brecht did of course stage plays by other writers at the start of his career, before staging his own work, but neither in his theoretical writings nor in his practice does he stop to consider the aesthetics of mise en scène. Rather, he speaks of the *Spielleiter* (director of acting) or of *Theaterarbeit* (theatre work). The mise en scène he limits himself to describing must tell the story in an ingenious way. The director must especially learn to recognise the contradictions of the world, choose a critical point of view, and finally change that world. Staging thus means recognising the dramaturgy of the work and finding the theatrical means both to illustrate it and, less importantly, to discover it with new eyes. For that to happen, one must know how to extract the story from the play, and thus clearly tell the tale. Mise en scène runs the risk of becoming a Marxist and Brechtian orthodoxy. This is indeed what happened with the epigones and the overly faithful readers of the *Modellbuch*, the reference book for Brecht's stagings, produced for use by future artists, and particularly associated with those operating in East Germany in the 1950s. The moment mise en scène only repeats a ready-made solution or only obeys the meaning imposed by the official politics of the moment, mise en scène freezes and dies, even Brecht's.

In one of his rare texts about mise en scène, specifically about the 'director of acting' (*Spielleiter*), Brecht, in a few lines, gives a radical critique of the main styles of his time.[40]According to Brecht, naturalism catches people in random positions, which thus have no relevance. Expressionism does not take history into account; it allows the characters to express themselves without analysing themselves. Symbolism, being interested only in the symbols behind reality, loses sight of it. Formalism is suspected of combining different elements into series of images that do not move the story forward. Brecht, who did not always escape these errors himself, still radically changed the function of mise en scène as well as our ways of understanding its practice.

1945 to 1965

Theatrical democratisation and decentralisation take place under the dual leadership of Jean Vilar, with *théâtre populaire*, and Jean-Louis Barrault, representing the 'official' avant-garde. For Vilar, 'the true theatre artists of the last thirty years are not authors but directors',[41] a declaration that does not prevent him from pushing for sobriety and austerity in the acting. For Barrault, the stage must reconcile itself with the théâtre d'art and with a scenography sometimes limited to pretty sets.

The rupture of 1968 and the political reaction of the 1970s

This coincides with the end of the economic boom and of theory, and the foretold death of the author (Barthes, Foucault, Lacan). Despite the narcissistic withdrawal of mise en scène into itself, US artists involved in performance art, music, dance or happenings (Wilson, Cunningham, Beck, Foreman, Cage, Glass) manage to open it up in order to expose it to performance art. This is also the great era of collective creation, with the Théâtre du Soleil and Ariane Mnouchkine, and similar experiments around the world. This rejection of the director nevertheless often goes hand in hand with the subsequent reintroduction of the director.

At this point, mise en scène sometimes conceives of itself as a signifying practice, an open work, and sometimes as 'stage writing' (Planchon's *écriture scénique*), which includes metatext. The 'discourse of mise en scène' is supposed to give the key to staging choices. Words considered too 'bourgeois' are avoided: *work, author, théâtre d'art, mise en scène*; instead, one speaks of *production, scriptor,* or of *signifying practices*. Rather than using the terminology of classical aesthetics, words like *event, collective creation* and *psychodrama* are substituted.

The le tout-culturel *('everything is cultural') era of the 1980s*

This, and the experience of French-style socialism between the arrival of Mitterrand and the fall of the Berlin Wall, puts experimental theatre, and even theatre itself, in a minority. Theatre becomes only one among innumerable artistic and cultural practices. The notion of mise en scène seems to dissolve all the more easily as it had to compete with performance art and all that the (Anglo-Saxon) word 'performance' brings with it in terms of pragmatism and infinite cultural variation.

Paradoxically, however, the artistic and institutional triumph of the director takes place, particularly the theatre of images of Robert Wilson. A gap forms between the sophistication of the practice and a lack of interest in theory, barring a few rare exceptions such as Vitez or Mesguich. In the same period, in the United Kingdom and the United States, the taste for postmodern or poststructural theory in universities and Derridean deconstruction rarely has any effect in the theatre world (except for the work of Richard Foreman and the Wooster Group).

The return of the text and of new writing in the 1990s

This can in part be attributed to the elevated cost of productions, a crisis of public funding and the fostering of writing. These phenomena led to a reconsideration of the role of the all-powerful director and a search for simpler and more minimalist ways of staging texts that no longer summon a flood of images and effects.

The closing of the gap between mise en scène and performance art benefits both sides at this point: performance theory and performance studies enlarge their domain infinitely, but sometimes lose a certain methodological relevance in terms of analysis. By returning to aesthetic objects and to theatrical production, they find a greater rigour, as well as tools already considered archaic, such as theatricality, whose usage dates back to Meyerhold, Evreïnoff or Copeau. But a continental and rather narrow view of the theatre, which is not very receptive to performances from the world outside France, needs performance in order to 'breathe' a bit, if only to test texts opened up in this way, inventing for them a blocking capable of 'untangling' a text seemingly too compact and barely readable on paper.

The question was no longer about knowing whether the author or the director possessed and controlled the text, or how the textual practice influenced the stage: it was more about knowing how the acting and stage experimentation assisted the actor, then the spectator, in understanding the text in their own way.

To parody Pierre Quillard's piece, we could call this essay 'On the relative usefulness of contemporary mise en scène, whether it be accurate or not'. Useful or not, this notion of mise en scène is definitely generalised, to the point of being applied to every domain of social life.[42] This leads us to question whether the notion has thus lost all its relevance. Even if the function of mise en scène has considerably evolved from the nineteenth to the twenty-first century, it serves nevertheless like an Ariadne's thread if we seek to follow the history of theatre. The different steps that have been enumerated here constitute a set of milestones and traditions that are not mere historical curiosities, but discoveries that continue to impact upon contemporary practice, '[f]or successful innovation inevitably becomes convention'.[43] The difficulty is not so much that of recognising these traces of the past, but of understanding why and how they are linked with new inventions, and as such participate in the renewal of theatre practice. Rather than writing the history of these borrowed traces and of their lineage, we will simply present a few aspects of theatre practice from the 1990s onwards.[44]

Can we do without mise en scène?

When the stage is bare, the night dark, the acting minimal, the voice neutralised, and the actor absent, is there still mise en scène?

We sometimes say, a bit hastily perhaps, that mise en scène is best when you don't notice it. Just as we say that film music is best when you don't hear it.

Must such facile sayings be believed?

The discreet charm of the *bonne régie*?

Is it the case that one genre, reading aloud, in a toneless voice, comes closest to this ideal of 'non-mise en scène', like 'non-violence', with a Buddhist attraction to the void?

Is it sometimes the case that a reading of a play by actors, script in hand, can be more engaging, more passionate, and more unforgettable than a staging that is too sure of itself?

But is this not, once again, to consider mise en scène as something visible, exterior and superfluous? As if it were something avoidable, which it would be better to do without? 'What the devil are you doing? Be more discreet', they seem to say.

At the frontier of the stage, and without denying its own status as representation, mise en scène is trying to be discreet; it is playing dead, but does that mean it is disappearing? It is often trying today to come (back) to the simplicity of reading, be it public or intimate, with invisible lips turned inwards.

What frontier is there between representation and reality? Is the frontier mise en scène?

2 On the frontiers of mise en scène

When almost all the possibilities of the stage have been tested, theatre sometimes likes to return to forms that are closer to reading than to performance. To get back to the simplicity of reading seems theatre's most urgent task. But is this even possible? Perhaps any onstage reading is already a representation of the act of reading, a mise en scène, however minimalist?

We will examine three borderline cases, where mise en scène tries to negate itself, in a reading onstage, a 'non-mise en scène', or an improvised mise en scène.

The stage reading

This is done with the script in hand, with one or several readers, who may or may not correspond to the characters of the play. More and more often, we encounter poems or novels read by a single actor.

This might be a stage reading per se, taking place in order to draw the audience's attention to an unpublished or as yet unstaged text, or to give a voice to a text that was not intended for the stage. Of late, actors have often been invited to read poetry; the genre of the poetry recital, which for a long time was not considered the best way to bring poetry to the people, is now invading theatres as well as non-theatrical spaces.

An illuminating exercise for the actor consists of using acting to distinguish several sorts of reading, and to find the sort that best suits the text to be read. Individual, silent reading is a recent invention. Until the end of the Middle Ages, people read out loud; silent reading appeared with the printing press: 'As the Gutenberg typography filled the world the human voice closed down. People began to read silently and passively as consumers.'[1] Reading to yourself, subvocalising (moving the lips and speaking a few of the words), constitutes a second step to reading at a moderate level, with the actor at your side, then reading out loud to an entire group, and finally projecting to the audience. What must be determined is the point at which the reading becomes truly public, projected for an audience that is outside the fictional universe.

Once the reading is done for an audience, the reader quickly becomes an actor since reactions to the words and the role in the fiction that is taking shape can be made out, or simply imagined. Antoine Vitez, with *Catherine* (1975), was among the first to have brought together the reading out loud of a novel (*Les cloches de Bâle*, by Aragon) and the acting of a text's characters. The border between reading and acting, between the player and the character, is impossible to draw, making every stage reading a display of speakers, and therefore a mise en scène.

And yet, even if the voice 'naturally' stages the text – since it necessarily gives a certain situation of enunciation – the reader can reduce to the minimum the visual effects, hide the dramatic choices, reduce the subtext, merely suggest some 'sketches for the staging' (Denis Podalydès). The voice must nonetheless control itself carefully: it limits itself to referencing the world by way of speech, rather than inscribing itself in the world, and participating in it. In reading the text, the reader onstage projects it into the space, creating and placing in the spectator's head a fictional universe that seems to come straight out of the words to mingle with what is shown on the stage. The reader, like the spectator, and without wanting to, 'takes off': beginning to play and to imagine an action, either real or purely imaginary. There are of course all sorts of possible readings, from the most intimate to the most acted out. Reading is not necessarily inferior to acting: the acting can be very discreet, while a reading can equally produce 'histrionics' (as Jacques Bonnaffé observes), as if the reader, especially if inexperienced, seeks to compensate by way of intonation for the apparent absence of movement and of dramatic acting. In the case of poetry – written to be read in the mind more than declaimed onstage and thus complete in itself – any vocal and gestural 'exaggeration' will seem redundant and out of place. On the other hand, a dramatic text being read remains an incomplete text waiting for a performer, and ham acting will be more acceptable than it would be for poetry.

Most readings that take place on a stage or in another space involve poetry, often read by famous actors, and this attracts a growing audience. Why is reading made into spectacle? And what has this to do with theatre?

It's a delicate question!

Strangely enough, there has been little study made of this genre of public reading of poetic or dramatic texts, as if it were a pre-aesthetic or preparatory form that is hardly worthy of our attention. And yet these actors, and the poets whose work is read, can teach us a great deal about the work (which is on the way to public recognition). This, surely, is the site of the emergence of meaning, where the poetic voice traces a theatrical path.

What is at stake in this public reading of poems is not only bringing recognition to unknown poets, it is also a question of making their voices heard, sometimes literally, when they are invited to read their own poems, but also figuratively, as many ways of saying and hearing their poems are revealed. The performance situation (when an audience attends a reading) forces the actor to choose a way of speaking, taking sides in terms of a possible meaning; the author realises for the first time that the text belongs to the other, and that it must escape the author in order to exist. Performance, the fact of achieving the enunciation of the text (using the linguistic meaning of 'performance'), and the fact of playing a certain version, with a particular understanding, make of poetry (or of any other text) a dramatic text waiting to be staged. The same goes for the audience: they are summoned to listen differently to what is either too well known, or too 'unheard of'. Thanks to the Russian formalists, we know very well that the poetic text always seems strange and unexpected, that it gives the effect of an object placed before one, as if external and observable from any angle. The point is no longer to interpret it, to reduce it to a signified, but to see it as a relative object, just as Tadeusz Kantor, onstage and alongside his actors, saw the staging as a landscape or an object to be shaped. Thus 'the poem becomes the object that is there between the actor and the audience and it is shown from several perspectives at the same time'.[1]

Non-mise en scène

This relativism of the object leads us to that of mise en scène, to the idea that it is better to limit the performance to its minimum in order to make the text heard. Some artists, such as Claude Régy, start with the principle of 'not staging': 'it should be more like going into labour; let go, knock down the walls, allow the free flow from far inside the author's unconscious, as well as the actors' unconscious, and thus, still without barriers, it reaches the spectators' unconscious'. The task of the director is therefore to 'remain suspended in the world of the written', 'to listen to the written'.[2] In order to do this, we must neutralise the 'spectacular' part of the performance and find the silence and stillness necessary for the actor's concentration. Régy would agree with Copeau's observation that 'The actor makes too many gestures, too many involuntary ones, on the grounds that this is natural. And always too much face acting. [They must] attain inner silence and calm.'[3]

The theatre, for Régy, is thus to be read in the text, which does not mean that we must return to dramatic literature, but rather that the mise en scène should be as discreet as possible in order that the spectator might enter the text:

> Provided that the staging does not smother it, the writing can constitute a dramatic element in itself, meaning that it transmits sensation and creates images. On hearing a text, the spirit generates a flow of images. The staging must remain minimalist in order to avoid formatting the spectators' vision and preventing the free development of their imaginations, as a result of what they hear and see.[4]

In practical terms, the spectator tends to become a listener – almost as if it were on the radio – relying on the actors' voices. The dim light of the stage and the slow delivery of the lines, far from sending the spectator to sleep, are supposed to sharpen the senses and focus the attention.

In his stagings of Duras, Fosse and Maeterlinck, Régy applies this system by slowing the diction and movement (as in the symbolist stagings of the late nineteenth century), and by leaving the stage in near-darkness, forcing the spectator to concentrate and to experience time differently. The director finds himself agreeing with the author whom he has best served, Marguerite Duras, leading to a 'theatre of voices with pauses and repetitions'.[5] Nevertheless, this non-mise en scène is still mise en scène: the tiniest variation of the lights or of tempo, the slightest movement of a finger, or the subtlest vocal inflection, take on huge proportions. It is thus merely a change of scale.

In a minimalist mise en scène of this kind, Phillip Zarrilli's[6] *Water Station*, based on Ota Shogo's play, we see figures moving towards a loud running tap for the entire performance: they drink or use the water in their own way. The slightest change of rhythm – either voluntary or involuntary – becomes a veritable 'mise en scène effect', and the spectator, concentrated and patient, constructs a possible story, without needing the help of a plot.

When this kind of minimal stage action is accompanied, as in Régy's productions, by a text delivered as a soundtrack playing slowly, speech takes on unexpected importance. The words spoken seem individually underlined and the listener is necessarily guided, corresponding to one of the classical tasks of mise en scène. The listener can thus get the impression that everything springs from the text, but this is only partially true: it is actually the actor, led by the director, who chooses what is to be underlined in the text – and these are precisely the choices of mise en scène.

'Non-mise en scène' is frequently the strategy chosen for non-dramatic texts, normally intended to be read and not requiring the support and the supplement of a staging. It becomes almost a necessity, given the inexhaustible richness of such texts, and given that such texts demand the greatest possible concentration, in every sense of the word.

This is the case in *Je poussais donc le temps avec l'épaule*, a montage of texts by Marcel Proust 'spoken' by Serge Maggiani under the direction of Charles Tordjman.[8] This is not a stage reading in the proper sense, since the actor speaks the lines without reading them, in the style of a narrator who speaks as if reading with difficulty, like a child who reads a text in a state of wonder at what they discover. It is often difficult to know – here as elsewhere – if the actor is living the text and speaking it or if he is reading and reciting it. Even though the actor is playing a role, that of Proust, he speaks in a way that is not at all 'natural', and seems more preoccupied with the precision of the rhythm than with the meaning of his words. And hence the sense that this is a reading, despite the recitation of a text learned by heart. As narrator-storyteller, he appears as the character Proust, but as reader, he appears as the child discovering the world and telling us about it, a child or an innocent with whom the listener might identify.

Here, too, this 'non-mise en scène' (according to quantitative and tangible criteria) is not a mise en scène, but rather its opposite: indeed it rests, almost literally, on the shoulders of the actor. Far from rendering the world of Proust, instead of giving a representation of the world of the novel, Serge Maggiani chooses to say the lines with a physical attitude that suggests the lightness of the reader faced with the immense Proustian body of work. The strange title, *Je poussais donc le temps avec l'épaule*, must be taken literally. Through his posture, his voice and his phrasing, the actor places himself in a new physical relationship with the text of the novel. This is not an attempt to incarnate Proust and his characters, but to find a body, a posture and a voice that can 'push time with the shoulder'; thus Proust's words are produced by a voice in the space, as if pushed along by an invisible shoulder. This shoulder pushing time, this effort to 'ex-press' the Proustian sentence, are made physically palpable by the clumsy stiffness. The stage arrangement (a white box with a screen at the back changing colour) and the actor's delivery, his place in space and duration, make felt the pushing and the physical contraction as much as the tormented but fluid complexity of the sentences. The contraction of the shoulder, of the neck, of the fingers physically signify the child's anxiety ('Mother would probably come'). Maggiani's work consists of preparing the listener for the Proustian sentence, of physically communicating the bodily effort of remembrance through stiffness and the sidelong glance.

This production is an example of the minimalist staging of non-dramatic texts, as well as of the role of the speaking body, in the reading as well as in the words uttered onstage. The body pushes the text, it gives it to be heard, pushing a certain meaning. We only need show this meaning by way of the acting or the voice. Staging a text is less about placing the text into the body than about placing the body into the text. The actor does not so much seek to characterise a character as to be inserted into the text in order to feel physically its unfolding and its trajectory; the actor must feel the resistance of the textual material when pushed by a body. The actor confronts the spectator who looks to the actor for a representative and an acting force in the fictional world; the actor pushes the body laterally in the verbal temporality of the sentence. Thus laterality replaces frontality: it seeks to follow the movement of a sentence rather than to represent a lost universe. The body, alone, recovers memory and experiences the worlds by testing it against the other's gaze.

Mise en scène and dramatic criticism

Mise en scène at the heart of criticism

From the concerned perspective of theatre theory, the question might be put in these terms: how does dramatic criticism, such as appears in the press and the audiovisual media, help one to appreciate (in every sense of the term) mise en scène? Instead of looking down on criticism, subtle theory should instead raise its eyes toward it – and it would gain a great deal in doing so.

Our theoretical hypothesis is that mise en scène is the most useful, and indeed the central, notion for evaluating a performance, not only for the purposes of analysis, but also for making an aesthetic judgement. The notion of mise en scène is nonetheless far from being universal, and the term, though internationally known, has a specific meaning in each cultural context. In France, mise en scène initially designated the passage of the dramatic text to the stage. Then it rapidly came specifically to signify the stage work, the performance and the show, as opposed to the script or the written score for the stage acting. To this empirical (and contemporary) conception of mise en scène must be added the one employed here, which is more precise and technical, theoretical and semiological, designating a system of meaning and options for staging. We should thus distinguish between performance analysis, which describes the various signs of the performance in an empirical and positivist way, and the analysis of mise en scène, which offers a theory of its overall operations. Dramatic criticism draws on both kinds of analysis, but of particular interest here is criticism wherein mise en scène is considered as a more or less coherent system. Such criticism is actually well placed to convey the options of mise en scène, to reveal its system: the *Konzept* (as Germans say), the dramaturgy (as Brechtians say), or what is known in English as the acting or staging style. The big challenge is to find out whether these global notions are still pertinent for work from the last ten years. The dramatic criticism envisaged here is primarily that featured in the daily press, but at least in a French context, we should also consider previews in weekly publications, radio and television programmes, and audience discussion groups on the internet.

Crisis of mise en scène, crisis of criticism

Until the 1980s, French critics were aware that their craft was caught between two functions: supplying information for the general public and engaging in intellectual criticism, destined for academics, industry professionals or artists themselves. For Thibaudet,[9] the model is a trinity with the following parts: 'criticism for normal folk, criticism for professionals and criticism for artists'. More often, however, the model is binary: thus Bernard Dort[10] opposes a 'consumer criticism' with 'another criticism (which is) both critical of the theatrical fact as an aesthetic fact and critical of the social and political conditions of the activity of theatre.' Criticism is thus 'equally outside and inside'.[11] Later, Dort[12] would go on to attempt a delicate dialectic between two types of criticism: 'traditional criticism, with a journalistic bent', of an 'ideal average spectator', on the one hand, and the 'scientific or academic' speech of 'Theaterwissenschaft or theatrology' on the other. The synthesis of these, the 'third party', who is 'both outside and inside', the 'concerned spectator ... must have theatrical knowledge, be it historical or semiological', a knowledge that the critic does not 'apply to the show', but rather 'subjects to the test of theatrical representation.'[13] Georges Banu returns to this dualism: for Banu, criticism depends as much on the 'enlightened amateur' as on the 'dramaturg in the German sense of the word', who 'disposes of a theory, a certainty ... that he stubbornly endeavours to realise'.[14] This French tradition probably resembles that found in many other countries, in other forms. It is in no way universal, however, and the German critic Henning Rischbieter, for a long time the editor of *Theater heute*, proposes an entirely different distribution of the tasks of criticism, which corresponds, he claims, to three premises: 1) that criticism is a branch of journalism and news; 2) that criticism has an economic impact; 3) that criticism produces a literary output since it requires an artistic talent in the writer.[15] The absence of reflection on dramaturgy or mise en scène might shock somebody familiar with the French tradition; we might wonder if this absence bears witness to a certain cynicism and eclecticism or whether, conversely, it is a position of extreme open-mindedness.

Criticism and theory

Another kind of interference concerns the old distinction between journalistic criticism and theoretical academic writing. It is unclear whether this interference is something we should be proud of, but clearly the distinction is becoming blurred. The printed press is no longer charged with providing an immediate response to stage events, it has been beaten to first place by the other media, and blogs and internet forums. Many critics now publish their accounts a week, a month or even a year after seeing the show. There are academics that follow and support this group or that trend, appearing to be the artists' accomplices. This is understandable, given that the university, in Europe and in the United States, has abandoned the practice of proposing theoretical models, instead opting to become the conservatoire of know-how and factory of the ready-made, of poststructuralism and the post-dramatic. Its image as the home of scientificity, impartiality, rigour, and even of intellectual honesty has suffered a great deal. The good news, however, is that critics (who live from one day to the next) and theorists (who live from one season to the next) are in the same boat, and can no longer be pitched against one another.

For the first time, mise en scène is asking the critic the right question – it is a question of trust: how can readers, as future or potential spectators, learn to decipher, or simply accept, the work? The question is aimed at critical experts as well as mere mortals! The raw common sense of earlier critics will no longer suffice. Their only response to the question 'What does it mean?' is to perform a pirouette: 'What do you see in it?' They are no longer in any position to provide a guide to the uses of mise en scène. The passing perplexity that, according to Banu, once guaranteed the 'regeneration of criticism',[16] has become the norm for everyone.

This being the case, it is not surprising that dramaturgical analysis and research on the choices taken by the mise en scène are coming to an end. The melting pot of genres (comic, tragic, grotesque, absurd), and the multiplicity of registers, cloud the issue. The critic must put forth a hypothesis on the functioning of mise en scène, its system or its main threads, in order to help the perplexed spectator. But such a hypothesis might be misleading, or might lose the spectator if it is revealed to be false or forced.

There can be no doubt the change of paradigm for mise en scène practice has rendered analytic grids ineffective, at least temporarily.[17] The structural, functionalist, semiological conception of mise en scène, which imagined the show as a spectacular text and a semiotic system, is no longer in circulation. This is not entirely new, even if French criticism has not yet taken note of it. Theatre seems to have discovered that the essential element does not reside in the result, in the finished work, but in the process, and in the effect produced. Mise en scène has become performance (and the English word 'performance' is indeed the only way to describe this): it participates in an action, and is in a permanent state of becoming. The spectacle must be somehow envisaged from both its extremities: its origins and its extensions. This enables us to understand where performative action comes from and where it is heading.

The object of criticism

Are we once again faced with a stable, graspable, describable aesthetic object? Has the object of analysis, mise en scène, once again acquired a tangible aspect? Has it become, like the art objects described by Yves Michaud, 'art in a gaseous state'? Are the products of mise en scène soluble in air, reducible to single aesthetic experience for the spectator? Such aesthetic experience is the only thing that remains when we turn away from the stage object in favour of its mode of reception. What is true for the visual arts is true also for mise en scène, which is made up of objects that are even more fragile and which disappear as time goes by: the works 'no longer aim to represent nor to signify. They do not refer to anything beyond themselves: they no longer symbolise. They no longer even count as objects-made-sacred but aim directly to produce intense or specific experiences.'[18] We are in a paradoxical situation as we face, or rather as we enter, the work: it is material, sensuous and physical. But at the same time, what counts is no longer this materiality, but rather the experience into which we find ourselves plunged. Thus the work dematerialises itself, becomes virtual, and prevents us from being able to distinguish its properties or its meaning. In the 1980s, the critic was at least guaranteed the presence of a body of the same generation.[19] At the present time, the critic has the slight sense of losing this empirical body, as the performance dematerialises itself and the spectator, recovering an imaginary body, withdraws into aesthetic experience. To put it another way, the critic's body is lost just as the spectator's body is gained (and it is hard to say who gets the better deal!).

This withdrawal is difficult to halt. Nevertheless, criticism, preoccupied with the description of representation as a whole, continually returns to the stage/d system. Mitter and Shevtsova's recent study of fifty theatre directors concludes with the authors taking a distance from the term directing (mise en scène) in favour of embracing the body in movement.[20] This corporeal action in movement must thus become the object of criticism of mise en scène. Instead of comparing text and its stage concretisation (as criticism has been doing for a long time), it is appropriate instead to reveal the logic of the body in movement as well as that of the space–time in which it is to be found. If criticism, and in turn the spectator, is preoccupied with the whole show, and not with the isolated details, they protect us from the effects of switching between channels (if I don't like something, I switch to something else). There remains nonetheless the extreme difficulty of reading and deciphering the show in its internal logic and in terms of its references to our world. It is difficult but not impossible.

New tasks for dramatic criticism faced with the renewal of mise en scène

In addition to this widening of perspectives (which dramatic criticism has in fact always practised), it is necessary to venture to give criticism new tasks, precisely in the domains that political correctness carefully avoids. What might these tasks be? Let us list just a few:

- To take on, and make explicit, value judgements. This is something which criticism, like theory, cannot avoid. To accept that there exists a risk of legitimisation when any discourse on an artist, a movement, or a way of working, is proposed, even if it is a negative discourse. Nonetheless to remain aware of the relativity of this judgement in giving the reader the possibility of contesting or deconstructing it.
- To have (and raise) awareness about the cultural identity of whoever passes judgement, while still allowing them the right to talk about what does not concern them (another culture, another milieu, another identity, another religion). To delocalise critics. To make critics analyse works that are foreign to them. To be untroubled by legitimacy, authenticity, fundamentalism, even by cultural nature.
- To reaffirm the importance of mise en scène and of the director as mediator between the work and the audience. As was said in the 1980s, when Vitez arrived at Chaillot: 'we will defend the function, the very existence of mise en scène, which is once again, today, contested in principle. We will not let ourselves get stuck in the ineffable relationship of the actor to the text and to the audience.'[21] Vitez's lesson has not been forgotten; it is as true for criticism as it is for mise en scène.

The critic, too, is a species in danger of extinction, and yet, like the director, the critic is essential as a mediator between the stage and the auditorium. The critic and the director are old comrades, old friends, each obliged to hear what the other has to say for fear of both becoming extinct.

Mise en scène thus remains in all respects the territory and the stakes of theatrical production and dramatic criticism.

Improvised mise en scène

If a non-mise en scène turns out to be very sophisticated work, which is tightly controlled by the director as well as the actor, then there is a strong chance that an improvised mise en scène will only turn out to be half-improvised. We should nevertheless take very seriously the desire of a director like Christian Rist[22] to propose a 'recital' (a provisional term) of Rimbaud's *Illuminations*, one that is not fixed in advance like a poem recital performed by three theatre actors. In fact, nothing is fixed from one evening to the next: not the choice of texts, or their running order, or the identity of their performer, or the meaning that each interpretation is supposed to draw from them. The lighting is set up in a random fashion; the duration of the performance varies according to the performers. The only fixed givens are the literality of the poems, and the stage arrangement specially designed for the piece: an amphitheatre in light wood around a central area covered in a light-reflecting surface. The audience is very close to the performers, who move around on the raised audience area as well as within the rectangular stage space where Rimbaud's works have been carelessly left, in the unlikely event that the actors might need to refer to them.

The improvisation in the diction of the texts is not limited to intonation or to any such antics. The improvisation consists of deciding when to speak, choosing a poem, and – importantly – finding an impulse. Unlike a text that is read, the text learned by heart is available in the body, ready to be mobilised at any moment. Each performer, in order to capture the decisive moment, must be sensitive to the other two performers, and must be inspired by the spatial and physical relationships being woven between performers. A word or a theme from a poem sometimes unleashes an impulse, motivates a movement, produces an effect of echoing, but such encounters tend to be accidental: they merely rhythmically relaunch the interactions. The approach taken to the texts resembles the approach to reading proposed by Rimbaud: literal and done in every possible way. Freed from linearity, the approach allows a network of poems to be heard and seen; the clashing and chance meetings of different sounds and themes sometimes fit together perfectly.

In the sphere of research, mise en scène has more than a hundred years of accumulating material and experience behind it. But the saturation of signs has been observed for some time: the symbolists were already complaining about it as early as 1890. Performance art, emerging in France in the 1960s, belongs to an Anglo-American cultural tradition, where it is commonplace, constitutive of performativity. And yet we

Figure 2.1 Les illuminations by Rimbaud, directed by Christian Rist.
© Christian Rist.

might well be witnessing a shift from theatricality that is too lavishly staged, to performativity, which is a prolongation of drama. The theatricality and dramaticity are indivisible in Western dramaturgy, and they are also what enable the comparison and confrontation between European forms and cultural performances and performance practices from the rest of the world. These three borderline cases of mise en scène – reading, self-negating mise en scène and relative improvisation – only confirm this diagnosis: good old Greek theatricality, which was banned as soon as it appeared, desperately tried to reduce itself to a minimum in order to survive, but also in order to join forces with ancient rhetoric and dramaticity, which also have Greek origins. Certainly, theatricality and performance do not exist in separation; only the dosage of each might vary. We might need to invent '*performise*'.

The French tradition, and more widely the 'continental' one, conceives of theatre as a representation linked to spectacle, to theatricality (a term used by the Russian formalists – as opposed to 'literality' – and by the directors of the early twentieth century, especially Meyerhold). In contrast, the English-speaking tradition only knows the term 'performance', which it uses both for the stage theatrical presentation itself, and for any kind of cultural performance, not only shows, but any activity accomplishing an action (a rite, a ritual, a ceremony, a game and so on). The arrival in France in the 1960s of performance art also marks the appearance of a performative conception of theatre.[23] From that point on, theatre was included in the category of cultural performances.

Ludovic Janvier rightly remarks that 'Poetry, theatre, prose ... all converge to move towards the vocal and the rhythmical.'[24] This convergence (one could almost call it a conversion) shuffles the cards, but doesn't reinvent them: reading is only possible if the reader is to some extent also a spectator of the actions being imagined. Accordingly, mise en scène, even when it modestly seeks to be forgotten, is dependent on the performative action. Theatricality, in its most recent canonical form, that of mise en scène, is no longer an accumulation of signs, an 'informational polyphony' (Barthes), but an action performed on different objects – those described by Janvier, and those of our other examples: the text read onstage, the text heard by the spectator, the poem revived by the improvised impulse of the actor.

What could be more French than the term mise en scène?
What could be more English than the term performance?

They cannot function as translations as one another, and cannot be converted into one another. And a good thing too, since this Anglo-French incompatibility is rather welcome/*bienvenue*, and we should build on it.

The incompatibility of mood allows us to imagine how each of the languages sees the world – and thus the theatre – in its own way. The French envisage the passage from the text to the stage, from the word to the act. English emphasises the production of an action in the very act of its enunciation: this is the 'performative' of Anglo-American analytic philosophy (in for example Austin and Searle).

But, in this multipolar world, the borders are coming down. French textual isolation is no longer *de rigueur*; English performative stage action needs a discourse to lend it legitimacy.

The short history of mise en scène bears witness to this secret struggle for power between two visions of the world, two ways of making theatre and talking about it.

Since the 1960s, the world has been moving more and more quickly. Performance has reached continental Europe. It has become a new way of doing theatre, or rather of denying re-presentation, illusion, and the pedagogical pretensions of theatre. Thus, the technique of 'classical' and continental mise en scène, which was patiently perfected by directors (from Antoine to Copeau, from Meyerhold to Vitez), became aware of its incongruence, in the Anglo-American performing and performative world, within the art of making theatre, or rather that of making performance.

A few international examples will perhaps tell us what we have gained in such *performise*, or *mise en perf*.

3 The difference between mise en scène and performance

Mise en scène and performance: a shaky couple

Playing on words, I propose to examine a very serious question: the way in which the two terms 'mise en scène' and 'performance' allow us, and also oblige us, to think about how a production is interpreted, and indeed about our very conception of theatre. The two languages, English and French, in fact see things very differently, and are more or less capable of describing the phenomenon of theatre as it constantly evolves. At various times in the history of the theatre, in particular over the twentieth century, words and concepts from different languages have been unevenly appropriated to capture changes in conception. At certain points, words cease to be appropriate, and we are likely to return to another linguistic and conceptual way of describing phenomena, switch languages, or even turn to neologisms.

The English term 'performance', as applied in the theatre, designates what is played by the actors and created by all the contributors to the show, meaning that which is shown to the audience at the end of a rehearsal period. The word actually stems from the old French word *parformer*, a synonym of *parfaire* (to finish, to perfect), and in French retains only the notion of an exploit, as in a 'strong performance' in sport, for example. In the domain of the arts, the French term 'performance' (translating as 'performance art' in English) designates a genre invented in the 1970s in the United States. In both senses of the term, 'performance' refers to an action executed by artists as well as the result of this action. An action is produced in any performance, as Andy Lavender suggests: 'Words, in the theatre, are not a matter of exquisite literary provenance but are part of the larger machinery of performance, which is movement-based'.[1] The English term 'performance' does not really find any equivalent in

French: even the word *représentation* (which is the usual translation) does not convey the meaning of the English word, and betrays an entirely different worldview. This dissymmetry has its advantages, as we will discover.

The French term 'mise en scène' is in no way the equivalent of 'performance'. Since the end of the eighteenth century, in fact, it has designated the passage from the text to the stage, from writing to acting, from page to stage. The implicit meaning is thus very different from that of performance. Of course, the notion of mise en scène also exists in English: when the phrase 'mise en scène' is not used, people speak of a 'production', or a 'staging', or use verbs: 'to stage', or 'to direct a play'. The word 'production' emphasises the making, from a technical point of view, of the object that is theatre. The terms 'to stage', and 'to direct' are themselves performative, as is 'performance'. 'To stage' indicates the idea of laying out, putting on stage, whereas 'to direct' is not only to lead and direct the actor, but also signifies leading the author and the play (in a certain direction). In France, nevertheless, the notion of mise en scène evokes, first of all, beyond the setting-up of the scenery, the passage from page to stage, then the opposition of the visual and textual, and ultimately the semiotic system of meaning that the show implicitly carries.

I suggest that studying this asymmetrical usage of 'performance' and 'mise en scène' – in English and French contexts – shows that the gap exists for profound reasons and has serious consequences, and that it ultimately reveals two conceptions that are incompatible (or at least seem so at first glance, since the situation has changed a great deal over the last twenty or thirty years). Before comparing this evolution throughout the twentieth century, we should briefly return to the notion of mise en scène and to the reasons for its appearance. Mise en scène (at least mise en scène that is aware of itself as such) emerged when it seemed necessary to show – via the stage – how the director could, and even should, indicate how a dramatic work (something too complex to be deciphered in any single and obvious way by a homogenous audience) might be read. Mise en scène, therefore, initially concerned literary work and not visual spectacle. It appeared at a time when language and representation through language were in crisis – a time of crisis like the many others weathered by the theatre. The emphasis shifted from the author of the text to the author of the mise en scène, notwithstanding that the interpretation of the latter would be decisive in giving a possible meaning to the play. This transfer of power 'authorised' the former stage manager, now the director, to run the operation, to control everything. This absolute power was only possible if the stage closed in on itself, if it formed an tightly coordinated system of signs. This was the case with symbolism, which had an obsession with the coherence of signs and a desire to be cut off from the outside world. But it was also a concern for naturalism, seeking to reproduce a self-sufficient homogenous milieu. In both of these sources of modern mise en scène, the aim was to make a counter-world, a more or less mimetic representation of the world.

In the United Kingdom at the beginning of the twentieth century the situation was not radically different, but the changes that took place cannot be summed up in the term mise en scène: 'production' seems more neutral, neither emphasising the passage from page to stage nor the systematic character of stage representation, but rather conveying the pragmatic nature of the operation. The notion of a performance largely remained dominant. It seems that in the UK terrain of images and meanings, mise en scène (the term is hyphenated in many English texts) is a typically French exercise of exegesis, of hermeneutics, or even signifies a decorating of the text. The French notion in fact holds little sway, seeming to be a specialised term, remaining foreign in common English usage.

If we review the last century, we note that our two notions do not have a fixed place: at points they are distanced from each other, and at points closer together, a symptom of shifts in ways of making theatre. There follow a few examples of such shifts over the last hundred years. Our preoccupation, beyond the task of periodisation (which is always tricky in the arts), is the evolution of the concept of mise en scène.

From 1910 to 1920

After the appearance (c.1890) of the first directors, the European avant-garde, particularly in Russia and Germany, built experiments around the space, the actor and the visual arts; they were not particularly interested in the relationship between the text and the stage, but rather in the set-up of the stage. Only expressionism was interested in the expressive powers of the actor.

In the 1920s and 1930s

Particularly in France (thanks to Copeau and the 'Cartel' to which he belonged, along with Baty, Dullin and Jouvet), mise en scène found its classic formula as the 'totality of the stage spectacle coming from a single way of thinking, which conceives it, orders it and finally harmonises it.[2] The author/ity changed sides: mise en scène closed in on itself. It became an autonomous 'stage language' (as Artaud put it). This was closely associated with the *théâtre d'art*, with its tradition of literary, and even elitist, theatre. In the United Kingdom, on the other hand, no clear and definitive distinction was made between experimental theatre and 'entertainment' (and this is still the case today). What counts is the idea of a performance, the performative realisation of an action, and not a judgement on the cultural level, be it high or low.

In the 1930s and 1940s

We observe, with Artaud and Brecht, a double rupture as regards the classical position of mise en scène. Artaud called for an autonomous stage, without regard for the passage of the text to the stage; he distrusted mise en scène, seeing it as an accumulation of signs; he sought the uniqueness of stage representation. Such a vision would find its logical conclusion in the happening or in performance art in the 1970s. Ultimately, Artaud's conception is not far from the idea of a work of performance art as being unrepeatable, active and present.

For Brecht, mise en scène (*Regie, Inszenierung*) did not itself have any aesthetic or political value: it was a notion linked to that of stage practice, intended to demonstrate the way in which signs and illusion are produced, the Marxian transformability of the world. What was important, then, was that the theatre be opened onto the world. Theatre became, like performance, a form in action.

The 1950s and 1960s

In France this period prolonged and concluded the classical conception of mise en scène with a double discourse – by turns approving and critical – represented by the figures of Barrault and Vilar. Barrault returned to the *théâtre d'art*, demanding a total theatre, and emphasising theatricality. This term, which had been in use since Evréïnoff and Meyerhold, returned to the surface in critical discourse and was used in opposition to textuality or literarity. This marked the beginning of the metaphorisation of the notion of theatricality and its extension into all domains, in parallel with the extension of performance into all social activities.

Jean Vilar, in his earliest writings (around 1950) was suspicious of directors who make the text serve them, rather than serving it. And yet he admits that 'the real dramatic creators of the last thirty years are not authors but directors'.[3] He feared that mise en scène might be demoted to a style, while it was essentially not a style but a moral code. He preferred that his actors 'indicate', rather than metamorphosing or incarnating, seeking to avoid at all costs a degeneration of the acting into a style particular to the director, which might be followed from one show to the next.

In parallel with this French evolution towards a greater theatricality and stylisation, the notion of performance did not cease its expansion into all domains of social life. Under the influence of anthropology, the notion of performance spread, little by little, to encompass all human activities. In the English-speaking world, in particular since the 1960s and 1970s, 'the theatre stage and world stage – two fields of activity which offer more than a semantic analogy – interrelate in a dialectical relationship'.[4]

The 1970s

This period marked a shift in the evolution of the activity of theatre and in the 'dialogue' between performance and mise en scène, leading to an imbalance, an incompatibility. What happened? Given the importance of this turning point, it is necessary to go into more detail.

With the appearance of semiology, at the end of the 1960s, mise en scène tended to be conceived as a system of meaning, a coherent ensemble, a work that is readable or describable by way of linguistics, decidable sign by sign, as in the classical mise en scène of a figure like Copeau. At times, theatre practice continued to follow a structural and semiological model, but increasingly it contested this method. The apogee of mise en scène as scenic writing, in the 1960s, coincided with the beginning of its crisis: it became a system that was too closed, too linked to an author, a style and a method of acting, too associated with the idea of 'reading theatre'.[5] The show's structure is christened a 'signifying practice' (for instance by Julia Kristeva), to avoid talking about the work, the author or the director, notions deemed too bourgeois. In the end, functionalist structuralism had not been left behind. Productions continued, for the most part, to function according to the same model.

There followed, in practice and in theory, a movement of reaction, of revolt, a radical critique of stage representation. Enter performance art, emerging in particular from the United States and the United Kingdom. At the same point, and in a similar spirit, poststructuralism reached Europe, and texts and shows began to be approached in a very different way. This change of perspective benefited theatre practice, in that it was inclined to reconsider all notions of dramaturgy:

character, stage, meaning, the viewing subject and the purpose of theatre. In such an atmosphere of crisis and questioning, performance became a way of challenging theatre and its literary conception, deemed too logocentric, but also a strategy for overcoming a semiology that is too preoccupied with the reading of signs and of mise en scène. A new word was discovered, at least in French: in this polemical context, 'performance' – in the non-technical sense of the word – became a handy tool for understanding how theatre opens onto the world: the empty space, the uncertainty principle, the 'play' in the mechanism of theatre, and its flexibility.

At the same time, semiological theory definitively distanced itself from early semiology, which was often based around the text or the mise en scène considered as a 'performance text', meaning a readable texture or web. In the 1970s mise en scène, in France at least, began to overshadow dramatic literature. Mise en scène still – and specifically – worked on texts, often classic texts, and not on performances in the English (or French) sense of the term. From the UK side, this period coincided with the appearance of the notion of mise en scène:

> What tends to fade from view is that alternative to mise en scène, the performance. Mise en scène was a more attractive object partly because it still could be made to behave like written text: while Keir Elam's *The Semiotics of Theatre and Drama*, notionally attends in part to action and the dramatic world it is underpinned by minute verbal analysis.[6]

From then on, towards 1966–68, under the unconscious influence of American poststructuralism, and largely inspired by the last masterminds of French thought, mise en scène and theatre practice attempted to reform themselves. And not without some difficulty, since the literary and authoritative models were deeply engrained in the French, and the aftermath of 1968 was a dark period of social reaction, one whose repercussions are still being felt today. Most theatre production went on its (quiet and decentralised) way. Performance, in continental Europe, was confined to a few galleries. The terms signifying practice or theatrical production remained theoretical visions without a future and without any concrete realisation, with the exception of the works of Vitez. By denying the biographical conception of the author and the director, by replacing this with notions of production, *scripteur*, collective creation and signifying practice, theatre did not, in spite of all this, produce any fewer striking works (a term that was forbidden at the time!).

The only domain in which performance made a real breakthrough was in 'physical theatre' (which was not yet known by that name), the theatre of the 'insurrection of bodies' ('*la révolte des corps*') (Dort), around 1968. It is nevertheless in individual performance, outside theatres and institutions, that the body had the means with which to express itself: 'The "performer" explores the limits of the body, a fragile frontier, between subject and world. Thus theatrical liberation will be the liberation of the body or will be nothing at all.'[7] But there are bodies and there are bodies! The exalting body is more American and English than French (Living theater, Schechner, Chaikin). France was happy just to channel energies and to theorise (for instance, Artaud via Derrida[8]), and did not manage to find a successor to this body onstage. Mise en scène's attempts to maintain its control over the bodies and performers were few. At the same time, in the United Kingdom and in the English-speaking world at large, the subject became the only agent responsible for the production of the body. This situation can still be seen today with groups such as DV8 and Complicite, or indeed in contemporary writing with 'potholers of the body' like Sarah Kane or Mark Ravenhill.

The United Kingdom, despite its insular status, was not sheltered from theory: performance was enjoying its happy – that is, pre-theoretical – days, and was suddenly seized by poststructuralist and postmodern fever, 'French theory': theory adapted to the needs of North America and reintroduced (perhaps even marketed) to the English-speaking world. At the same time, in France, the rejection of theory in the theatre world lead to theorists and practitioners ignoring cultural studies, critical theory and poststructuralism. There was little interest in racial or sexual minorities. While in the United Kingdom 'identity militantism onstage as well as in the streets'[9] supplied an abundant set of themes to authors and actors, French mise en scène clung to a Brechtian heritage and to critical discourse in the tradition of the Enlightenment (Planchon is one example of this). Mise en scène remained rather obedient to text-based theatre, awaiting the arrival of the theatre of images of Robert Wilson and the experimental work of Peter Brook (from 1971 onwards). The form of the complete (literary and subsidised) production, with a story and characters, continued to dominate French mise en scène. It did not lend itself to any mutation such as 'stand-up comedy' (born in pubs and alternative spaces, of which are very few in France). The storyteller's art moves away from theatre circles and only offers the slightest inspiration to directors.

For the same reasons, installation and site-specific performance had little resonance in continental Europe, and in particular in

France. The promenade performance of *Dell'Inferno*, directed by André Engel (1982), remains a notable exception. There was no French equivalent of performances by Mike Pearson or John Fox, and Mnouchkine (very sensibly) returned to a frontal stage set-up after *L'Âge d'or* (1975).

From the 1980s

In this period, the contradiction between mise en scène and performance became more obvious, but also became increasingly productive, as much from theoretical point of view as from a practical one. French does not have a word for 'site-specific performance'; the term '*théâtre de rue*' ('street theatre') refers to a very different vision of theatre.

(A) On the English-speaking side, theory oriented itself towards the reception of the spectator: it asked itself how the subject deconstructs the object and what distinction it is appropriate to make between masculine and feminine subjects.

In France, we had unfortunately not overcome a certain historical theory of reception, inspired by the German *Rezeptionsästhetik*, a theory that only examines the successive concretisations of a play; we have, then, stayed with a historical hermeneutic which defines the work as a series of variants. We were still convinced that the human sciences, with more and more sophisticated tools, would lead us to the right reading of the play. No wonder that directors would ceaselessly return to the same works with the hope (or the pretension) of finally finding the ideal formula. With readings and re-readings (Planchon), and their 'infinite variations' (Vitez), directors were at the apex of their power and at the height of their art.

(B) This interest in reception went along – in the Anglo-American domain – with an extension of performance to cultural performance, given that the notion lends itself, by way of its generality, to all anthropological events, while poor theatricality remained tied, in the imaginary of the language, to the other arts and not directly to non-artistic forms of social life. Since, paradoxically, France has no institutional equivalent of cultural studies, theatre was unable to benefit from this intercultural and postcolonial wave[10] ('postcolonial' is another term that is unknown in French universities and which would only reach the general public in 2005 during debates about colonialism, social exclusion and caricatures of the Prophet!). When Vitez, for example, declared that he wanted to 'make theatre out of anything', he simply means that we should use all kinds of text. He was not calling for a rethinking of ceremonies, rituals or other cultures; he remains attached to the literary, elitist and artistic universe of texts and to the universality of Western theatre. His colleague Brook had the task of introducing to the dumbfounded French actors with strange and foreign accents performing together, provoking a shrugging of shoulders and grinding of teeth amongst the Parisian intelligentsia. For Vitez, any text can become theatre; for Brook, everything is a performative action. This nuance is not without importance.

(C) The reorientation, since the beginning of the 1990s, of theory towards the spectator's reception led us gently towards a phenomenological approach to analysing theatre. This philosophy, applied by people like Merleau-Ponty to knowledge and the arts (specifically painting), seeks to determine what emotional and cognitive experience the spectator or observer has, and what physical sensations are transmitted from actor to spectator. Moreover, phenomenology is suited to the notion of performance since it is defined by the effect produced on the receptor.[11] In the face of this, a slightly archaic semiology continued to base its analyses on the systematised representation of a mise en scène. Nonetheless, all of this (the change in theatre practice, the influence of non-European and non-literary forms, the provocations of performance art and so on) was favourable to the adoption of performance as the new – theoretical and practical – model. Postmodern performance and the influence of Derrida's deconstruction offered a more serious challenge to the continental conception of what mise en scène is supposed to be. These two entities would soon be forced to hear what the other had to say.

(D) In the 1980s, Anglo-American performance theory adopted the relativism of Derrida and his followers, and conceived of any stage creation as a deconstruction of the dramatic text or of its own practice. There is a noticeable gap between the sophistication of the theory and the much more conventional stage practice. Conversely, in France, with supposedly 'intellectual' directors, like Vitez, Mesguich and Chéreau, deconstruction (which was not known as such or under this name) was put into practice. In Chapter 9, we will examine some practical applications of Derridean deconstruction and see how they distance us from (closed) mise en scène and bring us closer to (open) performance.

The current state of the performance and mise en scène relationship

Since the last decade of the twentieth century, the tendency to bring together mise en scène and performance art has been evidenced. The breadth and the importance of the phenomenon of performance continue to increase. According to Jon McKenzie, we have moved from the era of the discipline (in the Foucauldian sense) to an era of performance: 'performance will be to the twentieth and twenty-first centuries what discipline was to the eighteenth and nineteenth, that is, an onto-historical formation of power and knowledge.'[12] The growth of performance in all fields and as a new universal paradigm must influence our object of study and our way of comprehending it, in every sense of the word. It is as if this fragile object is lost in a mass of cultural practices. This mass – indeed avalanche – renders difficult any overall theoretical view, if only by way of intimidation, since it has become impossible to analyse all types of performance, at least if we use a single blueprint. Analysis becomes tricky, and theory is systematically rejected by some artists as well as the audience. Subversive theoretical thought sometimes takes on the disguise (or uses the weapons) of deconstruction.[13]

Three theoretical and practical examples will enable us to test a hypothesis of the epistemological convergence of mise en scène and performance. The solution is perhaps to reintroduce a bit of mise en scène into the study of performance, and to return to the criteria of theatricality (as defined in the past by Josette Féral),[14] to think once again in terms of fiction, scene, place, 'author-ity'. The solution is also to conserve an entirely semiological rigour in evaluating a specific work. Let us check this by way of three questions and five examples. We will examine the constitution of the contemporary text, otherness and embodiment.

The constitution of the contemporary text

Everybody knows, post-Beckett and post-Koltés, that texts are difficult to read 'on the page'; they need to be spoken in context, either actually onstage or in the imagination. But it is not enough to merely reconstitute a possible situation, it is necessary to test what the blocking permits in terms of textual breath, how the words can be distributed beyond the origins of the characters.

J'étais dans ma maison et j'attendais que la pluie vienne, by Jean-Luc Lagarce, is a good example. In order to make distinct the voices of each of the five women, the director Stanislas Nordey did not seek to characterise them ('so as to differentiate them' with details of behaviour or of costume); he gives each actress a rhythm that is both distinct and shared. The text is carried by successive waves; the overall rhythm is that of a chamber orchestra. The organisation of the voices makes sense, forcing the listener or the reader to progressively build the dramatic experience. Sense – or sensation – is constituted in listening, or in its fragility, in its close links with the vocal performance. The spectator has the sense of a flow, thanks to the overlapping of the lines (a new incantation from one of the women begins before the previous one has ended, continuing in the same style, and making it very difficult to distinguish the voices). The overall impression is that of an overall flow, as with a chamber quintet. This technique was also used by Joan Littlewood's Theatre Workshop, according to Clive Barker's account: 'In working on the units of action, there was a continuous overlap. Before one unit ended, the next had already begun. In many lines of dialogue there was a point at which the thought could be grasped without the full line being delivered.'[15]

Let us take another example: *Dans la solitude des champs de coton,* as staged by Patrice Chéreau. Beyond analysing the motifs, the progression of the 'deal', and the rising dramatic tension, the director confers through the acting a playful interaction, a rhetoric of verbal sparring (which he can illustrate according to examples of sparring that he borrows from the culture chosen for the staging). He creates a 'flow', in Csikszentmihalyi's sense of the word:[16] the sense of losing yourself in an action, of only being conscious of performing that action. Each actor experiences, and more importantly delivers, this flow, carrying Koltés's long sentences (which go on for a page or two on occasion), and being carried by them. It is as if the only preoccupation was to hold the sentence like a temporal and verbal substance that is almost physical. The actor, like the spectator, no longer distinguishes what belongs to the semantics of the sentence and what produces the stage movement and rhythm. As in Csikszentmihalyi's flow, they feel unified and masters of their lives in perceiving the text and the verbal and theatrical event. It is not so much about the delicious loss of ego in action as about the sensation of a performance giving an open text its identity and constitution. The intellectual reflection, of the actor and of the spectator, momentarily gives way to the immediate and intuitive pleasure of the moment. This is a sensation that we often find in Anglo-American performances (consider the work of Robert Lepage or Simon McBurney).

From authority to alterity

Nordey and Chéreau 'try on' the play, and this approach confirms something obvious – the text no longer has an unquestionable centre, and thus it is necessary to experiment with its topology, its atopia. We would be at fault however to believe, as was the case in the classical era of mise en scène (from the end of the nineteenth century to the 1930s), that the director is once again the author of the show, the central agency charged with restoring order or balance. This cannot be the case: on the one hand, because there is no metatext of mise en scène inscribed or buried in the play, and on the other hand because the interpretation always seems somewhat undecidable, indeterminate and deferred (to use Derrida's term). Subject to a 'destinerrancy',[17] just like the author before and the spectator after, the director's destiny is to wander from one place in the text to another; the places of indetermination are no longer fixed by history, there is no ready-made metatext to be found, or anything 'set in stone', frozen like a marble statue or celluloid film. The moment authority over the text or the performance is surrendered, the power of decision is transferred to the actor, and in the final analysis to the spectator's gaze. Performance reclaims its rights.

Postmodern performance is used to the practices of alterity since it includes within its walls different cultural models, distinct ways of thinking and heterogeneous materials. It presents these elements without seeking to unify them. The productions of Peter Sellars are a good example of this eclectic, and even erratic, technique. In *Les Enfants d'Héracles*, Sellars used a little-known tragedy by Euripides to consider the right to asylum in the face of the imminent Iraq war. A worthy intention indeed, even if the parabola of the play needed to be twisted somewhat in order to transmit this contemporary message. The king Eurysthée (called 'Président' to facilitate allusion to Bush) follows the refugee children and is ultimately sent to his death by Alcmène. The principle of otherness does not work well, and the Greek tragedy in no way vouches for the validity of the comparison. Certainly, the casting of actors with vary different origins does indeed suggest the question of political asylum and of otherness, and also poses the question of the Guantanamo prisoners, but the dramatic analysis does not clearly establish parallels with our time. Thus the immediate, frontal acting style transforms this show into a successful performance, but the system of dramaturgy and mise en scène severely confuses the political message and weakens this theatrical enterprise. Fortunately, this is rarely the case in Sellars's works, and the impact of his 'presentational' style (literally audience address) remains remarkable: he inspires the audience to think, even if this reflection does remain – so to speak – the sole responsibility of the spectator. The absence of authority thus does not necessarily contribute to the question of otherness.

Conversely, a mise en scène can very well be structured in a rigorous manner, in the old-fashioned way, and still be open towards a non-authoritarian discourse, favouring otherness. This is the case in the

Misanthrope, staged in 2004 by Stéphane Braunschweig at the Bouffes du Nord. His Alceste remains ambiguous, with none of the characteristics of an honest romantic character that is the victim of a corrupt society, he is pathologically jealous, a reactionary puritan, and as narcissistic as Célimène. His radicalism, 'his need for certainty and to possess the other'[18] is the opposite image of Célimène's refusal to engage with him. Their entrenched and opposing positions exclude them from the experience of otherness, love and sociability. The staging hints at this impasse, but at the same time does not claim to solve the enigma of the play, and shows itself to be more circumspect and tolerant than its irreconcilable heroes. It proposes a new kind of stage interpretation that leaves its options open while giving the spectators the keys to forming their own opinion. Thus, in our imaginary topology, this work is located halfway between mise en scène, which can be too authoritarian, and performance, which can be too difficult to read.

A body in pieces: Bulbary.

Embodiment

'Embodiment' is a typically English term, which is very difficult to convey in French. The term avoids the mystical connotations of 'incarnation', and is closer to 'incorporation' – one French translation might be *mise en corps*. To analyse the action and the gestures in a mise en scène or a performance, it is best to avoid reducing them to mere description in words, as did the earliest semiology and classical/mimetic mise en scène. Let us instead consider these actions, in the manner of an anthropologist like Kirsten Halstrup, as 'embodied patterns of experience'.[19]

In practical terms, space is considered as 'bodied' or 'embodied', that is constituted of bodies run through with social contradictions (revealed by the *gestus*), with different densities[20] (bodies are more or less dense, meaning more or less present according to their use at a particular moment). The body is felt by the actor and the spectator in terms of its qualities of totality or fragmentation: an entire body or a dismembered one, a body in pieces. Let us take the example of Marivaux's *La Dispute*, staged by Chéreau (1973–76). Adolescents who have suddenly been given their freedom look at each other in large mirrors and strive, like the infant of Lacan's mirror stage, to perceive and thereby constitute their corporeal unity. But ultimately every character on the stage is defined by a body that the acting tests and figures. All of the bodies are the playthings of an X-ray procedure: it reveals them in their perfectly stabilised state of mise en scène (which keeps its signs under control), or in their unstable state of performance (which is subject to the actors' improvisation or to chance encounters).

Be that as it may, performance theory and the renewal of theatre practice reveal the previously incompatible notions of performance and mise en scène. This connection is so marked that we might be tempted to invent the new terms *mise en perf* or *performise*. It is simple to diagnose this cross-contamination: it is not possible these days to create mise en scène without the reflections of performance theory, or to create performance without the possibility of analysing it in terms of semiology and phenomenology.

But what is the result of this cooperation and this hybridisation? To test it by way of a few examples, we will examine more closely the work of three UK directors who have confronted mise en scène in France: Simon McBurney, Peter Brook and Declan Donnellan. For good measure, we will also add two French directors who are immersed in another culture, Jean Lambert-wild and Marion Schoevaert (with Buyn Jung-Joo).

Four examples of cooperation

Simon McBurney: Mnemonic

It would not be difficult to locate in McBurney the trace of his time at Jacques Lecoq's school, and he himself mocks this legacy: 'I thought I was going to see some dance, or something …. It's this company that people said were really physical, apparently they used to be very funny.'[21] It is more worthwhile, however, to observe how McBurney uses several acting traditions, allowing himself to be surprised by the apparent incompatibility of techniques and styles.

The 'play' begins with some stand-up comedy: McBurney speaks directly to the audience like a circus barker, while also mocking participatory theatre. He takes pleasure in manipulating the auditorium, asking the audience to don the eye masks given out by the ushers, to recall what they were doing an hour, a day, a year ago. But this mischievous prologue does not last very long. McBurney quickly becomes the principal character of a captivating story. The plot combines several parallel stories, with each actor drawing on elements from their own life. Virgil, the narrator, tells the story of his friend Alice. Why did she leave and what was she seeking? What is the origin of the man found in the ice? A complex plot takes shape inside of which several tales intersect and merge, operating at multiple levels, clouding the issues.

A series of tableaux makes for a rather classical staging, thanks to the representation of collective actions within a space–time seeking a goal. Images are regularly created which are often beautiful and original, and might be unexpected in a storytelling dramaturgy, such as silhouettes seen through a translucent plastic curtain, or actors stepping over a table, one after the other. This is the paradox of this work: the blending of all these elements does not form a homogeneous discourse, no subject centralises or homogenises the materials, and nevertheless the cleverness of the dramatic structure allows a network of motifs to be set up, a circulation established without any necessity to locate the centre of the work. What began as performance, playing with the audience, and an unusual neoclassical mix of image theatre and physical theatre, acquires a neoclassical coherence, but without the slightest dogmatism, and thus a juvenile grace. *Mnemonic* is a perfect *performise*! An acting technique is thus staged. This is a rare phenomenon, since *performise* demands impeccable physical training, but without the refusal of mise en scène as something impure and superfluous found in Decroux, Lecoq or other teachers. Only a few hardy spirits – Complicite, L'Ange fou, Théâtre du Mouvement, or even Barba – have had the courage to detach themselves from their masters to create their own visual universe, in order to develop a method of mise en scène that is not reduced to a style or a manufacturer's label, in order to transpose the organicity of the actor or the mime into the overall staging structure.

Peter Brook: **Je prends ta main dans la mienne**

In his staging of Carol Rocamora's play (2003, Bouffes du Nord), Peter Brook intervened in the wake of much mediation, since the play is made up of citations from original letters by Chekhov to Olga Knipper, which are transformed into dialogue by the author. What is the possible perspective of a staging of these documents? Brook is known for his denials: mise en scène must not propose a personal reading or a rereading; it must not impose its choices, be self-serving, and so on. Protestation and modesty in directors is not unusual and should not be taken too seriously. This time, however, Brook seems to have been satisfied with a non-mise en scène. Such modesty would be admirable if the actors had themselves taken over. But they appeared instead to be left to their own devices, that is, outside the realms of psychological acting, good honest non-acting, ironic Brechtian quoting or postmodern pastiche. Where were they, then? In a no man's land between performance (where all experimentation is permitted) and mise en scène (where the actor must be given over to the whole); with ham or *boulevard* acting, the actor gives the audience what it wants and expects: reality effects, tender memories, the great feats of the great actor, and memories from previous shows such as *The Cherry Orchard* (*La Cerisaie*, which was staged in the same venue in 1981). Brook probably encouraged such strong performances (in the negative, sporting sense of the term), but appeared to give no acting direction, chose no recognisable perspective, and let the acting turn into a self-satisfied mechanism. This led to rather hammy performances by Michel Piccoli and Natasha Parry: they faced the audience a great deal, looked at it, and began their lines with false hesitations. The rare movements did not always make sense, as if the actors did not want to descend to such simple justifications. Mise en scène declined to intervene, even to regulate the direction of the actors, and direction was strangely absent without apparent reason (unless it was just to avoid bothering the two stars). Brook's lack of interest, his absolute 'discontrol', drove the actors to their own habits, like the worst examples of boulevard theatre.

In general the direction of actors is at the heart of mise en scène, but here the emptiness at the heart was not a zen-like emptiness that might create meaning. The direction of actors does not carry mise en scène, which is only the mainstay of the Brook style (the empty space, the absence of objects, the proximity of the spectators, the simplicity of actions). Such a mise en scène has the strategy of erasing itself, but the remaining performance is in no way a deconstruction, since what would be deconstructed? Neither the ambiguous writing of the play, as it is not ambiguous, nor the biographical lineage of the work, since the play is made in too traditional a manner to lend itself to such deconstruction. We are thus stuck between *mise* and *perf.*

Declan Donnellan: **La nuit des rois**

The case of a staging in France of a Shakespeare play with an entirely Russian cast brings us a little closer to the objective convergence of these two, French and English, conceptions, and might convince us of the advantages of successful *performise.*

Indeed, the success of this work (call it what you will) is dazzling: Donnellan could have instrumentalised the actors, used them to illustrate his thesis, and thus designed an a priori mise en scène. But this artist is known for his willingness to place the actor at the centre of the process, in order to avoid starting with a preconceived staging: 'One of the aims of Cheek by Jowl is to reexamine the classic texts of world theatre and to investigate them in a fresh and unsentimental way, eschewing directorial concepts to focus on the actor and on the actor's art.'[22]

Faithful to this principle, Donnellan begins with the homogeneous group of Russian actors, who at the start are presented in the form of a chorus: then, taking the groups one after another, he carefully leads the construction not of character but of transvestitism. We see each actor start acting, and construct his disguise instead of living it. The signs of femininity are placed without hysteria, with a certain distance but without parody. The same process applies to the diction of the Russian text: clearly spoken, it serves as the basis of all characterisation: according to Donnellan, the text contains impulses and modulations that can be expressed by the body and its movements. There is thus no a priori dramaturgical or psychological analysis, but a rhythmical placing that by extension forms the mise en scène in its entirety. This method resembles that of the diction, of declamation as it was done before the invention of mise en scène, but it is more simply a normative method to ensure the text is read well, it is a method for attaining an overall interpretation (close to the method of Jouvet and Villégier's recent baroque tragedies). The 'system' of the mise en scène is only visible at the end, when all of the rhythmic and dramatic cells end up forming a whole. As the mise en scène establishes itself progressively by way of a proliferation of cells, the metatext of any reading of the play is only perceptible at the end, which prevents any logocentrism of interpretation. This is an uneasy and miraculous balance of 'mise' and 'perf'!

This is not a question of formal acting, constructed with a sense of abstraction and permutation, but rather of a reflection on identity and masquerade. If, as Judith Butler suggests, gender is always a question of performance, a cultural construction, the simulation of the men playing women or playing women playing men (and in succession) marks their voluntary loss of identity. For them as for the spectator, there is no stable referent. It is thus useless to claim to grasp their mimetic representation, as a classical and well-intentioned mise en scène might do. It is better to organise a masquerade (not so much in a metaphysical, psychological and sexual way as would a figure like Genet) in order to pose the question of identity and of pretence. If, as Joan Rivière suggests in her brilliant article 'Womanliness as masquerade',[23] femininity is a voluntary masquerade, for Donnellan, masculinity is a masked ball where his actors hide and display themselves, construct and deconstruct. And this is in the spirit of the play, since the dissolution of identity, the impossibility of judging, the value of love, to cling to reality, to distinguish truth from falsehood: all of this is evoked by Shakespeare and given to be seen in this extraordinary performance.

The rich reflection of Donnellan in no way illustrates these theories, but it would be unimaginable without the preparatory work of critical theory, particularly as regards sexual identity and simulation.

Is there thus another difference here between 'mise' and 'perf'? Probably, but it is disappearing: the difference tends to reduce, since it is true that the direction of actors and performance are increasingly at the heart of the set-up of any mise en scène. These two ways of seeing and doing theatre are complimentary, as Donnellan, McBurney and Braunschweig show so well. When these two aspects predominate, we must fear an imbalance or a deficiency.

Les Coréens, *staged in Korea*

To test the rule of the complementarity of mise en scène and performance, we will take a final example: the 2006 staging of Michel Vinaver's *Les Coréens* (*The Koreans*), in Seoul, directed by Marion Schoevaert and Byun Jung-Joo.[24] This play from 1956 tells the story of a fictional episode from the Korean War (1950–53). In a 'présentation de ses œuvres', Vinaver describes it in these terms:

> After a bombardment, where everything appears to have been undone, where nothing remains except a few noises, a few gestures, and some debris, a life comes back to life. While a Korean village returns to its senses – but things are no longer the same – five soldiers patrol the surrounding underbrush, in search of a prisoner. They live their war as a dream, without recognising it. A sixth has been left for dead in a night battle. An eight-year-old girl finds him wounded and brings him back to the village. What follows – what happens in the village, and what happens to the soldier – is not an event inscribed in eternity. It is, surprisingly, the reconquest of today.[25]

The last sentence by the author is not so much a description as an interpretation of the play, and a rather obscure one at that. The staging, albeit Korean, did not make things much clearer. It did however invite one to consider the action as a collective movement, to go beyond the story of the only major character, Belair. This explains the choice of music, gesture and choreography, inspired by traditional Korean culture. The choice is perfectly legitimate, not only because it gave a plausible decor, bringing the referent of the play back to its place of origin, but particularly because the Korean rhythm of the music, movement and speech gave the work a stylistic unity, keeping it from an overly psychological or realistic interpretation. The mise en scène (or is it the writing, or even the dramaturgy?) constructed from the elements a musical score, a diction that was intoned and shouted rather than spoken, and a choreography of steps, movements and physical attitudes borrowed from traditional Korean dance. More than a dramatic *mise en jeu* of the text, this was an opera and a choreography, forming the precise score of a performance, rather than the mise en scène of an existing text. The text was kept almost in its entirety, thus remaining audible, and not reduced to the status of an opera libretto (with meaning taking second place to the music). Thanks to the possibility of retranslation, the text is malleable according to the requirements of the gestural and musical rhythm. There is a happy rhythmic meeting of the rewritten translation by Ahn Chi-Woo, the music composed by Kim Dong-Guen and the choreography by Park Jun-Mi. This meeting has been carefully prepared by the mise en scène as a *mise en énonciation* of signs from different registers: the metrics, the orchestration of Western (accordion, clarinet, flute, guitar) and Korean (*Buk* – a large drum) instruments, and the dancing or posed figures. The work prior to the composition of this new kind of opera, then the mise en scène, consisted of integrating these rhythms in frames that allow the organisation of a musical, choreographic and textual tale. The text, although often shouted in the same tone and with the same energy, does remain 'audible' (perceptible and understandable by the ear and the mind), but it is also very readily and very quickly integrated in the dance and music event. The play is thus plunged into a Korean 'bath', at least for non-Koreans: it is as much a question of intraculturality as of interculturality.

Matching the importance placed on ritual and anthropological interpretation by Vinaver, the staging reinforces the ritual dimension: songs and dances, masks, hoods, thick make-up, and allusions to shamanism via the two altars at which each character, and each performer, comes to meditate. These elements are not authentic, there is not concern for ethnographic accuracy; they are conceived in their aesthetic form, idealised and imaginary. This evocation of Korean gesture and sound is not the reconstitution (impossible in any case) of *Homo Korean*, both unobtainable and imaginary.

But which Koreans are we talking about? The directors, Schoevaert and Byun, and before them the Wuturi Players of Kim Kwang-Lim, do not for a moment claim to be reconstituting an authentic fragment of

Figure 3.1 Les Coréens by Michel Vinaver,
directed by Marion Schoevaert
and Buyn Jung-Joo.
© Kim Kwang-Lim.

Korea, but rather are imagining a few signs from Korean culture. A
largely fantasised Korean-ness, both for them and for us, but
convincing in aesthetic terms, is what these artists hope to create.
They inadvertently invent a new type of intercultural theatre, or a
more precisely intercultural theatre.

Interculturality is no longer – as was the case in the 1970s and 1980s
– a question of cultural exchange, of communication between poles
of cultural instances, or of conflict between dominant and dominated
cultures. In this example from Vinaver, there takes place instead a
meeting (less impassioned, because it is natural) between acting

traditions and written dialogue. The writing (already one step removed from day-to-day communication) lends itself to a certain stylisation of the stage, but demands an enunciation that is both energetic and unrealistic, in order to be integrated into the pure artifice and codes of opera which, like a traditional performance form, is regulated and codified.

This is a new intercultural meeting with both mise en scène (in the Western tradition) and performance, defined as a traditional and fixed form ('Eastern' or otherwise). This meeting is highly epistemological, and indicates a tension between two ways of 'showing doing', as Schechner defines the object of study which previously answered to the name 'theatre'.[26]

This meeting can be observed, and described in a sufficiently technical manner, by way of tensions between ways of moving, walking, speaking and giving rhythm to a text. The choreographer Park Jun-Mi creates a montage of several corporeal techniques:

- the duck-walk of a pot-bellied peasant, borrowed from traditional folk art
- the slight repetitive movement of a peasant's shoulders, a movement that is barely registered, but is likely at any moment to change into an elaborate masked dance
- poses held for quite a long time by the French soldiers, public officials, and sometimes a little girl (Wen-Ta)
- the stereotypical thick make-up of the peasants and officials, which seems to highlight the rigidity of tradition, ideology and uniform.

The actor-dancers, assisted by the choreographer and conforming to the general design of the mise en scène, gradually construct a style, an attitude and a tension characteristic of their characters. This establishes a corporeal technique that is both individual and in part common to characters of the same group. The technique solidifies itself in a corporeal tension in each posed body: from the lightest (Wen-Ta) to the heaviest (Kim). The public officials build into their steps and poses a violent movement (borrowing from Kung Fu), immediately connoting the sinister Chinese Cultural Revolution and the Peking Opera under Mao. Chinese influences enter the physical work, just as do gestures that 'quote' pro-American and North Korean posters. The fascist or communist body, totally controlled, also borrows from Western techniques of close combat. It thus declares its incompatibility with the bodies of the peasants, which obey an entirely different logic.

The work of the choreographer consists only of bringing these different bodies, models of the body, and types of movement and stillness into confrontation, to make a montage and to have them evolve according to the transformations of the character. Belair, for example, breaks away from the automatisms of his fellow soldiers, is humanised through contact with the little girl, and timidly joins the final peasant dance, but not without some ambiguity around such forced integration (he hesitates, is out of step, and stiff). The choreographic figure chosen sometimes surprises: the French soldiers, hooded like terrorists, at one point turn and jump in a Korean style, like a masked dance. Aesthetically, the movement is spectacular; dramaturgically, it is rather displaced, since it suggests an assimilation into the group of peasants. The problem lies in the coherence of the mise en scène rather than in errors in the choreographic performance. The choreography is first and foremost concerned with maintaining the rhythm, and perfectly succeeds in creating coherent ensembles of groups, who sometimes freeze in a tableau vivant or are led into a dance around a soup pot, represented by the Buk drum, with the dancers striking the beat.

The struggle for influence between (choreographic) performance and mise en scène shows itself in a vacillation between a very distant scenography (a high stage, which is far from the audience, whereas a village play would be staged in the round) and costumes and make-up that are very close to those used by Korean peasants in a past era. The shiny floor and the brand new auditorium both contradict the crude, rustic faces, and the costumes of the peasants. The stage apron, which is almost Shakespearian, seeks to bridge the distance, and the soldiers frequently overflow into the audience. And yet this universe remains foreign to Koreans, even to those who study Korea, as it relies on a symbolic, choreographed vision, and thus on an aesthetic performance of dance, realised on the neutral and abstract stage of danced opera.

Fortunately, the device of fiction helps us to penetrate this faraway, imaginary universe. Not the fiction of a 1953 Korean village, but that of a group of villagers participating in a ceremony, celebrating an already theatricalised, 'restored' (Schechner), and ritualised episode of the past; they do this *with* us rather than *for* us. At the start, the actors welcome us while shouting and frenetically moving clothes that we presume belonged to the dead. At the end, they take off their masks, then place the same carefully folded clothes on the stage apron one after another, before leaving this stage via the auditorium. A ceremony has thus taken place, in which we have actually participated, at least by proxy. Like the actors, throughout the show we have periodically meditated before the two little altars on either side of the stage. Such rituals pull the play towards cultural performance, towards performative action. They drag us away from the classical mise en scène of an interpreted text.

Nonetheless this example helps us to understand the struggle for influence between mise en scène and performance. Indeed, the spectator must choose between the reading of the story by way of mise en scène and the logic of danced and musical performance. According to Western logic, the choreography and the music must be at the disposal of the mise en scène. They must be composed according to the intentions or the overall choices of the mise en scène, without which they might become independent of the story and thus reduce the dramatic text to the status of insignificant libretto. And yet, in the work of Byun and Schoevaert, the text is neither modified nor cut. The framing motif of the sorting of clothes becomes a metaphor in the story, where restoration and order follow destruction and reconciliation. The interpretation of a few final key scenes (notably scenes 15, 17 and 19) is essential for the establishment of the story required by any mise en scène. The villagers, by way of the intermediary of Lin-Huai ('a forceful woman'; 'a heartless woman') decide to integrate Belair – who has just announced that he intends to leave – into the village community, reassuring him of his sexual potency. In a rewriting of Marivaux's *The Surprise of Love*, Vinaver shows how a couple, with their bantering and gallantries, and in thinking they have permanently taken their leave from love and desire, end up finding desire. But the action is more anthropological than psychological. The staging does not parody a Marivaux scene: in this translation and with this physical acting we are very far from Marivaux's flourishes, and therefore from the possibility of parodying them. The erasure of dramaturgical reading and of the critical signature of mise en scène are continued in the final scene, which the mise en scène treats in a manner more choral and choreographical than discursive and hermeneutic. Overall, mise en scène somewhat gives way to Korean opera: it imbues dance, music and the ceremonial with a cathartic power, a joy that is linked to the voice and the body rather than to the mind and to discursive interpretation.

By way of its coherence, its creativity, its driving force and its lyricism, the choreography and the music of Kim Kwang-Lim's neo-Korean opera tend to subvert, to subjugate and even to engulf the mise en scène. We know that opera claims to regiment everything, including the weaknesses of the director; it is the master of time and rhythm, and everything must be subservient to it. Music imposes a particular timing, a rhythm that dance translates into space, and the actors' bodies translate into figures and physical attitudes.

This allows us to continue to compare the 'Korean' performative way of putting things onstage and the Western method of subjecting them to mise en scène, distributing them according to a centralising and organising gaze. These *Coréens* are very Korean in that they give the impression of a performance for which objects, gestures and musical leitmotifs have been placed next to one another without the organising gaze of the Western director. From the Western point of view, we might get a bit lost amidst the juxtaposition of things onstage and inside the space–time of the show: the performance goes from one ensemble to another without logical, or even chronological, reason, as if it were an installation, as if mise en scène (in the Western sense) had ceased to impose itself and faded into the pseudo-Korean performance. This performance is also a performance in the sense that it constitutes an artistic, musical, and choreographical endeavour. It also recovers something sensual and unorganised. Mise en scène always basically remains an organised and conceptual system.

This is precisely what the theatre of deconstruction or the theatre of performance attempts to realise today: emancipation from the constraining perspective of the director, setting things out without privileging one point of view. This attitude coincides with a new interculturalism, one that no longer tries to control everything as Western mise en scène did when it mastered all the signs and had a single perspective. This new interculturalism inscribes itself into a multiple perspective or a disorientation (neither 'purely' Eastern nor 'purely' Western, it lacks any such direction). It is therefore a syncretic, professional and postmodern interculturalism. The signs that it employs are sometimes deliberately ambiguous, wide open, and not reducible to clear indications as they were in classical mise en scène. Take, for example, the hooded soldiers: are they an amorphous mass from any of today's armies or are they terrorists, and if so what kind? And the large drum transported to centre stage: is this a pot of food to nourish and regenerate the village, or simply a rallying point for the acting, a purely gyrating figure, turning around and around, in the real and the figurative sense? These signs are culturally polysemic indicators, they are not social or psychological indications as they would be for mise en scène. They provide a general and universal frame for a virtuoso and polymorphous performance. They definitively escape interpretation that is too discursive, too tied to the text, and too subject to the 'author/ity' of the director. They have us return to a state before mise en scène, that of technical know-how, standardised, and not tied to individual interpretation, but rather codified and perfectly mastered, as it would be in an age-old tradition. This return to a previous state – not yet individualised because it is interpreted by a unique and artistically responsible 'explainer' – is not necessarily a regression; it is a means of linking with Korean choreography, as if it had already existed and we were in the process of rediscovering it.

Gradually, two current temptations in the theatre can be grasped: that of performance and that of mise en scène. The temptation of performance is to freeze dramatic categories, characters and meaning, the better to work on form. Thus it calls on interpreters, instrumentalists, virtuosos and performers. The temptation of mise en scène is to appreciate, to judge and to interpret the contents and the nuances of the text, to show just how it is relative. It calls on actor-imitators who 'set up camp' in their characters. In this Korean production, the actors are first and foremost dancers who cannot simply be taken out of their choreographic routine, their formal codification, in order to be placed in a dramatic and theatrical situation and asked to play 'great scenes', to nuance and to interpret the story and to clarify the subtext and a situation. Everything leads us to believe that this play deliberately situates itself within abstract and anthropological performance, and not in historical or historicising mise en scène in the Brechtian way.

What does the play in fact require? In his introduction, Vinaver emphasises the fact that we not be preoccupied with the 'journey of the main character',[27] but that 'it is rather the whole play that must seek as it progresses to depict the advent of a 'new time', of a world freed from all process, open to any movement.'[28] Thus, the time and the action are not the anecdotal ones of the character in transformation, but those of a whole society, conceived anthropologically. The play and its stage treatment insist on the assimilation of the soldier Belair in another living tissue. This is thus anti-Brechtian theatre, and so is not located in political history, despite the names and the places. The play lends itself to the travesty of a culture that is other; in this case it is Korean, but it could just as easily be Thai or Irish. The play is to be found alongside performance in the sense of a formal endeavour and in the sense of an ahistorical codified form of theatre that is traditional, immutable in its unfolding and thus not at all dependent on a new reading by a director. The performative aspect is key, since the mimetic, political, ethnological and geographic requirements are very few indeed. Vinaver's play certainly refers to Korea, but without giving specific cultural markers in the text. This absence appears to have authorised the directors and the choreographer to attempt a reconstitution and a codification of Korean-ness in danced and sung performance, an imaginary and strikingly aesthetic Korean-ness.

Conclusions: performance studies/theatre studies

This Korean and Korean-ised example of mise en scène, *Les Coréens* by Vinaver might help us to return to the relationship between performance and mise en scène, and more generally to the difference between performance studies and theatre studies.

The project of *Les Coréens* has a double origin: it is 'Western' in terms of Vinaver's writing and the dramaturgical analysis and the direction of Schoevaert, and it is 'Korean/Asian/Eastern'[29] in terms of the Wuturi style of Kim Kwang-Lim, and the direction of the actors by Byun Jung-Joo (who is also named as director). It is not surprising, then, that the production is equally characterised by a double influence, sometimes hard to decipher and distinguish – the European influence of a theatre of text (that mise en scène, like the Sphinx, must decode), and a performative and performing influence (that produces the performance in this opera and work of dance-theatre).

For the last twenty years, under the influence and leadership of Richard Schechner, theatre studies and performance studies have stood face to face and compared methods and notes. A show like *Les Coréens* demonstrates that both approaches are valid, necessary and complementary, to understand the making of the work and evaluate its reception.

We must nevertheless not deny the epistemological difficulty of this meeting and coexistence. Theatre studies have made use of a whole arsenal from the humanities, most notably critical theory. Disciplines such as philology, sociology, psychoanalysis and Derridean deconstruction have proven their worth. Also, we must note a certain crisis of confidence, and perhaps the self-denigration of 'theory'. Theory has been found to be too Western, too Cartesian, too humanistic. It is accused of every evil since Adam and Eve, and is asked to take responsibility for colonialism and racism. It is true that the task of the humanities, like that of mise en scène, is to be critical, and even self-critical: mise en scène seeks to explain the work, to evaluate whether it can still be called a mise en scène in the true sense, or whether it is a cultural performance. Mise en scène claims to be located in history, to adapt to the requirements and faculties of the audience at a given time. The lessons of mise en scène assisted by dramaturgy are precious: the relativity of time, of era, of the gaze, of desire, of the effect produced: lessons not to be forgotten. But these lessons have in fact often been forgotten, and Marxist – or simply Brechtian – analyses have been simplified for the reading or playing of a work. After 1989, which marked the end of communism (just as

1789 marked the start of humankind's foray into the machine of revolutionary history), the humanities were somewhat discredited. It is true that, as Schechner has shown, that we currently have 'very little faith in long-term futurology',[30] but this is no reason to stop thinking; humanist study can help, if only to prevent despair.

On the other bank of the river, the performance studies side, which is wide open to the inexhaustible world of cultural performances, we might feel destitute, like Robinson Crusoe. There are few political approaches that allow the analysis of so many forms, too diverse and 'different' for our 'dirty Western fingers',[31] and particularly few approaches that go beyond merely describing the technical function of forms and their codifications. Now the 'performance model' that Schechner describes requires a definition – does it really operate on its own, without reference to Western dramaturgy? There is room for doubt! Certainly, we might observe this in *Les Coréens*: music and dance tend to constitute a pure language, cut off from culture while nonetheless calling on it. They do have an immediate, touching, directly emotional effect. But we should grasp the moment where this effect is translated into an impact on the meaning and the dramaturgy, and as a result on the mise en scène as a system of meaning.

In practice as in theory, we strive to reconcile or to confront performance (formal) with mise en scène (loaded with meaning, particularly political meaning). On the theory side, unproductive divisions like performance versus mimesis can be overcome. In the performative action that constitutes performance there can be effects of the real that immediately make a spectator understand that the fiction and the artistic form are also linked, by numerous mediations perhaps, to life (or everyday experience). In practice, this implies that the spectator can – and may desire to – oscillate ceaselessly between the joy of music or dance (the form and the rhythm where they manifest themselves), and finding the critical distance that takes care of reflection on the organisation of stage meaning. For Vinaver's Koreanised Koreans, the choice as the show unfolds to favour either performance or mise en scène is decisive. These Seoul Coréens clearly favour virtuoso performance. This is why it is sometimes difficult to think about the play in an interpretive mode, and to bring together the joy of the performance and dramaturgical reflection (an old European instinct). It remains to be decided – a critical judgement must be made – if this absence of a connection was done 'on purpose' or if it bears witness to a conception that is too unilaterally linked to the performance of Korean culture, called upon to perform miracles.

One final miracle: Vinaver's play inaugurated, in 1956, a radically new conception of the theatre: 'a theatre that abolishes all memory, which wipes the slate clean of images and meanings, which presents a world where relationships between beings and things are emptied of all depth, given without prolongation, literally recorded'.[32] So, instead of looking for meaning in the individual 'conversion' of Belair to Korean culture (to identify with some quest for meaning), it might be better to observe, as did the mise en scène, how the performative aspect of the acting, Korean opera-dance, contributes to the advent of this new time 'open to any movement'. The relationships between beings are expressed through movement, voice, choreography and particularly through physical attitudes: so many formal elements bring no subtext whatsoever, no depth, but 'knit together' a group of relationships that become a whole, the image of our world as a network. It is thus interconnected performance that triumphs over the individual as master of meaning. In this sense, Korean culture, as a metaphor, finds value and justification, but for postmodern, rather than ethnographic, reasons.

This shift from mise en scène to performance, which can be observed in the Seoul production of *Les Coréens* as in many other contemporary works, has methodological consequences: analysis goes from descriptive semiology to a phenomenology of the perceiving subject. But this shift is more of a union between two methods: semiology is an indispensable tool for the description of a work's structure, while phenomenology actively includes the spectator in its bodily and emotional dimensions. For the strange objects that current productions have become, this double method is a double check. We have now left the side of obviated meaning, we are faced with and inside examples of *performise* or *mise en perf*, which semio-phenomenology will perhaps help us to approach. Destinerrancy will surely ensue.

Scenography is the visible and material part of mise en scène. It is only one component among others, and yet is the focus of much research on theatre and performance-making today.

Space is seen as the barometer of time, as the chrysalis from which mise en scène emerges.

There is an underground struggle between scenography and mise en scène: since the appearance, or at least awareness, of mise en scène, scenography has been on the defensive, as if it had definitively lost the powers it acquired during the Renaissance. Often it identifies with mise en scène, seeking to go beyond the fixed frame and architecture of a space contained by the limits of the stage, as when it first appeared.

But are we still in the era of the *Revolutions of Stage Design in the Twentieth Century*, to take the title of Denis Bablet's 1975 book?* Has the scenography of the last twenty years renewed and prolonged the historical avant-gardes? Is it now exploring new paths?

A few concrete examples, albeit necessarily partial, will feed our thoughts on the subject.

In the theatre, as elsewhere, we should expect everything. Spatial disorientation at least helps us to reconsider our position in the world.

* Denis Bablet, *Revolutions of Stage Design in the Twentieth Century*, Paris and New York, Leon Amiel, 1976.

4 Tendencies in French scenography

If we closed our eyes for a moment to consider scenography in France during the 1980s and 1990s, what would we see?[1] The same vision as if we contemplated mise en scène: the same kaleidoscope of forms and colours, an infinite number of ideas, of confused spaces, an incomparable range of achievements. But we would necessarily acknowledge the impossibility of reducing this rich variety to any sort of system or making any sort of systematic review or anthology of the stage experiments that marked the past century. This is because – another revelation – we find ourselves at present in a baroque (or we could say postmodern) phase, in which old solutions are reused, perhaps to excess, and tested procedures are perfected. Of course there have certainly been some new scenographic forms invented, but the 1980s and 1990s were years of taking stock, of concluding, and indeed of the apotheosis of previous experiments. Scenography is the faithful barometer of these variations, and space is what reveals it. Luc Boucris has rightly pointed this out: 'Space informs communication. Everyone knows that. Yes, but how? Theatrical space, and its transformations, might well be a way into undertaking such explorations …. Informing and modelling space is now the concern and the ambition of the theatre-maker.'[2]

Scenography, in France and elsewhere, has become one of the most beautiful jewels of theatrical creation, the royal road for understanding stage work, for casting new light on the role of the actor, and consequently for evaluating changes in modern staging. As it would be impossible to describe these changes exhaustively or to enter into the technical details of scenic practice, only a few concrete examples will be considered here. These are not representative of every current tendency, but will nevertheless serve as typical examples from an abundance of work. Without seeking to be exhaustive, this quick overview hopes to show the relationship between these scenographies and the question of staging of the actor's body. A remark by one of the most talented young French scenographers, Daniel Jeanneteau, provides support for this approach: 'The theatrical space ought to be an emanation from the mind and body of the actor. It should not exist before the actor does.'[3] What we are looking at in a setting will therefore have no meaning except in relationship to the actor and the way in which the actor is placed onstage for a given public. This hypothesis, moreover, supports that of Jean-Marie Pradier, who speaks of 'ethnoscenology', which views the stage as an 'anthropological model of the body'.[4] Such a hypothesis will help us to envisage scenography in its relationship to the actor and the mise en scène, since, as Jouvet observed in his preface to Nicola Sabbattini's treatise,[5] architecture, dramaturgy and staging 'stick together'. To this trinity must be added the body and the spectator's gaze. We will, in the six examples that follow, look at how space situates the actor at the heart of the mise en scène, before bringing in the spectator's body and gaze.

Our case studies, though various and typical, by no means comprise a typology of scenography, nor even a representative selection. They provide only a preliminary orientation. It would be very risky to attempt any typology of this subject. Indeed scenographers generally profess no single method, nor particular style or given aesthetic, since they work with various directors or – where they collaborate with the same artists – work on extremely diverse projects. Certainly there are constants from one set to another if created by the same artist, but what engages our interest here is neither the style nor the career of the scenographers, but rather the different ways of experiencing space and transmitting it to the actor and then to the spectator. We should not need reminding that scenography is not the search for spectacular effects, just as technical performance is not an end in itself; the magnificence of the stage setting is only an 'infantile disorder' of theatre practice.

The choice of examples is to some extent arbitrary. Ironically, the selection is often dictated by the photographic documentation that theatres were willing to provide. From this material we have attempted to distinguish the following uses of space:

1   The powers of stage illusion (Collet/Demarcy-Mota).
2   Fantasy and the real (Peduzzi/Chéreau).
3   Crossing the image (Vigner/Vigner).
4   The echoes of space (Timar/Timar).
5   The migration of subspaces (François/Mnouchkine)
6   The silence of space (Jeanneteau/Ollivier).

This selection makes no claim to be representative of the whole range of current practice, and still less a typology of theatrical architecture – such questions must be left to one side. Note, however, that five of the six examples deal with recovered spaces: an ammunition factory (5), a church (4), a warehouse (2), former theatres that have been 'reused' (1) or left as they are (6). Only one of the venues, the Maison de la Culture in Créteil (3), was purpose built for performances.

The powers of stage illusion

With the staging of Pirandello's *Six Characters in Search of an Author* (2001, Théâtre de la Ville, Paris), Emmanuel Demarcy-Mota and his designer Yves Collet contributed to the reconquest of the powers of the image; they rediscovered the magic of the proscenium stage. During the 1960s and 1970s, the enclosed perspective of the Italianate stage became suspect, and the exodus of theatre from traditional spaces seemed to have sounded the death knell for this beautiful object of fantasy. The last two decades of the century, however, saw theatre return to the fold, to the power of illusion. Collet's set and lighting permeated every nook and cranny of the stage and auditorium, creating a flexible space, especially since the performance took place in a theatre like the Bouffes du Nord, where the playing space penetrates the audience space in the manner of the Elizabethan 'thrust' stage. The space alternated between close proximity with the spectators, and extending all the way back to the wall of the building, creating, by means of a transparent curtain, shadows and objects on both sides. In this way, many types of space were mobilised one after another: a near space where the actors watch rehearsals, a space in the middle distance on the playing platform, and a distant space for the summoning of phantasms and phantoms of the past. The set-up made use of two tableaux: a frontal space operating at various scales and a multitude of secondary spaces representing various places. The box stage was both recreated and deconstructed. Thanks to this mastery and malleability of space, the design and the mise en scène seemed to exhaust every possibility of the Western stage. They denounced and dismantled bourgeois illusionistic representation, even while pushing it to its limits and re-establishing it in all its attributes.

Such a scenography, with its variable geometry, is an exercise in style, demonstrating the powers of theatre: it reinforces the identity of the actor, and through the actor, that of the author. It draws up a end-of-century record and inventory of all the stratagems and possibilities of theatricality, taking them to absolute aesthetic perfection; it gives the actors back their performing space, their spontaneity and their freedom, and in particular the pleasures of ham acting and flirting with character. The body of the character, according to Pirandellian metaphysics (and the body of the actor tasked with embodying it) is reconstituted before our eyes: scenography once more places itself at its service, it presides over its creation, playing on the confusion between the body and its shadow. By way of identification, that is by way of recognition and empathy, the spectators 'communicate' (in a proper and a figurative sense) with the bodies; organising a perception of space, constructing the fiction from them and from themselves. Yves Collet exposes every possibility of scenographic art, and particularly its pictorial and fantastical function at the moment when, as in the prologue of Goethe's Faust, theatrical shadows approach and become embodied in the figures of the actors. Such fantastical figures seem to invade the interior space of the spectators, giving rise to a sensation where we can no longer distinguish between what we perceive outside and what we feel inside.

Many of Yves Collet's images are inspired by the aesthetics of the glossy images of the 1970s and 1980s, like those created by Chéreau, himself of the Strehler school, and also superb images of productions by Richard Demarcy and Teresa Mota. And yet, at the same time, any such phantasmagoria of images is called into question, or perhaps completed, by a totally different concept of staging, that of deconstruction, of a 'gentle rupture', of an illusion which is broken and then restored. This ambivalent procedure is also found in the work of Chéreau and Peduzzi, but with a completely different atmosphere and a much darker emotional colouring.

Fantasy and the real

Chéreau and Peduzzi, who have been collaborating for some forty years, have remained faithful to an aesthetic refinement of the image (after Strehler), which has produced great architectural plasticity in their work. They are not content with figuring a mimetic representation of reality: they create a crisis in reality by way of an excess of theatricality, a monumentality of setting and exaggerated performance by the actors. This contradiction of realism and fantasy, this oxymoron, was evidenced in the staging of Racine's *Phèdre* at the Ateliers Berthier, the temporary home of the Théâtre de l'Europe (from January to April 2003). In a voluminous industrial space rearranged as a bifrontal stage/auditorium, the audience was positioned rather uncomfortably on seating banks overhanging a narrow, long area. This area was stretched between the very imposing façade of Phèdre's palace on the one side, and the open space of the Ateliers Berthier (with its old lift and contemporary chairs, probably used during rehearsals) on the other. Thus the archaeological reconstruction of a palace and a prosaic and contemporary 'found space' were placed in confrontation. The set precisely and at full scale included one of the stone tombs from Petra in Jordan. The contrast between tragic fiction and prosaic reality, between monumental artificiality and everyday reality, inevitably disturbed the spectators, who were caught between the imaginary elsewhere of another time ('aimable Trézène') and the presence of bodies and objects.

In the same way, the actors were split between tragic immobility and the passionate transports of their characters. Shifts between the two poles of fiction and physical presence pushed the actors to play a double game, alternately formal (or even cold), and psychological (or even hysterical). The entire production followed the same principle: it created a distressing *chiaroscuro* atmosphere, and yet sometimes cruelly illuminated an action with a follow spot (as one might find in a circus or a music hall), thus breaking the atmosphere the better to emphasise some decisive physical action. Thanks to this double perspective of the scenography and the mise en scène, the body of the actress (that of Dominique Blanc, who played Phèdre, for example) conveyed the impression of wrenching, so characteristic of Racine. The impossibility of a frontal, framed, stable gaze created in the spectator a feeling of witnessing a tragic struggle whose stakes cannot be calculated. Peduzzi's scenography, the chiaroscuro lighting (André Diot noted that 'the diminished lighting makes the audience more attentive than if they could see clearly'),[6] Chéreau's direction and the double game of the actors, all relate to this principle of a doubled space: alternately presenting a distant fantasised image, and a near and immediate action. The distant fantasised image and the shock of the real are the two basic principles of this dramaturgy, and by extension, of the whole mise en scène. The spectators felt them in the body with the same tearing sensation, the same oscillation between the dream-like perspective at a distance and a close and painful rupture. This 'schizophrenic' body thus did not know where to take refuge: in the absence of the waking dream or in the painful presence of the suffering body? Scenography is sometimes governed by contradictory principles which can only be reconciled by mise en scène.

Crossing the image

Sometimes directors feel the need to design their own set in order to have it conform as closely as possible to their dramaturgical vision. And conversely, some designers sooner or later end up directing: Yannis Kokkos, Daniel Jeanneteau, Alain Timar and Eric Vigner in particular have moved from visual arts or stage design backgrounds to directing their own productions, as if they feared being absorbed by mise en scène: that is, by the interweaving and the convergence of two arts and two practices.

In staging Marguerite Duras's play *La Bête dans la jungle* (2001), Eric Vigner visually organised James Lord's stage adaptation, which Duras herself had revised for the stage. Given this series of rewritings, it would be impossible, and moreover of little interest, to recover the origin of the narrative, to evaluate the 'authority' of the successive adaptations, or to try to establish the story. The scenography took into account this entanglement of texts, their superimposition and their relative unreadability. It employed an analogous set-up: an image recalls beyond itself another image; a series of appearances forever opening onto new appearances. Each void opens onto another void. The setting vaguely suggested a medieval château and a virgin forest, though the spectators could hardly determine which was which. From time to time, a translucent curtain with a lighting effect would separate the stage from the house, encouraging the spectator–voyeur to pierce this mysterious separation, in order to penetrate a forbidden universe.

The male hero seemed to succumb to the taboo, to the ban on stating the source of his trouble and exactly what the beast hidden in the jungle represents. Is it some shameful illness, homosexuality, some consuming passion, indecision, or some other defect? This taboo was in any case figured visually by the impossibility of stopping on any one image, or of stopping the constant flux. Vigner's solution consisted of playing with the stage box as if it were an open space that magically changed as soon as it were approached with the gaze, as soon as any attempt was made to pierce the mystery of its series of images. The musical settings evoked by the soundtrack and the lighting design subtly transformed the nature and the fictional status of the locations; the mise en scène generated a series of immaterial sets and curtains, stage images in constant flux. Thus the set, in command of the operation, worked by means of illusion and suggestion rather than with real materials. Within this quasi-virtual image or hologram, the very real bodies of the two actors could be perceived, but they were to some extent absorbed – made unreal – by

Figure 4.1 La bête dans la jungle by Marguerite Duras, directed by Éric Vigner, Théâtre de lorient. © Alain Fonteray.

this visual phantasmagoria. For the real bodies, Vigner created a disturbed and vague setting, a place of entrapment which is more readily guessed, desired and fantasised than truly perceived and identified. The scenography and what Vigner has called the 'artists' bodies' were more fantasied than real, and they matched perfectly. The stage decoration was a mask and a hiding place designed to make a voice heard, to stimulate the imagination and the fantasy of the spectators, instead of flooding them with images and mental representations.

With this work by Vigner, scenographic art seems to have come to the end of its long trajectory in the West: it has reached the final stage (which symbolist staging had in fact already achieved), that of the dissolution of the bodies of the actors into the image and the reality of fantasy. This does not mean that the actors are transformed into marionettes; they preserve their body in flesh and blood, but their presence is unobtrusive, atemporal, and closer to the ideal than to the material – 'outside of all time and event'.[7] Actors' bodies nonetheless remain at the heart of scenography and of theatrical architecture. For Vigner, like most people working in theatre today, both are at the service of the actor. 'There is no ideal architecture', he proclaimed in

an article on this subject in 1999, 'There are only individual projects
… and as many theatres as there are actors' bodies.'[7]

The golden rule of scenography (to put itself at the disposal of the
actor, and not the other way round) is perfectly verified in the visual
creation of Vigner and most of his colleagues. But even while
remaining at the service of the stage concept, scenography has found
a new place in the contemporary theatre; a more challenging place,
particularly in its relationship to the text. Scenography is no longer a
matter of illustrating or explicating, but of producing a 'visual
imaginary', part real and part fantasy, which also grafts itself onto
abstract and sound elements. This particularly calls into question the
traditional hierarchies of the text, the performance of the actor, and
the general interpretation of mise en scène.

Such 'dehierarchising' is very apparent in the spatial and scenographic
work of Alain Timar, for instance in his staging of *Le livre de ma mère*.

The echoes of space

A 'dehierarchising' of the elements of staging proceeds with an original
use of space, extending into dialogue and sound. In his adaptation of
Albert Cohen's autobiographical *Le Livre de ma mère*, Alain Timar offers a
subtle montage of a filial story evoking the memory of a mother (Théâtre
des Halles, Avignon, 2003). Here, he does not put together a dramatic
tale, or a dialogue between the son and the mother, since – although
they use the first person – the words are more lyric and obsessive than
dramatic. To avoid the monotony of a long monologue, Timar invents
new modes of speaking. He dramatises the text by splitting the voice of
the narrator into two agencies: that of the protagonist/author of the
story, and that of the musician/composer, who commentates the
narrative by way of a double bass, or even by way of speech. This set-up
for the narration is supported by a set which moves and shifts, with large
abstract paintings, about 2 metres square, whose canvases are turned
around at the beginning and placed on three sides of a rather deep
frontal stage. These paintings come progressively to block off the large
horizon, to close off the space, to suggest tombstones or a high wall.
Timar does not put canvases on stage as painters sometimes do when
they work in the theatre: his canvases are not frozen as if one were
studying them in a museum, but are integrated into the young man's
narration and into the spatial arrangements that result from it.

This manipulation by the protagonist is by no means the only
action, and it takes place only during certain interruptions in the
dialogue. This spatial arrangement depends upon the enunciation of

the text and on the accompaniment of the double bass. The complaints of the son, the penetrating evocations of his memories, are given rhythm with the intrusions of the music. The musical composition is, however, much more than a simple accompaniment or a continuous bass note – it is a work in itself. It is not restricted to a commentary or a questioning of the son's elevated language; it penetrates that language, creating a musical space; it gives the spectators the opportunity to perceive the paintings against the sonorous background of music that is more amusing than tragic; it makes one hear the space of memory in an as yet unheard of manner. But the spectator/hearer has little time to contemplate each of these revealed paintings: this is not a museum, where they might be able to control the visual and temporal rhythm, either during the performance or afterwards. The spectators find themselves embarking on a dramatic action which makes use of musical, scenic, pictorial and gestural spaces according to the needs of the discourse of the mise en scène.

Scenography, in the broad sense, is a gathering of elements deployed in space and time, but such chronotopes do not form synthetic or kinesthetic units; there is neither fusion nor correspondence among them. Instead of a total work of art, or conversely a reciprocal distancing of the arts, the staging sets up an interplay of echoes among the visual and auditory signs, bridges between time and space. Time and space, music and text, the present and memory are reunited and melded. Staging is the search for the text's other; it is to make the series of signs of the performance work together in such a way as to produce a chain reaction and an effect on the spectator. This effect and this chain reaction are manifested in the son's lyrical complaint: they are extended and intensified in the vibration of the bow, but also in the chromatic and visual vibration of the painting and of the space. Creating a set involves predicting such chain reactions in empty space, transforming into time and narrative that which arises from spatiality and music.

With Timar, as with the other artists considered here, scenography can be seen as culminating in a global practice which can no longer be readily distinguished from the art of directing. According to such an approach, which is commonplace today, scenography (writing with the stage) comes to mean stage composition by way of actors, which is directed towards the body and mind of the spectator. The vibrant body of the actor reaches the spectator, who is like a sensitive plate that vibrates on all sides at the slightest breeze. It reaches it on all levels simultaneously: vision, hearing, intellect. At this point, we can no longer distinguish scenography, music and text.

The migration of subspaces

Thus scenography extends its power just as it loses its specificity. This is a sign of scenography's integration into the production as a whole. If it is the case that the greatest loyalties are artistic, the marriages between directors and scenographers seem particularly long-lasting. Ariane Mnouchkine and Guy-Claude François's relationship started in 1975 with the first staging of *L'âge d'or*. In that heroic era, the task of the scenographer consisted primarily of remodelling the interior architectural space of the Cartoucherie, of transforming the spatial relationships between the stage and the auditorium. But since the Shakespeare productions in the 1980s, the public space has remained the same: benches, which are uncomfortable (but convivial due to their encouragement of sociality); and the audience faces a very large stage, looking down on it from quite high up. From this vantage point, the audience can also admire Jean-Jacques Lemêtre's musical instruments, which are set out stage left. For *Le Dernier Caravansérail* (*odyssées*), Mnouchkine kept this same open, frontal space, but the various episodes would unfold on small wheeled platforms, pushed on and off by stagehands, and unceasingly moving around, as if to suggest that everything is in unstable motion, that the world (the stage) is vast, but that the refugees shown possess only a small share of it.

Like a number of rapidly sketched little vignettes, the short two or three-character scenes reconstruct typical situations from the world of clandestine immigration, with the damned of the earth sharing the same obsession: to leave their country and somehow get to England. For the spectator standing outside these events, the world is put together anew as an incessant mixture of the same wretched elements. On the wheeled *mansions* (going to and fro at the whim of the flow of migration) the bodies are narrowly confined, even though there is in fact plenty of space left in the wide world. Each *mansion* houses a foreign world, limited to some miserable shanty dwelling, a telephone booth, a small customs or police checkpoint. Yet each is nonetheless a world in itself, a universe evoked with a few gestures and some gibberish. The space is not mimetic, and yet the details of costume and movement are accurate; the attitude and the *gestus* of the violence are precise. These *mansions* in different shapes and sizes, seemingly hastily constructed, contain concentrated worlds, cultural universes that are distinct if unstable, tiny, drifting microcosmic islands.

The fourth wall of the stage is none other than the border that these unhappy souls are trying to cross, in order to join us. We understand their misery and the violence that is carried forth. Soon we no longer

Figure 4.2 Le livre de ma mère, directed by Alain Timar, Théâtre des Halles. © Manuel Pascual.

know with whom we should identify spatially: should we fear their invasion or rather stand beside them in their attempt to break through the frontier and share our space? We waver between the two worlds, and the scenography produces the same effect of constriction, of agony, as if we also begin to feel the earth giving way beneath our feet. Once again, we experience the close connection between dramaturgy, scenography, acting and the physical sensations of the spectators.

The silence of space

Fundamentally, we should not be surprised that scenography is perfectly integrated into current theatre practice, since its rapid growth coincided with the appearance of mise en scène. Today, scenographers see it as a site dedicated to words and to silence. For Daniel Jeanneteau, and many other practitioners, scenography is at the heart of mise en scène's set-up, but it knows that it must become invisible to avoid ending up as a work in itself; it must serve the text or the subject while remaining silent. As Jeanneteau puts it, 'in order to welcome in the word, space should avoid meaning; it should introduce a certain confirmation of the meaning but not the meaning itself. It is only afterwards, under the influence of the meaning given by the word, that space can offer to transform itself and to absorb meanings.'[9] Claude Régy, moreover, has sought to:

> maintain the mass of unconscious thought that stems from the text, and to make it join with the spectators' unconscious. In order for this encounter to take place, the staging must keep a low profile, must let anything pass through, in order that the spectators allow themselves to be invaded by the living matter of the writing, inventing and meeting the author in person. The audience cannot receive this word and create its own fiction unless it is fully ready with its senses alive. To speak in a low tone, or to plunge the performance into darkness are methods of encouraging this change of consciousness, to shift the thresholds of perception, and, perhaps, create new ways of hearing.[10]

Scenography and mise en scène here evidently work towards their goals in perfect harmony. A shared interest in silence and emptiness has guided both Jeanneteau and Régy in their scenographic and playful choices: they require an open, neutral and unmarked space. Such a space facilitates a hearing of the text that is as direct as possible, as if the aim is to realise the old dream of putting the author and spectator in direct contact. 'The space of theatre unfolds in the border region located between speaking and hearing.'[11] Here, then, it is not a case of Peter Brook's 'empty space', a very real space which must be conquered by ridding it of the trappings of the bourgeois theatre, but rather of a symbolic space, that of a text that is not immediately reduced to its meaning. Régy and Jeanneteau are less concerned with the stage image conceived as a presentation case for performing actors, than with an interior vision, their own and that of a future spectator.

In their collaboration for Maeterlinck's *La Mort de Tintagiles* (1997) or for Jon Fosse's *Quelqu'un va venir* and *Melancholia* (2001), they began by clearing as much space as possible around the actors, concentrating their attention and ours on the speaking body of the actor. The scenography is not so much about realising the visual idea of the play as about slowing down the trajectory of the actor and allowing the meaning to emerge slowly for the spectators. In the space emptied by Jeanneteau for Régy's actors to speak their words, the staging stimulates in the spectator a physical and psychical slowdown precisely similar to that of the actors, who appear to be in a state of hibernation. In the work of this pair of deconstructionists, known associates, fascinated by slowness and emptiness – and the same is true of the work of many of their peers – the scenography eliminates all superfluous decoration, all figurative imitation, in order to create an abstract space. This space is no longer tied to the dramatic action except in an allusive, but not metaphorical way. With Jeanneteau, as with many other contemporary artists, we witness a privatisation of scenography: not in the sense of the stock market, but in terms of an internalisation of the spaces presented by the spectator, a dematerialisation. Jeanneteau's work consists of what he calls:

> guiding the gaze toward new spaces of consciousness, internalising the high stakes weighing upon the characters by weaving subtle relationships between these beings and their environment, evoking spaces whose emotional power and beauty do not exist prior to the performance, perhaps inadequate ones from the point of view of realism, but developed according to an economy of the imaginary which tends to locate the real place of appearance in the mind of the spectator.[12]

When he designs for other directors, Jeanneteau finds a more figurative and symbolic image, as he did for *Pélléas et Mélisande* staged by Alain Ollivier (Théâtre Gerard-Philippe, Saint-Denis, 2004). Once again the movement was slowed down and stylised, the vocal delivery wilfully artificial and polished, but the stage figuring, the reflection of the water for example, continues the magic tricks of Strehler or Chéreau, with the aesthetic overkill and atmospherics of Maeterlinck's theatre of the unexpressed. And yet this dedication to a heightened fantasy image, seen at a distance, accessible only to fantasy, did not prevent him from having a gangway extending all the way across the stage at the front, where groups appeared in conversation in close up. Scenography, therefore, plays with proximity and with distance. In the background, the image created an atmosphere by means of obscurity, shadows and the reflections of the water, while downstage, on the gangway, actions were isolated and highlighted. The actors and their characters seemed tangible, tactile, physically present, and the spectator was invited to construct these subspaces mentally and to arrange them according to the needs of the staging.

Concluding remarks

Different principles of scenography can thus coexist perfectly well, provided that the spectator plays a significant role in their utilisation. The important thing remains the coherence of the dramaturgical approach and the harmony of the production with the space and staging. 'Once the curtain rises, it is the show – and only the show – that counts, most likely because of its appropriateness to the place and the manner in which it is produced.'[13]

The conclusion of this overview was predictable from the start. There does not exist in France, or indeed elsewhere, scenography per se; instead there are many different scenographic approaches. Even if these conclusions reveal a number of shared features, no typology of scenography can be put forward. We might therefore instead rejoice in the rich variety of visual work and its ever-increasing proximity to the art of staging.

Unlike in the 1960s, the theatre is no longer conceived as what French film director René Allio might call 'a machine for seeing', but is rather a point of exchange between the previously separated components of the production (actor, sound, text). The spectator must now spot the design choices in the staging, and follow the space in all its nooks and crannies inside the performance. Scenographers have had the sense to integrate the temporal dimension into their work, since as Yannis Kokkos has observed, 'the duration of the theatrical action is also the duration of a space. Space should be marked by time.'[14]

There is not, then, at least in France, any standardisation of scenography, and this good news has its corollary in another sphere: contemporary theatre architecture rejects the flexible spaces that thrifty and ignorant authorities imposed upon us during the 1950s and 1960s. After the *maisons du peuple* of the 1930s, the *maisons de la culture* of the 1960s and 1970s, and the versatile spaces of the 1980s and 1990s, will the theatre end up coming back to its own buildings, leaving these shelters to get back to the proscenium arch?[15] This seems to be the general tendency: the theatre is coming back – in the case of (rare) new builds – to halls exclusively conceived from the outset for theatre; both artists and spectators now accept the idea that there is no ideal place from which to see the performance and they can only 'verify at what point the perception of a performance alters according to how the place of observation in the auditorium changes'.[16] In spite of the persistence of the proscenium arch theatre, many theatre buildings seem past their best today, since the societies which engendered them have gone forever. Despite this cumbersome heritage, theatre must always be reconsidered and must find new forms and architectural styles.

In an analogous way, for scenography and directing, the idea of a central point of view, optimal for the spectator and for analysis, becomes relative. Both scenography and directing encourage a personal journey and individual discovery. Although the stage has often become frontal, or Italianate once again, the audience is encouraged to pass from one place or one zone to another, with free seating, and the 'customer' is free to construct the temporal, spatial and causal sequence of the scenes (as in the *Odyssées*). This is a far cry from the extreme stage experimentation of the 1920s or 1960s avant-garde, from the 'environmental' theatre of Richard Schechner, from the free circulation of promenade performance, alternative, subverted spaces. Still, current scenographic experiments, now more modest and less confrontational, are as exacting as those of the old avant-garde. They no longer attempt to blind the audience with science, with a shameless parade of chic equipment, a very high-tech or high-class decorativism, technological monstrosities worthy of Broadway or Hollywood. They rely much more than previously upon the imagination of the spectator.

If we were to pursue our inquiry into domains other than text-based or experimental theatre, and venture, for example, towards the visual arts, film, installation art and multimedia work, we would no doubt observe that innovation and funding have been turned toward these newer sites. Nevertheless, text-based theatre, artistic theatre and experimental theatre, which are often our concern, are still an essential part of scenographic research, and the theoretical radicalism of figures like Jeanneteau and Braunschweig is not at all unique in contemporary stage practice. By dint of extending its field of operation, scenography has grown so close to mise en scène that they can no longer always be distinguished. This is perhaps the sign of scenography's maturity, but also of its culmination, of its conclusion. We can now therefore return to the theatre with our eyes closed.

When a play has just been written, or when it has never been performed, how might it be staged?

No precedent can serve, no model, not even to challenge some traditional interpretation.

Everything has yet to be invented, as the act of setting such plays in motion shows.

Such freedom can be frightening.

But most directors know no fear. They have seen it all before. And even if they are caught between the fear of displeasing the author (often also a friend) and the fear of not finding a way into the work (or of only finding an easy way in), they are ready to give their word, pledge their honour, and stake everything on the text as they set it into motion.

But authors always want the last word; they supply texts that resist theatre, that are stage-proof, texts that prevent, or at least hinder, the process of stage conversion.

All in vain.

Directors in the 1990s and 2000s – daughters and sons of the great stage autocrats of institutional decentralisation and hermeneutic recentralisation – do not always get the last word. But they always get the last action, the last bullet; he who laughs last laughs longest!

So must we foresee what these artists concoct for the rest of us, spectators, transfixed by unheard-of texts and unspeakable images? Can we ever hope to catch up?

5 The *mise en jeu* of contemporary texts

This title immediately requires a couple of words of explanation, if not more. There are several different ways of playing a text, of setting it in motion (*mise en jeu*), and no single specific way of staging it. It is also better to talk in terms of 'texts', rather than in terms of plays, since the starting point of a performance is neither a dialogue nor even a dramatic action embodied by characters. And finally, 'contemporary' refers to texts written over the last twenty or thirty years, without specifying whether they are innovative or conventional ones.

But is there, we might ask, a specific way of staging contemporary authors? Can we discern one or more methods, or do we face a situation where, as one Koltès character puts it, 'There are no rules, there are only means; there are only weapons'?[1] These questions are not as rhetorical as they might at first seem, since we need to determine two things: first, whether new writing demands a new method of staging, and second, whether experimental mise en scène inspires new ways of writing. We might well be tempted to respond (cutting a long story short and remaining faithful to the spirit of our times), stating that there are as many methods of staging as there are texts, and so no theory could ever be capable of dealing with this diversity. But to claim this would be to forget that the history of mise en scène has, over a hundred years, accumulated numerous acting and staging techniques, techniques that cannot be completely ignored when staging the contemporary repertoire. Unable to forget a recent and remarkable past, but unable to completely break with it, we face specific problems when staging contemporary authors. It is not easy to separate the old and the new in this kind of staging. We know the classic methods of mise en scène, those developed from the 1950s to the 1980s (and notably for the staging of classical plays), but we are disarmed by the diversity of contemporary possibilities of *mise en jeu*.

If, for the time being at least, a typology of texts and of techniques of mise en scène should be avoided, a few particular examples can still be analysed. In the following pages, we will describe a few rules for the *mise en jeu* of contemporary texts, in order patiently to piece together the jigsaw of the current theatre landscape, to distinguish a few specific cases and to envisage – in the longer term – a panorama and then a typology of stage practices. The examples have been chosen almost at random according to particular encounters, recordings and personal taste, rather than in order to satisfy any overall theory and systematic view. These examples are concerned with already published texts, 'finished' texts: that is, texts no longer likely to shift as a result of a writing or acting workshop, and thus considered 'finished' by the author, even if the right to make slight modifications remains reserved. A dramatic text of this type is in principle not modifiable or adaptable; it constitutes the solid basis of the work of mise en scène; it does not wait for staging in order to exist, and is readable like any literary work. We are no longer, as in the 1960s or 1970s, in the situation of writing-in-progress, work that was developed in the workshop, and likely to be modified after things have been tried out by the actors. It has become rare, at least in France, that a text is produced collectively, or that actors are enlisted in the process of a text's elaboration. Such a luxury is rare these days, which is a source of regret for young authors like Emmanuel Darley: 'Ideally, the author would be able to work with the actors throughout the process of writing. To place one's words at risk thanks to the presence of the body and the voice before reaching a final version of the theatre text.'[2] The only thing that today's director has – as with the classics – is therefore the finished text, and perhaps also the living author, ready to respond to – sometimes indiscreet – questions, and all being well, actors who are happy to test the most varied and paradoxical hypotheses for the text's interpretation.

Despite the infinite freedom of interpretation allowed by contemporary texts, the 'solutions' adopted tend to be fairly modest, as if directors do not dare, or do not wish, to take the place of the author, to impose too personal a vision and attitude on a play that must first be brought to the attention of the audience via the stage. This probably explains why the staging of contemporary plays – even under the influence of very visible work on the classics in the 1950s, 1960s and 1970s – keeps a low profile, and seems to reject the excesses and the effects of mise en scène. The beginning of the 1980s marked a turning point: the crisis linked to the (visual and financial) excess of the stage led to a certain calm among artists and favoured the rise of dramatic writing, encouraged by the subsidy system, by residencies, and equally by the necessity of mounting lighter and cheaper productions. This crisis of theatrical production benefited the author: 'At the beginning of the 1980s, the French author was a being left alone, defending his own language and his individual imagination while, like Koltès, he faced huge changes in the contemporary world.'[3] Chéreau's stagings of Koltès, from 1982, and the untimely demise of Koltès in 1989, marked a transition from the golden age of showbiz mise en scène to the beginnings of new writing. This is clear in the example of *Combat de nègre et de chiens*, directed by Chéreau in 1983, and in the restaging of the same play by Dimiter Gotscheff in 2004 at the Berlin Volksbühne. Other examples in this chapter – productions of plays by Marie NDiaye, Catherine Anne and Noëlle Renaude, all staged between 2002 and 2005 – confirm these huge changes in the world as well as the difficulty of establishing a truly contemporary mise en scène.

Combat de nègre et de chiens[4]

Dimiter Gotscheff's production *Combat de nègre et de chiens* (*Black Battles with Dogs*) is different at every stage from that of Chéreau and indeed seems to contradict the author's own hypotheses. At Nanterre, Chéreau reconstituted an African environment: heat, haze, sounds, costume, European and African actors. The first staging of the play stigmatised white racism in a polarising way. Alboury, the brother of the victim, is a black Antigone, who has come to claim his brother's corpse. He kills Cal, the white murderer. In Gotscheff's version, towards the end of the play Horn, the white engineer, attempts one last manoeuvre to buy the silence of Alboury. Alboury, played by a white actor who is very ostentatiously disguised as a black man, enjoys imitating the stereotypes expected of him by white racists. He performs a masquerade in order to catch Horn, and reveals his baseness and his cheap tricks. Like an abject character from Genet, he gives the 'black' a voluntarily negative image, projecting the white's expectations, fears and aggression onto himself. He builds the character of a crude, dirty, unlearned savage. To show the functioning of racism and power, he demonstrates the construction of a fabricated identity, far from the essentialism of Koltès, and from Koltès's 'black and white' vision of racial conflict.

Gotscheff thus suggests that each of us is potentially racist, and that racial identity is only a construction from the other's gaze. Hence the reversal of all the stereotypes: the black sniffs the white, who dons a ridiculous grass skirt and so on, with disgust. Gotscheff (who, in the

1980s staged this same play in the realist style of Chéreau) thus turns this contemporary tragedy of clear ideas upside down, transforming it into a mocking masquerade, making only the point that every construction of identity is constructible and deconstructible. He certainly still denounces the racism and baseness of the whites, but does so by playing with identity and by giving the actors the possibility of creating and demolishing their own racial identity. Notions of fixed identity, of authenticity and of presence, are rendered ridiculous in an endless play of deconstructions and differences.

Thus conceived, Gotscheff's mise en scène challenges the presentation of the conflict. For this Bulgarian director, racism is not presented as ideological conflict, a contradictory vision of the world, but rather as a game of construction. Alboury is merely an empty construction, a projection of racists' hatred and fear. This construction, deliberately exaggerated and parodical, allows a denunciation of the way in which racists project onto the other that which they cannot bear, attributing it as signifying a defect in the other. By mocking the simplistic views of humanists and liberals, Gotscheff finds an entirely new level of fiction and draws on acting conventions closer to the music hall or to stand-up comedy. Africa is an empty blank surface covered in confetti, falling endlessly from the sky. Alboury is a white master of ceremonies who speaks directly to the audience with a microphone, puts on make-up in front of them, addresses them directly, and ends the show with racist jokes about blacks and Bulgarians. Gotscheff reintroduces Brecht in his own way, the Brecht of *Man is Man*: the subject is created in front of us, and theatre is a way of showing the construction of 'natural' identities, lending a critical distance.

In this way, it is not enough for the mise en scène to adapt to the flavour of the month: it completely changed the system of enunciation, reduced the text to a third of its length, and above all denounced its initial ideological functioning. It is unclear whether it even remains the same play. It is no longer about neocolonial exploitation, but about the construction of identity. It takes into account a change of atmosphere, the progression of globalisation. Under the guise of provocation and playfulness, it updates the play, adapts it to a new situation, pokes fun at the mimetic and moralistic presentation of racism, mocks political correctness, even while taking place on a subsidised stage. Gotscheff's provocation makes fun, not only of the 1980s and 1990s, but also of the way in which racism is treated in countries where political correctness reigns, such as Germany and the Anglo-American world. It signals a counter attack on petit-bourgeois and apolitical moralism and on thinking that is too correct to be honest.

Papa doit manger

Gotscheff updates an already old play, and this contribution oddly enough connects with the first production of Marie NDiaye's *Papa doit manger* (at the Comédie Française with director André Engel).[5] As this work is also about racism, it is worth reading it alongside the Koltès play. How does this play, and this staging, address the issues also present in the Koltès play, and how do they propose a different (albeit close) staging solution, in a context that is just as ideologically sensitive?

Marie NDiaye is an author of African origin on her father's side, but was born and has always lived in France. She is thus in no way an African writer or one from the francophone world outside France. The play tells the story of Papa, a black man returning home to his white wife after an absence of ten years. We quickly understand that he has come back only in order to extort money from her. He considers every action legitimate on the grounds that he 'must eat' (*doit manger*). We learn that he is ready to steal, cheat, lie, abandon the baby that he had with another woman, to live off the back of his daughter and go back to his former wife's home. The character is clearly unpleasant, but he has also always been the victim of the ordinary racism of his stepfamily. Maman maintains an endless 'inexplicable love' for him.[6] Will she take him back?

Papa doit manger is by no means a thesis play. It gives neither responses nor recipes, it obliges the director to take a position on the behaviour of the principal character, and thus on the story. Was it not the mission of mise en scène, or at least one of its missions at the start (towards the end of the nineteenth century) to enable the audience to understand a complicated or tangled story, to suggest the ideological and psychological stakes, to adopt a point of view on the reality and the fiction? In the last twenty years, it has been forgotten to some extent that mise en scène can also be an instrument for judging, distinguishing, pointing out difficulties or proposing solutions. As for the work of the actor, it consists of influencing our judgement on the actions and the characters. Bakary Sangaré, an actor of Malian origin, the first African member of the Comédie Française company, inhabits a character who is first likeable in his volubility and candour, then becomes frankly despicable. The text and the performance place the spectator in the position of Zelner, the friend of Maman, a caricature of the fair and honest teacher. This character provides us with a point of view on the action with which we can identify, and which takes as its theme our relationship with the other, with the foreigner, with the black person.

The colour of his skin fooled me.

I thought I didn't have the right to hate him. All hatred towards him is politically reprehensible. ...

He behaved badly, granted. But a Black, I told myself, is not responsible for his actions since a Black is first and foremost a victim.

There is no guilty Black man, I told myself, not on our land. ...

Everything is our fault, I told myself. ...

And if I dared, I would punch him in the face. ...

But can you hit a Black man? I'm not sure yet.[7]

Would the author, Marie NDiaye, be able to put these words into her character's mouth, could she morally condemn him, if she were not herself black? Of this too, we are perhaps 'not sure yet'! And it obviously depends on the context. Moreover, must we know the colour of the author, of the director, of the actor in order to know whether her critique of an unpleasant, but black, character is permissible? As soon as the audience knows that the writer is black, and provided it is assumed that the author is not succumbing to self-hatred and to anti-black racism, it will feel acceptable to judge objectively (and in this case, judge harshly) the conduct of Papa. André Engel seems to head in this direction, and this is the meaning of his mise en scène, it seems – to follow the text. But in the last analysis, it is for the spectators to judge.

If we consult Engel's notes on staging in the programme, we can observe a certain contradiction with what is apparent in the acting. Engel feels obliged – but is he really? – to find in Papa's character excuses that are not present in the text. Zelner, he writes, is supposedly obsessed with Papa's skin colour. But if Zelner is preoccupied with this skin colour, it is not (it would seem) in any racist way. Is the failure to criticise behaviour that could be morally condemned, for fear of being judged racist, not itself a form of racism, a cowardice born of fear of not being politically correct? This is perhaps ultimately the hidden secondary meaning of the play, and probably the most important one. In any case, in the programme, Engel defends Papa as someone who was 'abandoned' by his wife and rejected by his daughter because he was 'too heavy, useless and in the way'.[8] Like a good Brechtian, he interrogates the possible political meaning of the story: he sees in this abandonment a metaphor for what he calls the 'young African continent'. This seems more Engel's personal opinion than a truth found in the text. It is also a concession made to a theatre institution preoccupied with the idea that it will be accused of racism if it condemns a black character, just as the company believes itself to be above suspicion because it has just hired an African actor.

In comparing Engel's attitude with that of Gotscheff on the same subject, it must be acknowledged that French artists tend to operate with some delay, or some cautiousness. It is true that the Koltès play is showing its age a bit, and that debate around identity has come a long way, especially outside France; we are a long way from the 'romantic' position of people like Chéreau and Koltès on the 'young African continent'. The ravaging parody of Gotscheff stands in contrast to the more subtle and ambiguous irony of Engel. If mise en scène, like irony, is the art of saying without saying, we are, along with NDiaye and Engel, deep in ironic, rationalist and critical territory. The debate is open, even as the denial inherent in any artistic creation allows for it not to be determined; it is for the reader and the spectator to judge for themselves.

Le bonheur du vent

To judge for oneself is perhaps one of the goals of new writing: such is the friendly constraint, the gentle violence that the author imposes on the spectator. But what if the author stages her own work? *Le bonheur du vent,* a play written in 2003 and staged at the Théâtre de l'Est Parisien by Catherine Anne,[9] gives us the opportunity to study the way in which a text is transposed when the director knows, in theory, its every nook and cranny. Does the gesture of the writer occasion the same repercussions as the gesture of the director and his actors? Is a good director one who knows the tricks of the playwright's trade?

Freely inspired by the life of Calamity Jane, *Le bonheur du vent* tells the story of Jane. Jane had to abandon her baby to a rich couple, Helen and Jim. The three acts of the play turn around these three women: the mother, the adoptive mother and the daughter. The child goes from one woman to another, without being able to return to her biological mother after her adoptive mother dies. When the daughter learns the secret of her birth, her real mother Jane has already left for the other side, the banks of old age and of death. If such a story resonates so profoundly in us, it is because it concerns questions that are universally human: motherhood, attachment to the child, the heartbreak of separation, the death of the mother. These primordial emotions are raised in the text, as onstage, with great dramatic tension. The different scenes seem carefully prepared by the dramatic structure: the meeting, the near recognition, the moment when, the truth known, the mother and the daughter 'perhaps speak, despite the thousands of miles that separate them',[10] where the death of one coincides with the beginning of the life of the other.

The lightness of the writing – most often short free verses which are said on a breath – corresponds to a lightness of staging: quick and fleeting movements, scenes that are set up in a flash and disappear just as fast, minimal characterisation, a curtain that erases what has just been shown. Writing and acting coincide with the quickness and simplicity of the sketch: no scrupulously reconstituted Wild West, no bourgeois interior, no stagecoach attacked by Jane, and no story inscribed in a recognisable time or space. A few words set the scene, a curtain that is suddenly pulled closed creates a place that disappears no sooner than the curtain is drawn. A few lines, a bit of costume or a sound from the soundtrack, and immediately the outside world appears and gives meaning to the words. 'On the barest of stages, we seek to show the exterior traces of interior worlds.'[11] In the empty space of the stage, only at times limited by the stage curtain, dense and enigmatic words arise fleetingly to create a period, a situation, a place, a moment of life. Hence these focusing effects, close-ups, zooms on certain points in the text. Takes of different lengths, as in the editing of a film, appear one after another and give the performance its rhythm. The acting emphasises close-ups on a single facial expression, a single gesture, a single aspect of a relationship with another. Assonances, repetitions, snappy turns of phrase, summary phrases, words that sum up the play ('I prefer the happiness of the wind to the comfort of houses'),[12] all create a phenomenon of regularity, of abstraction, which we could say 'sets' the text on the stage, stabilises it, avoids its having to account for itself with a heavy illustration.

On the huge stage of the Théâtre de l'Est Parisien, on the playing and writing surface, the sketch is as much visual as it is discursive. Writing fosters this quickness of the sketch and the line, moments of rupture and of silence, moments where the echo of the words becomes audible. One example among many others:

JANE: No need for money
Money always buys
I get by
Keep your cash Jim thanks for coming over
Out
Everybody out
I want to be alone.[13]

The absence of punctuation does not prevent pauses: in fact it facilitates them and makes them necessary. There is no syntactical ambiguity, only awareness of units of breath, which help organise the thinking. The typography of the play is like breathing, it helps the actor find phrasing, and later a gestural language. Marie-Armell Deguy's acting physically renders the out-of-sync phrase, a structure that is as much respiratory as emotional and semantic. The clearly visible rhythmic structure, which is also relatively and slightly modifiable by the voice and the body, becomes the basis of an interpretation, by way of accumulation, of the whole staging. The staging does not stem from a diagram or from a pre-existing image, brought in from outside by the director. It develops unit by unit, by a series and accumulation of exchanges, as the result of a reading that from the start seeks to lean on the attitudes and movements of the actress as much as on her accents and intonations.

Since the author is also by training a director and an actress, the rhythmic structuring and the blocking of sequences take place at almost the same time. One supposes that Catherine Anne as director does not need to look for the meaning of her text, and that she naturally finds its rhythmic foundations, its tempo, its phrasing and its intonations: in short, the entire psychomotor set-up which must be the basis for any attempt at a staging.

Rhythm gives the text its meaning. This is even more so in a work where silence carries such importance, giving us a chance, according to Michel Corvin, 'to see the carnal silence of mise en scène indirectly influence writing'.[14]

Undoubtedly, mise en scène confirms, and also displaces, that which writing proposed. Each enriches the other without claiming to be the first or the foremost. The body of the author extends into the body of the director, then into the body of the interpreter (the actor as well as the spectator). The possibility remains for those who will come after to read differently and to reactivate an interpretation. An 'exterior' director will thus move anything that tends to become stable, to become anchored to the text, or is just a bit too self-assured.

A tous ceux qui ...

Whether the mise en scène is the work of the author or of someone different, attention must be paid to the discursive and rhetorical texture of the text. The director cannot dispense with reading the text, analysing its punctuation and rhythm, taking account of its linguistic and discursive traces. This attention given to texture appears more important than bringing in images or external impulses, at least for the staging of texts performed today. Additional proof is provided by the staging of Noëlle Renaude's play *A tous ceux qui ...* presented by Claude Maurice and Joël Collot at the 2005 Avignon festival.[15]

Directors from the company Art Mixte, who also play all thirty roles, had the good sense to set these speeches – punctuated by toasting – at a table for a banquet or a family party. The guests seem to speak to each other and the setting and period are very recognisable. This staging choice corresponds perfectly with Noëlle Renaude's advice to stick closely to the text:

> One must speak up in order to take the floor. Love the suspense that punctuation allows. Develop a taste for the exchange of words, for hesitation, for intrusion, for the risk taken when language tells us stories? If you know how to look, everything is right there. And the character, if there is one, will always turn up in the end.[16]

This advice is basically the same as that of Copeau, when he was seeking to recover the breath or the silence of the author, of Jouvet when he sought 'sentiment' or the respiratory difficulty of Molière, of Vitez reconstructing his 'master's voice'.

Such directives can be very useful in order to enter the lexicological and rhythmic world of an author, to avoid throwing oneself at the character and making that the axis of the narrative. Actors may well be impatient to find their characters, to lend them a body and a voice. But if they wait for a while – if their director manages to hold them back, to temper their desire, if they listen for suspense, silence, changes of rhythm – they will acquire a more structural and global vision of the play and will better establish an overall construction, inside which the character can safely emerge.

The writing of the play follows this double principle expressed by Noëlle Renaude: a very rigorous overall structure, and very strong mimetic character effects. The fact that the monologues are delivered by characters who are increasingly old helps us compare the different points of view according to age, gender and the social origin of the speakers. Thanks to the description of a single event given by different voices, we get to know a rather homogenous set of figures. A network is woven bit by bit: allusions, verbal tics, period ways of speaking, similarities. But such a colourful portrait gallery rather encourages the actors to mark the differences, if only in order to shine in the arts of metamorphosis and imitation, arts in which Maurice and Collot excel.

Indeed, character effects are what stand out at first reading, at first impression in this first attempt at a staging. Noëlle Renaude was able to pick out the tics of common speech of the period. This does not mean that her writing is naturalistic and phonogrammatical; the testimonies are not simply written from the perspective and linguistic competence of the character; linguistic verisimilitude or lexical precision are not sought in the phrases. Thus, for example, when Baba (four years old) speaks of his 'sister Lili who died five years ago amidst historical chaos',[17] it is not only he who speaks, but an invisible narrator, feeding him the monologue. The testimony is not historical or authentic, it does not seek to deceive as to the origin of the speech. The author is recognisable at every level: lexical, syntactical, discursive; but the narrator is so discreet that the speaker seems completely to be on the spot. Her rhetoric enables her to infiltrate the other's discourse to work on it from the inside, to complete it, to contradict it with irony, and to refer to other accounts.

The task of Maurice and Collot is to find the tone and voice of their creations, but without neglecting the form and rules of writing. Their movements are minimal and always relevant. The rhythmical setting of the text is so coherent that we recognise a certain dynamic from one character to another. To rediscover the spirit of a period demands that the actors grasp a specific colour of voice, a way of holding the body, and a common pronunciation; this is to transcend the peculiarities of the actors and assist in the overall reading. At every step, the actors invent a period body: a way of moving, of contracting, of hiding from the sight of others, of getting angry. They end up constituting a living documentary on a vanished time, which lives on in the memory of those born just after the war. Looking for the *habitus*[18] of the bodies, its 'socialised subjectivity',[19] they intuitively find this movement, this corporeity of a past time, they are its embodied encyclopaedia.

If the acting consists of giving believable indications to each figure, the staging reconstructs the puzzle of words while assuring the unity of the gestures and behaviours. Claude Maurice and Joël Collot maintain the writing of Noëlle Renaude and their own work in an unstable balance between a rather abstract overall composition and uncontrolled realistic notation. It is a delicate balance: if the composition is too rigid, the acting becomes formal and risks losing its flavour; if on the other hand the acting choices are too mimetic and slavishly imitative, the overall impression and spirit of the time will no

Figure 5.1 À tous ceux qui... by Noëlle Renaude, directed by Claude Maurice et Joël Collot, Théâtre Jean-Vilar Montpellier. © Jean-François Guiret.

longer feature. Guided by Noëlle Renaude's advice, they find an unexpected equilibrium and their work preserves all the promise of the writing.

It seems that the key to a 'successful' staging of Noëlle Renaude's texts consists of finding a sufficiently simple, coherent and abstract vocabulary for the gestures and the mise en scène, allowing the spectators to orient themselves, however complex the text or the countless characters. This was confirmed in seeing Jean-Paul Dias, directed by Frédéric Maragnani, playing the *Quarante églogues, natures mortes et motifs*.[20] In order to interpret the various roles, Dias found a more or less abstract gestural system, in the manner of Decroux's corporeal mime. This was not only because of the overalls with long white lines emphasising the outline of the body and its postures, as in Decroux's mime play *L'Usine*, of which a film remains, but particularly thanks to the mastery of postures and of very economical gestures. As is the case with Decroux, every sequence begins with, and returns to, a centred and balanced body, marked by a point on the floor and an imaginary centre in the body. Fortunately, Jean-Paul Dias avoids the flaws of Jaques-Dalcroze's eurythmics and any absolute correspondence of sound and gesture.

Figure 5.2 Jean-Paul Dias in *Quarante églogues* by Noëlle Renaude, directed by Frédéric Maragnani. © Frédéric Maragnani.

Dialogue

For more than a century, we have heard talk of a crisis of dialogue in Western theatre. Should this be taken seriously? Is dialogue not always, and necessarily, in crisis?

This supposed crisis concerns communication as question–response, the ping-pong of everyday conversation: the comings and goings of words have actually become rare in contemporary dramaturgy. In the strict sense, and in life, there is dialogue only if two speakers, two psychic entities, two subjects receive and emit – so exchange – words. In the theatre, this ideal exchange has never really existed: there is always some speech that, far from being exchanged, is thrown somewhere or other. Language is thrown, and is lost, but it is not lost for everyone, at least not for the spectator or auditor.

Nevertheless, it has a bad press lately: it is assimilated into traditional dramaturgy, even into *boulevard* theatre, at best into the dramatic form which, according to Szondi, has been in crisis since Ibsen, Maeterlinck and Chekhov. New authors try to write against dialogue, something they do not always achieve. As for theorists, they do not employ the term without a certain malaise, preferring instead, in describing new forms, the term 'voice' (a *'partage des voix'*, as Jean-Luc Nancy puts it), 'polyphony', 'chorus', or 'chorality'. Numerous non-verbal, gestural forms, such as 'live art', performance art and installation art, get along very well without dialogue.

To account for these examples of new writing, it is best to avoid typologies of dialogue, as theatrology once proposed, since a typology often remains based on so-called 'normal' communication, on the mimesis of human exchange and thus on precisely the model of communication that such writing seeks to go beyond. It is equally unhelpful to wish to distinguish categorically the dialogue from the monologue, as was the case in classical dramaturgy. It is preferable to oppose linked dialogue (such as Racine) and unlinked dialogue (such as Büchner). It is still more judicious to invent new tools in order to grasp the latest developments. Thus 'chorality' points out that theatre no longer limits dialogue to verbal exchanges, and that the classical chorus has metamorphosed into an assembly of figures collected in the same space–time in order to speak, but also in order to keep silent together and to intervene at rather arbitrary points (think of Marthaler's works).

Within mise en scène, dialogue has an entirely different character. It is no longer really confined to the exchange of words. Once it is put into enunciation, interaction between all of the materials, signified and signifiers, becomes the rule. Is this still a dialogue? Only in the metaphorical sense. It is rather the genesis of mise en scène, the orchestration of exchanges and the placement of a network of signs. Thus there is a 'dialogue' of silences, changes of rhythm, sonic and visual echoes, of all the different elements of the performance. Once the text is embodied in a body, music, rhythm, it is no longer its own, it is as if transported, it echoes with all the signs of the performance, and from this interaction mise en scène is born. Mise en scène, sometimes prolonging writing, conjoins or disjoins elements of dialogue, prevents all contact, or on the contrary weaves together the dialogical elements with the other elements of the stage. Once it is placed inside the interactivity of the stage, dialogue explodes, opening itself up to polyphony. New writing only ever anticipates this dissemination, sometimes to the point of being so pulverised that the mise en scène feels the need to patch things up and stick the pieces back together. It is thus equally stage practices and changes in the conception of human interactions – and the two are obviously linked – that cause dialogue to evolve.

Where is dialogue going? It never ceases to be reconfigured, while it once seemed to be in danger of becoming extinct. It reckons with the evolution of human relations: both easier and more coloured by autism. Do we still wish to live together, to speak, to 'exchange'? But at what price? What is left for us to say to each other, and are other people still concerned? These are the questions we must ask ourselves, before we even look for new forms of dialogue.

Vinaver and mise en scène

Vinaver is wary of any mise en scène that buries the text under images and actions. He claims that mise en scène has, over the years, become a *mise en trop* ('a staging of too much'): too much stage interpretation, too much useless acting. And yet 'the text requires only one thing: to be heard as distinctly as possible on stage'.[21] But this is only the case, of course, if we can agree on what is meant by 'to be heard'! Is it simply a question of being perceived aurally or rather one of being understood intellectually? For Vinaver, it is primarily a matter of listening, but this is only useful if the listener and the spectator understand what the text and the author are trying to do. Therefore, the risk of saying too much by way of the stage is constantly present.

So what exactly makes Vinaver so suspicious? Is the *mise en trop* also the placement of a trope (if we add an 'e'), or the work of a *Misanthrope*?

There is a *mise en trope* when the mise en scène considers itself as a trope, that is, as a stylistic figure used to say – in a decorative and rhetorical manner – what the text itself is already saying. Such a staging might, for example, include a visual or stage metaphor, employed to illustrate the text.

The *Misanthrope*, as in Molière's play, hates mankind, just as the director basically deeply despises texts and seeks to replace them with an original stage commentary.

So where is Vinaver located in the recent history of mise en scène? According the Vinaver, the director, since the 1960s, has often been the absolute master of the theatrical enterprise; text is used as the pretext for the director's own creation. Thus the director becomes the creator of a stage work that is specifically designed to dispense with playwrights, as Edward Gordon Craig predicted as early as the start of the twentieth century. But by the late 1980s, Vinaver, author of a study on theatre publishing,[22] helped to put a halt to the invasion of directors into the theatrical institution and the rehabilitation of the playwright. He thus participated in a reassessment of the functions of mise en scène. Mise en scène loses some of the autonomy it had fought so hard to win. Vinaver reintroduced the concept of norms, arguing that there are any number of 'perversions' of the text by the staging, but also 'right' ways to play the text.[23] But can we judge whether the mise en scène is right or whether it has been perverted? Implicit norms seem to prevail, but what are they? Vinaver does not specify the role and contribution of the director. We can, however, venture to guess that one of the main tasks of the director is to find a situation of enunciation to be inserted into both the proposed fiction and the fiction imagined by the audience. Yet there exists, on the part of Vinaver the author, a deliberate desire not to write for a future mise en scène. In the words of Vitez, Vinaver's text is not soluble in mise en scène; it does not dissolve like sugar in water (insoluble suggests something that does not dissolve, and also something for which there is no solution). These 'insoluble' texts are nevertheless 'stageable' – they can be put on a stage. But there is no universal recipe for mise en scène: 'So what should it be? Having seen many directors work, including the greatest of them, I am still unable to say. What should life be? How would you answer that?'[24]

Conclusions

From these isolated examples, it is very difficult to generalise and to define the main principles of staging contemporary texts. We will thus limit ourselves to pointing out a few key tendencies, hypotheses more than theses, impressions more than scientific and definitive conclusions.

- We have not been able to establish that stagings of contemporary work have invented new methods that radically differ from those employed in staging classics. And this is especially the case today, as the gap, or perhaps the difference, between classical and modern is increasingly narrow. The approach is perhaps less spectacular, there is a tendency to guide and assist the actor, to avoid the lavishness of scenography and the sometimes burdensome reflections of dramaturgical analysis. This focus sometimes leads to 'conceptual' staging, founded on a basic and repetitive idea, which is not particularly sensual, and which, despite its intelligence, quickly becomes fastidious.

- Should we give mise en scène another chance, avoiding the limitation of a dramatised reading, where words are just placed in the mouths of the actors? These readings are sometimes second-rate stagings: the play gets heard as an excuse to avoid staging it later. We should not settle for the actor-as-reader, nor confuse the results of a workshop process (however exciting they may be) with the public presentation of a work.

- Mise en scène seeks a middle way, between large-scale showy productions (with matching budgets) and the staged reading or a performance (where the actors only speak the text). So, from Vinaver's *mise-en-trop* ('a staging of too much'), we have nearly reached the *mise-en-pas-assez* (the staging of too little).

- While one might speak of a mise en scène style in tackling the classics, one instead finds a *method* in contemporary work. As a *method* that is only suitable for the play to be staged, or at most for one specific author's work, it is hard to reuse and resists any theory. Indeed, we never speak of the *style* of a director who specialises in contemporary work. Every staging of a new text requires the reinvention of a space, an action, a rhythm; these are not foreseeable when the text is merely read. Rhythmic work on the voice and its stage performance are more important than the meaning of the text.

- Conversely, certain of today's authors are performed according to a recognised and tested method. This constitutes a victory of method, or even of the 'discourse on method', but also presents a risk of sclerosis when it becomes the norm, reappearing from one production to another, seeming rehashed. For instance, 'Vinaverian acting' attained a kind of formal perfection (with Françon or Vinaver himself – and with the help of Catherine Anne in their recent production of *A la renverse* and of Gilone Brun with the staging of *Iphigénie hôtel*), but seems no longer capable of pushing the play to its limits.

- It is thus vital – in order to avoid any premature canonisation, or fossilisation – to encourage more iconoclastic experiments. According to David Bradby, this is already the case for Vinaver in the United Kingdom. And a good thing too! The acceptance into the repertoire of authors like Koltès, Vinaver, Minyana, Renaude and Durif might very well accelerate this process of canonisation and encourage the standardisation of acting style. We await with impatience ideas from the next generation of directors.

- New methods and approaches to mise en scène might remain to be invented, even while writing is experiencing unprecedented growth. Irritated by a frequent point made by the audience (but also by directors) that there are no more authors, Eugène Durif throws the question back at them:

    There are perhaps few directors who are capable of taking care of today's texts, of giving them an opportunity to be heard and seen, with jubilation, in a state of constant desire. These texts are being created today, and new, singular, imaginative, theatrical approaches remain to be invented for them.[25]

    It is not easy to describe these new approaches, precisely because the director renounces absolute control over the choice of material.

- One such approach, for instance, involves the place of ideology, of meaning and of the making of specific points. Ideology is no longer presupposed, known in advance, accepted – it is rather something to be discovered or invented by way of theatre. What does Gotscheff have in mind with his white and black masquerade? What does Engel think about anti-white racism? What about Vinaver? Does he really remain neutral when quoting the discourses of others? The directors' stagings have in any case at least examined the problem, instead of considering it already resolved. Theatre is a hermeneutic instrument for getting to know politics, not a field for the application of politics.

- This is why mise en scène, for the last twenty years, with classics and with hypermodern plays, has kept a low profile. It no longer claims to contest or reconstruct the world, nor to produce its own universe capable of rivalling the world. The director no longer has to be a 'cultural critic'[26] describing and defying the world. The director is more of a deconstructer, a blurrer of generic categories, a go-between,[27] as Cantarella puts it. The only demand placed on mise en scène is that it must set theatre in motion, particularly in conjunction with the scenographer: 'we work on measuring the temperature, the consistency of the materials that appear to us in the texts. I might, for instance, say: "this text reminds me of something fine and taut," or "Whiteness should be read into this text."'[28] Faced with contemporary writing, the critic is often disarmed, having neither the tools nor the legitimacy to make a judgement, leaving the spectators to make up their own minds and evaluate the staging according to their own subjective criteria.

- Where, then, has mise en scène gone? Writing has absorbed a large proportion of it, as if, in advance, the author had already resolved numerous questions of staging: ambiguities that cannot be removed, characters that cannot figure, constant changes of key in the acting, of conventions, and of levels of reality. The director is no longer the master of the acting, or at least not the only master, but rather merely the author's and the actor's partner, a person of no importance. It has become almost impossible to separate writing and mise en scène, even if the old division of labour continues to define the functions of author, actor, director (and spectator). *Mise en jeu* ('setting in motion' or even 'playing') might indeed be a better term than mise en scène.

- In spite of everything, mise en scène from the last twenty years sometimes manages to influence writing. Not in the old-fashioned way, with the text emerging from a workshop as the trace of a stage practice, but because today's acting experiments question, challenge and provoke the text that must be interpreted; the text, on the page, is barely readable. It is natural for mise en scène to illuminate the text, but here it is a more fundamental question of making a text readable, constituting it, and literally making it exist, in particular in terms of its interactions with the rest of the production.

- The mise en scène itself can sometimes be just as unreadable (and thus incomprehensible) as the text. We can celebrate this in the name of artistic freedom, but we might also regret it, since the audience often feels the need if not to understand, then at least to enjoy incomprehension. Often authors do not find their director, and thus their audience; sometimes, having found them, they leave the spectators dumbfounded: mute and deprived of a right to reply, as if the artist were telling them, 'love it or leave it!'

- But paradoxically, when the mise en scène remains unreadable to the exegete, it is still possible to go back to the text to examine the way in which it inspired the work of the director. Such investigation is the preserve of professionals and theorists, who have the luxury and freedom, the production run being over, to return to the text. This is a kind of 'reverse logocentrism'.

- There is another paradox: literature is no longer, in the well-informed theatre sphere at least, the natural and sworn enemy of theatre, the scarecrow that stops theatre from flying off into the heavens of the dramatic. It has become the force that prompts and provokes mise en scène, it gets theatre out of its rut, and forces it to find a means of defending itself. Some time ago, Heiner Müller celebrated literature's return to favour: 'I am convinced that literature is useful in resisting theatre. Given how conditioned theatre is, only an unmanageable text can be productive and catch its interest.'[29]

Mise en scène only survives and renews itself if authors, such as Heiner Müller, invent texts that constitute challenges for the theatre. And this is what today's writing desperately seeks to achieve.

The debate on the clash of cultures, multiculturalism, identity and community rages on.

Theatre cannot keep up. It is disoriented – surely it has always 'naturally' practised a mixing of languages, of cultures and of traditions? It feels overtaken by sociocultural reality, blamed by it – is it sufficiently intercultural? Does it look after its minorities? Has it moved away from Western domination? Has it colonised minor forms?

Western intercultural theatre seems to be stepping back – this is rejection as much as regression – in the face of a world that is shifting and that no longer recognises theatre. We are moving away from the intercultural optimism of Brook or Mnouchkine in the 1980s. At that time, when everything was cultural, one could believe in the meeting of civilisations, the fraternity of peoples, the universality of theatre language. Artists, enthusiastically and without a care in the world, rubbed shoulders with the most diverse array of cultural sources. Politics was to be replaced with the idea of *le tout-culturel* ('everything is cultural').

This heroic time seems far away now: today other anthropological experiences occupy the terrain, planting mines and clearing them at the same time. It is thus that the video-graffiti of Mexican artist Guillermo Gómez-Peña addresses and redresses all of the big questions of cultural anthropology, with cutting humour and apparent nonchalance, but also with striking political astuteness. Gómez-Peña's *fronterizo*, frontier worker character, is not only the figure of the Mexican becoming accustomed to North America, he is that of every human torn between identities that both free and imprison – a borderline case, one might say.

The light, mobile and forceful form of the video or televisual sketches is suited to urban guerrilla skirmishes. Such a form hardly exists in Europe, where art is often caught between the elitist *théâtre d'art* and more vulgar types of entertainment.

Thanks to this form, intercultural theatre gets a second wind. Censorship is subverted, the imagination and the taboo are liberated, identities come together. The paths of the social and the political are located by way of personal experiences.

Surely anyone would welcome such a breath of fresh air?

6   The intercultural trap

Rituality and mise en scène in
the video art of Guillermo
Gómez-Peña

Until the start of the twentieth century, the idea that theatre
originated in ritual was considered incontestable: recall the 'goat
song' and its continuation into Greek tragedy. Such theories are now
being challenged.

If we were to examine the numerous performative practices that
exist – and notably those that would once have been called theatre
traditions – we might observe ritual elements belonging to each
cultural context. Due to a lack of anthropological and linguistic
knowledge, scholars tend to trace everything back to such ceremonies
and ritual forms. Anglo-American performance studies sought to
take on the Sisyphean task of identifying and describing these
'cultural performances'.

At almost the same time, in the 1960s, the theatre world sought to
bring together – in terms of the motifs presented as much as the
performance styles involved – ceremonies, games, myths and rites
borrowed from these traditional cultures. The audience was invited to
take part, or even to replace the actors.

It might seem strange to study the role of ritual in theatre production
and contemporary performance artwork, since it is difficult to imagine
that ritual could be at the service of theatre. Nevertheless, for more
than forty years, numerous works have been inspired by existing
rituals (sometimes parodying them), or indeed have invented their
own rituals. Is this a sign of maturity?

Instead of giving an overview of these practices, we will examine
Guillermo Gómez-Peña's *Video Graffiti* as sketches that parody existing
or made-up rituals.

It might be necessary to establish what connection exists between
ritual and theatre. But the word 'theatre' is already an obstacle to
reflection since it refers to Western forms of representation. The word
'performance' covers everything – Western theatre, ritual, ceremonies

and all possible cultural performances, thus the link between theatre and ritual is not hard to see!

For fear that we might be crushed by the Sisyphean rock that is the panoply of performative practices, we will here observe only a few ordinary rituals linked to the life of a Mexican or a Chicano, and also to the life of any person who is displaced, 'humiliated and insulted' (as Dostoevsky puts it). The only risk, then, is that of being crushed under Gómez-Peña's sombrero.

Instead of conducting a general study of contemporary possibilities and forms of interculturalism, and in order to avoid pointlessly being exposed to the ire of the guardians of the temple of foreign cultures (so readily 'exploitable'), we will take an example where the clash of cultures is already the very object of the work, an example that is embodied by its author and performer: Gómez-Peña's *Video Graffiti*, available as a DVD published by La Pocha Nostra. This will serve as our corpus, or even our habeas corpus.

The *Graffiti* are short sketches produced in the last ten or fifteen years, and represent a veritable treasure trove, a representative sample of the work of Gómez-Peña; they are diverse in the forms they have taken over time. It is these treasures that we shall unpack, then use, seeking to understand how rituals are both embraced and subverted by the different performers involved. Thus we will hope to understand the effective and the parodic use that performance and contemporary theatre make of ritual.

The forty or so sketches, lasting on average one to three minutes, are detailed in the DVD menu in a highly learned and theoretical way, as if the author was intentionally, and not without irony, borrowing categories from anthropology and Anglo-American critical theory. The following categories can be found:

1   Politics of language.
2   Identity crises.
3   TV gone wrong.
4   Reverse anthropology.
5   *El cuerpo politico* (the body politic).
6   *Lo personal tambien es politico* (the personal is also political).

This thematic classification tends to erase the real conditions of production of the sketches. The short commentaries on the DVD do not illuminate the past political situation either. For an art that is so anchored in its political situation, such dehistoricisation is problematic: any interpretation would require the reconstitution of the socio-political situation of the past and that of the present.

Each of the six groupings addresses the same question, testing or confirming highly complex hypotheses:

1   To speak Spanish and English is an advantage for Chicanos, and a threat to English speakers. Language is a passport and a weapon.
2   People are troubled by their multiple identities.
3   Television does not explain reality, it distorts it.
4   Reverse anthropology studies the observer as much as the observed object.
5/6   Nothing is personal: the body too is shaped by politics.

This classification and the titles of the sketches lead to a reading that is necessarily reflexive and theoretical. This is true to a different degree each time, however: some sketches are almost commentated upon by the narrator, while others keep their mystery and force the spectator to risk an interpretation. In the face of such diversity, we can only limit ourselves to a few questions on ritual, on 'reverse anthropology', on the body's varying identities, and finally, at the end of a long journey, on mise en scène as the theatricalisation of rituals.

Current context

Before analysing the sketches, it is worth examining what happened in the 1990s. Since the fall of the Berlin Wall and the end of communism, globalisation has everywhere become apparent. One unexpected consequence, according to Carolina Ponce de Leon, Gómez-Peña's wife, is a recolonisation of the arts:

> Globalization has led to the recolonization of the art world and turned the multicultural landscape into a hip backdrop. The global art world is a colonizer captivated by the strategies of decolonization.[1]

As a result, we should beware of discourses claiming to be postcolonial, which in fact often merely revive 'primitive art' with a neocolonial twist.

Alongside this ambiguity as regards colonisation, we observe, paradoxically, that artists tend to keep their distance from all that is intercultural, and that theoreticians have growing scepticism in the face of a general theory of 'exchange'. Local knowledge (as Geerts calls it) is considered preferable to any general theory. The observer – anthropologist, cultural analyst or mere spectator – is invited to participate in the functioning of the work of art, which brings the artists and the users closer together, but blurs the roles, giving the audience the illusion of participating in the creative act. Additionally, there is a lassitude in the face of social questions, and a lack of compassion towards underprivileged people and cultures.

> In the past years, performance art audiences have experienced an acute case of compassion fatigue. They have grown ever more intolerant of intellectually challenging and politically overt work, and at the same time much more willing to participate acritically in performance art events which allow them to engage in what they perceive as 'radical behaviour'.[2]

In such conditions, foreign cultures seem only of interest to these audiences if they appear as identities in conflict, and if they can be embodied in real or invented people: as is the case for Guillermo Gómez-Peña, an artist of Mexican origin, who has lived in the United States for thirty years. Gómez-Peña's situation shows very well how the art of intercultural performance of recent times is tending to replace intercultural mise en scène (of the Brook variety), thus attracting a new audience.

The fad for identity play is both a positive sign, since these subjects can be addressed without the moralising of the 1980s, and a negative sign, betraying a lack of interest in politics and morality.

> Unlike their postmodern, multicultural or postcolonial predecessors, the new global impresarios needn't be concerned with ethical or political boundaries. Ethics, ideology, border issues, and postcolonial dilemmas – they all belong to the immediate past, a past too complicated to recall in any serious manner; a past which can merely be sampled as style or excerpted as motif.[3]
>
> Regardless of the country or the city where we perform, the results of these border performance experiments reveal a new relationship between artist and audience; between the brown body and the white voyeur. Most interactions are characterised by the lack of political or ethical implications. Unlike, say, ten years ago, when audiences were oversensitive regarding gender and racial politics, our new audiences are more than willing to manipulate our identity, overtly sexualize us, and engage in (symbolic or real) acts of cross-cultural/cross-gender transgression, even violence.[4]

Conscious of this new context, Gómez-Peña's videos of the last ten years or so seek means of analysis and of resistance in order to take recent developments into account. 'Ethno' and 'techno', two notions normally considered antithetical, are brought together to observe the impact of new technology on ethnographic identity, and to design the new human being in the age of shifting identities.

But how can we be Persian in the era of the internet? Or indeed Chicano, Mexican or North American?

Gómez-Peña seeks, he claims, a space equidistant between artistic practice, political activism and anthropological theory. Each corner of this equilateral triangle is made up of a set of questions that interfere with the others while remaining dependant on them: the practice is made up of open signifiers in search of a possible signified. Activism goes from a signified (of pre-existing ideas) in order to illustrate it with a signifier (of artistic forms); theory – either anthropological or socio-semiological – hangs between signified and signifier, it tests new ideas by way of performance art and it takes inspiration from performance art in order to clarify and situate its current state. In the end, it is the spectators who must determine the borders between these disciplines:

> It becomes necessary to open up a *sui generis* ceremonial space for the audience to reflect on their new relationship with cultural, racial, and political Otherness. The unique space of ambiguity and contradiction opened up by performance art becomes idea for this kind of antho-poetical inquiry.[5]

The spectacle of these videos readily convinces us of one thing: we must, in turn, run this 'anthro-poetic' investigation, and determine the proportions of ritual and poetry contained in the *Graffiti*. We should undertake this task in a minor key and an inquisitive mood.

Ritual?

Do Gómez-Peña's mischievous sketches summon ritual? Probably not in the sense of a 'flow in shared experience of ecstatic otherness',[6] as the religious or mystical ritual is usually defined. The spectator is not invited to share in sacred knowledge, to participate actively in some more or less secret ceremony. Theatre, in any case, is often defined in opposition to ritual: 'While theatre confines itself to saying things about relationships, ritual does things with them, and what it does is to reinforce or change them.'[7] On the other hand, however, we often define ritual in general terms as 'a formal set of human actions which function primarily at a symbolic level'.[8] And this graffiti does indeed show symbolic actions whose effect on reality we can observe, at least in the mind of those who undertake them.

What actions are undertaken in this way? Numerous characters are dressed in an extravagant manner, painted green, blue, black and white, or covered in tattoos. They chant incomprehensible formulae, seeming to observe a ceremony that is as timeless as it is impenetrable, and that must simply be followed. We might think that such games are mere secret rites. We know that 'the rite must complete a task and produce an effect by making use of certain practices to capture thought, leading one thus to "believe in it", rather than to attempt to analyse its meaning'.[9] This is very much the case for the repetitive and empty actions of the figures in the technological rites of *Border Interrogation* or those of *Chicano Virtual Reality*. In reality, these rituals are immediately parodied. They are reminiscent of an advertisement (for Benetton) or a holiday brochure. In *Cha-cha-manic Dance*, which mixes cha-cha-cha and shamanism, a slow and depressive dancer executes a few clumsy moves; it is an anti-cha-cha-cha performed in front of an unstable camera, before the long textual and spoken credits roll, with the names of the sponsors of the products. We are reminded of Lévi-Strauss's comment that 'Ritual always has a maniacal and desperate side to it'! Tourists and ill-informed citizens see the Mexican as a savage enacting incomprehensible and troubling rituals. In *Authentic Apocalypse Aztec Dancer*, the dancer seems to obey the orders and is happy to be as exotic as possible: he takes on, and accentuates, all the stereotypes one expects of him.

However this parody of ritual reveals a very sophisticated method. We can therefore distinguish different ritual practices, which are always parodical. For example:

- *The 'scientific' presentation*: El Psycho-Linguist explains in Spanish how to declare a sexual attraction for the other in a language that you do not speak, and thus take advantage of your bilingualism. This little speech is subtitled with instructions in English for monolingual English speakers.
- *The school presentation*: in *Geography Lessons*, Gómez-Peña, in the role of teacher, knowledgeably lists the cities of the world to which Latino-Americans have emigrated, the places they have colonised.
- *Recourse to language:* in *Language, my passport*, he recites a personal *cogito*, a series of certainties that end with a vibrant 'I talk, therefore I am, period.' The literary form of these litanies is that of a prayer, a recital with multiple repetition of the same formula: 'Language, my passport'. We see a gagged man, but continue to hear the text.
- *Smoking practice*: in *Mexercise*, a group of smokers is in a circle as if for a yoga session on breathing, but the exercise consists of learning to inhale cigarette smoke as deeply as possible.

All of these (supposedly) ritual actions are, as we see, subverted from their aim, parodied by way of an inversion of terms, executed according to a 'reverse anthropology'.

Reverse anthropology?

Or should we say 'upside-down anthropology', in an upside-down world? Gómez-Peña in any case wrong-foots classical ethnology, which identified 'primitive peoples', just before they disappeared. But he has a critical objective: these 'savages' are not Rousseau's 'good savage', nor the savages of Artaudian cruelty. They are 'artificial savages', reconstructed for the museum in the shape of Gómez-Peña, Coco Fusco and Roberto Sifuentes: they are displayed in a diorama as if they were survivors from the wild presented to the public. These 'savages' are constructed and deconstructed for the purpose of a critique of alienation.

Not only does Gómez-Peña not claim to study Chicano culture and the phenomena of acculturation that occur in contact with another language and culture in any scientific way, but he also takes pleasure in subverting, with irreverence and humour, the habits and stereotypes of his compatriots and his new fellow citizens. He observes forms of expression and greeting, gestures of affectivity, everyday behaviour, all of which are ritual, 'in the sense that their form and meaning is culturally determined and inherited, not spontaneously generated'.[10] He goes on to exaggerate each characteristic, treating them as stereotypes, and describing them by way of new technology. The *virtual Chicano*, the *Mexican Macho*, the *designer warrior*, are all parodic figures in his imaginary museum. In *Ethnic Profiling*, Cyber technology is combined with a shaman's helmet complete with animal horns. The virtual reality helmet changes nothing: the Chicano, with or without the helmet, remains a suspect and a delinquent for life.

If the tropics are indeed *tristes*, reverse anthropology nonetheless avoids sadness in favour of humour: fake rituals allow an awareness of how the world works. The quest for authenticity is merely a Western fantasy of representation of the other, a form of ethnographic pornography for (sexual) tourists. Such 'ethnographic porn' channels the desire to see 'authentic savages' outside of time, stuffed like wild animals. In *El Designer Warrior* (1997), we see Gómez-Peña applying the make-up of an authentic Indian, and we hear an indigenous language, which is in fact gibberish that sounds like Nahuatl, but with recognisable words such as 'Benetton', 'Nafta', 'Calvin Klein'. The English commentary, a female voice off, drives this home: 'Dear voyeur, do you like it more when he steps outside of your present in order to appeal to your desire for authenticity? Are you into ethnographic porn?'

The principle of the inversion of signs is one of the characteristics of this practice of reverse anthropology, and of this romantic irony (in the style of Johann Ludwig Tieck). As often, the personal case can be taken as a generality, and at least as an object of observation: an English-speaking journalist (who is of course performing herself, and is not authentic) interviews the performer, and places on his neck the necklace which she previously used as a lead; the camera operator is asked to reverse the perspective, and the journalist is asked questions. This reversal of perspective, which is of course staged, is as eloquent as any long speech about ethnocentrism.

The same reversal takes place in *Dual Citizenship*. Gómez-Peña reconstitutes the process of his appearance before the US authorities to obtain naturalisation: the video is filmed like a documentary, but the text states that the scene is a reconstruction. We see the author and his future wife Carolina waiting, and they are then received by an Asian-American employee. But, in a comic twist, the employee turns out to have read Gómez-Peña's books, and is a fan. The application is immediately accepted and the couple celebrate with a long and apparently juicy kiss! To reverse anthropology is, then, added humorous autobiography staged for the camera. The reconstruction only films the different stages of the ritual of naturalisation: waiting, worry, the critical moment, reversal, the victory kiss …. Fans of authenticity will be reassured to see that at the end of this long kiss for the camera – just before the final 'cut' – there is an uncut half-second where the lovers 'really' smile, laughing in the face of their victory and the 'hidden' camera, as if the 'authentic' erotic body shows it is never defeated, despite its multiple identities.

A body with variable identities?

If the human body, exposed to the hazards of social life, always becomes 'a sort of database for culture',[11] it comes as no surprise that it takes on all kinds of changing identities. In *Video Graffiti*, the Chicano or Mexican bodies assume all imaginable identities. It is not so much a question of the physical and individual body, but of the social body. As such, there is no point in asking if the body is in itself, or essentially, white, black, black and white, green or blue, half-Martian and half-Smurf, and so on. It is more a question of determining the social and market value that the body acquires in social exchange, of evaluating how it is perceived by itself and experienced by others. As Mary Douglas notes, 'The social body constrains the way the physical body is perceived.'[12] Gómez-Peña merely marks and distinguishes the difference, in a parodic mode: he enjoys frightening the townspeople by adding more and more stigmata to the 'foreign' bodies. For example, the sketch *Evolucion Alienigena* presents a green and speckled body, more extraterrestrial than foreign. This battered and ostracised body finally stands up and becomes a fascist doing a Hitler salute and spewing forth Nazi slogans. In *Authentic Apocalypse Aztec Dancer*, a warrior, inspiring terror and derision, dances naked, his penis wrapped in ribbons, with all the accoutrements of a warrior as represented in folklore.

In *Hoodoo Possession*, an androgynous being, filmed on an old 8 mm camera, puts on the black and white make-up of a black and white minstrel (the infamous 'blacked-up' singers and musicians), before mixing the two colours, smearing his face and blurring the limits of racial identity, leaving the observer to meditate on this strange exercise in hybridisation.

The different identities correspond to a plurality of experiences that the individual can have in a single day. They take place in an unexpected marriage of ethno and techno, in a new division between the living and the virtual. The body reconstructed in the laboratory, in *Border Interrogation*, is nothing new, however: it turns the virtual bodies over to the very real border police, and recalls the actual lives of Chicanos.

Basically, once again, the leopard cannot change its spots! Despite all these new identities, Chicanos remain alienated. And they are losing their traditional identities.

The same goes for the identities assumed by all these characters. Traditional identities, ethnic and political ones in particular, lose all relevance. As the Mexican sociologist Roger Bartra confirms, 'As far as Mexico is concerned, I am convinced that we are faced with the problem of constructing postnational forms of identity, to use Habermas's formula.'[13]

At a more modest level, that of Gómez-Peña's *Graffiti*, a similar process is at play: the characters from the sketches are of variable identity. Even Guillermo's charming little dog, a Chihuahua, tells us (in *The Most Famous Mexican*) that he is tired of constantly changing identity on the internet. The ethnographic caricatures exhibit the museum's frozen identities, a series of characters that it is forbidden to touch. Identity is modifiable, adaptable to the context and to the situation. In *Trimming One's Identity*, Gómez-Peña, his head crowned like the Statue of Liberty, a pair of scissors in his hand, trims everything that sticks out of his body: hair, ears, nose, tongue. He thus must hope to provide the identikit photo of the good American, with a well-groomed identity. Commodity culture and market culture trim our appearance, our body, our thought, in the same way. Physical identity resembles Pierre Bourdieu's notion of *habitus*: a way of holding the body in certain attitudes, a type of behaviour judged appropriate in a social context, an internalisation by the individual of practical and corporeal punishment that the individual considers 'natural', but that is in fact dictated by society.[14]

But this *habitus* – often translated in the theatre as the gestus of the characters – is in no way fixed. Each element is somehow made up of multiple identities. With Gómez-Peña, we can note four principal components:

> The composite identities of our ethno-cyborg/personae are manufactured with the following formula in mind: one-fourth stereotype, one-fourth audience projection, one-fourth aesthetic artifact, and one-fourth social behaviour.[15]

Of course, the value and the importance of each of these four components varies in each case. But they do enable us to establish some kind of typology of sketches, according to the hierarchy and the weight of each of the four components.

Let us take *La Kabuki Club Girl*, in visual terms one of the most successful sketches on the DVD. A good quarter is made up of the aesthetic artefact, of the beauty of the photograms and the lights, and of the perfect synchronisation with the music. The stereotyped part is less evident, precisely because the visual quality of the images is so high. The component of social behaviour is crucial, but difficult to evaluate: if you know the rigorous form of the kabuki ritual, you will be shocked by the club dancer's half-open clothes, which resemble the stereotype of a geisha. The alternating montage of black and white shots of Western models confronted with the gaze of Africans is more enigmatic: we are put in the position of Africans discovering a culture that is exotic and beautiful, but not explicit. The video works according to the principal of 'cracked' representation: the contrast between the face and the body of the Japanese woman, between the lively colours of kabuki and the black and white of the fashion parade in sub-Saharan Africa. As for the final component – the projections of the spectator – this is certainly important, but is hard to predict. For each clip, it is easy to measure the relative proportions of the four components, and to differentiate between the more formal works, and the overtly political and militant sketches.

In doing this, we enter the domain of a formal and ideological analysis of the work, and the field of the interpretation of video. The notion of mise en scène is thus useful if we conceive of it as the theatricalisation of ritual, as the aesthetic expression of symbolic actions.

Mise en scène as the theatricalisation of rituals?

A detailed analysis of the videos is beyond the scope of this study, since they possess a great deal of aesthetic and political sophistication. We shall therefore simply summarise some of the principles of the analysis.

- We should first of all distinguish each of the forms used: filmed performance, video made especially for the television or the cinema, video poems with work on the filmic matter itself, parodies of historical styles (MTV from the 1980s, for example), 'video exquisite corpse'. Certain works (*La Kabuki Club Girl* or *Cha-cha-manic dance* or *El Christo de Samoa*) are characterised by a specific use of video: fluidity, graphics, a remixed soundtrack.
- We have seen that where rituals are staged, this is always done in an ironic way. On the one hand, it is never really about existing rituals from Mexico or elsewhere, but more a question of the rituals of everyday life, repetitive and empty actions whose formal rigidity recalls traditional rituals with maniacal repetition or a playful side, maintaining the pretence of completing a symbolic action. On the other hand, it is not unusual for a ritual or a transformation to be 'theatricalised': that is, shown in a framework other than its original environment and for a theatregoing public. In that case, its efficacy is not necessarily destroyed by theatricalisation, but is sometimes threatened by it.

  > Speaking of the theatricalisation of ritual implies nothing about its efficacy, though there may remain a problem if the very theatricality of ritual or the obviousness of its playacting undermines belief in its effectiveness.[16]

For Gómez-Peña's *Graffiti*, the objective is in no way that of conserving the (highly problematic) efficacy of the parodied ritual, but to use these forms to make us aware of our cultural habits and of their relativity. Paradoxically, the playful side of the parodied rituals reinforces the identity of the community that is the target of parody. In this respect, we should acknowledge the enterprise as a success. It remains to be seen which community is concerned, and whether this community is in fact in constant evolution. To the non-Chicano, it would seem that the community is clearly in excess of this original group. This is why, as communities scatter, mise en scène must be able to adapt the work of art to less specific audiences. In art, however, success is always relative. In this kind of theatricalisation, success is also anthropological: it consists of theorising that which ethnology would take years or volumes to even demonstrate. This *mad mex* immediately finds the means for humour to reach this theorisation in situ, with all the denial that humour suggests: it is by no means certain that the reflection is correct at a theoretical level, but the phenomenon is at least pinned down, and the point is made subtly. For the spectators, that is what counts (and who cares if moralists and scientists object to being outwitted, if this shaman cannot be pinned down).

Gómez-Peña often returns to his 'original sin': that of having left his family and his country to come to the United States, and for the last thirty years, to have made of his life a continuous and unending performance. If this 'sin' could in no way be redeemed, no more can Gómez-Peña's sense of guilt and the feeling of always being left behind by a changing reality, at least in his position as theorist, as an immediate commentator on a history that cannot be denied. While he complains (the classic complaint) that the critics do not understand him, he also legitimises himself as a theorist as he makes steps towards an analysis of society and its identities. He could serve as an inspiration to other artists in very different cultural contexts.

• It would be a mistake to attribute any success in legitimisation to 'reverse anthropology', since it is only in the work on form, on signifiers of acting and staging, on the enigma of certain sketches, that theory can progress. There are clearly two methods in the construction of sketches: to give the conclusion or even announce it before the dramatisation (as in *Binational Boxer*) or to refuse to conclude, leaving the observer to guess and continue their enquiry. In *White on White*, on the other hand, the valorisation of the forms produced without a definitive or preconceived idea constitutes the heart of mise en scène. While *Binational Boxer* is a transparent allegory on the schizophrenia of the author, *White on White* is a symbol that is much more difficult to decipher, and thus is richer. We recall Heiner Müller's comment, 'The author is more intelligent than allegory; metaphor is more intelligent than the author.'[17] Mise en scène should not display knowledge of the author or the director; it must leave a space of interpretative freedom for the spectator. But just what is this freedom of mise en scène?

- 'Mise en scène' might be the wrong term for these videos, since nothing is actually put onto a stage. The notion nonetheless merits that we consider it for a moment. The performer is present at all points along the assembly line: author, actor, theorist, activist and, worse still, professor. There is not, as is the case in Barba's Odin Teatret, the outside gaze of a director judging and correcting the work of the actors or 'dramaturg' actors, who have produced their own script. This is both a disadvantage and an enormous advantage. Distance is sometimes lacking in the work of Gómez-Peña, and there can be a sense of repetition or of redundancy. But conversely, this gives him the ability to split into a performer-character and a commentator, particularly in the sketches about the power of language, in *Censurado* or in *El Psycho-Linguist*, where he gives himself the luxury of addressing the spectator from the video ('me captas?': 'do you catch my drift?'), adding meta-commentary to the different levels of enunciation. This procedure of adding is common: on-screen text relativises the visual message. This is also a typical feature of mise en scène as the permanent relativisation of meaning, like the ultimate modalisation of what is said.

- Mise en scène takes on the task of constructing all these levels of meaning and making them interact. The stage is not an allegory of an already known situation, but a search for a new meaning; mise en scène is like graffiti – an unfinished work: freedom in the line, fragility in the form, spontaneity in the expression. Since it is provisional, erasable and dirty, graffiti gives a first impression from which it is difficult to escape. Ironically, it acquires unexpected depth and a gravitas. Graffiti acts the innocent, but nevertheless leaves traces.

- Mise en scène consists of a fine-tuning of meaning, in a given moment and a given context. But nothing about this ritual is absolute. In a staging, there are continuously decisions to be made, choices to be respected, actions to be completed, habits to be observed, in order that the performance will happen. The conjunction of these various phenomena lends the whole its meaning.

- Is mise en scène (the mise en scène of this graffiti, for example) not at the same time theatrical, performative and ritualistic? It is theatrical because the scenographic, visual and signifying means must be found; it is performative because all the actions must be performed; and it is ritualistic because the actions must be completed according to a predetermined scenario. As a result of its having these three dimensions (theatrical, performative, ritualistic), mise en scène always remains fragile, provisional and revocable.

Mise en scène is necessary for the purely performative and active dimension of the ritual, since it brings with it the fictional, aesthetic and dramaturgical dimensions – in a word, it brings theatricality. Thus both the stage, filmic or video object, and the gaze of the observer find themselves ironically confronted with these facetious rituals or serious farces. Irony is the principal figure of mise en scène, it is a way of using the stage to say the opposite of what is said verbally or apparently, a way of parodying everything in order to explore all its facets. Ritual is humourless, forcing us to follow a ceremony that we have not created and that bores us, even if it can also be fascinating at times. Mise en scène keeps us destabilised, and keeps us standing to attention. It places our gaze and our bodies in a frame – a museum display, a mask, a role of idiot or false idiot (Schweyk!), ironically suggesting the opposite message, or at least the *other* message.

We should strive not to turn mise en scène into a ritualistic or religious way of thinking. Mise en scène protects us from the incredible performance that the postmodern world expects of us! It is thus pointless to make of mise en scène the baroque metaphor of the divine arrangement of mere human actions. From this perspective, each graffito erases the previous ones, it is a snapshot, a poor man's photograph (taken without a camera), a step towards a never-completed performance, which is never equipped with every possible supplement nor completely completed. Every graffito is a palimpsest – it erases the previous one to mark a new paroxistic state, the new world (b)order.

To stage such Chicano (or other) rituals is always a question of finding an arrangement with reality: I rearrange life in order to make it artistic, I rearrange art in order that it touch on life. I make my arrangements, I adjust my sombrero, and I am on my way.

Is mise en scène a French, or even Parisian invention?

Not entirely: it is the conclusion of a whole European theatrical movement that sought to control the signs of a production in ever tighter ways. Since the world's becoming, that is, since there has been acting; since forever, then.

What about other, non-European cultures? Their traditions are not governed by the same laws. The weight of playing traditions or of dance is too strong to allow a rereading, a reinterpretation and an autonomous work, thus a mise en scène.

European expansionism of the nineteenth century, the bridging of cultures, and theatre's interest in 'faraway' traditions all emerged at the same moment – towards the end of the nineteenth century – as mise en scène. Is this a coincidence?

Can we export mise en scène? And how? Can it be franchised? Does it reinvent itself in non-European productions? Many Asian artists (notably Chinese, Japanese and Korean) claim the influence of Stanislavski, Brecht, Kantor or Wilson.

Instead of exporting mise en scène, or imposing our theoretical savoir-faire, let us rather imagine how 'they' import it and adapt it to their needs. What is really important to them?

Is it so easy to see from another's point of view?

An Asian point of view, and even Korean?

The curiosity is currently on our side. But what use have they for our tools to read our texts or their own, to continue their creative processes? What use are our clumsy and primitive implements? Do they help get to the flesh of the meaning?

7   Theatre in another culture
A Korean example

In a foreign culture, you immediately perceive what is foreign (to you). But do you grasp what is familiar, notably in a culture or a work that you know to be 'other' and to come from far away? Is it easier to discern what is common to everybody or what is foreign to you?

What is the situation of theatre as it is practised today in Korea, and how should it be approached? Will it stay forever foreign to us? It remains for us to determine whether the Western notion of mise en scène finds an equivalent on the contemporary Korean stage.

If we conceive of mise en scène as the putting into practice of the dramatic or scenic work for a given audience, according to the aesthetic of a director, then it is easy to imagine that the historical and cultural conditions of our two countries might lead to very different results. But as regards theatre performance, either literary or visual, the results are not really very different. When viewed from France, we would expect that the Korean artists, hungry for information, are very familiar with European or American work and that they have managed to assimilate it into their mode of operation. But has European theatre not in fact come closer to Asian forms too? In these times of globalisation, artistic discoveries happen almost simultaneously.

A season in heaven

In any case, the theatre fan, and the cultural *flâneur*, hope to spot cultural difference as much as to grasp the aesthetic principles of Korean theatrical life. Of the thirty or so shows that I saw from September to December 2003 in Seoul, I will mention only a few examples, those in which the mise en scène seemed be based on principles distinct from those to which a European spectator is accustomed.[1]

A large section of contemporary productions in Seoul is made up of classical European plays, from Shakespeare to Molière, from Ibsen to

Chekhov. It is always exciting to see how these world classics are approached and sometimes revised by Korean artists. In his staging of *The Cherry Orchard* by Anton Chekhov, Yoon Young-Sun approached the work from an entirely different cultural and temporal context. In a difficult and limited space, he recreated a homogenous universe with a naturalistic style of acting. Kim Hye-Min's costumes in a harmonious beige and white monochrome reinforced the unity of a universe which both recalled the sepia-toned Russia of the late nineteenth century and created a world of its own. However, the characterisation did not bring out one character above another; it did not offer a new reading of the play, or a personal response from the director on the deep meaning of the loss of the cherry orchard. One could consider this timidity as a mark of respect for the complexity of the play, but, from the perspective of Western staging, it was a shame that this version did not make the spectator discover, although seeing the work for the umpteenth time, an as yet hidden aspect that might become the director's trademark. We implicitly expect that an interpretation will reveal something new, or at least that the director will not be limited to making a copy of the Russian original, that he will tell us how he imagines this object of desire: the cherry orchard. What is at stake today in the metaphor of the destruction of the cherry orchard? Should the staging not have adapted the play to the contemporary Korean context, arranged the bodies, the ways of speaking and moving, and of expressing emotion? This would seem possible, given that the actors are Korean and their shapes and faces are those of today. In short, the cultural transfer and the interpretations might demand that Yoon more clearly take a position.

What we enjoy onstage, whatever form it takes, is to be able to be at once submerged by chaos and sensitive to an invisible order that governs the performance, and that bears the name of mise en scène. This is what a foreign spectator experiences in watching performances in Seoul. Not understanding the language only adds to the pleasure of the chaos, without sacrificing the hidden order of the stage, which remains present. But this mixture of chaos and order is common in experimental productions, which make up the brilliant avant-garde of the professional Korean theatre troupes.

Thus, in Yoon Jeong-Seop's staging of Hwang Ji-Yoo's poetic text, *Material Man*, at the Chayou theatre at Seoul Art Center, the city's largest theatre, order was visible in chaos. Yoon, known as a scenographer and now as a director, achieves a perfect integration of the space, the stage movement, the soundtrack and the poetry. More than theatrical mise en scène, with story and dialogue, this is a question of *performance* and *installation*. Wong's poetic text, which tells the story of people killed when a department store collapsed, does not need to be staged, interpreted, concretised by the acting; it needs only to be heard, 'installed' in a formal frame and an adaptable space, spoken more by *performers* than by actors and dramatic characters. We see the influence of Robert Wilson in the perfect mastery of space and light. But unlike Wilson, Yoon highlights and lets us hear the poetry of a contemporary author. His staging and his scenography (and here it is difficult to separate the two) consist of placing two parallel tracks opposite one another: the sequence of images and the unfolding of the text. The space is in no way mimetic: it is created by variations of lighting and the indications of the soundtrack. Unlike the classical usage of Western mise en scène, the stage does not conceive of the text as a material that is more plastic and musical than literary and semantic. This work is more a performance than a theatrical show; it does not aim for symbolism, explanation or resolution of the textual enigma. In Seoul as in Paris, the spectator is not always used to seeing a text inscribe itself in a space independently of its speakers, or overcoming notions of story and exchange of dialogue. This kind of production remains in the minority, here as there.

What France and Korea have in common at the beginning of the twenty-first century is experimentation in acting techniques, scenographic designs and new media. There results from this an insistence on the body of the actor in motion and a certain erasure of the text as origin and aim of the theatre.

Most of the time, the shows are conceived for a fairly broad audience. Some 'high-end' shows, like *The Last Empress*, a musical which has enjoyed worldwide success since 1996, are typical high-quality examples from the production line, and use today's hot talent. Evoking the magnificence of imperial life, this court intrigue wins the admiration of the middle-class audience. In this representation of a glorious past, everything combines to produce a harmonious and tasteful work. The ballets, halfway between choreography and martial arts, are perfectly organised: the use of the large stage at Seoul Art Center is optimal. The light, discreet scenography is malleable thanks to the lighting design, and responds exactly to the needs of the acting and staging. It equally constitutes the frame of this ideal palace and the stage onto which the movement and the figures of this turbulent story inscribe themselves. On this stage all the expected cultural ingredients take their place: soldiers of the imperial guard, Japanese occupiers, ladies in waiting, *mudangs*. The lights produce delicate monochromes and the magnificent costumes by Kim Hyun-Sook maintain a subtle balance between historical accuracy and contemporary form and tone. The very melodic and highly sentimental music is always pleasant and never dissonant. This very neoclassical composition borrows a Western rhythmic and melodic structure, while also producing an effect of Korean traditional music, fused with contemporary sources. Like the scenography and the gestures, the music is elegant and harmonious, but also rather fabricated and artificial. Voices amplified with microphones lose their fragility, and are at the mercy of musical recording. The great success in terms of the cultural industry and export commerce takes place at the expense of artistic experimentation. As for the mise en scène, it fulfils a significant ideological function, because it passes on – in a brilliant and almost subliminal way – the following message: *The Last Empress* incarnates the desire for Korean independence in the face of the great superpowers, the virtues of aristocracy, the resistance of an entire people to Japanese imperialism, the end of imperial splendour. Thus this beautiful stage gives a nostalgic, idealised vision, conforming to Korean history, but paradoxically at the same time concluding that it is necessary to be open to foreign influence and to find one's place among the other nations.

This idealisation of the past is not the rule, even for plays which, like *Wuturi*, are inspired by some popular tale and rewritten with today's words. It is not a question, then, as for our French classics of the seventeenth century, of keeping the same text while creating a new staging, but of entirely rewriting the legend, adapting it to our times and according to current understandings. It is a question of creating a new play: the stage interpretation will vary, as it does for us, from director to director. Unlike in Europe, the publication of dramatic texts in Korea only goes back as far as the beginning of the twentieth century.

Wuturi, written and directed by Kim Kwang-Lim, is inspired by the legend of the giant baby and of the moving of the mountain. The text is perfectly integrated into the show – it appears to be its organic voice, as if it came out of the acting. The show harmoniously brings together all the means of the stage. The poetry of the writing does not prevent the story being told clearly. Music, dance and movement give rhythm to the speech, bringing vitality to the whole production. The gestures are made up of attitudes, poses, tensions: danced steps borrowing from martial arts and from an acting tradition that can be compared to our *commedia dell'arte*, with coded, but also modifiable, expansible gestures; it is not unlike the comic theatre of our times, inspired by Italian comedy, but open to its era (a comic approach that Jacques Copeau and Ariane Mnouchkine have sought to establish). Sometimes the actors take steps that are very much anchored in the ground; sometimes they skip from one foot to the other, the back arched, the trunk leaning forward, the shoulders going up and down with every shift of contact with the ground. We recognise the typical steps of a traditional dance. But this return to traditional acting techniques is not only a search for identity (as in the 1970s); it is already the confirmation of an identity which is at once cultural and professional in Korean theatre. We have seen this ground covered since the 1960s. In the 1960s in Korea, the focus was on translating, and sometimes imitating, Western theatre; then, throughout the 1970s and 1980s, it was about finding a more Korean identity, notably by way of political theatre; from the 1990s, after the end of the dictatorship, mise en scène replaced traditional forms in the wider framework of intercultural world theatre (Brook, Mnouchkine) and found its natural place on the international stage. Authors and directors like Hwang Ji-Yoo, Yoon Jeong-Seop, Kim Kwang-Lim and Yoon Young-Sun, whose works we discuss here, have perfectly found this place.

In another mise en scène of the same play *Wuturi* (significantly performed at the Cartoucherie de Vincennes, in September 2004) a new director, Lee Sang-Woo, emphasised the grotesque and the effects of modernity, bringing about a clear change of tone and an impression of a greater proximity. This is further proof that the director, just as in Europe, holds the key to the overall interpretation and gives their own vision of the tale. Indeed, it was amusing to watch this troupe work on the stage of the Théâtre du Soleil, where, in the 1980s Mnouchkine invented her own intercultural style, and to observe the originality of Korean interculturalism, with the postmodern humour of Lee Sang-Woo and his actresses parodying American cinema as a bonus.

This same Lee Sang-Woo is a legitimate author whose burlesque comedies, such as *The Hunt of the Pig*, are satires of country life and of political corruption. The play is craftily constructed around a parallelism of situation: two restaurateurs, two observers, the mute village belle who shares her attentions between the two parties. The mechanical progression of the effects and the situation, the speed of the acting and the changes in rhythm are those of farce as much as of advertising or television comedy sketches: we see the same heavy, slightly hysterical acting.

Korean theatre seen from afar

To prepare the French spectator for a journey to Korea, to help with the assimilation of such a large body of information, we should examine how the Korean and French societies support their theatres, what cultural and intercultural context this creates, and what kinds of mise en scène allow this to be revealed.

Figure 7.1 Kim Kwang-Lim, *Wuturi*, directed Lee Sang-Woo.
© Patrice Pavis.

Where is the society going?

Or rather, put more modestly: how does the society behave as regards theatre? After the surrender of Japan (1945), the independence and partitioning of the country, the civil war (1950–53), reconstruction, the Northern as well as Southern dictatorships, and finally the democratisation of the South from 1987, Korea has known – more than most countries – a dramatic past and extraordinary expansion.

Since the process of democratisation, Korean institutions have aimed to make their culture known across the world. Students, artists and intellectuals have a great thirst to discover the world, to draw on other traditions, to try out Western working methods in order to better find their own way. We Europeans must respond to these insistent demands while benefiting this momentum, in order to rethink our own methods and our conception of the performing arts.

The difficulty is obviously to make recent stage works taken from a Korean context accessible to the French public; such works are always more interesting than those made for export. The invitation to France of Korean productions (other than dance, music or cinema) is certainly a decisive first step, but it needs to be strongly supported: surtitles, pedagogical programmes of introduction, workshops, and discussions before and after the shows. As for practice, an even more expensive, although more effective, method would be to invite Korean directors to direct French actors, in order that everyone test various acting techniques, and new ways of thinking and working.

Going in the opposite direction, and thanks to tireless cultural facilitators like Choe Jun-Ho – the current artistic director of Seoul Art Centre, translator and assistant to invited directors, such as Eric Vigner or Daniel Mesguich – the reciprocal relationships between artists will progress more effectively and will last longer. Many Korean intellectuals or artists studied in the United States, and a considerable number in Europe; many students have chosen France or Germany for training in the arts. Theatre is often the pilotfish for a society: it helps it to stay aware of its evolution, and to work out its direction. The dramatic situation of a play or a show is no doubt fictional, microscopic and deformed; but the theatrical relationship – the link between the audience and the work – reveals the sociality of the moment. This relationship is not easily transferable from one culture to another, but is nonetheless essential for evaluating the life of the mise en scène. In transmitting texts and productions, we are particularly sensitive to the relationship of language to the body, sound, rhythm, the 'gestural' of language, the 'word–body relationship' (which is determined by its affectivity and its sociality): subjects more or less manifest their emotions and their social identity, their *gestus* and their *habitus*. In working with real texts and bodies, to go from one country to another might offer few surprises. Perhaps we are cousins? Or 'soul mates'?

Is this emotional and spiritual proximity the fruit of a professional identity which subjects all artists to the same affects, the same worries, the same hopes? In any case Korean artists from the non-commercial sectors are like France's *intermittents du spectacle* (that is to say alternating between periods of work and of unemployment, although Korean artists are not covered in the case of long periods without work as is the case for the French *intermittents* within the benefit system), despairing in a precarious economic context. The working conditions of Korean artists are more difficult than those of their French colleagues, since theatre is barely subsidised at all. The young people, and the parents of pupils, thus require extraordinary courage and energy in order to continue to create. Many do throw in the towel in Korea, even earlier than their French counterparts – these French colleagues survive thanks to an illusion that they will end up making a decent living from their artistic work.

What is theatre for? Koreans might answer this question in various ways: partisans of the commercial theatre sometimes see it as a formal game, entertainment without consequence. Young people, on the other hand, consider that literature or theatre can change someone's life or offer explanations of current socio-political issues. Theatre people in France stick to the idea that theatre has, or should have, an impact on society. Ironically enough, one of the rare recent plays with a resolutely political message – *Daewoo*, by François Bon – tells the story of the closure of the Korean factory in Lorraine and the disastrous consequences for the women who worked there. In Korea, more even than in France, *théâtre d'art* is a minority response to the all-powerful media. Some young theatre-makers would gladly return to the difficult period of the 1970s, when plays, despite harsh censorship, dealt with political issues and thus contributed to the struggle against the dictatorship. Even though the form was sometimes too simplistic or direct, theatre demonstrated its vital necessity each evening. And yet this period already seems very far away (except to those who lived through it). Young people are not nostalgic for it in the way that Avignon audiences or figures in French cultural politics are nostalgic for Vilar's *théâtre populaire* of the 1950s and 1960s. If the young Korean audience is not always nostalgic for a golden age comparable with that of Vilar's theatre, it is not stuck in an esoteric avant-garde either. Basically the situation is the exact opposite of that in France. In Korea, the dichotomy is no longer between popular or elitist, but rather between commercial or artistic, which takes the debate into different territory.

Where is culture going?

This difference of attitudes, of motivations and of reactions is all the more discernible as regards the conception and the role of culture in current stage practice.

It will come as no surprise that culture is not the same in France and in Korea! But what differs just as radically is the conception each country has of its own culture and of foreign cultures, of traditional culture and interculturalism.

After Westernisation, between 1950 and 1970, years of dictatorship pushed artists to rediscover, as a form of resistance, truly Korean traditions: shamism and *Kut*, masked dance, *Pansori*, martial arts. Directors like Kim Sôk-Man, Kim Kwang-Lim, Son Chin-Ch'aek and Oh Tae-Sok consciously positioned themselves in this intracultural tradition, but they also see themselves as part of the contemporary era, resolutely turned towards the future. Kim Chong-Ok – who speaks French and trained in France in the era of *théâtre populaire* – talks of a 'third theatre', which is a meeting (or rather a clash) between traditional heritage and Western works. In the same period, in France, we did not observe a similar return to the source. From the 1920s to the 1950s in France, there was increasing fascination with 'oriental' culture (notably Chinese, Japanese and Balinese culture). Korean civilisation remains a missing link in this Western infatuation with the Orient. This gives another reason to discover at last wonders hidden for too long.

Since the 1980s and 1990s, relationships with culture and the intercultural have radically changed. In Korea, interculturalism gladly allies itself with pop culture, the cultural industry and globalisation. In France, on the other hand, Mnouchkine or Brook, for example, advocate a brand of interculturalism that precisely rejects such commercial realities. By way of traditional Eastern cultures, those directors seek the supposed origins of theatre, resulting in a conception of human relationships that is more essentialist than political or economic. In recent years, since the beginning of the twenty-first century, the cultural question has been a burning one. Despite the official discourse, intercultural theatre does not interest theatregoers and theatre-makers very much. They are – rightly enough – suspicious of multiculturalism, community identity politics and fundamentalism. They only hesitantly experiment with groups or cultures, fearing accusations of racism, neocolonialism or – at best – paternalism. Thus cultural exchanges within France have diminished, with the abandonment of all multicultural artistic projects in the *banlieues* (suburban housing estates), where Eastern cultures and vestiges of such cultures coexist, often ignoring one another or even fighting. Thus is created in each of us, or in each different group, a 'voluntary inner *apartheid*', a cultural ghetto whose sad face, in the fires and the isolation of the *banlieues*, has recently been exposed.

One paradoxical consequence of globalisation is that French society no longer manages to integrate and absorb populations of foreigners and those who see themselves as foreign. French cultural identity has become a suspicious, if not colonialist or racist, notion. Conversely, Korean culture is ethnically homogenous, and is historically unified (despite the partition); it is religiously varied but tolerant, culturally diligent and disciplined. Thus national identity keeps all of its meaning in Korea, if only in contrast with its counterpart, Western culture and indeed what Koreans call 'international theatre'. Not fearing to conquer the outside world in terms of economics, and even feeling obliged to do so in order to survive, Korean society maintains a seeming unity, which is sometimes tainted with nationalism. While Korea's artists are curious about other cultural and artistic traditions, sampling only what is useful to them, without guilt nor a sense of sin, the French, obsessed with the decline of the great nation, fearing for their future and their retirement, feeling themselves downgraded on the world stage or at an individual level, no longer manage to situate themselves or evaluate themselves in comparison with other cultures.

In such circumstances, theatre plays a role of a 'cultural probe', sounding out practices and forms from elsewhere, in miniature and in a playful mode. In France, the very positive – even enthusiastic – reception of *Pansori* and traditional dance and music has already prepared the terrain for stagings of Korean or universal texts. This was noticeable in productions such as *Wuturi*, by Kim Kwang-Lim, a mixture of traditional acting and texts rewritten in today's words. From a similar angle, Eric Vigner, in his staging of Molière's *Le bourgeois gentilhomme*, used Korean music and dance. From the French perspective at least, these touring productions were very warmly received. We should nevertheless compare this with the reception of the same shows in Korea.

For *Wuturi*, seen in Seoul, the surprise was not the form of the traditional acting (well known since the 1960s and 1970s) but the modern resonance of a text rewritten in today's language. For the same Wuturi seen and 'read' with surtitles (written by Han Dukwha) at the Cartoucherie de Vincennes, the surprise was the virtuosity of the acting, and not the story or the contemporary writing style. This is a classic case of cultural misunderstanding, of transference and change of perspective. As for 'our' *Bourgeois gentilhomme*: in France the production managed to pass for a charming – some might say irritating – orientalist vision of a French classic. The Lorient audience, who already knew the Molière play well, were delighted with its 'enrichment' via Lulli's music, played on traditional Korean instruments, and via the Korean (or supposedly Korean) dance; they did not worry whether the borrowed elements were 'correctly' Korean, 'Japanese-inspired', or just 'oriental'. These concerns had however not escaped the notice of the people of Seoul, whose zealous anti-orientalism meant they risked turning their backs on Molière (deemed too invasive), or on the staging (too inspired by 'the Orient'). Whatever the cultural misunderstandings, this first collaboration was essential.

The next step, which is trickier because it necessitates more mediation, might be to welcome and eventually even incite stagings of contemporary Korean texts in French translation. Without even realising it, and so in all innocence, French and Korean artists might thus discover a natural way of treating the cultures, and trying out new acting techniques. This is a challenge that is all the more vital in France given that mise en scène – as a concrete use of the theatre apparatus – has experienced a moment of doubt and crisis for the last fifteen years.

Figure 7.2 Wuturi by Kim Kwang-Lim, directed by Lee Sang-Woo.
© Patrice Pavis.

Moreover, the encounter with other traditions leads us inevitably to ask
questions about Western-style mise en scène: Where does it come from?
What is it for? Does it exist in Korean practice? And since when? Is it
merely stuck on top of a very different tradition? And conversely, how
does the Asian conception of performance, martial arts and dance
influence the European practice of stage interpretation?

Where is mise en scène going?

It is for Koreans to say at what point Western theatre first arrived in
their country. But we might suggest that a distinction be made between
European or US dramaturgy on the Korean stage, and the beginnings
of a truly Western conception and practice of mise en scène by
Koreans. There is general agreement that mise en scène in the
European sense (that is, the interpretation of a text or of the
performance by a director responsible for the signs and the meaning)
was 'imported' into Korea in the 1920s and 1930s, in particular by
Hong Hae-Sang, who had studied Western theatre in Japan and
transmitted this practice to a new generation of Korean artists. For
mise en scène in the French sense, the gap between Korea and Europe
is only fifty or so years wide, and yet the difference in spirit is

considerable. In the home of Descartes and Racine, classical theatre is considered literature. The performance, and *a fortiori* mise en scène, are considered to have derived from the dramatic text. Only towards the end of the nineteenth century would the 'great reversal' occur, and it became accepted that a director gives the play an original meaning and a second youth. In the 'Land of the Quiet Morning', however, the different forms of traditional theatre (*yeonhi*) are cultural performances, not a text to be performed. It was only through classical and modern Western plays that Korean 'theatre' became rooted in literature and could in turn claim the status of a dramatic text willing to receive the most diverse stage interpretations. More recently, since the 1990s, 'new writing', either French or Korean, is the object of all attempts to find a stage practice to confer this or that possible meaning: it is no longer, then, a question of setting off from a canonical text that is readable and constituted in an established meaning to be concretised in a performance.

A new generation of directors is practising a staging style that is as radically distanced from the fusional and intercultural model as it is from political theatre. Examples include the staging of Hwang Ji-Yoo's *Material Man*, by Yoon Jung-Seop, the staging of Philippe Minyana's plays by Robert Cantarella, and the staging of Noëlle Renaude's plays by Frédéric Maragnani. These constitute examples of the convergence of writing, acting and staging in French–Korean practice.

Between mise en scène and performance

The European spectator, in the habit of searching productions for the characteristics of Western mise en scène (staging choices, coherence of signs, reinterpretation) will not see, in the artistic and cultural performance in Seoul, any mise en scène in the strict sense of the term (as a reinterpretation of a classical text). Such a spectator will, however, be very sensitive to the visuality of theatre, and to what, in the 1960s and 1970s, became – in Europe and the United States – performance art: a work that is not a slave to text, but which emphasises instead the action accomplished by the actors and the visual and rhythmic coherence. So does this mean that in France there is textual mise en scène, and in Korea, spectacular performance?

Things are not so clear-cut, but it is definitely the case that Korean productions do call on dance and music more often, and that the relationship with text is less fetishistic than it is in France. Authors and directors like Yoon Jeong-Seop, Lee Sang-Woo and Kim Kwang-Lim, among many others, went straight to stage work, to performance.

Indeed, they were not required to deliver an umpteenth interpretation of a classical play (without the right to change a single word). They have the freedom to work on space or on acting, to invent a scenographic and playing situation that highlights the entire show, rather than the dramatic text alone. The Korean artist is no prisoner of traditions of interpretation and acting style, and so is freer, as well as more eclectic, risking new directions, even where these seem incompatible. An obligatory stage of theatre work in the west has been skipped: dramaturgical analysis in the Brechtian mode. Moreover, the philological stage of respectful reading (in the style of Copeau) had already been skipped. Thus, free from philology and dramaturgy, the Korean artist reaches the level of the postmodern phase, with its grandeur (the direct and easy relationship with the work) and its servitudes (eclecticism, formalism, apoliticism). The Korean producer freely adapts to commercial demand – for musicals in particular, the goods are delivered without too much thought, according to the internal and international market: hence the Nanta group and its amusing but quickly tiresome parodies of the Samulnori percussion orchestra. The French artist, on the other hand, is more reserved, more torn. The dramatic text and the mimetic and literary tradition cannot (as was witnessed in Avignon in 2005) be dispensed with completely, despite a will to embrace visual arts or spectacle alone; the artist knows that the audience get left behind. This is why, in France (and this is not the case in Korea), postmodernism and deconstruction are seen as aberrant or suspicious practices, only of use for a few dreamy members of the autistic avant-garde. In this way, the contribution of Korean experiences like the dramatic installations of Yoon Young-Soon, the political farces of Lee Sang-Woo, and the stagings of Im Yŏng-Ung, Park Jung-Hee and Han Tai-Suk, would be a precious asset for French artists and spectators. We would see a different division of roles between author, director and actor.

And this is why Europe and the United States have so much to learn from Asian performance, from traditional forms, but also from 'theatre' as it is currently being invented and practiced in Korea. 'Our' theatre might also benefit from this.[2]

We go to the theatre to see living actors.

And so we are surprised, and sometimes disappointed or even unhappy, when the stage contains more audiovisual media than it does tangible bodies.

Media surround us; they encircle us. But what do we really know about their effects on our thoughts, imagination, language and art?

We find media useful in our daily lives, but we feel a certain distrust in seeing them used in theatre performance: is the little life that remains in the theatre at risk of being devoured?

Our inherent fear of machines returns: we fear they will eliminate what is still human, in us and on stage.

That is certainly what we thought, in the 1960s, when Grotowski defined theatre as the encounter between an actor and a spectator, or when Brook searched for the human link.

Since then, however, we have become accustomed to seeing media on stage. Since the 1960s, theatre practitioners have learned to tame these media, to use them wisely, to integrate them into dramaturgy and mise en scène. In order to overcome our irrational fear of media, it is worth analysing a few productions where audiovisual media are used, to examine how the spectator perceives the images produced. Media disconnect and reconnect us with our own body. Through live performance, we physically experience the mutations of the world and of our bodies.

Neither the body nor language can escape media: both are infiltrated, penetrated by media. We should, however, avoid any notion that either the body or language is a pure and authentic entity, in opposition to the impure and invasive media.

Mise en scène is a configuration of verbal and nonverbal signs, of physical and mechanical actions. Such signs and actions do not escape the grip of the media.

Should we limit ourselves to picking out, and then describing, the media used in a particular performance? Let us instead observe how media contribute to the construction of mise en scène.

8 Media on the stage

In contemporary mise en scène, media are ubiquitous, and therefore we do not always notice them. What is a medium? And in what forms do media appear on a stage?

Theatre and media

By 'media', we mean 'any communication system that allows a society to fulfil all or a part of three main functions of conservation, long-distance communication of messages and knowledge, and the updating of cultural and political practices'.[1] Dramatic writing and mise en scène undertake these three functions of the media: writing enables communication and conservation; the stage organises the continuous updating of texts and performance practices. In this general understanding of the term *media*, *theatre* is therefore very much part of media. It even constitutes a medium par excellence, and its most common components are themselves also constituted of different media. Mise en scène, once it puts texts or acting choices into practice, must call upon numerous media. It updates or re-updates cultural practices, it communicates sensations and meanings to spectators, and indeed it conserves texts or actions, or at least their material and conceptual interpretations.

Nevertheless, we find it difficult to speak of theatre as media, since we persist in seeing it as a 'crossroads of the arts' (literature, painting, music), or even conceive of it as an autonomous and synthetic art. Thus, the moment we refer to theatre and the media, we implicitly suggest that not only is theatre part of the media that it dominates and precedes, but moreover that the technological media, and new or old technologies (video, film, the projection of images) 'invade' the inviolable space of the performance, itself limited to the acting, or even to the hearing of the text. This suspicion, this defensive attitude, reveals an essentialist conception of theatre: the theatre, for example, of Grotowski, of Kantor, of Brook or of Mnouchkine. But has theatre not always made use of technologies of all kinds? And are these technologies so distant from the notion of media?

Live performance

The very dated term *live performance* might be useful for politicians charged with attempting to distribute subsidies within a bureaucratic cultural structure, but it is less so when trying to describe the current state of the performing arts. The term suggests that there can be a clear separation between first, all of the stage events that require 'living' actors in 'flesh and blood' (theatre, dance, mime), and second, 'the media', concerned with recording and mechanical reproduction by every audiovisual means.

'Theatre', to use a generic and neutral term, at least in the West and according to the Aristotelian conception, is the only art using the body and the voice of the human being to create a fiction and imitate human actions. What could be more living than an actor facing us, whom we could – in theory – interrupt or touch, and who addresses us by way of the body alone, the unmediated voice, and presence in the flesh? Through our silence and our nervousness, we have a tangible effect on the actor. And conversely, this living body, through its movements, its physical and sexual force of attraction, stimulates us, even if we do not know how its effect actually differs from that of the filmic or mental image. We know very little about the kinesthetic transmission of the actor: only dancers and dance theorists have tackled the question. With their help, we have learned to evaluate the impact of the living body in motion, and take part in a merciless wrestling match, a fusional interaction, a living bond which, although marked 'fiction', is kept at a distance. An entire branch of theatre studies, the study of 'organized human spectacular behaviors', or Jean-Marie Pradier's 'ethnoscenology', is concerned with 'the inextricably tangled history of live performance and the sciences before the dawn of the encounter with Asia'.[9] It seems crucial to study the effects such bodies have upon us, in the tradition of Grotowski and Barba. Until the 1960s or 1970s, we were, naturally enough, Artaudians, and felt that the actor's body was the key to theatrical representation. Such a position implicitly suggests that the body is worth more than any media or cinema. This received idea sometimes makes us forget the cultural and mediatic environment that is the body's habitat; it uncritically equates the body with the real or with truth.

Still, the true challenge to live performance has come, at least since the 1980s, from audiovisual media, whose presence at the heart of live performance has consequences for our perceptions. Thus, the change of scale of an image, which is a familiar procedure in photography and cinema, can lead – when that image is onstage – to spatial and corporeal disorientation for the spectator. In the competition between the filmic image and the 'real' body of the living actor, the spectator will not necessarily choose the living over the inanimate – in fact, quite the opposite! The eye is drawn by what is visible at the largest scale, that which never stops moving and holds the attention by way of constant shifts in shot and in scale. Such is the lot of live performance, and such is the challenge to theatre: to render, in spite of everything, living presence and its forces of attraction.

But that is not all. The challenge is to question the traditional and clear-cut oppositions between the living being and the (media) machine, between present and absent, between human and inhuman. Does the presence of the actor mean that the actor is visible? And what if the actor is invisible, in the wings, or acting behind a sign serving as a screen, captured by live video and projected onto some part of the set? What if the actor is on the phone or filmed on a webcam on the other side of the world? Such an actor goes through the motions of presence; we can imagine their presence, even if we cannot directly perceive it. We should distinguish physical and spatial presence from the temporal present of performance, its live aspect. The live does not depend on media: a television broadcast or a video can be live – that is received in the very moment of its production, just as theatrical production is live. The actor can thus be absent from the stage space, and nevertheless be present, in an entirely different place. Presence is no longer bound to the visible body. If I am on the telephone, I am present – live – but obviously absent in the visual space (if, on the other hand – I dare say – I am lost in thought, my body is there, but I am not there – my mind is elsewhere, absent for those who might want to talk to me).

Many productions that make use of the internet establish communication without any actor present onstage, but rather use a remote actor connected live. The Wooster Group, for example, moves between a flesh-and-blood actor and that same actor, except now recorded; this takes place to the point that it makes no sense to ask if the production is live performance or media recording. The Australian performer Stelarc plugs a third, computer-operated, hand into his 'real' body. His human body is certainly present, partially living, but it is no longer itself – it is remotely controlled by computer. The limits between the natural body and the prosthetic body controlled by artificial intelligence are no longer clear. What is more, the old distinction between live performance and programmed, mediatised performance no longer holds true, if indeed it ever did. As the media – literally – penetrate our bodies in all their forms – implants, probes, pacemakers (perhaps *soulmakers*, soon enough?), microprocessors, Korean-Japanese implanted mobile telephones – as our attention and our imagination become colonised and distracted by the dominant media of our time, the old-fashioned categories of the human, the living and the present become irrelevant. Our perception is entirely determined by intermediality. We are in the posthuman (Hayles),[3] or even in the postdramatic (Lehmann).[4] We can no longer distinguish between live presence and recording, flesh and electronic components, a being of flesh and blood (as the poet might have put it) and a performative cyborg (as performance scholars would say today).

Live performance is surely always influenced, infiltrated by different media, but that does not mean that it necessarily reproduces them. It betrays another essentialist attitude if we ask 'Which came first, the live or the recorded?' It is better instead to observe how elements that appear by turns living and frozen come together in a performance the moment it is constituted as a meaningful confrontation, as is the case with mise en scène. This is because mise en scène precisely constitutes a mediation between the immediate and the media, the live and the prerecorded, the living and the lifeless, matter and spirit. Mise en scène always seeks to bring together the principle of living authenticity and that of recordable repetition: to appear authentic and unique at each showing, despite being created in order to be identically repeated, whatever the audience and the place.

Instead of preserving these old-fashioned distinctions between the living and the lifeless, the human and the machine, it would be wiser to consider instead the process of embodiment, of incarnation that performance and performers must necessarily undertake in order that there be 'theatre'. This process of staging the body distinguishes theatre from straightforward reading or dramatic literature. But such an incarnation goes hand in hand with a process of disembodiment, a dis-incarnation, with the necessary abstraction of any signifying process, a production of signs, a *mise en signes*. Mise en scène becomes the tool and the field necessary for understanding what emerges from this encounter between living and mechanical reproduction, between concrete and abstract, between matter and spirit.

Should we fear that the human being is no longer at the centre of the work, that media have driven us into the posthuman, into the postdramatic, or that the subject – creator as well as receiver – has gone off the radar, and become just a programmer at the service of computers? Not in the least! The moment that this programmed and programming subject begins to examine the relationship between signs and things, the difference between the living and the lifeless, the moment they are fictionally reincarnated in their creatures, they become directors once again, become human again because they make mistakes, they renegotiate without prejudice the powers and the illusions of theatre. Of course, in doing so, the new media landscape and the reconfiguration of post-Brechtian, post-semiotic theory that emerges must be taken into account, in particular, as regards the binaries signifier/signified, and materiality/immaterial information. This remains a question that mise en scène can tackle, manage and resolve.

Technology/media

The stage has always called upon *technology*, on machines that transform the world by way of *techné* in its human-made environment: amphitheatre, architecture, machines for moving objects, instruments for making sound or light. *Techné* (technique, craft) should be opposed to *épistémé* (that is, knowledge). Is the difference between different media a difference of scale or of nature? The media are always communication machines, technologies that are ever more effective at circulating information. We have, for the last sixty years or so, been living in what Régis Debray calls the '*vidéosphère*', the 'period initiated by audiovisual technology: the mainly screen-based transmission of data, models and stories'.[5] For the stage, this is illustrated by the growing use of 'new media', of recent computer technologies that participate both on and around the stage.

Multimedia performance is not simply an accumulation of arts (theatre, dance, music, projections and so on); it is in its true sense the merging of technologies in the space–time of representation. Cybertheatre, created with the help of the new media and computer technologies, is the use of media in theatrical performance, and is also particularly concerned with the internet's capacity to produce virtual spaces.

It would be impossible to describe here the range of new media used in today's theatre. In any case, the most important thing for mise en scène is not the intrinsic performance of the media, but rather the effect of those media onstage, in particular in the case of film projections, the digital-video image, virtual images, and new media (both present and yet to come). New technologies of information and communication (NTIC) are bound to the computer, and are more concerned with cybertheatre than with live performance.

Other media in performance

As examples of media, we should include technology used in the preparation of a performance, such as recorded sound, light or surtitles.

These days, sound is rarely produced live in the wings; it is prerecorded using the latest technology. The resulting soundtrack accompanies the show. It is sometimes too 'present', and is redundant compared with the visual elements, and usually appears in the role of arbitrator, in order to establish meaning and produce sensations. What results is a 'soundscape',[6] a sound-landscape comparable with the set itself, with reliefs and nuances of space and color. Since the end of the 1970s, actors have had microphones hidden about their person; these not only increase the volume of their voices, but also rework them: adding reverb or distortion, mixing the voice into the sound landscape, and giving the actor a different emotional tone.

Lighting, since the emergence of electric lighting in around 1880, has been subject to spectacular changes. Lighting designs involve the entire production, and also particularly contribute to atmosphere. Here too, computing is essential in order to produce and memorise the smallest changes of light or mood. This creates a theatre that is entirely computerised, where everything is tightly controlled, which paradoxically brings us back to the notion of *Gesamtkunstwerk*, a total work of art, even while mise en scène does all it can to distance itself from this notion.[7]

Surtitles – another technical development whose impact on the spectator has yet to be properly measured – constitute the perfect example of a technology and a use of media that changes our perception almost without our noticing it. To read surtitles is, of course, optional, but it is difficult to resist doing so, even if we understand the language being translated for the display. Surtitles can be more or less discreet, and can be integrated into the production's visuals like calligraphy. Some directors, such as Dominique Pitoiset,[8] work on the translation as well as the integration of the surtitles with the staging and the visuals of the production. Surtitles can add another level of perception, reintroducing – in a way that is sometimes iconic and sometimes ironic – the text of which theatre people were so suspicious back in the old days.

The audiovisual media remain the most visible media in contemporary productions. To retrace their appearance, and their history, would be too heavy a task here: a few spaced historical landmarks will give us a sense of direction.[9]

Historical landmarks

- The first experiments with audiovisual media go back to Meyerhold (*Hidden Earth*, 1923). Piscator used projections (*Flags*, 1924), or films (*In Spite of Everything*, 1925) to complement, or to contrast with, theatrical representation. Walter Gropius developed in 1927 a project for a total theatre that embraced audiovisual media. In the United States, Thomas Wilfred staged Ibsen's *Warriors of Helgeland*.

- The scenographic creations of Josef Svoboda from 1958 onward, with a multiscreen and a Lanterna Magika, marked a crucial new step toward the use of video, something that became widespread at the start of the 1970s. Jacques Polieri, in his '*vidéo-ballet-spectacle*' of 1964, *Game de sept*, showed video on a large screen. His 'eidophore', a large-screen television projector, allowed him to create close-ups.[10]

- From the early 1970s onwards, film projections disappeared, replaced by television screens used to diffuse video. As one of the first users, Hans-Peter Cloos, admits, television screens were often used as a gesture of opposition to bourgeois theatre. In the 1980s, video very quickly became a means of renewing stage narrative, of replacing an absent actor (as in the Wooster Group's *LSD*), or of bringing acting into confrontation with its screen representation (*Route 1 and 9*, 1981, and *Brace Up*, 1992, by the same group). Mabou Mines used video for *Hajj*. In Germany, in 1979 the director Hans-Günther Heyme made an *Electronic Hamlet* with the video artist Wolf Vorstell.[11] Until the 1980s, the relationship between theatre practitioners and video remained uneasy and uncomfortable: artists tended to accumulate television sets in the space, in the style of Nam June Paik, or of Peter Sellars in his early installations (the immense cross made of television sets in his staging of *Saint Francis of Assisi*, 1992).

• From the 1990s, theatre artists such as Robert Lepage, Peter Sellars, Giorgio Barbero Corseti and Frank Castorf began a new phase in the use of video: video is no longer limited to the margins, or used as mere provocation, but takes its place at the heart of a stage set-up, and instigates a new way of telling stories by means of theatre. In this sense, video has become no longer an end in itself, but a new departure point for unknown lands.

• Since 2000, we have been cured of our anxieties about using media – it has even become rather banal. Christian Schiaretti's staging of *Ervart ou les derniers jours de Frédéric Nietzsche*, by Hervé Blusch, is typical of a tendency to use virtual scenery projections ironically, as if to replace the flat cardboard scenery of yesteryear.

For Robert Lepage, media is always at the service of the story being told, far more easily and directly than is the case for his European colleagues. In *The Andersen Project* (2005), Lepage the actor takes all the roles played by the virtual images. The media are all the more effective in that they are integrated into a dramaturgical function, an art of telling, a search for the identity of the character. Like film music, such media can be said to be most effectively used and integrated when we do not even notice they are there. Just as our lives constantly and uninterruptedly call upon such prostheses, recent mise en scène seems to have assimilated media. This is a long way from trashy videos, filling the screen with disposable images, shot in order that we immediately consume and then rapidly dispense with them.

Possibilities for video on stage

Shooting and projecting video is obviously much easier than shooting and projecting film. Improvements in video image quality, in particular due to the advent of high-definition video, in part explain video's current success. There is no point in opposing video and film in order to seek out their essence, but it is useful instead to point out a few properties of each. According to Frédéric Maurin:

> there remains an opposition, it is in televisual terms between live and recorded broadcast; in cinematic terms, it is between the close up and the off-screen; and, in psychoanalytic terms, an

opposition between the process of narcissism (the image as doubling) and that of fetishism (the image as substitute for lack).[12]

Thus video returns a narcissistic reflection, while film encourages fetishism. This comparison recalls one made by Stéphane Braunschweig, who notes the very conceptual and barely illusionistic uses of video onstage: 'Television, as an object, is much more conceptual. It emits a sign. On screen, on the other hand, the sign is instantly absorbed in the fiction.'[13]

Effects of media on our perception

The presence of audiovisual media onstage has consequences for our perceptions, both short and long term. The change of scale, well known in photography and in cinema, leads to a spatial and corporeal disorientation for the spectator, which can be more or less pleasant or unpleasant. Trickery gives the regressive pleasure of the marvellous, as in the cinematic work of Georges Méliès.

As stated earlier, in the competition between image and real presence (video and actor), the spectator does not necessarily choose the living over the inanimate – far from it. Rather, the spectator chooses that which is visible on the largest scale, what keeps moving, and thus grabs the attention. This is precisely what is at stake in the conflict between living actor and image: the challenge made to theatre is to help the actors find their presence and their ability to present themselves. Jean-François Peyret notes this with regard to video in his shows:

> Place an actor onstage; then project a video image; the spectator's gaze will immediately be drawn to the image. What will bring the gaze back to the actor? The promise of what emotion? This is for me the only question left in the theatre, since theatre can no longer draw its strength from its representative powers, and still less from its powers of illusion, but rather must draw on its capacity to present itself, and, I might even add, its capacity to empty the gaze of what has already been seen, or seen too much.[14]

For Peyret, and also for Lepage[15] and Braunschweig,[16] it seems obvious that the 'problem' of the media onstage is not the elimination of the human or the question of presence, but the kind of identification that video, cinema or projection allows the spectator. It is a question of seeing how this identification differs from that of theatrical representation (if the notion can even be maintained). In the cinema, the spectator identifies with the character, whereas in the theatre identification is directed toward the actor and towards the audience as a community. The real presence of the actor on stage is not absolutely vital to the spectator, and it is in no way proof of the 'ontological' superiority of theatre over audiovisual media. The phantasmic power of the cinema image, and the plasticity of video as it takes hold of the acting and links to the outside world, constitute a real challenge for theatrical reality: the bodies are present in the spectator's imagination, but cut off from the spectator's concrete experience. And yet, as Peyret rightly points out:

> Bodies in the cinema are stronger because they are lost, out of reach, out of real presence, more phantasmically present because they are absent. So the links are perhaps broken between the visible and the living, which is undoubtedly the challenge that the world of images (real, computer-generated, and virtual) makes to the stage. The key point of any phenomenology of perception was, according to Merleau-Ponty, that all vision takes place somewhere inside the tactile space. Can we still be sure of this? Is there still a tactile space?[17]

This question goes to the heart of the spectator. Can spectators re-centre on themselves that which the media seeks to decentre? Can spectators delocalize perception and resist returning it to a stable and tactile place? Cybertheatre eliminates the notion of a stage and of a spectator inscribed in a stable and ultimately tactile space. The spectator is no longer in the representation of an exterior and existing reality, but in the simulation of virtual theatre. And so the spectator has definitively abandoned the stage and auditorium screened-off for protection, in favour of the screen as site of projection or of transmission (in the case of digital video).

To stick (itself a very tactile term!) to the use of video on the theatre stage, we should observe audiovisual media in relation to theatre mise en scène and ask a few direct, but simple, questions.

Suggestions for the analysis of media in mise en scène

A few simple questions:

• Are the different media identifiable, visible and shown, or are they instead hidden, kept from the (non-specialist) spectators' view? Do we see the technical apparatus or are we under the spell of the marvellous?

- Are media produced live, such as, for example, a live video that retransmits the acting? Or are they prepared in advance to be inserted into the theatrical performance at a given, fixed or arbitrary moment?
- What is the ratio of audiovisual media to live performance? Is the presence of a living or visible actor necessary in order that the performance does not become an installation, an interactive film or cybertheatre? A semantic distinction, perhaps? Is the presence of a human being with a – visible or invisible – body, which is potentially tangible, necessary in order to speak of theatre? And, on the other hand, is live presentation really the hallmark of theatre? Can machines not be used live? Thus we should perhaps distinguish the living from the live, which in the media use of the term does not mean 'living' but rather 'produced in real time for the receiver (of theatre and of the media)'.
- What is the relationship between the different media? Can they be separated clearly? Or do we move smoothly from one to the other?
- In what historical moment of the evolution of media is the work situated? In a moment of competition or of intermediality? 'In the phase of media competition, dialogue concerns the survival of the media, in the phase of intermedial experiments it concerns the development of new ways of seeing.'[18] We seem most often to be found in the latter situation: the different media provide us with new ways of seeing the world.

These simple questions, even more than their answers, lead us to a few theoretical conclusions, which are mere working hypotheses.

Working hypotheses

Should one seek to know and to compare the specific properties of media? This can certainly be useful, but it is often difficult – for the normal spectator at least – to identify and thus to describe the media at play in a production. Even when this is achieved, this will not explain their functioning, and still less the effect produced (in the same way that to describe a production 'exhaustively' proves nothing!).

As Christopher Balme shows,[19] the media have no specific ontological essence, they are merely provisional and changing constructions. There is no such thing as 'the televisual', 'the theatrical' or 'the filmic', contrary to what Philip Auslander suggests.[20] Paradoxically, it is easier to study the exchanges between the different media, and their interactions, than it is to study a single medium in isolation.

Intermediality is the study of such interactions, and is the discipline that hopes to account for them. Theatre and theory have left essentialism behind; insistence on the purity of medium, that of Grotowski, Brook or Kantor, ended with the 1960s. Balme speaks of a 'paradigm shift that can be described as the displacement of the specificity of media, a shift towards intermediality'.[21] Intermediality is linked to the capacity of the spectator to perceive each medium differently, and to accept receipt of several more or less mixed messages.

The relationship of stage immediacy to media remains to be established. According to Philip Auslander, the live form is paradoxically modelled on the mediatised form that influences it. According to Auslander, a historical reversal takes place: 'Initially, the mediatized form is modeled on the live form, but it eventually usurps the live form's position in the cultural economy.'[22] Thus, 'historically, the live is actually an effect of mediatization, not the other way around. It is the development of recording technologies that made it possible to perceive existing representations as "live."'[23] It is undeniable, as Auslander observes, that, 'the ancient Greek theatre, for example, was not live because there was no possibility of recording it'.[24] This category of the live is thus historical, and not ontological. In this respect, Auslander is right to relativize the notion of the live, not to make it the absolute origin, the voice (in Derrida's sense) which, according to Western metaphysics, is supposed to precede writing. Basically, Auslander discovers that the live is a relative category, and that it does not exist without its opposite, the recorded. This discovery of dialectics (no white without black, or good without evil) should not be an excuse to push the paradox to the point of saying that the live is a construction and a consequence of media. Auslander easily exposes Peggy Phelan's position – according to which theatre defines itself ontologically as that which cannot be reproduced – as betraying an essentialist conception of theatre that does not take into account the evolution of art and the media.[25] But to see the live as a product of media is a step too far. Is it not enough to note that supposedly authentic forms of theatre are indeed influenced and deformed by the impact of media?

Alongside the theorist Matthew Causey, we would suggest that the theses of Phelan and of Auslander are both equally problematic:

> Phelan disregards any effect of technology on performance and draws a non-negotiable, essentialist border between the two media. Auslander's material theory and legalistic argument overlooks the most material aspect of the live, namely death. ... The supplementing of live performance with mediated technologies of representation

creates a system which can alter the spatial, temporal system through being present and absent simultaneously.[26]

Following Causey's logic, we suggest the following compromise: live performance is always linked to different media and thus influenced by them, but it does not reproduce them mechanically and does not precede them either. Mise en scène (as it has been defined here) constitutes a mediation between the live and the media. It actually tries to bring together, and at times to confront, a principle of authenticity and a principle of repetition of the same: it strives to appear authentic and unique for every performance, but at the same time is 'fabricated' to be identically repeated, whatever the necessarily different audiences may be.

Remediation, or representation of one medium in another,[27] traces the modification of a medium caused by borrowing the conventions of another medium. In the case of twentieth-century mise en scène it would be easy to show that the stage constantly adopts procedures borrowed from technological media, such as the cinema and more recently video, and that it adapts them to the concrete needs of the time. The close-up, editing, and montage are examples of filmic techniques perfectly adaptable to the theatre stage.

Instead of opposing theatricality, choreography, music, voice, shadow theatre and so on, and instead of listing instances of cinema trickery, computer trickery and projection trickery, we should rather – as we will see in the analysis of *Paradis* by Dominique Hervieu and José Montalvo, below – attempt to grasp the strategy of their interaction: 'Intermedial thought does not consist of erratically cementing specific criteria of media; rather, it asks what function of usage, what convention of perception, what effect, what aesthetic strategy, and what aesthetic experience, is to be found actualised in and through a medium.'[28]

In the example of *Paradis*, the aesthetic experience is that of a mediation of the body, the artists' as much as the spectators', a mediation between principles that are normally antithetical: the true and the false, the live and the filmed, the classic and the popular. This mediation is at the same time a remediation and a remedy for spectators' tired bodies, a social remedy to allow styles, cultures and different corporealities to dance together and coexist. This 'social remedy' consists of erasing differences, cultures and divergent corporealities by way of movement and beauty. Suddenly receptive to changes in our conventions of perception, the spectator, an immobile dancer, follows the movement and identifies with it, as if the movement had taken on a political dimension, thus cementing together the genres and classes, the media and the arts, and being transported by them.

This remediation is thus not abstract, but embodied; it takes place according to a series of movements and physical actions, and manifests itself in the effects produced upon the spectators. There is thus a series of images, of visual effects, with a great 'force of affective actions',[29] but these images are always embodied by the (real or filmed) bodies of the actors. They evolve in time, not as isolated actions, but as a vectorised series of moments of different intensities.

In this respect, the analysis of media and of images must take place with attention to what Marie-José Mondzain calls the 'political sociality of the emotions'.[30] This analysis thus always leads, in the end, to the judgment and evaluation of a given community.

Armed with this fragile theoretical toolkit, we should set about conquering the world (that is, describing productions where the audiovisual media participate), undertaking a quest in the style of Don Quixote.

Three examples

Paradis *by Dominique Hervieu and José Montalvo*

We now analyse a short sequence from *Paradis*,[31] starting at the moment when an Antillaise dancer repeats '*bene sikine*' to the arrival onscreen of an old lady, which brings to a close an extract from Vivaldi's opera.

Against a blue background, addressing the audience with words of obscure meaning, and launching the music with the recommendation that it be delivered '*avec elegance*', the dancer performs a brief solo that is almost a physical feat in itself: spectacularly moving her pelvis and contracting the muscles of her buttocks, demonstrating striking mobility. All this becomes a counterpoint to the 'celestial' opera music, and then to the pure 'angelic' voice of the singer.

Thus begins a game of *trompe-l'oeil*: four dancers seem to lift a curtain and discover a stage, but this stage is merely a screen upon which two identical groups of three dancers perform, visible too thanks to film projection. Each of the three dancers expresses herself in a different style: hip hop, classical, African.

The media (projectors) are hidden from the view of the audience, the illusion is near-perfect – the actions seem to happen as if by magic, without us knowing why or how. We can hardly distinguish the real dancers from the filmed dancers.

In the next sequence, animated projections of animals – a dog, a donkey, a snake, an elephant, a tiger, a crocodile – cross the stage. As they cross, they encounter real dancers who follow them or try to avoid them. The scale of the animals varies, from a very large snake to a giant dog, to an elephant of normal proportions. The filmed dancers mingle with the real dancers, trying also to avoid colliding with the animals; they sometimes go inside the screen, and come out from behind it as filmed images or as real people. This sequence follows the dynamics and rhythm of Vivaldi's music and vocal work. Rapid gestures, virtuosity, pure voices and baroque music are the vectors of emotion, and allow the spectator to take off.

Two of the dancers, a man and a woman, come and stand in front of the screen, then struggle to avoid a huge double shadow that threatens to crush them; it is a filmed shadow, which might be the shadow of a man with heavy boots. The two dancers then run toward the forestage, and step in front of a light that projects their shadow, very similar to the previous one, which is also determined to crush the 'real' dancers who have joined the struggle. The music is drowned out by the terrified cries of the dancers, until the final calm, when an old woman arrives, a filmic image that freezes during the last measures of the musical sequence.

Thanks to Vivaldi's music, *Paradis* recovers all the powers of nascent opera. The marvellous and the sublime defeat the material; they conceal the workings and transport us into a marvellous world where anything is possible. The sequence is structured according to a classical dramatic progression: introduction and prologue by the Antillaise dancer, the *peripeteia* of the advancing animals, the intensification of the danger and ultimate defeat of the 'baddies', the final return to calm, and the simultaneous halting of the music and movement. This classical narrative gives the spectator a complete kinaesthetic experience. The media are perfectly integrated into the core of the performance, and the entire stage becomes a singing and dancing body. The movement and gestures are indexed to temporality, rhythm, and all kinds of unconscious perceptions linked to voice and the invisible.

The persistent theme of the sequence, and of the ballet as a whole, remains the unending struggle between real dancers and their virtual images. The filmic image is used to 'crush' – by means of its stature and its constant changes of scale – the frail shadows of the dancers. We witness a struggle between marvellous virtual images and the reality of flesh and blood dancers, who are at times virtuosos, and at times frightened or screaming. But this struggle is a trick, since the way in which the animals are represented avoids all realism and any fear-inducing effect. The conflict is just for fun, as is the coexistence of styles and social groups represented: a stylistic, ethnic and sociocultural consensus. Who could argue with that?

Sometimes the use of media is clearly more critical and combative, as if the medium abandoned its illustrative and sedative function in order to confront ambient reality and wake the spectator from mediatic slumbers. Indeed, this will be the case in the next example, from Frank Castorf.

Crime et châtiment *by Frank Castorf*

In several productions, and particularly for *Crime et châtiment* (*Crime and Punishment*), Castorf films his actors continuously. Their image – which is fairly blurred and unclear – appears projected on a screen or onto parts of Bert Neumann's set. The faces are often shot in close-up and thus nothing escapes the lens, including wrinkles, dirt and sordid details. The video is a planned intrusion into the stage's intimacy, where normally we can watch, but never see things close up. The video passes straight through the actor, as if the actor were invisible; it exposes any breach of the rules or of manners to the audience, like video surveillance. The actor is not supposed to perform for the camera, and thus is recorded as if without knowledge of it. The camera operator puts together a few images without claiming to be exhaustive, as would a sports reporter seeking to bear witness to and exhibit the performances. The camera delivers details that are invisible to the naked eye or considered private or taboo. Obviously, however, the actors are aware of being filmed. They must act as if they did not know and also give themselves over to the technical demands of the camera.

Live recording is not, or at least is not necessarily, a critical distancing in the Brechtian sense. It is more deconstruction, or even demolition, than aesthetic and political alienation. This is a 'vivisection by live video',[32] without the ideological false consciousness or the pedagogical pose that might say, 'Look at what I managed to show you about the actor, all the little stage secrets that this ham actor wanted to both reveal and hide!' The actor does not escape the camera. And yet it is also Dostoevsky's characters that are probed, chased, given the camera's truth serum: does Raskolnikov, when interrogated by the police officer, know what the officer knows? And is the police officer pretending not to suspect him or is he psychologically torturing him? The camera adds a dimension of analysis, of suspense, and of authenticity to the dialogue from the novel.

Whether or not there is any (voluntary or involuntary) confession, video offers the spectator a second perspective on the stage and on the stage event.

It is our perception that produces the world – this is what demonstrates the second perspective of live video on the stage. Potentially, its alternative perspective gives us the possibility of rendering visible what escapes control, when as always in the theatre, we exercise a degree of control. The cameraman's gaze, which touches things via the lens, guarantees the possibility of participating by its sheer presence; it guarantees that we will witness an authentic event. Thus the live use of video gives the special possibility of leading the mise en scène towards a heightened now: in this integrated simultaneity, degrees of truth and discovery that we could otherwise never imagine are made available to perception.[33]

For Castorf, the video gaze follows and heightens the frenzy of the acting, brings crisis to the actor and breakdown to the performance: it is an epic technique, perhaps, but not necessarily a Brechtian one in terms of its political dimension. There emerges a new and reinforced relationship between the actor and her character: is the character dirty, or does the actor end up dirty? Who is lying? How can we find out the truth? What are the signals in this reportage on the actor at work? Old questions of theatrical aesthetics continually reappear with new clarity; they demand that the spectators decide on an instant response. Perception is ceaselessly upset, profoundly and lastingly, while in *Paradis* it was flattered and confirmed in its certainties. To the distilled, sanitised, infantilised, idealistic and rather silly illusionism of *Paradis* can be opposed the dislocation of identities, and the open fracture of social and interpersonal relationships, of Castorf and Dostoevsky's hell. If *Paradis* calms the subject, recentres its scattered perceptions, Castorf's hell feeds on contradictory and shocking impressions. Projections and *trompe-l'oeil* trickery in *Paradis* heighten the exhilaration of the rapid and virtuoso movement thanks to the euphoric music of baroque opera; they offer a kinaesthetic physiotherapy for social relationships, albeit an illusory one. On the other hand, the clashing images of *Crime et châtiment* induce a fragmented perception of the body, challenging any imposed harmonisation of human relationships.

The Passions *by Bill Viola*

In order to test out some of the possibilities of intermediality, and to expand our understanding of theatre and media, we will examine a few of Bill Viola's video installations. These works are displayed in numerous museums, and their photographic trace obliges us to imagine a moving image, even if it is one that unfolds very slowly.

The Greeting

Before *The Passions* series, Viola experimented with a technique of slow motion, starting with what seemed at first to be Renaissance paintings. In *The Greeting* (1995), he films a group of three women from a low angle; the scene is inspired by Pontormo's painting *The Visitation* (1528), which evokes a meeting between Mary and her cousin Elizabeth, as told in Luke (1: 39–56). In real time, the sequence cannot have lasted longer than forty-five seconds, but here it is stretched over twelve minutes. It is not a faithful reconstruction of the painting, as found in the traditional theatre exercise of creating a *tableau vivant*. The four characters of the painting are here reduced to three; they are not immediately identifiable and it is not necessary to identify them in order to appreciate the video (just as we can today enjoy a painting without knowing the identity of each biblical character depicted).

A comparison between the painting and the video remains nonetheless useful, if only in order to evaluate the choices and possibilities of the painter and the video artist. The general meaning of the scene, and the situation, remains the same, as does the system of gazes. The differences, however, are every bit as relevant: the costumes are brought up to date, and the faces and bodies appear contemporary. How does this work? The hairstyles are contemporary European ones. The poses, the configurations of bodies, the gazes and the emotions all produce an effect of contemporaneity. Even the bodies and faces are subject to historical time: they evolve and remind us of modern morphologies. The fact that they move so slowly allows us to observe their dynamics and their trajectory all the better. Slow motion gives their movement a grace and a precision that would normally go unnoticed. Immobility *par excellence* – of the type found in painting – is the subject of video art of this kind. The natural opposition between immobility and movement is challenged: 'everything moves' (as Jacques Lecoq puts it). Movement, and not stillness, seems to be the norm. Or, to borrow from Henri Matisse's conception, 'immobility is a movement placed at a level that does not involve the bodies of the spectators, but rather their spirit'. We need to use our imaginations to understand that life can be frozen into a painted image.

With video movement, which animates or reanimates painting, Viola resuscitates people and things: an art of Lazarus, where bodies and life can be reborn at any time. In the darkened space of the audiovisual installations of Viola and Petrov, a sense of surprise and anguish greets the visitor. The high-definition video image gives the momentary illusion of an old master. The only thing that betrays the visual trap, beyond the tiny and barely perceptible motion, is the modernity of the faces, the bodies and the movements. We recognise – and therein lies our pleasure – the presence of actors in flesh and blood before the camera, staged for the occasion, only slightly disguised as New Testament figures, as if they do not successfully 'represent the antique' (Barthes),[34] since their corporeality and their appearance remain contemporary.

Thus we must study mise en scène in the filmic sense: the way in which objects and bodies are arranged in the space, the way in which the arrangement is guided both by the imitation of character from painting and by the necessary organisation for the camera. This staging – one that emerges from the pictorial source, from the visual and scenographic reconstitution, and from the way of filming – is to a large extent concerned with the representation of bodies. It is necessary, then, to analyse the gestures and gazes. As an example, we could compare how Pontormo and Viola represent the embrace of the two women. The painter captures the eyes of the four women at the same height, which initially seems to place them on an equal footing, but the gazes of Mary and Elisabeth are the only ones that meet, while those of the two servants remain attentive, but exterior. The video artist has twelve minutes in which to show the exchange of glances, to prepare the embrace, to kinesthetically allow the coming together and the vibrations of the bodies. Since the camera is fixed, with the observer facing the canvas, the system of gazes appears clearly, and the observer has the impression of watching a theatre scene that has secretly been filmed.

The theatrical mise en scène reimagines and recreates the meeting by way of pictorial data, it sets into enunciation (in space, in rhythm, in 'flesh') the situation of meeting, the only obligation being to show hands that touch or arms that embrace. More directly and precisely than normal speed, slow motion reveals and deploys emotions that are often unspeakable or unreadable, which move between the two women, and between them and the two servants. Thus slow-motion video unfolds a scene formerly played for the camera under the guidance of the spontaneous theatre director Bill Viola. Viola's starting point is an intuition about the corporeality of the characters in Pontormo's painting, and this intuition is transmitted verbally and mimetically to the actors, who are thus able to retranslate it into – and with – their own bodies. The difference from the theatre or film actor is that Viola takes the pictorial mode of representation into account, particularly in his figuring of the bodies. This cooperation and imbrication of both the media and the arts has little to do with linear intermediality (the reproduction of one art by another); rather, it produces a work in its own right, and obliges us to imagine interactions between media themselves and between the arts.

Each of the video works tackles a different theme and approaches a specific question of intermediality. Here are a few emblematic examples.

Anima

In *The Passions*, Viola conserves the principle of representation of the face and body in a form that the gallery viewer might initially mistake for a painting. These 'paintings', like a troublesome hallucination, turn out to be high-definition video recordings. Inspired by the famous lecture by Charles Le Brun on 'the general expression of passions of the soul' (1668), in *Anima*, Viola deals with four fundamental emotions: joy, sadness, anger and fear. Filming a man and a woman separately, he leaves each actor to express their emotions by way of the almost invisible transformation of a facial expression. The result is the impression of an emotional continuum, of a morphing effect, as if it were basically impossible to distinguish and dissociate the different human emotions. This absence of rupture, unlike Le Brun's drawn plates or the logical descriptions of the passions by Descartes, suggests that the affects are actually joined together. Viola uses slow motion to demonstrate the fluidity and continuity of the emotions, to question the supposed authenticity of the passions, to suggest, by contrast, the building of a character by a virtuoso and a 'cold' actor.

Contemporary theory distinguishes several categories of affect: first, the affective intense emotions or states such as anger or fear; second, feelings like love, hope, or jealousy; third, affective tonalities like joy and sadness, 'pure affects, without any representative content, without any immediately apparent cause'.[35] Viola's actors seem to be primarily concerned with intense emotions and tonalities of affect. They need not actually feel emotions, but only show their expressions at their own tempo. The subsequent slowing down, far from diluting these emotions by stretching them, indicates precisely the nuances, thresholds, and transitions that – to the naked eye – would remain invisible. We must not forget that the video artist films a constitution of affects, and not real affects as we experience them in real life; rather, he artificially reconstitutes the actors' fabricated emotions, in order then to rework them by way of slow motion, framing and camera angle. Video media modify the perception of the spectator, and they renew the theory of the actor, demystifying the natural, showing tricks and strings, and confirming the artificial character of all representation.

Emergence

Another moving painting, *Emergence*, inspired by Pieta de Masolino (1424), is a video representing the resurrection of Christ. This is resurrection, but also birth, or rebirth, in the world. The body of Jesus emerges from its tomb, reborn, as if the water has just broken, where life already flows over a new world. The body of Christ, which is classical in proportions and posture, and with its eternity made visible, lends the scene its harmonious plasticity, its intemporality, its eternity.

But 'which body' (as Barthes might have asked) are we talking about? It is at once the *anatomical body* (intact, young, muscular, naked with innocence, self-assured or even arrogant, defying the ban on nudity), the *ethnological body* (which is here not given a type according to a particular culture, but rather a universal – Greek, perhaps – idealised, aesthetic), the *aesthetic body* (or 'human body that is the object of artistic representations'),[36] the *historical body* (specifically modern: 'the clothing, or, in some cases, the controlled, and overseen absence of clothing, has the function of signifying the new body, the modern body').[37]

From a Christian perspective, the resurrection is a miracle, a mystery that grounds faith and establishes the dogma of eternal life; from the aesthetic perspective of this video, and generally of all of Viola's *Passions*, we can more readily speak of the *marvellous*, that which provokes astonishment, or even admiration from the observer. Such admiration, in the face of these video works, consists of 'the surprise that means that the soul carefully considers things that seem rare and extraordinary to it'.[38] Each visitor to these painting–video installations must feel some admiration for the technical and aesthetic prowess of the pictorial image magically brought to life. The marvellous inhabits the laws of our real world: a painting does not move, a human being cannot move so slowly and refer to so many things that until now have gone unnoticed. We do not perceive, or we do not want to perceive, the mystery of these magical transformations. We surely do not doubt that Viola and Kirov have more up their sleeves, but we choose to accept and enjoy the marvellous without demanding any explanation, and we accept it as something that we pretend not to understand. We enjoy the logic of the material, without seeking explanations, without necessarily imagining that artists are illustrating their ideas on the

Bible, on art or on the world. Our pleasure in the face of these videos is in no way an abstract reasoning, or a search for final causes. Rather, it leads us to an incarnated understanding, to a sensory and haptic experience according to the logic of sensation and of material. In the same way, movement can only be perceived, evaluated and finally 'grasped' if we are not trying to conceive it uniquely with our logic, but also with physical, and haptic, imagination. Is such not the calming effect of these videos, of the art that emanates from them, and of art in general? Silence, slowness, concentration and Buddhist-like spirituality are the final outcome of this advanced technology, this intermediality that brings us into contact with the marvellous in creation.

Catherine's Room

Combining studies focused on the expression of emotions, this series of works deals with episodes from the Bible seen in the context of a characteristic action. Viola creates a temporal sequence: he situates himself at different moments of the day, of the year or of life, but lets each animated image have its own logic and distinct atmosphere.

Catherine's Room captures the figure of Catherine four times, in sequences each lasting a few minutes. The moving paintings follow on from one another like images in a comic book, forming a cycle of day to night, life to death, prayer to rejoining God. The visitor can choose the order of viewing, although the four phases are presented in chronological order. If we 'read' from left to right as in Western writing, the narrative logic is clearly sketched and corresponds to the philosophical or religious message. Each painting is situated in a distinct temporal framework with its own rhythm and particular atmosphere.

But what exactly are we perceiving, and upon what is our perception founded? We continue to ask ourselves this question, which belongs to an old order, long before intermediality, when we felt the need to categorise everything into literary genres, into arts, or into media with clearly defined outlines. Today we tend to imagine that each medium calls upon a certain type of corporeal experience, of physical imagination: that is, of distinct bodies that the user may mobilise, when the time comes. What body allows us to 'absorb' this videographic work?

The *static body*, placed before the fixed and painted image, is a body that is susceptible to disappearing in contemplation.

The *dynamic body*, which becomes animated immediately when the painting reveals itself to be a video: this is a body that follows movement by imagination, itself participating in the movement (albeit internal and not in an externally visible way). This is a body that projects itself into movement, identifies with it, and follows it in order to seize it.

The *moving body* moves within the space of the installation, jumping from one scene to the next. This body is disoriented by parallel actions, torn by the ruptures of the split screen; it tends to become fragmented, but it follows an overall logic, that of the cycle of life, giving it a certain unity.

The *cyclical body* is a pensive body, that of a narrative without beginning or end, since each episode is endlessly reused or repeated, like a myth or a parable of eternal recurrence.

Between these bodies, or between these corporeal and temporal experiences, there are spaces, thresholds, changes and milestones for intermediality, empty spaces that are neither painted nor embodied, where the imagination of the receiver can precisely find its place. 'I am interested', says Bill Viola, 'by what the old masters did not paint, by the steps in between.'[39] Is this a question of thresholds of perception, of turning points, or simply of the unstated, the unpainted, which the dance of bodies and the media draws and composes for the benefit of the spectator?

These few examples challenge the distinction between arts, between media, and between types of bodies supposed to perceive them. They inspire us to look for the limits, the artistic thresholds, between the media, but also between types of bodies, but we never manage to grasp them.

Viola's high-tech video serves a mystical, marvellous vision, a vision filled with wonder. Intermediality is perhaps little more than a change in our corporeal perception. A medium has perhaps no existence or is of no interest until it is received and embodied by the receiver.

In order to understand what happens in these strange transmutations, the notion of mise en scène is highly useful, if not indispensable. Indeed, it is as if the paintings are restaged (mise en scène again): they keep the same theme, the same constituents, but the staging adapts their style and their figuring to the spectator's habits of perception and expectations. Thus, Viola gives his vision of things, indicates his attitude, while pretending to quote the story to be told; he leaves the imprint of his own interpretation. Viola sees himself as a continuation of, and a return to, the humanist values of classical painting – refuge, solitude, spirituality, a sense of beauty, the sublime – thus countering a certain postmodern or postdramatic cynicism.

With *The Passions*, Viola returns to the classical theory of affects: he continually asks how to produce them, transmit them and receive them. A sense of the sublime and of the pathetic marked the efforts of

Descartes and Le Brun to define and represent emotions, postures, facial expressions and basic narratives. But how can we now share these emotions, these passions? If the stage is, as Marie-José Mondzain suggests, the site where impassioned pathos is shared,[40] it remains for us to establish how this sharing requires a new universal theory of the effect produced (*Wirkungen*) – a theory of the passion, in every sense of the word this time.

Where does passion come from? And in the case of Viola's *The Passions*, how do technology and art, allied under the sign of theatre and of the actor, produce such an impact, such a powerful effect, on the spectator? A theory of the spectator's affects is certainly premature, even if it has solid precursors in classical aesthetics. For each video, we can certainly ask which passions are foregrounded and what form our reception takes: surprise, fear admiration and so on. We also learn how the interaction of the media contributes to a re-evaluation and reconfiguration of the classical passions of painting and philosophy. The spectator, who is the object and the source of affects, becomes the key to a phenomenological analysis, which runs the risk of becoming a new impressionistic theory of sensations and emotions. It is therefore appropriate to link the aesthetic object firmly with the passions/ reactions felt by the spectator.

General conclusions

The use of media is not a simple question of technique or of form, but is related to the global meaning of mise en scène. But technique and form should not be a secondary concern, and we should avoid a limited conception of technology in the theatre.

- The contrasting examples of *Paradis* and *Crime et châtiment* demonstrate that there are opposing means of drawing on the different media. The usage of the different media should be analysed in the context of a given mise en scène where the media acquire their meaning. In order to evaluate this usage, hermeneutics reveals itself to be a means of predicting the impact and integration of media on and in the performance.
- Do we need a theory of the image in order to analyse a production? This remains to be seen and of course it depends which theory we end up using! The stage event – the series of physical and scenographic actions wherein the media can intervene – is much more than a series of visible images. We should avoid placing all emphasis on visuality and visibility, and should look at the invisible

as well: time, sound and voice. Marie-José Mondzain claims that the entertainment industry is all about:

> the hypothesis of the all-visible, of showing everything. We are located in a totalitarianism of vision. The only thing that exists is what we see, at the time when we see it. This gives huge power to the owners of visibilities, who control the notion of spectacle in pure terms of visibility, and not in terms of the invisibility that is the essence of spectacle. The essence of spectacle is not visible because it is time.[41]

- Instead of establishing a general theory of media (an undertaking that is problematic and indeed titanic), let us instead offer a provisional theory of mise en scène and of the variable role of media in its constitution. In order to do this, we ask a few simple questions. How does a stage, film or auditory event function for a given spectator? How do the new audiovisual media lead us to a renewed perception, to the gaze turning on itself? How, for example, do videos or projections force us to rethink or 're-feel' our usual theatrical impressions? In the example of *Paradis*, we noted that the projections and trickery intensified the rapture of the virtuoso movement accompanied by euphoric music. It is a simple heightening, then. And it has a physiotherapeutic and anaesthetising function: to reduce pain, but not remove its cause. The media contribute to reconstituting identity and corporeal unity. In *Crime et châtiment*, the live video sometimes has a Brechtian function of alienation; it controls our purely theatrical perception, which has become too imprecise and unreliable. The frenzy of showing everything (as in reality television) implies a certain sadism of attention and engenders a body in pieces. Thanks to the media, our relationship with the world is reconfigured: it is as if we inhabit it in a different way. In *Paradis* (lost!) we are 'high up'; in *Crime et châtiment*, our punishment is to crawl, to be constantly returned to the pit of sordid reality revealed by the camera following the guilty party.
- Media disconnect and reconnect spectators with their own bodies and with their situations in the world. Far from being destroyed by the media, mise en scène is reshaped, recreated and relived by it. Basically, mise en scène is itself situated equidistant from performance (which is live but cannot be codified) and technology (which is reproducible but lifeless).

We naturally conceive of the work of mise en scène as that of the patient construction of representation and of a show. Mise en scène, an open and polymorphous object, becomes an aesthetic object for an audience after all its elements have been tuned. It is also – at the same time – a deconstruction of our habitual ways of seeing and reading, a distancing of representation, what Brecht would have called an alienation, or rather estrangement. What is the difference between the two conceptions?

Deconstruction is much more than an alienation effect. Brecht never leaves the mimetic representation of the real, although the real in question is a stylised one inside critical realism. But the moment we question, as Derrida would, any such logocentric representation, the moment we interrogate the text or the performance about itself, beyond its metalanguage and its dramatic or scenographic language, we enter deconstruction.

Deconstruction contests the authority of language and of logos to interpret the analysed object, it attempts to break the 'closure of representation'.

There is much representation in the theatre, and many limits.

Mise en scène lends itself to these games of construction and deconstruction because it takes shape in the same moment in which it is received. It possesses means of commentating, manipulating and demystifying the process of production and the reception of its object in situ, by way of the actor/spectator/critic/hermeneute.

Derrida loves 'D-' words: Différance, Destinerrancy, Destruction, Decentring, but also Dissemination and Dissociation (a term borrowed from Freud). These tools of Défaire (undoing, Deconstruction) keep us at a distance and deliver us from destruction, without ever becoming pragmatic, methodological, or regulatory tools.

In order to understand Derrida without Deifying him, and to De-ride him out of his own philosophical seriousness, a few specific theatre productions deserve our attention, and should be our point of departure.

All work and no play make Jacques a dull boy.

9 The deconstruction of postmodern mise en scène

We should probably start by deconstructing the title of this chapter and the ambiguity it contains! The point is to examine how postmodern mise en scène might be deconstructed, but also to consider how mise en scène itself enacts deconstruction. Let us play immediately with the prefix 'de-', in the passive as well as the active sense. Since the three terms of the title are in no way univocal, the programme will inevitably include errancy, or 'destinerrancy'. Nevertheless, the sole aim of this chapter is to take up the Derridean notion of deconstruction as a tool to analyse the functioning of a few theatre productions by directors such as Vitez, Mesguich and Chéreau.

But what is the object that is deconstructed or due for deconstruction? It might be a text to interpret on a stage, but could equally be the mise en scène itself, the way in which the mise en scène takes shape, or unravels, coming undone before our very eyes. If a mise en scène, in the classical or primitive sense of the term, is a total work, one that is unitary, harmonious and centred, then its deconstruction (in the Derridean sense) consists of finding and inducing its possible fragmentation, its contradictions, its dissonances and its decentring.

Borrowed from architecture, from masonry in fact, the term 'deconstruction' designates in the proper sense 'dismantling', the taking-down of a structure. Derrida first used the term in 1967 in *On Grammatology*, inspired by Heidegger's *Destruktion and Abbau* (although Heidegger did not seek to criticise logocentrism per se). When quizzed on the meaning and origin of the notion, Derrida was not very willing to provide a definition, despite friendly requests:

> What people retained of it at the outset was the allusion to structure, because at the time I used this word, there was the dominance of structuralism: deconstruction was considered then at the same time to be a structuralist and anti-structuralist gesture.

Which it was, in a certain manner. Deconstruction is not simply the decomposition of an architectural structure; it is also a question about the foundation, about the relation between foundation and what is founded; it is also a question about the closure of the structure, about a whole architecture of philosophy. Not only as concerns this or that construction, but on the architectonic motif of the system.[1]

Is this pro- or anti-structuralist gesture not ultimately that of mise en scène, which builds a more or less closed or open, centred or decentred, system? Mise en scène is by turns described as a coherent sign system, or as an event without limits. Indeed, *Mise en scène* is what happens, without us necessarily knowing where or why. This is a characteristic of the unconscious work of deconstruction. And it is exactly this that emerges in a conversation between Derrida and Elisabeth Roudinesco. The latter suggests that the term refers to:

> a work of unconscious thought ('it deconstructs itself' [ça se déconstruit]), and consists of undoing, without ever destroying, a hegemonic or dominant system of thought. ... To deconstruct is in some way to resist the tyranny of the One, of the logos, of (Western) metaphysics, and to do so in the very language in which it is articulated, by using the same material that one displaces and moves for the purposes of reconstructions that remain in motion. Deconstruction is 'what happens' [*ce qui arrive*], without our knowing whether it will arrive at a destination, etc.[2]

This beautiful and complete definition – given in Derrida's presence and not rejected or indeed deconstructed by him – does not only apply to philosophy and literature; *mutatis mutandis*, it also applies to theatre. But should this be limited to so-called 'postmodern' theatre?

The category of the postmodern is convenient, but not very relevant. We can undoubtedly agree on a few characteristics of the postmodern in the arts and in literature, but we must take care not to consider them (or reduce them to) deconstruction! In literature, the postmodern is characterised by a mixture of registers, genres, stylistic levels, by a hybridity of forms, and a high degree of intertextuality. It enjoys being parodic, playful, and irreducible to any ultimate meaning. If modernism made a clean break with the classical tradition, from Baudelaire to Kafka, for example, postmodernism reintroduces representation and a taste for narrative, but at the same time challenges the possibility of representing the real, particularly the 'grand narratives' inspired by Marxism, Freudianism or the other canonical models. In the theatre, mise en scène that is postmodern (a term used more in North and South America than in Europe) does not have any one homogeneous style or defined genre, or even a given period. At most it has a certain attitude, a certain gaze. Faced with such artistic blurring, why not use the trusty tool that is Derridean deconstruction? Deconstruction possesses no arsenal of stable rules and properties, but it has at least been the object of solid analyses and we can check its usefulness by way of specific instances of mise en scène.

Moreover, deconstruction, like poststructuralism, is often defined as the theoretical and critical answer to postmodernism. Thanks to deconstruction, mise en scène solves problems in the making of meaning, and at the same time the spectator and the theorist test their methods of analysing postmodern performance.

Examples have been chosen according to both their diversity and the different properties of deconstruction that they reveal. From Vitez to Castorf, as well as Régy, Chéreau and Marthaler, there follow a few instances of mise en scène conceived as deconstruction.

Impossible erasure of the palimpsest

The *trace*, for Derrida, is the place where the presence of an element is conditioned by a series of absences. What language represents is never there. It is conspicuous by its absence, through the trace of what is neither visible nor tangible. In psychoanalysis, the memorial trace carries the unconscious mark of incidents inscribed in memory. This trace, present and absent, allows us to understand how stagings do not come into being in a void but are interconnected by a whole network of quotations, allusions, polemics or simply involuntary traces. This is even more the case in stagings of the same play, which becomes a sort of mystic writing pad, the Freudian *Wunderblock*, retaining traces of previous works or experiments. It is not rare for an artist to stage the same work several times in a career. Traces are not pure quotation, reminiscence or 'interludicity' – they are displacements from their place of origin, their identity, their presence. Mise en scène and writing are not repeatable. Even a new staging of a work displaces what had seemed to be the best solution, and can only refer to previous and provisional readings.

Antoine Vitez was one of the first stage 'deconstructionists', particularly on the classical stage. If, since the advent of mise en scène, the relativity and therefore the potential deconstruction of the work is well established, the poststructuralism of the 1970s meant that deconstruction was to become a tried and tested technique to turn the play against itself, so as to unleash the infinite series of possible readings, a series that in practice ends up being just a few possible solutions, limited in number.

Vitez saw his stagings as part of a body of work, despite the significant differences between them; he envisaged them as variations on a theme, if only because they were all superimposed on his memory. He specifically wished to stage (or to show?) the traces of this memory: 'What I stage and put onstage is precisely that: my memory.'[3] This memory is also what we know of the works, their history and their interpretation. The classics are not contemporaries whom we can pretend not to know. We should not let the classics intimidate us, nor should we suffer intimidation (as Brecht suggested with regard to the petit-bourgeois audience so in awe of the past); and yet we also risk an inverted intimidation that would have us believe in the contemporaneity of the classics, in their eternal youth.[4]

Thus, not only does each new version of a work fail to erase totally the previous ones, but according to Daniel Mesguich, every interpretation thereafter forms part of it, and writes itself into the infinite series of successive versions (as with Mesguich's stagings of *Hamlet* in 1977, *Romeo and Juliet* in 1985, and *Lorenzaccio* in 1986). Certain theatrical pieces, like the works of Carmelo Bene, consist first and foremost of variations on a single, simple action, and no longer, as is the case in theatre for popular audiences or Brechtian theatre, on the representation of conflicts.[5]

Deconstruction and the reconstruction of tradition

To deconstruct tradition is not to destroy it: it is to extract its principles and confront them with today's principles. In acting, to observe a tradition consists of reinstating a vocabulary of gesture, a phrasing or a pronunciation from the past, as directors such as Eugène Green or Jean-Denis Monory do with great precision in their baroque reconstructions of Racine.[6] But this is not reconstitution-reconstruction as practised by Antoine Vitez. In his production of *Andromaque* in 1971, Vitez reinforced the rhetoric of the alexandrines; he respected it scrupulously; he obeyed the rules of euphony. The aim was not to imitate nor to get as close as possible to the acting tradition, it was rather to understand the role of the rules in the constitution of character and of the tragic. Vitez swapped the roles around, and the actors would give the name of their character as they took on a role: 'The actors play several roles, the roles play several actors.'[7] In the style of Derrida, Vitez confirms that the play does not have an already known meaning that need only be translated for the stage: 'We can't put *Andromaque* onstage as if its meaning existed in itself, and as if it were enough merely to translate it.'[8] To put the play onstage is thus to begin to deconstruct its traditional image, while already reconstructing a possible reading. To do this, the site of the discourse and commentary must be displaced: they are no longer at the centre of the play, but in the margins, on the side. It is a matter of showing, rather than including. This decentring is vital, since mise en scène no longer claims to capture the centre of the play, or to be in a position of overseeing, of explaining: the discourse of mise en scène remains in the margins of the performance.

The undecidability of meaning

With the work of Bernard-Marie Koltès, from the beginning of the 1980s onwards, the principal of decentring writing and acting finds a magnificent testing ground. In *The Solitude of Cotton Fields*[9] – which appears as a philosophical, rather than dramatic, dialogue – is a pastiche of the classic philosophical disputes, and of the mock-heroic style of seventeenth- and eighteenth-century high literature. The piece's postmodern irony consists of placing the fundamental rules of dialects and dialogue into the hands, and the mouths, of two misfits. A rather explosive mix forces the spectator to reconsider any categories of the sublime and the vulgar, the philosophical and the commercial. We are not given the alternatives of true and false in the resolution of conflicts, but in the play of *différance*:[10] the conclusion, the solution and the encounter are endlessly deferred. The pleasure and the perversity of the game reside in the fact that the characters' philosophical arguments are so equally matched, as well as in the apparent impossibility of a conclusion ever being reached: the author, then the actors, keep the reader and spectator in suspense, giving them the illusion that they will end up solving the enigma of this 'deal' and will resolve this conflict-without-object. Chéreau and his actors avoid specifying the nature of the deal. Of course, the stage interpretation cannot avoid giving clues, but its tactic is to immediately take back everything that it has just suggested.

Whenever the dramatic play opens up a path, it ultimately proves to be a dead end. Spatially, every bit of territory gained is immediately lost, and vice versa. The actors (Pascal Grégory and Patrice Chéreau) defer explanation for as long as they can, while giving the illusion that they are passionately seeking it. This *différance* manifests itself in the space between interrelating elements, precisely in the distance that the actors put between each other, in space as well as in time, in order to continue the approach and maintain the conflict, without ever revealing the motivation. It is not, then, a question of distinguishing between the characters, whose discourses sometimes seem interchangeable, even though they are designated in the text by antithetical markers (Client/Dealer), nor is it about spotting their differences. Rather, it is a question of deferring the characters' true encounter, of deferring the moment where we understand the set-up and bring our suspense to an end. Action, space and time coincide in this lost search for otherness, corresponding to *différance*. '*différance* is not a distinction, an essence or an opposition, but a spacing manoeuvre, a "becoming-space" of time, a "becoming-time" of space, a reference to alterity, to a heterogeneity that is not born of opposition'.[11]

This *différance*, this deferral of every solution and of every meaning, is thus confirmed by mise en scène. Chéreau's performance is the supplement to a textual strategy which, unusually, neither adds nor explains anything, and offers no position of oversight to illuminate the text. Koltès's deconstruction, then that of Chéreau, who follows in his steps, lays ruin to Hegelian dialectics, and its *Aufhebung* (its resolution), in a way that makes any synthesis of the two positions impossible. In doing this, both the text and the mise en scène introduce a radical otherness: returning every proposition to its double, preventing access to the other, precluding any victory of the one over the other, denying each human gift or exchange. Chéreau applies Derrida's directives to the letter: he does not give the game away, and thus stops Hegelian dialectics in its tracks. In the end, he introduces the principle of radical otherness inside oneself.

We know that the deconstruction of literary texts throws into doubt the possibility of textual coherence, guaranteed by either the author or by the reader; and that deconstruction seeks the little details, the grain of sand that blocks the machinery of explanation. Yet in this play as in its staging, the grains of sand are many: the slightest discordant gesture, the tiniest stage effect, any imperceptible halt in the flow of the actions and images is susceptible to contradict, to 'contra-play' the nice harmonies of the text, and to ruin any overall explanation. *Différance* is thus equally responsible for delaying, even invalidating, any meeting of lines of force, networks, vectors of signs – it refuses any overall view. It is inscribed into many contemporary productions, becoming almost a postmodern trademark. The actor who thus rejects any psychological or social identification at the same time refuses to become a readable and stable bearer of signs. Fleeing any concrete dramatic situation, the actor prefers to remain in an abstract configuration. Hence Chéreau's recipe: despite a few reality effects (costumes, rags, speech patterns), the two actors move around according to almost geometric trajectories, describing abstract straight lines or parabolas. But, as is the destiny of representation, their destination will never be reached.

Crisis of representation and chorality

If deconstruction does not always achieve its goal, it is because the object to deconstruct remains strongly attached to mimesis (and especially in the theatre), particularly the kind of mimesis that emerges from a pre-existing text given to be heard and illustrated on the stage. One attempt to reject mise en scène as mere illustration of a text is François Tanguy's Théâtre du Radeau. This company gives itself the rule of never illustrating, or rendering understandable, any pre-existing text or scenario. They offer us works of performance – not stagings – that put the spectator in a waking dream, perceiving only scraps of the dream conveyed by actors who may well be there in flesh and bone, but who often appear as mere shadows, silhouettes or figures of uncertain existence. Whatever is made figurative is deceptive, and the figurative work of these actors completely avoids the trap of frozen representation.

The Théâtre du Radeau's *Coda* (2004) is based on a deceptive impression of depth: we perceive – indistinctly at the back of the stage, and then increasingly clearly as they approach the audience – anonymous figures, in gowns and hats from another age, murmuring a few words addressed to an unknown receiver, with voices often drowned out by background noises or music coming from an inaccessible room overhead. Scraps of text are discernible, without our being able to work out any story or plot. Panels, cut out in a sawmill (unless we are already inside the sawmill), figure onstage to establish a rhythm in space and a blocking that does not suggest any totality. *Différance*, or deferral of any meaning, proceeds through a very tightly knit network of different sign systems, or rather of signifiers that go from one material to another without ever reaching a final meaning. A very marked spacing is produced – this is visible in the arrangement of the figures, and also temporally, as we jump from one motif to another. But this itinerary takes shape thanks to a very focused circuit of affect – that is, effects produced upon the spectator: beyond the terror and pity proper to tragedy, the spectator is constantly assailed with new affects bound to the search for clues that quickly reveal themselves to be illusory and lead only to the next image or musical motif, in a continual digging motion, fit for an 'archaeology of the frivolous'.[12]

Is this mise en scène? Not in terms of its usual meaning, the representation of a pre-existing text or other material. This example is more like an installation seen from a distance (and thus which cannot be entered at any time or be viewed from every angle). This installation inserts itself into a shared space–time continuum that we enter via long-distance perception as much as via the imagination. The observer is thus free to distinguish forms and movements in this space–time, since 'the respiratory rhythms and movements form, construct, deconstruct, and relaunch concrete elements from which the perceptions construct the directions of meaning'.[13] In practice, the observer distinguishes the different, stacked, superimposed, successive and misaligned elements, which either overlap or are scattered far and wide.

A *coda* is that which 'drifts from the musical figure of the reprise of the motif at the end of a piece, extended here to theatrical movement: welcoming, gathering, tying together, untying'.[14] The spectators are always required to sort and tie together their own perceptions, not knowing if these are shared. The spectator's task essentially consists of accepting new visual and auditory sensations, brought together within a fragile and ephemeral community. In the place of the singular gaze of the director, vectorising these materials, we find a collection of images and sounds presented as chorality: all the elements of stage representation are considered without predetermined hierarchy. This chorality is not the sharing of words; instead, it brings together stage events and inaugurates a new way of being in the world and of receiving it together. The materials, texts, sounds, lights and silhouettes are unfolded and deployed before us, held at a distance, which is the only sign that still distinguishes between theatrical vision and a visit to an installation. We are confronted with a surplus of signification, a 'floating signifier': 'the *overabundance* of the signifier, its *supplementary* character, is thus the result of a finitude, that is to say, the result of a lack that must be *supplemented*'.[15]

This '*suppléance du manque*' (supplementing of the lack) leads to a *supplement*. In the Western metaphysical tradition, the sign is supplementary in that it seeks to compensate for the loss of the origin, the absence, the void. The presence of the sign and the abundance of the signifier, whose trace can be detected in the work of the Théâtre du Radeau, is therefore the consequence of the loss of meaning. Hence an abundant and endless supply of stage writing attempts to fill in for the loss. But, according to Derrida, writing is not a substitute for speech: like a degraded supplement that has taken the place of presence and the voice, it is always already there as a supplementary, if not superfluous – and thus aesthetic – bonus. In *Coda*, the stage writing possesses this quality of a signifier in constant growth: the signifier does not refer to a pre-existing and stable signified: it invents itself in its perpetual mutations. But what about stage writing, Régy's stage writing, that aims precisely to empty the stage and the actor of all expressiveness, of all possible predetermined meaning? Is it possible to reconstruct before deconstructing?

In praise of the void and of slowness

For his staging of *Comme un psaume de David* (2006), Claude Régy begins by making a void. He creates a huge square around which the audience is seated in two rows, with total darkness surrounding Valérie Dréville, the only performer. A very faint light, the source of which is invisible, hidden by a false ceiling, allows us to discover the playing area bit by bit, and particularly the four sides. The actress walks with very slow but regular steps along the outside line of the square, occasionally using a diagonal to reach the centre below the source of light and the music. She speaks extracts from the thirteen 'Psalms of David', in which David confesses his 'failings' to God.

What the spectator notices first and foremost is the extreme slowness of the moves and the speech: 'two syntaxes are troubled – that of grammar and that of the theatre'.[16] In dilating time, in slowing the tempo of the speech, as well that of the steps, Régy seeks to alter the perception of the spectators, to cause them to lose balance, and often their nerve as well. The loss in fact goes beyond his wildest dreams: Valérie Dréville masters her physical moves, and she maintains the concentration necessary to perfectly outline a geometric path. But the human voice cannot be treated like magnetic audio or video tape that is slowed-down to deform the articulation. Verbal delivery is not regular, but is subject to constant changes of speed. The actress cannot utter sentences by spacing out the words, keeping a constant flow; constant slowness cannot be maintained, acceleration – in order to reach the end of a sentence and to ensure semantic understanding – is inevitable. Thus, the act of listening often becomes painful for the listeners, not to mention their frustration at not being able to follow the semantic meaning of the sentences and verses. Claude Régy and Henri Meschonnic, the translator, explain this discontinuity of delivery with all the necessary stops, calls, interruptions, of prophetic discourse: this diverting of language, 'bothers people a great deal ... those who cannot accept not to understand or 'get' the meaning. They always ask us "what's it about? What's it saying?"'[17]

Unlike the previous examples and despite our expectations, this mise en scène does not lead us to a deconstruction of the text or of the stage. In fact, the 'spacing', the 'becoming-space of time' of which Derrida speaks with regard to *différance*[18] produces no strategic reversal to interrogate or even to discover the meaning of the Psalms. This text may be conceived as 'a spiritual experience', 'a spirituality without allegiance, that is not hijacked by any religion',[19] but that does not mean that it is 'turned back to front'. At best it is used in a decorative way, like a piece of music that is perfectly performed, but is void of meaning. Cut into tiny pieces, uttered in a no man's land that is cut off from the real world and from any mimetic dimension relatable to the present situation (unless you consult the programme), these Psalms do not reach the listener, while the mise en scène wants to give us direct access to the Bible conceived as pure poetry, without visual, political, philosophical or religious discourse.

On the other hand, we cannot deny – if we get over the irritation of hearing words without grasping their overall meaning – a certain 'poetic hypnosis'. This hypnosis occurs when the listener agrees to follow the flow of the text, and gives up trying to detect any directorial intention. In receiving the Psalms almost as pure poetry and music with a somewhat semantic dimension, the spectator is close, albeit by another route, to the spirit of deconstruction, which aims, by way of opposition to Western metaphysics, to overcome oppositions between intelligible and sensory, inside and outside, subject and object, spirit and matter, reason and passion, speech and writing, philosophy and poetry. In his 'unlimited arrangement', Régy strives to reach the point where, 'light and shadow are treated, not as two opposed notions, but as unified matter'.[20] Thanks to the lighting, the stage architecture (little more than the square and the heavens suggested by it) begins to sing, or in more prosaic terms, to know that it takes part in the construction of the universe of meaning. Voice and light, silence and obscurity, full and empty, abstract and concrete become this 'unified matter': the geometric design concretises the divine (or poetic) design.

The question concerns whether the subliminal perception of light, of verbal poetry, and of all these mystical unions will really change the vision of the spectator; if this sensorial experience remains truly cut off from any religious or metaphysical pretension, and whether it can join the Derridean critique of logocentrism, of the '*parole soufflée*' (the 'prompted word' or 'breathed speech'), of presence and representation, and particularly the mimetic representation of the Western theatrical tradition. In other words, the question is to ask whether deconstruction is at work (or at play!).

We may have our doubts. Irony and self-reflexivity do seem to be lacking. Régy still believes that meaning, text and poetry will appear as long as we respect the ceremony of slowness, of light and of concentration. We are not far from the essence, from essentialism, as if slowness and darkness had some inherent value, as if they lead to the unveiling of meaning. This brings us to a metaphysics of presence, to a purity of presence to oneself through the word, a nostalgia for a full, poetic, universal, naively humanistic speech.

There are thus, according to Derrida:

> two interpretations of interpretation, of structure, of sign of play. One seeks to decipher, dreams of deciphering a truth or an origin which escapes play and the order of the sign, and which lives the necessity of interpretation as an exile. The other, which is no longer turned toward the origin, affirms play and tries to pass beyond man and humanism.[21]

Régy locates himself in the first interpretation: he is suspicious of the sign, and does not deconstruct it; he basically seeks an origin prior to the word and history; he remains within Western metaphysics. Others, like Antoine Vitez for example, work with play and with repetition, with citation and with irony.

The degraded ritual of repetition

Since *Murx den Europäer* (1993), Marthaler's productions have avoided linear representation of a story illustrating a preexisting text. They are not productions conceived as a synthesis and simultaneity of signs, like Barthes's 'informational polyphony', or as a hierarchical performance centred on the directives of a director. Rather, they are performances with neither beginning nor end (meaning you cannot make head nor tail of them), events that drag on and on, intercut with ruptures, surprises or unanticipated effects. Thus, with events that are both unending and syncopated, and which are always perfectly mastered by the actors as much as by their 'conductor', we think we can escape the 'closure of representation' which, according to Derrida reading Artaud, plagues theatre and Western metaphysics alike by isolating them from all outside influence. But we still have to grasp the meaning of this ritualistic waiting: it remains an opportunity to perform repetitive and boring actions, but also to experience poetic, lyrical and even sublime moments. Repetition, *ritornello* and all the old refrains are here elevated to the summit of the art of theatre and music.

Seemannslieder (*Sailor's Shanties*), first staged in 2005, is emblematic of postmodern posturing, being both trivial and sublime; it is a degraded ritual, but one that is also magnified through repetition. In a sailors' bar, a group of sailors and their wives meet to sing folk songs. They form an involuntary chorus, all the while deprived of their drug of choice: they yearn for the sea, for voyages, and especially for affection and the human community. Although no character stands out, each still performs when the time comes, and each number is delivered with great seriousness and the most subtle precision. The evocation of the sea by those who have stayed on dry land, the women's homesickness and the strange raucous tone of the Dutch voices all produce a beautiful choral effect. As in Wagner's *Flying Dutchman*, the members of the chorus appear condemned to repeat the same actions, yet here without hope of redemption. Only occasional – and sometimes burlesque – incidents (pratfalls, sudden reactions, little revolts in the humdrum routine of everyday life) come to disrupt these rituals, without any hope of success or improvement in the situation.

And so, without knowing it, these simple sailors are in fact victims of the closure and crisis of representation. For on the one hand, they are anchored to their everyday habits, their common places, their absence of perspective; and on the other hand, they nevertheless try to leave their old ways behind, to deliver themselves by delivering a masterful vocal or physical performance. Their failure is that of mise en scène confronted with performance. Their characters are quickly put in their place; they do not manage to stand out, or to propose any individual number – they return instead to anonymity. Likewise, the mise en scène manages to disrupt the routine of mimetic and frozen representation; it tries to free itself from the control of the director, leaving the way open for the actors; it welcomes their ruptures, their incidents, and all that deconstructs, or at least disturbs, classical representation. Mise en scène does not, however, manage to transform itself into performance, since it falls back on a frozen performance controlled by a director, who dominates and eventually closes mise en scène, since he – like the spectator – is a victim of the 'fate of representation': 'To think of the closure of representation is to think of the tragic: not as a representation of fate, but as the fate of representation. In its all gratuitous and baseless necessity. And it is to think why is it *fatal* that, in its closure, representation continues.'[22]

For Marthaler, representation also continues, even if this voyage on the seas always offers the most beautiful surprises.

To exit representation

If the cracks in Marthaler's representation are not sufficient for it to become performance art, open to manipulation by the actors, for Frank Castorf representation attempts a final procedure, more radical still, whereby it will exit from itself: live video cameras irredeemably dismantle and deconstruct classical theatrical representation.

In his adaptation of *Crime and Punishment*, the director of the Volksbühne closely follows the story of Dostoevsky's novel, even though he transplants it into a contemporary German context. For almost the entire performance, a video camera endlessly tracks downstage actions, while itself remaining invisible from the auditorium. It retransmits some of the images onto large external screens, or onto part of the set, and thus reveals the hidden face of things, giving a reversed perspective that the theatre spectator must put back in place and into perspective according to the appropriate scale. The spectator perceives things that there is normally no time to see: the actor at work, complete with ticks and imperfections, with a degree of implication in the story, and a certain virtuosity. Transformed into an intrusive camera, the spectator's gaze leaves no intimacy to the protagonists. With the appropriate means for the times in which we live (rapidity, real-time, efficiency), live video explodes the frontal representation of traditional theatre; it delegates the principle of objective analysis by somehow inserting itself into the theatrical object, which thus loses its primacy, its aura, and its immediate presence to the benefit of the live video image, which is certainly blurry and approximate, but is also immediate and striking, like the 'surgical' strike of a missile. The medium transforms and magnifies – but also parodies and alienates – the actors' performance. The gaze provokes that which is gazed upon, but never from a distance, from any point of view exterior to the object, such as would describe and exhaust it definitively. Only partial, albeit unpleasant, truths about reality emerge from this practice. The gaze is never totalising and profound; it only ever scratches the surface of appearances, ruining any notion of a definitive, final or 'polished' rendering, and any claim, perhaps, of ever knowing the ultimate ends of things.

The actors' lack of intimacy, and their inability to salvage classical theatrical form, also become the subjects of this detective story. The reader thus takes the place of a detective pursuing the guilty party, Raskolnikov, without ever wanting to make an arrest: sadistic pursuit is more tormenting for the criminal than the immediate or metaphorical arrest of our relationship with the media. The intrusion of a camera into the private sphere of the actor, taking from the actor any capacity to imitate a character, reveals (or produces?) an acting style that is both invested and pathetic, detached and disembodied. The frame of the camera becomes a limited, but protected, space inside which the actors can invent their own scores, and even improvise, and use psychological or physical characteristics or images, yet without soliciting identification from the spectator, and without being submitted to the figuring that is demanded. The frenzy of the acting, its rapidity, and its immoderation, worthy of Greek *hubris,* are less the signs of psychodramatic identification with a role than they are evidence of know-how, histrionics, and even ham acting designed to impress the audience (who in any case are not fooled by such a performance, by this athletic form of acting). The immoderation, and the frenzy of revelation, recall the work of '*perlaboration*': that is, the work of symbolising and working through something in oneself: the task of the individual in analysis, or indeed of the character in search of itself, and thus of the 'committed' spectator, seeking 'in some way to overcome the unbearable darkness that inhabits him'.[23] This process, which is thus available to the spectator, has clear links with the process of catharsis.

Deconstructing representation

To say deconstruction is also implicitly to say reconstruction. Mise en scène cannot merely undo and criticise a text or a production, but must also reconstitute it and comment on what shows up as an already considerably deconstructed text. Such is the case in dramatic writing like that of Sarah Kane, and notably her very last play, *4.48 Psychosis.*[24] To find such a balance seems to have been the delicate and necessary task of Park Jung-Hee in her recent and remarkable staging of the play in Korea during the 2006 autumn festival at the Arko Theatre in Seoul.

Dramaturgical choice

Kane's play is a long monologue, subdivided into sequences that are each separated by '…', and sometimes articulated in a series of questions and answers without the name of any speaker being supplied. The monologue can seem autobiographical in that it warns of the suicide the author herself was unable to avoid. It is nevertheless not an authentic or purely autobiographical document, nor is it the author's suicide note. It is a text of great stylistic sophistication, a very formally intricate poem that it is difficult to imagine coming from the hand of someone about to end her own life.

Figure 9.1 4.48 Psychosis by Sarah Kane, directed by Park Jung-Hee.
© Park Jung-Hee.

The female director perfectly respected the author's last formal wish by offering a visual poem, equally masterful in terms of acting, scenography and musical accompaniment. In this sense, the staging was able to avoid the raw document, the psychodramatic, documentary and clinical aspects of this fatal episode. Absolute control over the signs, notably those of the behaviour of a suicidal person, gave the production a sublime, essential, and almost mystical and ceremonial aspect. This choice perfectly respects the strategy and spirit of the play, its attempt to go all the way with the analysis, to 'touch the essential self',[25] to name – without holding anything back – the reasons for despair, while maintaining a perfectly mastered form. The search for the causes of psychosis, the pitiless analysis of the self, the fragmentation of the text, the uncertainty of the identity of the speaker or speakers, all of these elements contribute to the extreme deconstruction of the play. Nevertheless, the formal coherence and the uncompromising logic of the reasoning lend this personal experience a universal value, allowing the readers to see themselves, to identify themselves, and ultimately to reconstruct themselves. Reconstruction of the other by way of the narrator's self-destruction is not the play's smallest paradox. Park Jung-Hee's staging manages to find the scenographic and formal means to allow the spectator a pathway towards reconstruction, or even reconciliation.

Figure 9.2 4.48 Psychosis by Sarah Kane, directed by Park Jung-Hee.
© Park Jung-Hee.

Reconstruction

Reconstruction of the other must go via the aesthetic work of this staging and via a reconstruction of the text, which is fragmented and deprived of any identifiable address from one 'character' to another. Taking a position on the origin of the words, Park Jung-Hee calls on three actors to play three characters, or at least three different voices or three different selves. To the principal self of the narrator responds the self of the doctor; and the self of the other, the little internal voice, responds to the narrator. The play does not in any way state the origin of the words, and therefore the number and identity of the characters. The figure of the doctor, in charge of supervising the mental health of the others, is almost evident in the 'dialogues' marked by dashes. The figure of 'the other self', played by the second actress, is not obvious: she 'double-crosses' the figure of the principal self, who is precisely searching for herself.

The dramaturgical choice of having these three actants certainly renders the play more readable by dramatising it, but has the serious disadvantage of complicating the search for the self. The choice implies that we can discuss, make arrangements, and reconcile ourselves with the other in ourselves, while the narrator specifically cannot settle the score with herself and those who, with the best intentions in the world, want to cure her. The scenes where the doctor intervenes quickly become anecdotal or banal, conforming to the cliché of a detached psychiatrist or of the free-floating attention of a psychoanalyst. Fortunately, the acting struggles to diminish reality effects, and leaves room for the possibility that the two supplementary roles are in fact little more than the mental projections of the narrator (as is suggested after all by the text).

The problem with the stage interpretation of a text so difficult to grasp is that it can be too dominant and can swallow the words, which cannot withstand any stage illustration. The play seems to confirm the postdramatic idea that a text does not need to be staged: 'Just a word on a page and there is the drama.'[26] In order that there be not only drama, but also theatre – a presentation onstage for an audience – we must pass through, and even over, the body of the actor. The body of Kim Ho-Jeong, the actress embodying the principal self, is in no way marked by illness: it is young, supple and relaxed. Calmly and elegantly fixing her hair into a pony-tail, the narrator is far from the stereotypical image of the mental patient. The other self, the double of the patient by definition, struggles to find her own identity. At times it mirrors the principal self – the same trousers, the same behaviour, the same rejection of the doctor – and at times marks its distance: attacking, sword in hand, its double, as if it wanted to touch it, identifying it/self at long last. The reconstruction of the text, in its explicative and dramaturgical dimension, helps the spectator to find a place in the struggle against psychosis. The director has chosen a radical dramaturgical intervention: the addition of characters and the identification of the psychic forces in action. Fortunately, this is counterbalanced by other classical factors of deconstruction such as dissemination and decentring, abstraction and the void.

Dissemination and decentring

The scenographer (Chung Hyung-Woo), dramaturg (Lim Yoo), lighting designer (Jo Sunghan), and director (Park Jung-Hee) manage to disseminate the different fragments of words from this three-voice monologue into the entire stage space and within the temporal block of one hour. They have carefully followed the unfolding of the text, despite cutting a few passages that are poetic (and difficult to translate), and have clearly distinguished zones corresponding to moments of the confession. From the back of the stage comes a shadow – the double of the self. From a pit in the stage, shaped like a coffin or an analyst's couch, comes the doctor, seated behind his patient. An immense compass confirms the impression of a geometrical and well-ordered world that is cold and implacable, denouncing any deviation and any curve. The dissemination of speech in the space corresponds to the decentring of writing: there is no response to the questions of this character faced with itself. In an act of *différance*, in the Derridean sense, the enigma of the self, whose 'face is pasted on the underside of my mind',[27] are never attainable; their grasp is endlessly deferred. Thanks to a series of confessions, but also dispossessions, the moment of suicide is postponed, deferred, but also prepared and planned. The rhythmical pulsation of the performance renders these dispossessions, in constructing each sequence between blackouts and short musical interludes, according to a pattern of hope then despair. The very precise lighting, which is almost surgical, cuts the shadow and the light into geometrical shapes, isolating a part of the face, one quarter of the stage, one self from the whole character. Going from the word on the page to the presence on a stage, Park Jung-Hee transposes verbal architecture and poetic typography into an abstract choreography around a trio of actors. Word, light and musical sound come together before moving apart again, suggesting an ongoing quest for identity. Unlike a dramatic poem, which takes place in our heads, a performance should make manifest, illustrate and explicate what is subtle and immaterial. Thus, the acting out – only discretely suggested by the line 'please open the curtains',[28] recalling perhaps Goethe's 'Mehr Licht' ('more light') – is translated onstage by the advancing of the woman towards the blinding light of the stage lamps. This creates a somewhat melodramatic effect, which must be hard to avoid as music that is more intense than usual underlines and punctuates the final exit.

The cry of silence, the void of the heart

The musical compositions of Choi Jung-Woo, played live by his band, Renata Suicide, give an image of the void and of the silence of death. Based upon Maurice Blanchot's notion of 'the impersonality of abstraction', the contemporary composition, made up of minimalist percussion in the style of Buddhist music, is never illustrative. It never underlines the text by way of any particular emotion or leitmotiv. Rather, it creates empty and silent frames for the listener. The idea behind this discreet music, which is hardly audible during scenes, is to give an impression of the void, like a Buddhist monk using the monochord and obsessional percussion of a wooden bell. This purity

Figure 9.3 4.48 Psychosis by Sarah Kane, directed by Park Jung-Hee.
© Park Jung-Hee.

of sound, and the (apparent) simplicity of the melody make us sense the empty form, the pure signifier, over which the character fears having lost control: 'How can I return to form/Now my formal thought has gone?'[29] The poem reduces itself to a pure play on the signifier, but one which nonetheless makes sense. Hence 'still ill',[30] meaning 'still unwell' but also suggesting the stillness, the immobility of the unwell. The absence of sound and of movement – that is, death – plays on the signifier to produce a formula by which its sound, its elision, leaves only the 'ill', the illness soon leading to death. The music matches the staging: music and staging do not render one another redundant here, but rather cast light on one another. We see the music, and we hear the void of death. All that remains is the sparkling beauty of form, that of the drama and of the mise en scène.

Postmodernism, or else nothing

In terms of form, the acting, the scenography and the music have erased all cultural references, Korean or otherwise. The themes explored are profoundly universal, and so is the way in which psychosis, voluntary death, depression and the lack of love are figured in the production. The figuring closely follows Western postmodernism, which claims to have an international identity: a sanitised one perhaps, but one that at least avoids imposing any narrow identity. From London to Seoul, from Paris to Shanghai, we can identify with this psychosis that makes us fear excessive psychologising and parochialism. It takes all the formal mastery of Park Jung-Hee and her excellent collaborators to convey the universality of human distress to the Korean audience. The formal beauty of *4:48 Psychosis* and of this Korean staging, the sense of authenticity and lucidity, are the ultimate arms against mourning, despair and eternal regret.

Conclusions: 'To have done with the judgement of god' (Artaud) and with deconstruction?

These contemporary examples reveal a constant to and fro between deconstruction and reconstruction. There must always be a construction, that is, a writing in the Derridean sense, a writing that is not the trace of preexisting speech.

- There results a decentring of the director, who is no longer at the centre of everything, and most notably of meaning; who no longer masters any absolute subjectivity that can translate into all the decisions and choices of mise en scène. Vitez, one of the first deconstructors, in the 1970s, clearly marked the epistemological shift in theatre practice: the director is no longer the point of origin of the mise en scène, but rather the point of arrival for the actors. 'I no longer consider that a theatre work performed onstage is the illustration by actors of a design conceived by a director. No – the design varies according to the actors.'[31] Since Vitez, this idea has come a long way. The former position of the director-as-creator is now endlessly critiqued as absolutist and authoritarian: Alain Françon calls this the 'vision of a "visionary", of a seer, of a fantasist, of a "sensitive", it assembles a "we" by way of its authority alone, and leaves no room for hearing, or broad thought'.[32] Amplified hearing and broad thinking are, so to speak, the aims of decentred mise en scène: an untied mise en scène, free from the autocracy of a director – in other words a deconstructed mise en scène. If the productions remain tightly controlled, they are no longer, as was the case in the 1960s and 1970s, under the control of an absolute subject. Control was transferred to the actor a long time ago, and even to the spectator, who is put on the spot. The postmodern coincided with the relativism of the 1950s and 1960s, which was also the era of performance art. Deconstruction (in the 1970s and 1980s – what the Anglo-American world calls poststructuralism, with Derrida as figurehead) regained the territory left fallow after the hardcore structuralism of Lévi-Strauss and Benveniste (and was also the academic response to postmodern impressionism). The move to place the spectator once again at the centre, after the necessary structuralist and semiotic stage that was 'theatre studies', brings to a close this evolution towards deconstruction, in philosophy and in the arts.

• The spectator – now to be found at the centre of (phenomenological) theory and (performative) practice – is the object of all the attention and desire: it is the spectators' job to parry, repair and prepare the performance that they choose for themselves.

• Examples from the limited selection of work discussed here prove at least one thing: deconstruction is not a style of mise en scène, in this case a postmodern one. Rather, it is a procedure that attacks the postmodern and restores a particular way of working and a critique of representation. A good example perhaps is the return of representation after presentation. The 'presentation of self' (according to Goffman's formula) was well suited to performance art, which sought to present directly, without the trickery of mimetic imitation; the actors would speak of their own 'true' lives, playing no character and presenting their own problems. Examples from this body of work re-establish theatrical representation with all its ancestral rights. Castorf tells and reworks the procedures of the detective enigma in Dostoevsky's novel; Marthaler finds, beyond derisory songs, an authentic lived experience; Chéreau pretends to tell endlessly the story of two tramps; Tanguy evokes well-known images from Central Europe, from literary myths and visual traditions; Vitez returns to his actors a sense of French seventeenth-century diction and stages a *mise en abyme* of theatre, counting on knowledge of forms to access the story; Régy makes of the Psalms a universal poetic text.

In all these examples, deconstruction is certainly at work, and in a number of ways, but we always end up with reconstruction, with what

Derrida calls the 'fate of representation': the reconstruction of a fiction, of a limit, of a sign and of a closure. For theatre, this entails that deconstruction has not eliminated the director but has simply given the director new tasks in order to found an 'emancipated representation'.[33] This requires multiple tasks, or perhaps an infinite number of them, as these six examples clearly show. Vitez uses acting, exercises or sketches as a space for dismantling the rhetoric and desire written into the violence of language. Chéreau, following Koltès, invents a homeostatic mechanism so as never to determine the meaning and resolution of a conflict. Tanguy is more concerned with deconstruction than with construction, quoting and undoing all cultural references in which the spectators are immersed, but he nonetheless labours to rebuild them within a discourse following its own logic. Régy does not trouble himself with deconstructing writing; he remains bound within an essentialist discourse on a text which – thanks to a unique set-up (silence, darkness, slowness) – is supposed to speak for itself. Marthaler deconstructs the theatrical exchange by way of a chorality that ends up restoring a link between isolated and melancholic individuals. Castorf deconstructs classical representation at a distance, the better, perhaps, to re-establish the meaning and direction of culpability and to reinstate the story of the novel by way of a frenetic acting style and onstage camera surveillance. In this way, with the exception of Régy, whose regimen is a different one, the directors' deconstruction is Derridean in that it does not take place in the after, in 'post-', be it postmodern or postdramatic, or indeed at the point of the death of philosophy or the end of history. The closure of their production, just like the closure of metaphysics for Derrida, is in no way the end or the destruction of theatre (or indeed that of metaphysics); it is rather the beginning of a new way of doing theatre (or indeed philosophy).

In the end, and finally, our best theatre – contrary to a frequently expressed opinion – destroys nothing. It deconstructs, and often reconstructs. We could literally apply what Jacques Derrida, in one of his final texts, wrote about deconstruction: 'Deconstruction does not seek to discredit critique; it in fact constantly relegitimates its necessity and heritage, even though it never renounces either a genealogy of the critical idea or a history of the question and of the supposed privilege of interrogative thought.'[34] Mise en scène that deconstructs its object by interrogating the object's functioning as much as its provenance does not renounce the critical virtue of theatrical performance, or its capacity to interrogate and contest the real.

The old dream of the actor is to do without the director.
The old dream of the director is to transform the actors into marionettes.
Fortunately, such dreams do not come true. It is difficult, and inadvisable, to present oneself to the audience without first having been seen by an outside eye. And a human is not a puppet, but a breathing, thinking being.

This does not stop many an actor from wanting to work, alone in the studio, on a monologue or mime show, to seek to control every point in the production chain, from the original idea to the final delivery of the work in different places.

Theatre of gesture (physical theatre), founded on the mastery of the body, has become its own genre, competing with and sometimes eclipsing the 'mise en scène machine'.

But – and this is the paradox of physical theatre – this mastery of the body by the solo actor brings us straight back to the demands of mise en scène. And even performance art, advocating a non-fictional use of the body, often comes back (hence Marina Abramović) to theatricalisation and total control over the mise en scène – a closely supervised body.

10 Physical theatre and the dramaturgy of the actor

The English term 'physical theatre' designates a type of performance that emphasises the actor's body, rather than their words or their mind.[1] *Le Théâtre du geste* (*Theatre of Gesture and Movement*)[2] is a possible, albeit approximate, French translation of this formulation, but it mainly refers, as is the case in the book which bears the name, to mime and its variations. Whatever we call it, physical theatre is a genre that turns up in many Western experimental art forms. Thomas Leabhart, mime and former student of Etienne Decroux, defines it thus: 'Physical theatre, however, attempts to describe a type of hybridized non-cultural theatre which places emphasis on physical virtuosity but not exclusively dance, and which, although if often uses words, usually does not begin with a written text.'[3]

The practice of physical theatre has a natural place in a book dealing with contemporary mise en scène, since the 'theatre of gesture' constitutes a large part of current stage work, while also challenging the director's control. Indeed, physical theatre does away with directing, delegating to the actor the power to build a complete score, and to put together what Barba called the dramaturgy of the actor. Physical theatre is in the hands of the actors, who thus invent a new way of working.

Physical theatre has a long history, starting in the 1960s: in that period, the notion almost always referred to Antonin Artaud and his critique of bourgeois and psychological theatre. And yet Julian Beck, Peter Brook, Charles Marowitz and Jerzy Grotowski had not read *The Theatre and its Double*, at least at the beginning of their careers, but were, like Artaud, keen to read theatre texts in a radically different way. Grotowski asked his actors to be aware of the action behind the words, to feel in themselves the trajectory of language. Brook always considered that the word did not begin with the word, but rather that it was a final product born of an impulse. When staging *Dionysus in 69*

(1968), Schechner was primarily interested in the breath and the cry of the performer. Writing about *Deaf Man's Glance* (1972) by Robert Wilson, Louis Aragon, in an open letter to André Breton, spoke of: 'those who I won't call dancers or actors, because they are all that and something else: experimenters in a science still nameless, that of the body and its freedom'.[4] For Barba, the word only makes sense if it emerges from a 'decided body'.[5] All of these artists are thus convinced of the physical basis of theatre.

This chapter does not pretend to be a history of physical theatre, especially since it focuses on the 1990s. Since the 1960s, the genre has evolved a great deal: it has moved away from Grotowski and Brook's anthropological theatre, and many other forms have emerged of which we will give only a few isolated, but representative, examples. The conception of the body underpinning each practice will be examined, and we will ask how, in the more recent experiments, the body is formed. What relationship does it have to the Other, particularly when physical contact is made? If it is true that the unconscious speaks through the body, the spectators must read these bodies in order to understand what is revealed of their own unconscious, and of ours.

From *May B.* (1981) to a recent production by the Théâtre du Soleil, *Les Ephémères* (2007), physical theatre embodies many identities. It increasingly moves away from what Bernard Dort in the 1960s called the 'rebellion of the bodies'. The idea of the body as response to the alienation of the mind has had its day. Seeing body and text as strictly opposed has lost some of its relevance. The rebellion was not to everyone's taste in any case, and was certainly not to everyone's liking: in particularly, it was not appreciated by mime artists such as Decroux and Lecoq, who were more concerned with the rigour of gesture. Lecoq mocked this 'revolt of the hunchbacks'[6] and had his doubts about Grotowskian purism. The polemic about *expression corporelle* in the 1960s and 1970s has not yet found any peaceful resolution. Only at the end of the twentieth century did physical theatre begin to be seen in a different light, taking its unchallenged place within contemporary mise en scène.

Before addressing the new status physical theatre has enjoyed since the 1990s, it might be appropriate to briefly mention the dance-theatre of Maguy Marin, since the seed of the physical theatre of the last few years of the twentieth century can be found in works such as *May B.* The through-line will be the question of the body, the implicit conception we have of it, and the sense of touch as a barometer of people's proximity.

May B. by Maguy Marin: touched by the other

With this choreography, one of the most performed pieces in the world, Maguy Marin celebrates a rare happy meeting of dance and theatre. A group of zombies, whose faces and bodies are white as alabaster, and frozen in hieratic attitudes, move only at the signal of a whistle or of Gilles de Binche's popular fanfare. 'Finished, it's finished, nearly finished, it must be nearly finished' – the only words that come out of their deformed mouths are borrowed from Samuel Beckett's *Endgame*. This end is less the end of the show than that of humanity, judging by the sorry state of decrepitude in which the figures vegetate. Their bodies are treated as a bleached material, mixed like plaster, like creatures moulded by the sculptor Georges Segal, who captured the everyday gestures of his fellow citizens. Each of these ten figures 'without qualities' blends into the group, a homogeneous block of desolation, a collective living carcass on its last legs. The group moves as a bloc. Each individual does the same little mechanical and repetitive gestures. The bodies are dirty, repulsive, vulgar, deprived of individuality and humanity. But they can also help each other, look at each other, seduce each other, even if they never manage to extract themselves from the plaster of the clan or from the ore of the body.

The art of movement finds an ally in the living sculpture in its quest to figure out or to disfigure the human being in its petrified solitude and its imprisonment. The group of zombies dances as well to fanfares as it does to classical music: it stays on the beat simply but correctly. *May B.* plays on the ironic contrast between the refined music of Schubert (*Das Mädchen und der Tod*) and the vulgarity of the gestures that keep the beat. These cripples, casualties of life, can no longer move except collectively, responding to sonar stimuli: drum rolls, and the sounds of sliding or tapping feet. In the spirit of Beckett, whose plays obstinately refuse to 'mean anything', Maguy Marin allows us intellectually, but also 'kinaesthetically', to understand this emptiness and this dehumanisation. The alienation of the group is less metaphysical and individual (as in Beckett or *butô*) than it is social and collective. Despite having snouts, silhouettes and the walk of a troll, each disfigured character remains a peer, a likeness, a brother: a figure of our disarray and our wandering; they are part and parcel of our social reality, of our day-to-day existence. But just who are they? Outcasts? The 'nouveaux poor?' Casualties of globalisation? For so long devoted to existential absurdity, in particular of the Beckett variety, or to postmodern abstraction, the stage recovers its mimetic dimension, beyond the choreography of pure movement.

Maguy Marin still belongs to the tradition of Béjart, her former teacher: all that moves is placed at the service of a situation to be unfolded, of a story to be told. The collective body of this chorus expresses the dehumanisation, the gregariousness, the mechanisation of behaviours and ideas. With frequent stops, moments of silence or of musical interlude, the choreography constantly goes from individual to group. At regular intervals, the group movement, a dance that relies upon a fanfare or symphonic music, causes the group to take off, to leave its apathy behind, to go into a very tight figure that transports the spectator out of theatrical fiction and toward the domain of choreographic virtuosity. The gestural and choreographic score proposes extremely precise attitudes, postures, moves and movements. What emerges from this, once this choreographic device is assimilated, is the group's ultimately theatrical characters, emanating from our social universe – an army of the elderly, who are in pieces, but are still alive and happy to be alive.

If the body is the barometer and the metaphor of the state of the world, then *May B.* is the tragic-comical reversal of the liberation of the body that was so talked about in the 1960s. Contact between bodies has become problematic, parodic, and repulsive.

Remaining in the domain of *expression corporelle* as it has evolved since the 1960s, the next thing to tackle is *Itsi Bitsi*, an autobiographical show devised and performed by Danish actress Iben Nagel Rasmussen of the Odin Teatret.

Itsi Bitsi: the dramaturgy of the actress

Indeed, the performance (first shown in 1991, with guitarist Jan Ferslev and accordionist Kai Bredoldt) is set in the 1960s. Iben Nagel Rasmussen evokes the period of her life spent in the company of Eik Skalø, poet and singer – 'the Danish Bob Dylan' – who committed suicide in India in 1968. She recalls moments and visions from this era by way of characters and roles from the Odin Teatret, from 1966 onwards. The autobiographical narrative, then, constantly draws on gestural and vocal scores from previous performances.

Two scenes in particular shed light on Rasmussen's way of working, which is worth considering in terms of methods of *training* and rehearsal ('the Journey and the Old Woman' and 'Kattrin the Mute'). It is appropriate first to become familiar with the method of training and of rehearsal. The experimentation takes place by way of gesture, voice, words and sounds, in order to 'find the character': 'it is as if the character was a space that I must discover little-by-little in myself as the creative process unfolds, and in which everything can be found: actions, feelings, words, sounds …. I recognise this space within my body.'[7] Language and gesture are not separable at first. The actress must elaborate her character at the so-called 'pre-expressive' level, before conveying a particular meaning in the subsequent montage: 'The character was ready before we began the montage work. All her ways of walking, sitting, using her arms, using sound, were very precise physical actions without specific meanings and thus they could be used in various contexts.'[8] Not only does the actress find her own materials, she also has the possibility of elaborating them, 'in such a way that the director need not give directions according to a specific idea of the performance'.[9] She therefore maintains, at least at first, control over her dramaturgical choices.

Consider, for example, the scene of the old woman's journey. Rasmussen is tethered like a horse with a red blindfold, a kind of blood trail that gets longer and longer. The dealer, who is a pimp and a mobster, holds the reins and controls her movements, keeping her hooked on drugs. He only loosens the reins in order to imprison her; his tricky manoeuvres preclude any hope of escape. Dressed in a black evening gown, speaking with a soft voice and an ecstatic smile, which contrasts with the horror present in the words describing a descent into hell, Rasmussen recounts her memories of the trip and tells of her drug addiction. This sweet, stylised, theatricalised and artificial voice heightens the materiality and the musicality of the words. We might think that it belongs to an ancient and codified acting tradition, and yet it is purely the invention of this actress.

If the body of the dealer is easily identifiable, semiologically readable, by way of its attitude and its social *gestus*, Rasmussen's voice is less about meaning than about the effect it produces. It is the result of an impulse, a movement, a rhythm and a phrasing that belongs to her and her alone. From this voice and this body going ceaselessly on and on towards death, the spectator receives a physical and kinesthetic impulse. The mute body of this woman, de-socialised, depoliticised and cut off from history, nevertheless transmits powerful vibrations to which the spectator reacts before even deciphering the signs. 'Kinesthetic response occurs prior to a semiotic one',[10] Simon Shepherd and Mick Wallis note, echoing Bernard Beckerman's reflections on the theatre experience: 'our bodies are already reacting to the texture and structure of action before we recognize that they are doing so'.[11]

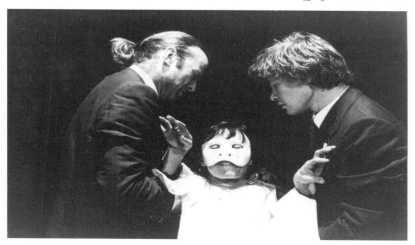

Figure 10.1 Iben Nagel Rasmussen, *Itsi Bitsi*, directed by Eugenio Barba.
© Østergaard.

Figure 10.2 Iben Nagel Rasmussen, *Itsi Bitsi*, directed by Eugenio Barba.
© Tony d'Urso.

In 'Kattrin the Mute' (sequence XI), Rasmussen reconstitutes a moment from Eugenio Barba's production *Brecht's Ashes*. She creates the figure of Mother Courage's daughter who saves the town of Halle by sacrificing her life. Kattrin is mute, but is far from deaf to the ills of the world. Her unarticulated cries and the alarm bell sound the alert. Having remained in contact with the world, she has managed to preserve the child in herself and is unaware of the violence surrounding her. Her body is incomplete, and seems to be that of a simpleton, of a young girl who yearns for a child, and who has been disabled by war. She pays for the temptation of goodness with her life. Her body as well as her age will remain frozen in memory, which she expresses in the testamentary poem she borrows from Brecht:

When you delight me
Then I think sometimes:
If I could die now
I would be happy
Till my life's end.

Then when you are old
And you think of me
I shall look as now
You'll have a sweetheart
That is still young.[12]

The body frozen in eternity and in memory is quickly idealised and essentialised. It is an abstract, undifferentiated body, untouched by time, a 'sacrificial offering' of a body, but one which is asexual, of uncertain gender, negated in its desire for love and for maternity, a body humble in heroism and which has no choice but to become the last defence against violence and destruction. This body is feminine, but it might be ceaselessly rendered virile through ill-treatment: the damaged, deep voice is forced, like that of a man: deprived of femininity as instructed by Mother Courage in order that she does not seduce men, who represent a constant danger of rape, castration and murder.

For Grotowski, in his theatre production phase (until 1968 to be precise), the body of the actor had this same neutralised gender. The incandescent body of Cieslak in *The Constant Prince* revealed suffering and Christ-like sacrifice, but it remained a sexually undifferentiated, essentialised body. Despite its total exposure, its sacrificial self-penetration (to use Grotowski's term), this orphan and mystic body lacked sexual otherness in the form of desire for the other. Kattrin/ Iben directly inherits this undifferentiated body of Grotowskian origin, a body pushed to its limits by exhausting training, more virile than feminine. But with her commentary on the period seen from the vantage point of 1991, she distances herself from the cumbersome heritage of the 1960s. She establishes a link with the 1980s and 1990s, and observes the liquidation of utopias, of the spirit of 1968, and of the individualist illusions (drugs, free love, anarchism). Her critique of the utopia of 1968 is explicit, as is the awareness that her generation was sacrificed, as a result of its idealism, by those who betrayed its ideals (and who did so perhaps inevitably, because they did not, like Eik or Kattrin, stay forever young).

And yet Kattrin – and thereby Iben – seeks her voice and her path: she seeks her femininity and her maternity in a masculine world of rapists and murderers. She seeks to get away from her too virile training, from a too demanding sacrifice, from a forced integration into either the world of men or – almost as bad – the world of asexual angels who lack their own voices, or indeed have only a voice imposed by men, in order to survive in the face of threats, a uniquely physical voice which never reaches the stage of the symbolism of language.

Les étourdis, La cour des grands by **Macha Makeïff and Jerôme Deschamps: the body in bits**

Etourdis ('scatterbrains'), *grands* ('big kids'): speechless characters from a world where all that is undertaken joyously fails. These are 'boarders': 'They are locked up but they keep forgetting it.'[13] Such disarticulated or chunky characters are just like us: we envy their innocence, and in forgiving them we absolve ourselves. Their – often shapeless or voluntarily deformed – bodies are immediately noticeable due to their physical properties and behaviour that departs from the norm. Deprived of articulated language, they possess many other ways of expressing themselves. Although always ill at ease, tortured by their superiors and by stupidity itself, they are also a virtuoso instrument in the hands of jugglers, acrobats, opera singers, capable of stunts, turn, tricks and striking displays, involuntary physical feats.

The *Etourdis* are simpletons who know not what they do. They obey the stupid orders of a choleric and unpredictable boss, they cause terrible disasters with the innocence and poetry of the naïve. They do not realise that they are in this world, at least in the social world; they keep it up for as long as they can. The *Grands* represent for them the others: the authorities, middle management, the obstacles in their path.

A failing body prevents them from completing even the simplest task. And thus the performance has no through-line of action, no story and no argument. It is made up of a series of gags, of battles between the weak and the powerful. Each episode of the soap opera ends in another failure or an unexpected physical feat. Hence the impression, confirmed many times, that the piece is not able to tell a story, but is only ever repeating a single situation. But, on the other hand, it is the bodies of the actors that are the source of all further developments. The idea is not – as was the case for Rasmussen – to tell the story of years of individual training, or – as for the Théâtre du Mouvement – to systematically explore the possibilities of gesture. Rather, it is a question of bringing about the embodiment by the actor-performer of the indefinable and non-speakable malaise of an entire epoch. It seems easier today to express this malaise in a grotesque and clowning manner than to suggest a global (or specifically Brechtian) analysis of it (which would demonstrate, by way of interposed *gestus* and alienation, the contradictions of the world of work while also lecturing the audience). Attacks of a burlesque and mocking nature, and even 'class' mockery born of the spectator's social and intellectual superiority, might actually be more effective, and definitely funnier. The breathtaking rhythm of the 'Deschiens' performances is on the pulse of today. The audience is in tune with these run-down creatures, too stupid to not be mocked, but too fragile to be truly despised. Basically, the audience fully understands the creatures' disarray in the face of new working conditions: as soon as the audience recognises their anxiety, their mode of passive resistance, it laughs (so as not to cry) and accepts, without condescension, the creatures' fears, their little fixations, their tics, and their small pleasures. The feeling of superiority and contempt gives way to empathy and tenderness.

The question of the body, then, can only be posed within the overall system of identification and of the becoming subject. A body is carried and constituted by a person or a subject. Its exposure is linked to a narrative, to a way of telling what will become of humans, and finally to a vision of the world. Despite the exposure of its imperfections, and its freak effects, this body remains within the frame of representation. It is still the body of a character and the instrument of the actor; its meaning remains symbolic and mimetic, and not literal.[14] Precisely in order to go beyond the limitations of physical expression caused by dramatic conventions, forms of performance art and body art decided, as early as the 1960s, to use the actors' bodies 'for real': that is, directly and literally.

From the body art of the past to the multiple identities of the present

Body art was hot, and had its heyday on the heels of performance art, in the 1960s and 1970s. Performers would break theatrical illusion using their bodies directly, and not so as to convey a fiction. They would seek to go beyond the limits of their bodies, subjecting them to provocative, and even painful and dangerous, treatment.

The art of photography bears witness to earlier experiments, from as early as the 1920s. Around 1927, the photographer and actress Claude Cahen posed as a moustachioed weightlifter, playing on sexual ambiguity, and making fun of the traditional division of the sexes.[15] Forty years later, Caroline Schneeman did a series of provocative performances. 'At a public lecture, she continually dressed and undressed herself, asking the audience, "Can an art istorian [the absence of the 'h' is intentional] be a naked woman?"[16] What credibility can she have when speaking?' In 1979, with *Interior Scroll*, Schneeman went to the limits of provocation and unrolled a long strip of paper from her vagina. In the same vein, but in a (more) feminist and militant spirit, the Viennese actionist artist Valie Export, with *Panique Générale* (1969), performed an action in a porno cinema. Armed with a machine gun, and with her genitals exposed, she announced that 'sex' was available, while threatening potential takers with her phallic weapon. 'Real' sex produced a different effect on the men than filmed sex: such was the experiment's (admittedly predictable!) conclusion.

For self-inflicted suffering, the prize undoubtedly goes to Chris Burden, who was in the habit of directing violent actions against himself. In 1974, in a piece called *Trans-fixed*, he was even crucified on the roof of a car, a Volkswagen Beetle. Stelarc, an Australian performer, is gentler with his body; while he may suspend it like a side of beef, he does distribute the weight over several hooks! The contact with the material goes as far as it can go: crucifixion, hanging or the repetitive plastic surgery that radically transformed Orlan's face.[17] Any advance on that? The limits are reached and the divorce from theatrical fiction might seem to have been consummated.

Towards the beginning of the 1980s, violent and dangerous actions seemed to have gone out of fashion. The body as a simple piece of meat had lost its appeal. The next step, then, seemed obvious, and involved the machine. Stelarc, considering the human body to be obsolete, a low-performance hangover from the past, sought to replace it with a more reliable prosthesis. To this end, he built a third bio-technical hand, which responds to the impulses of a machine (*The Third Hand*).[18]

Since the last decade of the twentieth century, the hardcore body art of the 1960s and 1970s has moved on: it has almost entirely disappeared in its primitive form and now allies itself with questions of identity (sexual, racial, social and so on). From the perspective of Derrida's deconstruction – or following a truly postmodern approach – the way in which the actor combines diverse identities in a piece is now on the agenda. The body becomes a laboratory of mixtures, hybrids, unconscious relationships between constantly shifting territories of identity. This body is the object of everyone's desires in erotic, as well as epistemological, terms. It is the marker of contradictions of identity that we cannot yet think of or reconcile. Each type of identity presents serious problems. Thus the notion of race, while regularly employed in the United States, is taboo in continental Europe, since the notion has often been used in a racist manner. The notion of sex is replaced with that of gender, which facilitates feminist thinking, still barely used in theoretical thought on theatre, at least in France. The notion of social belonging cannot – or at least cannot exclusively – be reduced to social contradictions. Nor can it be reduced to the often simplistic illustration of social determinacy, as in the choice of *gestus* supposed to embody class difference.

This generation of performers and 'devisers' – even if such work actually began in the 1960s – distanced themselves from any purely literal use of the body. In the last decade of the twentieth century, it reoriented its research towards a partial return to the symbolic instead of just being concerned with the body and the event. It no longer excludes from the outset the use of text or a reliance on character. It often invents a new way of telling. It takes some distance from the literalness of body art to turn towards texts (both modern and classical, treated in a physical and carnal way), while it remains attuned to the meaning of such texts and the feelings that they convey. The next example is a staging of Racine's classical play *Andromaque* by Michel Liard. Can you imagine a more physical interpretation?

Andromaque on the cutting edge: Michel Liard's art of looking and listening

Centre-stage is Oreste, head shaved, body coiled, gaze turned inward, arms crossed, touching, nobody to embrace.[19] He is physically and verbally supported by three other actors playing the principal characters. They form a chorus in charge of the role and the text of Oreste's confidant Pylade.

The entire tragic universe is concentrated upon this *tableau vivant*, on these autocontacts and the way in which each person touches the others – literally or emotionally – with a specific physical tension. Oreste, on his knees but sitting on his heels, is ready to move on to other hopes and other crimes. Hermione, on the right, is waiting for news, and is not really involved. Andromaque, on the left, is tense in her painful efforts to find her way. Pyrrhus masterfully dominates the situation: his role as Oreste's superego means that he guides Oreste more than he supports himself, the better to bring him back to reality.

This tableau, and indeed all of Michel Liard's mise en scène, reconciles the bones (classical dramaturgy, and its solid coherence) with the skin (that of an Artaudian theatre 'that wakes us up: nerves and heart')[20] 'addressed first of all to the senses instead of being addressed primarily to the mind as is the language of words'.[21] The members of the chorus and Oreste support each other. Each gestural fulcrum (hands, gazes, postures) corresponds to a vocal, rhetorical or rhythmical fulcrum in the alexandrine. These do not coincide: the body does not have the same needs as language, and one does not rhythmically reproduce the other. And yet they support each other. The physical work, its postural points of support and its contacts, operate as anchors to the language of passion; conversely, the expression of the passions and the diction of the verses both find reference points and rhythmical conformations in moments of postural immobility. By often performing on the floor (kneeling, lying down, squatting), the performers physically explore the contact points, the tensions, the impulses, the bounces and the rejections of our bodies and of the imaginary body of the group. They experience in a concrete way the drives of the whole body: not just the skeleton, with its constrained or liberated postures, but also the skin and the flesh that shine in the game of language and of seduction.

The union of bony stiffness and shining skin, of physical rigour and the rustling of language, becomes the very flesh of the Racinian word, with the regularity of the alexandrine and the surprises of rhythm. It makes up the beating heart of this physical and vocal universe, the site of passion and drive.

Is it skin or bone that controls flesh? Who can say. Flesh is there, luminous and rustling. Skins burn, hearts flare up. When they touch, hands transmit imperceptible orders, conscious or unconscious. At that point there is no way to distinguish the inside from the outside.

Michel Liard's actors speak the alexandrine impeccably, always finding the necessary gestural points of support needed for a good articulation of the text. Their bodies are strictly like ours: these are not the depressed or overexcited bodies of the 1960s and 1970s, nor are they bodies with the clean, cool and trendy look of the 1980s and

1990s. Rather, these are bodies in equilibrium and of variable intensity, which put the verse back in its straitjacket. Sometimes, at certain moments of crisis, the straitjacket bursts due to the force of passion and of the momentarily troubled language.

Thus the Racinian Mandala[22] comes into being: a world where opposing forces rule, a positive one here, a negative one there: a world that this mise en scène illustrates without knowing it. The passions, (a), (here: love, jealousy, anger) are (emotional as well as muscular) impulses, 'the will to seize', and they are immediately countered by the intellect, (b), the analytic consciousness in search of knowledge. The sensation, (c), or rather, 'a bloc of sensations, that is to say, a compound of percepts and affects'[23] that here manifests itself in the skin's willingness to expose itself, is countered by a logic of comparison, by a usage of concepts, (d), which 'jealously' defend their rights.

At their point of intersection, the four contrasting elements produce an empty form, unconscious and ignorant of itself: the form of tragedy, of the tragic universe. This form is the place of the miraculous balance between all these instances, in particular the bones and the skin – a perfectly ordered dramaturgy and a perfectly 'breathed' textuality.

This *Andromaque* staged by Michel Liard demands that the actors (like the spectators) be located inside, at the heart of things, as well as outside – on the side of the skin and the side of the bones. It overcomes the Western dualism of expressivity that, before Roland Barthes' article 'Dire Racine' and the work of 'Barthesian' directors like Vitez, Villégier or Mesguich, would clog up Racinian interpretation with numerous expressive effects.[24] Diction is no longer conceived of as a decoration stuck to the obvious and lasting meaning, but is seen instead as that which constitutes the meaning. Meaning and expressivity cannot be separated. Liard's mise en scène transports the actors (and later the spectators) across the alexandrines and the bodies, mobilising their understanding of the bony solid structure as well as their fleeting sensations of the skin. The mise en scène marks a balance between depth and surface, bone and skin, a balance that contemporary works rarely achieve because they get carried away by the burning interiority or – on the contrary – get stuck in cold formalism.

When Racine is so magnificently spoken and given to be seen, it is as if the spiritual bone structure of our unconscious were directly articulated on the delicate skin of the alexandrine and the bodies. It is as if bone and skin were meeting in an undetermined place, always a somewhat secret one, that the actors must find by way of their practice and that the spectators must seek on the surface of things. Conversely, a well-pitched voice, an appropriate point of support, a

Figure 10.3 Andromaque, directed by Michel Liard. © Vincent Jacques.

correctly held attitude and a tactility that is fully accepted will impact upon the intelligence of the text. Thus the entire universe of Racine (the inextricable interdependency of the different points of support, the inextricable interdependence of caresses and blows, drives and words) appears on the verge of taking flight all in one piece, as if it were no longer necessary to distinguish the three stages of the body any more than the different degrees of meaning.

The notion of 'physical theatre', as radical as it may have been, has moved over the last thirty years towards territories which might previously have seemed hostile to it, such as the staging of classics or of political theatre. It returns to one of its starting points: collective creation, not the French 1960s kind, but something closer to the notion of devised theatre: that is, a theatre creating all of its material, following a logic of progressive construction of the signifier. This shift in physical theatre away from the former collective devising corresponds to the Théâtre du Soleil's current work, from *Le Dernier Caravansérail* (*Odyssées*) (2004) to the *Les Ephémères* (2007).

Les Ephémères du Soleil: inventing collectively

The notion of devised theatre only arrived in the United Kingdom in the 1990s, linked to postmodern experimentation. Devising is 'a method of making performance that is often non-text based and includes the collaborative participation of the whole creative company in all stages and aspects of performance making'.[25] This definition can be applied to the Théâtre du Soleil's recent approach with *Les Éphémères*. In fact, not everything in the production was developed collectively with the group of actors, as was the case with *1789* (1970), where no director oversaw the entire process. The work started with microprojects conceived and developed at a local level, which were framed then edited (in the filmic sense) by Ariane Mnouchkine.

We should avoid a tricky genetic analysis of the different little scenes (this should be left to first-year students or to retired and learned professors: they alone would have the time to be present for the entire process – a titanic task, or a lost cause). Instead, we will continue to study the conception of the body underlying this enterprise.

The body of the actor is literally given to us on a platter. Two actor-stagehands push a small, often circular, wheeled platform onstage. Two or three characters are already engaged in an action, a dialogue or a silent situation that we can quickly identify. The wheeled platform crosses the stage lengthways between the two sides of the audience seating, which looks down; it resembles an operating theatre. The platform turns continually on its axis and moves longitudinally at the same speed. Thanks to this constant 'tracking', each spectator gains personal access to the intimate scenes. Each feels directly addressed by them. The smallest detail takes on great meaning. The rotation is generally slow, but varies slightly in speed from one scene to the next. It depends on the stage atmosphere, which is primarily created by Jean-Jacques Lemêtre's music. The movement of the chariots becomes almost a choreography in itself, a theatre of objects: at the end of each 'act', the platforms cross the stage to take a bow as the public applauds. This very ordered ballet clearly serves the dramaturgy of each fragment, and to a lesser extent the general dramaturgy, which recalls ephemerides: calendars whose pages are torn off each day. Throughout the slow rotations, the spectator experiences the pleasures of the voyeur, discovering the characters in all their facets, and following the progression of their consciousnesses and their thoughts, moving thoughts and lives that come together as we watch. The ephemeral is by definition short-lived, hard to grasp, momentary. It materialises in a brief moment when time stops, in a cinematic dissolve, or even in a close-up on a hidden aspect of existence. It coincides with *illuminations, with satori*, with unhoped-for meetings, and acceptance of and for the other. As in the chronophotography of Marey or Muybridge, every movement is as if reconstituted in a series of shots, intermediate stages, ephemeral impressions.

Figure 10.4 Les Éphémères, Théâtre du Soleil and Ariane Mnouchkine.
© Charles-Henri Bradier.

In a deliberately confined space, which is stuffed with objects and encumbered by podiums, the movements of the actors are minimal and all the more significant. The spectacular, expressive, visible, expansive, theatricalised body of the Soleil as it was before, with its productions of Shakespeare or Greek tragedies in the 1980s, seems distant. With a miniaturising and concentrating effect, the character appears in its day-to-day, minimalistic, typical environment. For certain actors, there seems to be an obsessional reconstruction of the past, which is necessary for the emergence of the memories and the words, a sort of trigger in the Stanislavskian vein. This process of reconstitution and concentration is not without risks, since it readily deteriorates into a standardised production line of television sketches, which creates an effect of immediate recognition and overly familiar situations, and panders to a rather lazy audience. Fortunately, these 'solar' actors have learned to resist temptation, and succumb to it only very rarely. The system whereby scenes return in the second half, with stories picking up where they left off (such as one about echography for example), sometimes leads to excessively long, repeated, gratuitous moments. But overall, the fresco of life gliding past in the stage space is impressively and precisely rendered. Is this the return of a theatre of situations? Not, in any case, in terms of any realistic or homogenous work. The fragmentation, which is the fate of this kind of montage, is compensated for by way of unity of tone and of theme, by the little scenes being placed in a network by the magic wand – and the whip – of Mnouchkine, following Ariadne's thread.

Let us take an example of this very successful synthesis of personal expression, the dramaturgy of the actor, French-style body art, and traditional stage representation. In 'Sandra's Birthday', Jeremy James plays the role of a transvestite celebrating his birthday one evening while babysitting a little girl (Galatea Bellugi). Answering the telephone, the character reveals that he finds painful the fact that he was born a man and would prefer to be thought of and to dress as a woman. His family and friends are not thrilled with his change of identity. The little girl is the only one who understands him, and she defends him from her friends and her father. The very aggressive father, having come to collect his daughter, suddenly bursts into tears, and collapses onto the sofa. He needs the consolation and physical support that the transvestite cannot give him, except in a silent and compassionate way. We learn that the father lost his wife and child in a car accident. But are grief and pain the sole reasons for his collapse? Or is it frustration at seeing that his daughter prefers the company of the babysitter, and the fact that she desperately lacks a feminine and maternal presence? These sudden and public tears also speak to the 'woman' looking after his child: they are an acceptance of his change of gender, of his difference, an awareness that sorrow is the most equally distributed thing in the world. Sandra's embarrassed modesty, his hesitancy in touching or consoling the father, the way in which the transvestite watches television, with the little girl sleeping on his lap: these are nonverbal behaviours that the spectator is given to read. The pleasures of theatrical representation lie mainly in the interpretation of characters' non-verbal behaviour, but also in the involuntary clues that the actor leaves on the body, like an unconscious form of body art.

The stage and the body of the actor are always the site of public exposure. By its very definition, the transvestite body gives itself to be seen. This occurs doubly in the theatre. A camp person is a ham actor: affected, effeminate, displaying poor taste and kitsch demeanour. Camp parodies heterosexual behaviour to illuminate its constructed and performative aspects. There is none of this in Jeremy James's acting. He is in no way parodic, and rather, it seems, seeks to create the image and the gestures of a woman with all the usual stereotypes: being well-dressed and a good housekeeper, baking a cake using the family recipe. In this transvestitism the secondary sexual characteristics are the object of our attention: we are faced with a work of body art because we are confronted with the real and constructed corporeality of the actor. The actor works at literally presenting the appearance, deciding how those traits called masculine will be shown or neutralised in cross-dressing. Physical features (being tall, having a deep voice) are not masked or adapted to feminine norms. The body is not provoked or forced in an unfamiliar direction. There is no violence as there might be for an explicit,[26] defiantly displayed body, which would provoke a debate on pornography or sexual politics. We are far from the provocative displays of Caroline Schneemann or Cindy Sherman, even further from the systematic naked exposure of the woman in the work of Japanese photographer Nobuyoshi Araki,[27] and further still from Gómez-Peña's geisha, with its parody of representations of elegance.[28]

In this French-style body art, as practiced by Jeremy James, the body is not explicitly shown and displayed. From the outset, it is placed in a narrative, at the service of a dramaturgical idea. Sandra has no other ambition than that of being accepted by all, adults as well as children; of entering normality, and a *petit bourgeois* normality for that matter.

This episode, masterfully performed by James, is characteristic of the recent evolutions of body art and of the dramaturgy of the actor. This signals the end of radical thinking on the body, but the body's meaning must still be determined. Is it a restoration of the old order, or a more subtle subversion? With great insight, Shepherd and Wallis see it thus:

> A plausible narrative runs that while in the 1960s counter-culture the body was naïvely deemed to be a resource of unalienated humanity, the 'return' to the body in the 1990s was predicated upon the deconstructionist understanding of the 'body in discourse' developed in the theory decade of the 1980s.[29]

This general observation helps us evaluate what we glimpse in James's scene about Sandra's new identity: the body makes a visible comeback in the symbolic order of language and of the narrative. What really matters to Sandra is not so much the literal and biological body as the identity, the gender, that the desiring subject feels. Sandra accepts the negative gaze of the other (that of the little girl at the beginning, that of mocking children, that of disapproving fathers), but he subverts it without the other realising it. The transgression of sexual roles and identities has been accepted for a long time by the character, and the others are coming around to the idea. Even if his own father refuses to talk to him, the little girl's father suddenly drops his defences, himself becoming an object deserving of pity. Sandra is eager to be himself, not to please others. He knows that this amounts to true acceptance, confirmed the moment they are able to change the subject. The problem for the character is how to make it so that the other, the one who accepts, does not lose face. How can he console the other, reassure the other, hold the other in his arms? This summons an ironic reversal of the body's situation and status: the transgression of the past must now reassure yesterday's well-meaning norm, a norm that is less self-assured these days, because it has lost its reference points and its certainties.

The art of narrative, here more than elsewhere, is the art of not saying everything, of leaving things open or merely implied. Most of these 'ephemeral' playlets reconnect with the theatre of silence as well as with the 1970s 'theatre of the everyday'. As in that theatre, the playlets introduce realist details into a narrative that does not seek to pass globally for reality. Real objects, and words really heard or pronounced, become part of a narrative system invented by the actors themselves and then by the director. Unlike the theatre of everyday life, the short scenes speak of autobiographical experiences. These are dramatisations of lived events, which are then shaped by the Soleil's actors.

Compared with Robert Lepage's art of storytelling, the Soleil's narrative approach might seem laborious and classical, even if it is true that each fragment obeys its own laws and sometimes finds indirect and original means of getting its message across. The – partially recorded – incidental music by Lemêtre, however clever and virtuoso it may be, often takes this too far: it coats the work in a sickly sentimentality, falling back, systematically and heavily, on one musical *leitmotif* – an old recipe from the world of film music. This unreasonable use of the *leitmotif* underlines what should simply be suggested by the acting.

The art of narrative is also the art of *montage*. Montage is found within the shot, in the first instance, as each sequence decides what is shown or said, hidden or silenced. As in all writing, there is a choice to reveal or to mask the motivations of the characters, to conclude or to maintain ambiguity. The tracking shots and the relativeness or reversibility of the point of view induce a relativity or a finesse that perfectly match the ephemeral nature of things. This is also the art of 'global montage', that of the dramaturgical organisation of the whole. This becomes manifest in the second half, once the network of all these figures starts to be established. This connection is nonetheless more anecdotal than dramaturgical. It produces no story, no central image, no overview. The fugitive nature of things easily convinces us that any point of view is only provisional. More than a decentring, more than a deconstruction, *Les Ephémères* offers a decentralisation, a delegation of directorial power to the actors working in the ephemeral world of memory. This return to a preoccupation that is at once decentralised and collective is a good thing. Collective creation is here much more than 'devised theatre': that is, a theatre imagined by a collective agency, a non-directive agent, working from what is found in the group and not from a preconceived idea. However, it must be pointed out that there exists no written history of works collectively developed by theatre companies. The observation of mise en scène and of the directors' choices will thus have to be helped along – completed and reinforced – by better knowledge of collective work. Does this mean a return to genetics? Or just the beginning of genetics?

The example of a 'theatricalised' performance constitutes the meeting of physical theatre and the dramaturgy of the actor within the art of performance – a performance which tends to come back to a mise en scène, to a de-monstration of controlled actions. This, like *Les Ephémères*, confirms the impression that physical theatre has changed its identity since the 1960s, that it has disguised itself as something else. Since the concluding decade of the last century it has invented new forms – the dramaturgy of the actor is only one of many possibilities. The notion of physical theatre has perhaps had its day: although useful in the 1960s as a reaction against the imperialism of dramatic literature, the term has lost some of its pertinence and its effectiveness since everyone now readily acknowledges the presence of the body in any kind of performance.

If body art and performance art seem to us children of the postmodern and postdramatic era to be historical genres, almost museum pieces (at least in the literal sense of the word), it is because a new model of the body has taken shape. It is no longer the 'savage' and 'unshackled' body of the 1960s, nor even the explicit body dear to Rebecca Schneider or Caroline Schneemann, but rather an imaginary, hybrid, fantasised body, mixed with language and discourse in search of multiple identities and of a multipolar subject. This embodied subject no longer has any need, for the sake of affirmation at least, to be placed in opposition to the spirit, the text or technology. In the same manner, theatre no longer feels obliged to convince us that it is physical, linked to the actor, made up of 'embodied events'. Theatre has so well integrated (and embodied) this corporeality that 'physical theatre' in the strict sense of the term is no longer a relevant category, leaving theatre free to pay a visit to other genres. The staging of a classic is sometimes more sensuous and physical than a fossilised *mimodrame*, and contemporary writing often urgently needs, if it is to be understood, to spread its sentences and its rhetoric (its wings), as if it were a question of body parts or modulations of the voice. Artists like Robert Lepage and Simon McBurney have shown that the use of media can be grafted onto human presence, the art of storytelling, and a literal use of the human body.

The infinite extension of 'embodied' theatre – whether it be called 'physical' or 'gestural' – must include appropriation by the postmodern theoretical debate on multiple identities, a debate that in a way takes us directly from the stone age to the schizophrenic postmodern condition, to a prosthetic body, mixing animal flesh and computer parts, seeking to make happy cyborgs of us all.

A large portion of theatre programming consists of plays from the classical repertoire.

It is often by way of this repertoire that spectators have their first experience of theatre. Our relationship with the repertoire is ambivalent: intimidation and rejection sometimes, uncertainty almost all the time.

Have we taken leave of the past? Even directors no longer fully believe in their powers. Nor do they still believe in any obvious method of interpretation. It is as if we have all lost our sense of direction.

Does the solution for performing the past reside in 'presentism'? Or in the postmodern and postdramatic future?

11 The splendour and the misery of interpreting the classics

'It cannot be denied that the problem of directing classics, as such, has gone away. Yet these texts remain very present on the stage. Is there no specific approach any more?'[1] Anne-Françoise Benhamou asks this question in her introduction to a remarkable 'Dialogue with the Classics' in the journal *Outre scène*. These observations, and this question, expose the problem perfectly; they summarise the current situation, but they also oblige us to put forward a few hypotheses on the staging of classical plays over the last twenty years.

What is a classic? A classic, according to Hemingway, is a book that nobody wants to read, but everybody wants to have read! One could add that a classic is a work that everybody read in class, but that nobody wants to talk about, since memories of school theatre trips still weigh heavily on everyone's mind. Our memories are classical by nature: the child's first play, and the very beginning of art, surely remind us of the significant moment where a unique and founding event attains the status of an example and marks us for life. Any such example is short lived, however, since less and less time is required in order for a work to be declared a classic: 'Funnily enough, twenty years suffices for a work to become just as old as the *Aeneid*. Despite the precautions he took in order to survive (photos, tape recordings, notes), Brecht himself has become ancient, and no less difficult to decipher than Molière.'[2]

Every epoch, every culture has its own conception of the classics. In France, the category of the 'classical' emerged in the nineteenth century, differentiating the classical from the romantic. 'Classical' describes both an aesthetic category and a epoch: 'the Century of Louis XIV', as Voltaire put it. It refers to Antiquity, to values considered to be absolute and universal. From an aesthetic perspective, it privileges order, harmony, and coherence. Seeking a balance between reason and affect, it obeys rules pertaining to decorum and verisimilitude.[3]

We will take the term 'classical' less in the historical sense (of the seventeenth century) than in the sense in which it has been used by directors in the last hundred years: a 'classic', a text to be rediscovered, a text that has been staged numerous times, taking the meaning given by Italo Calvino: 'The classics are those books about which you usually hear people saying: "I'm rereading ...", never "I'm reading ...."'[4] We could make an attempt at a history of the interpretation of classic works over the centuries up to the present day. And we would soon see that Racine and Molière were performed differently in the eighteenth and nineteenth centuries than they were in the century of Louis XIV. In the theatre, the classics thus have a long history of the conditions of interpretation. To this must be added the reputation of becoming a new category with the progressive emergence of mise en scène over the course of the twentieth century.

Mise en scène, towards the end of the nineteenth century, became aware of its powers, and of its capacity to (re)read texts performed countless times, or indeed those that had fallen into oblivion. It was at precisely this point that directors felt entitled to cast their own light upon plays from the repertoire. It is on these centuries-old texts that mise en scène honed its strategy to reconquer universal literature. This development can only be understood, as Didier Plassard shows, in the evolution of education and of the 'social grounding' of the general public.

The golden age of the classics would not take place until after the war, from 1945 to 1965, in the wake of the *théâtre populaire*, when theatre benefited from being seen to have a positive role to play in educating people and contributing to political change, particularly when 'French society sought to catch up in terms of the average age of school-leavers.' This era was followed by a 'period of contestation (1965–1975), when schooling started to become more democratic, then by a period of acculturation (1975–1990), when the university doors were opened to a growing proportion of those who would thereafter become the principal theatre audience'.[5] This phase, which we could say began in 1981 with the Left's taking power in France, was that of *le tout-culturel* ('everything is cultural'), that of intercultural theatre, and that of theatre that, as Vitez put it, was 'elitist for all'. It corresponds with the height of 'directors' theatre', and directors often secured their power by staging classics. The fall of the Berlin Wall in 1989 was followed by a period of instability, of criticism, of globalisation, but also of challenges to cultural relativism and the anthropological theatre of the 1980s (Grotowski, Brook, Barba, Mnouchkine). The catchphrase seemed to have mutated into 'egalitarian theatre for me':

a theatre that demanded equality of opportunity, but only where it was self-beneficial, an art of mass deception, whose weapons were impossible to find. This crisis of classical thinking and analysis is not without a future or lacking grandeur. It is our task to unleash the potentialities that are often buried in pessimistic or cynical discourses, and to work out the future of a theatrical illusion.

The 'classical effect'

Since the discovery of the great works, after 1890 and even more from 1950 to the 1960s, the notorious 'classical effect' created an sense of intimidation, owing to the prestige of the classics and their virtue of inclusivity for those who attended (and respected) them. But this effect no longer plays the same part: the spectators come to imagine themselves on an equal footing with the classics, able to understand them immediately and without any effort. This reversed intimidation creates the illusion that the classics are now at our level and that it is enough to consider them to be contemporary for this to be the case.[11] The classics are thus no longer a sign of cultural elevation, of social climbing, of integration into the middle classes. There has even been talk of 'bowdlerizing' them, in order to bring them in line with the norms of political correctness (which already happens in the case of extracts used in schools). Certain plays, certain scenes and certain staging ideas have been put to one side, lest they shock or fail to get past the fundamentalist censors. Others are annexed by this or that community that denies that they have any universal value. A festival like Avignon is moving away from its origins in *théâtre populaire*, and certain journalists worry that artists have become abstruse navel-gazers. This leads a distant observer such as Régis Debray to ask, 'Which is better, people deprived of art – an idea that terrified Vilar – or rather art without people, an art that is autistic and proud of it? The two have moved in together.'[12] The classics are equally victims of the disappearance of popular art and of the hermetic nature of contemporary art.

A tricky typology

Since the 1990s, we have struggled to distinguish between the varieties of stagings of classics. The historical distance is perhaps still too short, but the various 'methods' and ways of performing the classics are no longer in any way universal and systematic. In attempting to study pre-1980 stagings of classics, the following range of possibilities might be noted:[13]

1   Archaeological construction.
2   Historicisation.
3   Recuperation.
4   Signifying practice.
5   'The play in pieces'.
6   Return to myth.
7   Denial.

This typology was based on the specific conception that each kind of stage work was made from a dramatic text (until the 1970s). At that time, we argued that each conception concerned:

1   Following the text to the letter.
2   The story told.
3   The material used.
4   The multiple meanings.
5   The deconstruction of the rhetoric.
6   The myth where it takes root.
7   The direct relationship the text is supposed to establish with the audience.

It might be worth revisiting these old categories, if only to observe how much the practice of the 1990s distanced itself from them, but also how much effect they had without knowing it.

Archaeological reconstruction

Archaeological reconstruction of a performance, as it appeared when it was created, has always been an illusion, believing itself to be the very representational ideal of the classical work. Sheer technical difficulties meant this approach very quickly gave up trying to construct the past and reconstitute the acting style. Since it could never be perfect, reconstruction sought only to be a stylistic exercise, a useless distraction, a model of representation that 'distances the audience from the text and seduces it not with the story or language, but with the exoticism of the performance.'[14] Reconstruction quickly became imposture, a purely formal enterprise, preoccupied with archaeological details and not sufficiently interested in the relationship of the work to the contemporary audience, and thus with the concretisation engendered by the change in reception. Paradoxically, the audience turned away from it, finding itself distanced from the work and distracted by a vision from the past.

It is necessary to distinguish this rather naïve reconstruction from performances based on baroque declamation by Eugène Green or Jean-Denis Monory. In his reconstruction of *Mithridate,* Green primarily worked on the declamation and the gestures, careful to speak and to have others speak the text according to what he considered to have been the diction of verse by Racine's actors. He reconstituted a group to recover the sensation of Racinian poetry by way of period sounds, and a very codified system of gestures and postures. Such work is admirable in spirit and makes us pay attention to the technical identity of the piece. Nevertheless, because we are used to the dramatic structure and the chosen hermeneutical option being made manifest, we suffer the effects of withdrawal, deprived as we are of the pleasures of reinterpretation. Alternatively, what is required is the art of imagining the scene, as we would do when we simply read. But such an approach is only a 'three-dimensional reading', an interpretation of the work: meaning, and the imagined stage, are sorely missed. And are they not what counts?[15]

Historicisation

This is the exact opposite of archaeological reconstitution. It consists of staging the play from the point of view that is ours at the present time: situations, characters and conflicts are shown in their historical relativity. The ordering of the events of the story is such that we find a story that still concerns us today. As early as the 1960s, in the middle of the Brechtian honeymoon, voices like that of Vitez warned of this tendency of trying to explain the present too much, by forcing the plays to say what suited us at the time. Vitez was suspicious of and mocked the 'actualisation (of the Left, of course) and pseudo-Marxist reconstitution'. He also mocked the 'actualisation of the Left: explicit associations between the play and the events of our time (Creon wearing an armband with a swastika …)', and 'Pseudo-Marxist reconstitution: demonstration of the class struggles of 1399, as they might be imagined (with the considerable risk of getting it wrong)'.[16]

These reconstitution procedures, borrowed from the Berliner Ensemble, and also used by Joan Littlewood and the Roger Planchon in the 1960s, have become very rare in contemporary practice. When they are employed, it is only ever through a taste for anachronism, and without didactic pretensions. An entire coherent (and heavy) system of allusions, supposed to establish historical bridges between the two times, is now absent.

Recuperation

Recovery of the text as material was the most radical method for treating the dramatic text as sonic matter or as a set of polysemic elements (capable of being combined to produce multiple interpretations). Putting to one side musical compositions, where the text is actually reduced to a collage of sound elements, the sum of which no longer makes any sense (in the semantic sense, clearly), the text is basically never reducible to 'material' (the buzzword of the 1960s and 1970s). Brecht liked the idea of using classical text as a material, but he knew that this was not possible, since the notion of ownership remained strong: 'This obsession with ownership prevented us from discovering the value of the raw material of the classics, which could have allowed us to render them usable once again; the fear of destroying them reduced to nothing every effort made in this direction.'[17] This fear, one might say with hindsight, was not without foundation: it is exactly what occurred in the 1960s and 1970s when directors like Robert Wilson used texts, classical as well as contemporary, as simple 'word scenery', the better to focus on the production of images. The result certainly justified sacrificing the text, since these very visual productions were more beautiful than anything imaginable on stage. Nevertheless, this approach could no longer be seen as a rereading of the classics. The abandonment of the conception of the text as a recuperable material, which one might situate at the beginning of the 1980s and the moralising discourse of political correctness, still did not lead to the disappearance of the theatre of images – quite the opposite!

When Wilson staged *Fables de la Fontaine* at the Comédie Française in 2004, the text was certainly audible, and correctly pronounced by the actors, but the image and its overwhelming beauty erased, so to speak, the 'letter' of the text; the images changed any notion of (re)reading the *Fables*, leaving the ancient kingdom of literature for the kingdom of visual art. Even German dramaturg Hellen Hammer agrees:

> the guiding line and the themes chosen are the fruit of an architectural and musical enterprise. Playing on the contrasting situations: gravity/lightness, burlesque/seriousness, comedy/ tragedy, pessimism/optimism, length/brevity, silliness/wisdom. Playing on contrasts of size (lion/insect), or of amount (one, two, three, or a whole group of animals).[18]

The image-with-sound replaces the dramaturgy of the word.

Figure 11.1 Thérèse philosophe, directed by Anatoli Vassiliev.
© Patrice Pavis.

Sometimes stage practice, the way in which a text is enunciated (here it is chopped up without apparent reason) produces no meaning at all and thus does not offer a text to be reread, nor even to be read. In order to avoid immobilising the literary text, fetishising it, or venerating it like something untouchable, Vassiliev ends up crushing it, undoing its rhythm to the point of disfiguring it, giving flight to the otherwise impossible meaning (like a frail bird riddled with lead). Instead of breathing new life into the text, this chopped-up acting distances us, and prevents its becoming fiction, its metaphorisation, and the emergence of possible meaning.

The signifying practice

This is a consequence of the technique of recuperation. It implies that the text be open to the greatest possible number of meanings, to a plurality of meanings that contradict one another, complete one another and echo one another, irreducible to a final overall meaning.[19] Plurality is maintained thanks to the multiplication of stage enunciators (actor, music, rhythm, lighting and so on) and by way of a refusal to make a hierarchy of sign systems and thus to interpret. Peter Brook praised the Shakespearean form as being open to 'infinite interpretations', 'a form deliberately as vague as possible in order not to offer an interpretation'.[20]

This eulogy to openness is a classic of our times. It marked the arrival of the critique of semiology in the 1960s, attacking the principle of the coherence and closure of the work. This has multiple results, like Anatoli Vasiliev's staging of Molière's *Amphitryon* at the Comédie Française in 2002. In that staging, during an interminable scene, the actors performed with long batons and flags, then circulated all around the space. Their diction faltered at arbitrary moments, not following the syntax. The overall rhythm of the performance kept changing. Such fragmentation has no clear dramaturgical meaning, and thus seemed gratuitous and random. This stylistic exercise prevents us from any reading of the story, from any interpretation. Similarly, in *Thérèse philosophe*, performed at the Odéon's Ateliers Berthier (2007), two actors chopped up the text of the novel, taking turns to speak fragments cut mid-sentence, an operation that lent no meaning to the sentences, and in fact had the opposite effect. The stage machine functions well visually, but in terms of diction it becomes a very clumsy rendering of the body-machine.

The 'play in pieces' (mise en pièces)

To borrow the title of Planchon's experiment with Corneille's *Le Cid* (1968),[21] this is a practice that has become familiar, a deconstruction (before the term existed) of classical dramaturgy, a fragmentation of the text, that has been very common over the last forty years. Since the end of the 1970s, we have sought to reconstruct performances in bits and pieces. Even back then, we could already sense that collage, which is so easy on paper or in the game of chosen bits of scenes, would not automatically produce convincing results, either for the senses or for the intelligence of the text.

The return to myth

This was for many directors of the 1960s and 1970s a way of going directly to the essential core of any story, to the myth that inhabits and nourishes it. Myth was taken in the metaphorical sense of the source, the root or the resonance suggested by the text. Thus, in stagings of Polish classics, Grotowski sought the hard kernel, the link of the myth to the individual or collective unconscious. Far from archaeology or actualisation, he sought in the classics the forgotten myth and the buried memory of the human being.

This *topos* of the 1960s hardly works at all today. Nowadays, nobody dreams of reducing writing or representation to its mythic substrata. Most of the time, mise en scène shows the detail of writing; it is attentive to form and not just to universal themes. It is rare that tragedy, Greek tragedy for example, is reduced to abstraction, to a universal mythos.

Denial

Denial of mise en scène basically constitutes its natural situation: mise en scène is always present, but it wants to pass as invisible. Faced with often difficult, or even partially unreadable, classical plays, whose conditions of representation remain barely known, mise en scène is tempted to play its last card: to trust the actors alone to speaks the texts 'without a cultural filter', without the meta-discourse of an overall reflection on the play and its time. And yet there is no neutral, universal or immediate reading: the audience will definitely hear the letter of the text, but the meaning never goes without saying.

The end of the radical, fascination with the present

This attempt at a typology for classical productions of the 1950s, 1960s, and 1970s was already very problematic at the time. It was even more so for the 'exploded' productions of the 1980s and 1990s. Times had changed. The approach taken with texts from the past lost its radical and pugnacious nature. This happened for two reasons, according to Anne Françoise Benhamou:

> The classics remained present, but it is as if the questions involved – and the polemics – linked to their staging had vanished: either that historical questions no longer spoke to our times of 'presentism', or that the temple guardians and advocates of fidelity to the work had disappeared under fire from modernity, or, who knows, from postmodernity.[22]

Why have we taken leave of the past? Why do we entertain such suspicion of the past, and why this cult of the present? Is it a question of the acceleration of changes, their concomitance at the global level of the planet, the advance towards technological and commercial profit, the lack of awareness of past experience and its devaluation and decline, or even the impossibility of dramatic analysis, the absence of future perspective?

To live in the present is not so easy, even if that is the aspiration of the actor and the spectator, and even of the author.

The actor

The actor lives in the present, with the task of returning all fiction to a real act, that of a human being in the *hic et nunc* (here and now) of the acting. This obvious state of affairs can be seen with a great deal of actors and directors (especially those who have fallen for the charms of performance and the performative conception of theatre). Many, such as Jean-François Sivadier, note the importance of sharing in the theatre:

> Sharing is essential in the theatre. Sharing time and space. And it is never easy. I always try to interrogate the nature of sharing between the actors and with the spectators. In fact, this is largely about the idea of being in time with the audience. If I am in the space and I have the impression that the actor is not responding to a fictional image but rather facing me and a text and a space, I will have the impression of being next to them on a stage.[23]

In *La Mort de Danton* by Büchner (Avignon Festival, July 2005), Sivadier began with all the actors facing the audience, as if he wanted to start from their reality as actor and citizen in order to interpellate them and involve them – little by little and without rupture – in Büchner's fiction. The actors then kept this personal presence, like performers: concrete actors and citizens first and foremost, before being at the service of the fiction.

Such devices are now commonplace. In his staging of *Hamlet* with only three male actors, Arpád Schilling also worked on the temporal and spatial presence of the actor. It is not about offering a new reading of the play, nor indeed a reading of any kind! The story can still be followed, but numerous quotations of the other texts, and especially a constant changing of the different roles of the play, make any linear reading difficult, if not impossible. What counts for the three performers is to keep a distance, to maintain contact with the audience at all costs, despite the Hungarian words, the long and literary subtitles. The performers struggle to make us live in their enunciation, their actor's performance, their presence and their art of contact. They have given up on developing roles, being at the service of the author and his intentions. They claim to become coauthors of the show and address us as partners in the play. They make us read a few passages from the brochure and keep us awake by way of endlessly renewed jokes. This exercise in virtuosity, this actor's feat which is always in time with their partners and sensitive to the audience, is remarkable, but – if we are allowed to ask – is this still a staging of Shakespeare? Is this *Ham-let, Let it be ham* or *Hum-let*? Is it an exercise in ham acting, or a permanent and pleasant 'humming' on the nearly musical themes inspired by *Ham-let*? Does the hypertrophy of the enunciative function at the expense of the enunciations not preclude any rereading of the play? This is probably not the objective. Is the fact that they 'say' that they are performing *Hamlet*, without it being given to be understood, enough to keep us happy at present? This exercise in virtuosity and presence will be appreciated by those who already know the play, or indeed by those with no desire to get to know it, or even to get to know it better. There is no question of rereading: the performative function, which was captive for a long time, now occupies all shores.

The spectator

The spectator is directly affected by the invasive presence of the performer. Spectators will feel flattered, or on the contrary irritated by such solicitude. In affording direct, spontaneous access to the text – and thus voluntarily limiting all explanation by way of stage actions, any conception that would risk masking things – does the director not have too much confidence in the spectator's faculties? If only concerned with the enunciation, with enjoyment of the moment, the spectator risks also giving up all that the play could offer today, including an understanding of the work and of the world. Sometimes the miracle does happen, however. The spectator is interpellated at the deepest level, and the spectator's field of knowledge is also widened. When, in *La Mort de Danton*, the actor Ernst Stötzner stands before the audience and addresses it as would a French actor speaking to the audience about the problem of the *intermittents du spectacle*,[24] we listen with even greater attention, and his defence of terror seems to speak to our predicament. The political weight of this speech, although the result of chance, is all the more apparent. Not all direct addresses to the audience, Brechtian or otherwise, possess this power, but they at least force us to break referential illusion in favour of a vigorous awakening of critical, or even political, consciousness.

The author

The author is the third, and indispensable, term in this new equation. Anne-Françoise Benhamou notes that 'in the 1970s, under the influence of structuralism and of the supposed "death of the subject", the figure of the author had almost disappeared from literary theory, and, as a result, from the staging of classics. Today it is making a comeback.'[25] This comeback is noticeable not only in the declarations made by directors, but especially in the way in which the notion of author allows for the fragmentation of materials to be overcome, and recovers a coherence beyond scraps of text. Stéphane Braunschweig makes the same remark with regard to his research method:

> To work on the text as a text is to presuppose that there is a coherence – with all the contradictions. This is to claim that this thing has been thought, intended, even unconsciously, and that it forms a whole: the whole of an author.[26]

In his *Misanthrope*, Braunschweig reconstitutes an 'entire', uncompromising Alceste, and not just in terms of temperament. The 'author as a whole' is Molière's global and structurally ambiguous conception: his Alceste is sincere, but also fanatical and therefore dangerous. He is pitiful, childish, endearing, but also immature, ridiculous and egocentric. The challenge is not about knowing whether the character resembles his creator, but rather about asking how he might figure in the quest for Molière. And this is indeed the question, since the dramaturgy of this production was able to reconstitute the sense of a whole. Of course, this dramaturgy is only perceptible thanks to the actor: the actor is the interface, by way of imagination and physical appearance, between the exterior world and the text anchored in a particular time, present or past. As an intermediary and a conductor, the actor makes the link between the text and the outside world, which is the responsibility of the director. The actor, then, is surely both faithful and unfaithful, the official representative of the author but also the director's stowaway.

And yet coherence, here resulting from a global and rigorous reading, is not always there when needed, even when the mise en scène is coherent and well set up. This was the case in Ibsen's *Hedda Gabler*, directed by Thomas Ostermeier at the Schaubühne (2005). The play was skilfully updated. It was taken from its naturalistic Norwegian milieu, and moved to our time and a German bourgeois (neo-European bohemian yuppie) interior. If we believe the programme (uncredited), Hedda commits suicide because she fears seeing her plans for the future annihilated by the unexpected return of Lovborg, who might take her husband's professorial position. This is clearly nonsense if you read the play: Hedda kills herself to escape the blackmail of Judge Brack, because of her disappointment in love, because of her distain for the mediocrity of her entourage, and in no way for fear of social disgrace, supposedly corresponding to 'our collective drama'.[27] In fact, the stage interpretation says something else, and it is not as erroneous as the programme suggests: Hedda's motivations remain ambiguous, more linked to existential despair than to economic considerations (but how can we know?). In any case, this reading (which might be that of the dramaturg Marius von Mayenburg, credited as such in the programme) does not do justice to the 'whole of the author': it projects current preoccupations and obsessions – foreign to Ibsen – onto the play. What thirty years ago would have passed for a 'productive' reading, a 'rereading', a discovery that would renew our knowledge of the text (as we used to say!) now shocks us like an abuse of power: an unsatisfactory reading, or even a self-satisfied one.

But this self-satisfied reading has not become the rule. Rather, the opposite is true: the mise en scène often stops short of forming too daring a thesis, or one too contemporary, or too peculiar to a single director. Theatre no longer flatters itself with the illusion that it makes us better understand the world, and even less that it transforms it with the powers of art.

Living increasingly in the present, the actor, the spectator and the author change the rules of the game: the classics are no longer a simple thing of the past, that we have once and for all filed away in separate boxes. Let us try then to sketch a few new forms of mise en scène from the last twenty years.

New forms for old questions

The re-emergence of the body

In the classical play, the body is supposed to disappear behind the meaning and the words. But when the words are pronounced onstage and carried by the actor, the body reclaims its rights. We need only think of the numerous stage interpretations of Racine in which the body plays a central role. Here are a few examples.

In *Bérénice*, the choreographer Bernardo Montet and the director Frédéric Fisbach use both actors and dancers.[28] According to them, the body is quicker than the word: 'At times the body, the movement, the space can speak better than words.'[29] The presence of the body, then, comes from the text, which is prolonged in the bodies. Dance and theatre coexist without one swallowing the other. Dance with text heard over a loudspeaker establishes an atmosphere, makes the story familiar, before we hear theatrical speech. The words are exchanged, the bodies are distanced from one another or separated by a window; Titus and Bérénice only come back together for a brief moment, before their definitive separation.

Figure 11.2 *Iphigénie*, directed by Ophélia Teillaud. © Guy Delahaye.

In a staging of *Iphigénie*, Ophélia Teillaud uses diction perfectly while demanding a physical acting style to carry the language. Far from seeking the key to a new reading, as in the work of Barthes, Goldman and the other structuralists who survived the 1960s, this work places side by side, then integrates, two lines of research. The first is a diction that is not 'archaeological', as with Eugène Green – but which respects the rules of the alexandrine without limiting it to serving as abstract music – and which therefore allows the emotions of the character in situation to emerge. The second is a mode of expression onstage that allows the moves, the clashes, the blockage, the conflicts of the bodies in revolt to be seen and felt. This confrontation is subtle, almost peaceful. And indeed, the declamation is not cut off from the body; it is always tied to bodily expression, which is no longer, as in the 1960s and 1970s, an individual, 'expressionistic', unhinged and disjointed form. The impulses and the passions of the body, for example Achille's anger and desire, Iphigénie's juvenile obedience, or the mute, massive sturdiness of Agamemnon, can immediately be felt and are conveyed to the spectator.

Racine's play thus finds itself revived, and inhabited in gesture and impulse, treated as the origin and the arena of bodily impulses, and of the military and patriarchal order. Cruelty, in Artaud's sense, finds its origin in the violence of situations (sacrifice, murder, the desire for power), which are incarnated in the constraint of the alexandrine, of etiquette and of the story. Owing to the rotating position of the women (the men are more stable), the female body becomes interchangeable and global, reduced to the same age and the same appearance: it is both vibrant, liberated, aesthetic and tortured, exposed and consumed, sacrificed on the 'naturally' feminine altar, rendered unto the perversity of the power games. The choleric Achille and the ambiguous Ulysse are powerless in this story of feminine sacrifice that is beyond them; the challenge ends well, even though it ends badly. This production integrates and reconciles an intimate knowledge of the text with individual physical work by the actors.

Luc Bondy and Patrice Chéreau's stagings of Racine's *Phèdre*, respectively in 2002 and 2004, differ in their specific use of the body. Bondy's actress, Valérie Dréville, wears a tight dress of gold hoops, like a golden prison for her tortured body. Her appearance suggests an archaic, savage, mythical origin, which is of course true of the daughter of Minos and of Pasiphaë. The diction is informed by the very gutsy Artaudian acting. Valérie Dréville's diction respects the form of the alexandrine, but the other actors' diction, in particular the actor playing Hippolyte, is very 'psychological', hesitant and lazy. Conversely, Chéreau's actor, Dominique Blanc, is much more contained in her visible emotions and bends under the pressure of the alexandrine. Her acting, and more still that of Eric Ruf and Michel Duchaussoy (from the Comédie Française) is very masterful, attentive to the rhetoric of the line and, we could say, more 'Vitezian' than 'Chéreaudian'. Only Patrice Chéreau managed to make known and felt the intimate link between the alexandrine as a straitjacket of language and the body subject to the law of language.

The reappropriation of classical language

The formal language of the alexandrine, in tragedy as in comedy, represents a vital symbolic issue. Most of the time, the actors respect its form, particularly the number of feet and diereses. The care taken with correct diction does prevent a modernisation or updating of the context of the play in any case. This can be observed in the productions of Stéphane Braunschweig, or tested in the work of Benoît Lambert in his staging of *Le Misanthrope*. The option is no longer to modernise or to conserve. Perfect diction of the verses renders the stage anachronisms and the leitmotiv repeated by all at different times ('demeurez, je vous prie' [stay, I pray you]) funnier still. Respecting the letter does not prevent unexpected twists : 'De vos façons d'agir, je suis mal satisfait' [Your way of acting leaves me unsatisfied] declares Alceste to Célimène at the start of the second act as he puts his clothes back on, which gives a new meaning altogether to satisfaction. Oronte's eccentricities (a rocker and a dancer), the contemporary costumes, the microphone-assisted songs by Célimène's admirers – all these very effective jokes do not hide the issues of the play, but displace them into a current context, yet without simplifying the original story. The point is to show, as Lambert suggests, 'how Molière's language remains audible, when it travels through contemporary bodies. And the point is thus to follow the confrontation between inherited learned culture and the smuggling culture that we have made.'[30] The balance is miraculously maintained and the audience, notably a young audience, seems to make a link between its world and that of Molière.

Reconstitution in baroque declamation

In addition to Eugène Green, directors such as Jean-Denis Monory and Bénédicte Lavocat strive to reconstitute baroque declamation.

La Ruelle des plaisirs is a montage of erotic poems by Ronsard to Saint-Amant, from Belleau to Louise Labbé, spoken and 'interpreted' in baroque declamation by Bastien Ossart and Bénédicte Lavocat, and directed by the latter. This is a very pleasant and refined journey through little known erotic poetry from the sixteenth and seventeenth centuries. Delicately undertaken, the show never descends into vulgarity thanks to the elegant distance that is constantly maintained between the word and the thing, between the often crude, if poetic, language and the poetic, if fundamentally crude, thing.

The ironic distance between the word and the act is also that of literary disguise as practised in the seventeenth and eighteenth centuries. Within a dazzling and spiritual form, daring, taboo and sometimes ridiculous sexual realities are discussed. This little show is, from this point of view, a great success, a rare gem: the two actors manage to suggest 'the thing', with poses and attitudes that are perfectly executed, without physical contact, at the border between the ridiculous and the serious, the pathetic and the parodic. The women take on the expected stereotypes of female restraint, fooling nobody, while the man is consumed with love, but at a measured pace, calculating its effects. The declamation of the poems is more than a recital: the choice and organisation of the poems and songs constitutes a dramaturgy of the relations between the sexes, of female desire, as they are envisaged, in the past and in the present day. Everything is in the man's head, in his book, while the woman, despite the coded play-acting, keeps a sense of reality. She pushes the man into a corner, and, exhausted by many repeated attempts, the poor man is forced to give up. Thus this unexpected feminine constraint: one must betray, abandon the lover in order to go who knows where, wherever desire may call:

> Me dois-je préparer à ce funeste jour
> Où malgré mon ardeur fidèle
> Le destin me contraigne, à la honte d'amour,
> A trahir mon amant, l'abondonner tel quel?
> Hélas, je n'y puis consentir,
> Et toutefois il faut partir.[26]

Baroque declamation here functions perfectly, since gesture, which seems, and which already in its era seemed, rather artificial and specious, serves this idea well. In slowing the impact of the crude words and sexual realities, it is like a filter: it assists with the stylisation and allusion, it embellishes and distances the freed word. This slowing does not harm the dynamics of the mise en scène, unlike the declamation of a tragedy or, more still, a comedy.

Thus this declamation acting is very problematic for the staging of a comedy such as *Le médecin malgré lui* (The Mock Doctor) by Molière, directed by Jean-Denis Monory. For comedy, in fact, this acting produces the opposite effect: it halts and sometimes annihilates the comic effects, notably the verbal ones. It prevents us from reacting like clockwork, provoking a sort of delayed reaction, giving us a '*goutte à l'imaginative*' ('imaginative gout'), as Roxane says to Christian in *Cyrano de Bergerac*.

Such are perhaps the limits of baroque declamation when applied indiscriminately to all genres. For a tragedy like *Andromaque*, staged by Jean-Denis Monory, baroque acting gives access to a poetic language by concentrating on the expression of the passions. The slowing, the effects of 'peasant' French or Québecois amuse us and distract us a bit; we attribute them to historical truth and end up accepting them. This asceticism and heightened concentration make us appreciate the Racinian dramatic poem. Emotions are held for an instant in the actors' poses, the passions are written into their physical attitudes, pathos vibrates even in their fingers, the positions of their limbs and fingers correspond to very precise thoughts and emotions. But for a comedy, and all the more so for a Molière farce, the baroque operation is less justified, remaining a literary curiosity: the place is robbed of vitality since the animated movement and the liberated body of the straightjacket of declamation and of codified gesture are seriously

Figure 11.3 La Ruelle des plaisirs, directed by Bénédicte Lavocat, Théâtre de la Fabrique. © Pierre Hajek.

lacking. On the other hand poetry, and even more that of an effective dramatic montage like this one, lends itself admirably to this antiquating fantasy that is baroque declamation as soon as it encourages the spectator to concentrate on the language of the passions or on the allusions of erotic poetry.

'Recontextualisation' of mise en scène

As in the case of Benoît Lambert and of Stéphane Braunschweig, mise en scène attempts to bring the past and the present together, rather than to separate them. 'Recontextualisation', the 'transposition of dramatic action into new spatio-temporal referents',[27] thus takes place in an environment familiar to the contemporary audience. For Lambert's *Misanthrope*, our time is represented by the group around Alceste, always present on the stage, indifferent to all that happens in the foreground. He smokes, sings, enjoys himself, far from the negative image that he is trying to project. In the same spirit, Braunschweig's *Misanthrope* is not put back into its historical context: it literally returns our reflection in a giant mirror. Gestures, behaviour and costumes help us to locate ourselves in today's world, while the diction makes no concession to lazy contemporary language. As with Lassalle and

Braunschweig, the diction is highly correct without becoming archaic; it helps the understanding of the play's mechanisms. Vocal precision is thus not uniquely formal, but it helps in understanding how the character and the author's thoughts are formed.

Radical or relevant recontextualisation?

If recontextualisation of the story appears legitimate, particularly for comedies, it is nonetheless 'successful': the most radical is not necessarily the most correct. When Ostermeier sets Büchner's *Woyzeck* in a giant sewer in a great Eastern European metropolis, he definitely finds a powerful metaphor for the current situation of his anti-hero, but this changes the system of characters. Woyzeck is less the victim of the stupidity of the army and the medical profession, but rather is a punchbag for the mafia and all manner of dealers. We wonder why he rapes Marie after having murdered her. The violence of the tableaux, their visual coherence, their aesthetic qualities, and the assemblage of musical extracts (a live rap sequence as an extra) cannot hide the limitations of the dramaturgical analysis. We could say the same of Frank Castorf's productions: stylistic coherence and provocation are certainly to be expected, but they obscure rather than illuminate the play. Or could it be that dramaturgical analysis has lost all significance and relevance?[28]

Not always, and not necessarily! The dry humour and provocations of Christoph Marthaler, a slow hurricane coming in from Switzerland, prove the opposite. In his staging of *Les Noces de Figaro* (2006) at the Paris Opera, he created (with his faithful companion, scenographer Anna Viebrock) an entire universe of daily banality. We are in the impersonal entrance hall to a Swiss government building. The count is a doorman in uniform. Susanne is a waitress in a white apron. In the glass cage of the lodge, staff seem to be busy. A stammerer is only able to sing when given a vigorous slap on the back. The recitative is taken care of by a *lunaire* individual (Jörg Kienberger), a kind of Groucho Marx making some glasses on a tray sing and vibrate: a musical number not universally appreciated by the music lovers. By way of a kind of 'Deschiens effect' (from the name of Jérôme Deschamps and Macha Makeïff's first actors), Marthaler creates a visual world of everyday boredom, with ordinary creatures that come close to idiocy, but are rapidly 'sketched' from life with humour and tenderness. He opposes, like fighting dogs, two antithetical universes: petit-bourgeois mediocrity and the sublime music of Mozart. This desecration was not to the taste of all the season-ticket holders, and quickly turns to easy devices. But this complicit wink is never merely pure provocation or open parody. So who is being mocked? Not so much ordinary folk but rather us, the supposedly cultivated spectators who seek beauty in sublime works and who are incapable of finding it in the everyday.

A new relationship with tradition

The interpretation of classical plays depends upon the relationship that theatre has with tradition. This relationship continues to evolve, since the past is subject to continuous reevaluation and since the reader and the director possess tools that are also evolving as time passes and methods of analysis change. We are far from the somewhat naïve conception of the 1950s and 1960s, which claimed to renew the works of the past and to 'modernise' and 'dust' them. Vitez mocked such 'housework':

> Nothing seems more stupid than this idea: to dust the classics. As if, under the dust the meaning could appear naked, pure, shining, and golden. No – that's not how it works. There are fashions, traditions, schools... and style always hides something else, another, generally political, issue, and not necessarily linked to the works' own political ideas, but rather linked to their forms.[29]

This issue is political – Vitez is right – and it must be located in the forms used, the forms of acting and staging. Directors can choose to get as close as possible to the object and to the way in which the play was first performed, or conversely, turning their back to these circumstances, can invent a mode of acting disconnected from its original model.

In his staging of Racine's *Mithridate* with baroque declamation, Eugène Green recreates 'a theatrical art forgotten for two centuries':

> we have rediscovered that any text read or recited in public used to require 'eloquent speech', which led to a diction and a pronunciation that were totally different from the diction and the pronunciation that were the norm in everyday conversation. The declamation was close to song, and Lully, the creator of the French Opera, invited his singers to hear Racine's actors. Theatre acting itself served this eloquent speech, with gestures and facial expressions seeking to underline the words and highlight the conflicts and the passions.[30]

Today's spectator would probably be surprised by this style of declamation, which might appear archaic. But, according to Georges Forestier, the seventeenth-century audience felt no less distanced from this 'eloquent speech',[31] which they experienced as an artistic and artificial code. Thus, the twenty-first-century audience should concentrate on the vocal and visual performance, and give up on discovering a new reading of the play and reading the emotions of the characters beyond the codifications of facial expression and held and codified attitudes of the 'declaimer'. The lines of the face and the attitudes are magnified with candle light, and are also readable 'in the light of' the painting of the time. This reconstituted form, although not always historically accurate, is at least close to its origin. It has the merit of obliging us to reread this 'dramatic poetry', imagining its vocal and visual performance.

Most of the time, the interpretation no longer has any relationship with tradition. Sometimes the play is chosen in order to settle scores. This is often the case in the mounting (or 'sacking') of Frank Castorf, who knows only too well the audience's petit-bourgeois penchant for witnessing with morose delectation the live destruction of a masterpiece that was a childhood favourite. With *Meistersinger*, 'inspired by Richard Wagner and Ernst Toller', Castorf chose the opera that 'was not merely by chance the quintessence of the national-socialist Gesamtkunstwerk in 1933'.[32] He produced it with a trashy, 'degenerate' (as the Nazis and Stalinists used to say) scenography, and the contrast with the Wagnerian music and scenery was all the more striking and provocative. Thanks to a Trojan horse, the actors literally enter the Wagnerian monument. The stage gags continue, Toller's revolutionary quotations lose all their meaning, and become involuntarily parodic due to their excessiveness. The idea of incorporating 'foreign' quotations in a work, as employed by Godard (in the 1960s) or Mesguich (in the 1970s), has lost its power to provoke as well as its critical justification.

But tradition is often, and more prosaically, for directors, 'daddy's' tradition, that of the previous generation. For Castorf, Ostermeier or Thalheimer, the point is to react against Peter Stein, Claus Peymann or Peter Zadek's *Regietheater*.[33] In France, the fathers seem more ignored than execrated. Nobody would dream of coming out against Copeau or Vilar, or even Chéreau or Planchon. Directors in their forties would be more likely to reject the *théâtre d'art*, a 'well-made', critical and coherent theatre. Many consider themselves nonetheless, and rightly, to be in the lineage of the *théâtre de qualité*. It is not a question, as for these directors' German counterparts, of aversion to all authority, of revolting against the discipline and the critical or political ambitions of the fathers. Directors like Fisbach, Sivadier, Lacascade and Braunschweig at least agree on the necessity of taking their place in the continuity of the staging of the repertoire.

The fact remains that these directors, whether French or German, demonstrate a clear suspicion towards the previous generation. They no longer believe in a global 'interpretive system (such as Marxism, psychoanalysis, feminism)'.[34] They are not, a priori or in principle, hostile to theoretical analyses inspired by the humanities, but they no longer claim to lend the work staged a global or definitive explanation. That which, thirty years before them, appeared obvious – the universality of the image, of trans-linguistics, of expressive gesture, of (theatre as) celebratory event – is no longer obvious, either for them or for current theory. The 'theatre of images', which owes much to Robert Wilson, has lost much of its aesthetic relevance. Intercultural theatre, created by actors with different cultures and languages, by Brook in particular, has become the object of – sometimes unfair and demagogical – critique by nonetheless very 'Westernised' intellectuals, and cannot move on. *L'expression corporelle* ('movement'), coming from the 1960s counterculture, and the festive celebration of the early Théâtre du Soleil, now seem too approximative and poorly mastered by the young artists involved.[35] Their ideological presuppositions, for example the freeing of the body and the individuals, find themselves challenged.[36]

Tradition, as we know, is not what it was: it can no longer be conceived of and seems dubious. But every artist, willing or not, must reappraise any relationship with this tradition. To describe these recent shifts in the interpretation of classics, a few components of the performances are examined below. What changes are provoked, and at what levels?

Operating on the classics

Changing time and place

Such changes have almost become the rule: the frame of the play is thus ours. Either the actors wear our clothes and imitate our ways of speaking, or else they adopt an attitude towards action that seems familiar to us. Paradoxically, we are almost surprised to find the principal character of *L'Avare*, played by Michel Bouquet, and directed by Georges Werler, in a bourgeois seventeenth-century house.[37] The mimetic effect, the illusion of the representation of objects and behaviours transport us to an imaginary world where a 'period Miser' naturally reveals his avarice, in words as in deeds. The mimetic effect extends to the whole production: no detail, no anachronism ever disturbs our impression. The naturalism of the scenery, and the mimetic and vocal skills of the actors provide the pleasures of naturalism, while leaving the audience free to admire the star actor's craft. Michel Bouquet makes his Harpagon more sickly than comical, as if the point was to find medical excuses for his neurosis. He is amusing more because of his excesses than because of the ridiculousness of the situations. There is no room left for pure acting and theatricality in this sombre drama. It is always difficult to mock the afflicted, even an imaginary invalid. The famous voice of Michel Bouquet, so strong in his weak body, reinforces the impression of the character's real interior suffering. We feel sorry for this miser, with his psychosomatic illnesses, but this is at the expense of liberating laughter.

The evening is pleasant, but not at all restorative. It lacks lightness. And then, all the side-effects of the theatrical enterprise are too visible: the ushers expecting and requesting tips, the luxurious glossy programme, and especially the all-too predictable aesthetics of a faultless, compact and coherent performance, the star actor who everyone has come to see play the Miser.

What a contrast with another production of *The Miser*, by Andreï Serban:[38] the abstraction of the scenery and the absence of specific reference offers us a more universal and essential perception of avarice and of the violent relationship between owner and owned. The absence of univocal marks forces the spectator to imagine the situation. Hands sticking out of the screens to touch the Miser and monochromatic mobile screens are the visible instruments of representation and theatricality. And this allows the spectators, forced to construct their own 'scenario', to focus on human passions in order to interpret these playful actions. The actors' task consists of making the spectator understand that the story and the passions of the play are universal, and that they should begin by reading the organisation of the signs, without relying only on mimetic representation, and thus the options of the mise en scène must be clarified.

Changing the story

The story (a Brechtian concern) is established according to what the performance has to say to the play. This question is rarely raised today, as mise en scène no longer seeks to impose its reading, but rather prefers to open up the play to multiple interpretations. Dramaturgical analysis, although very popular in the 1960s and 1970s in Germany and in France, has gone out of fashion. The difficulty of telling, or even of lending coherence to a text in the era of deconstruction, leads some directors to give up on any attempt to tell a story, for fear of simplifying reality. Only those who still ask themselves (or ask themselves again) what meaning the author sought to create are able to tell a story and to construct a performance on the resulting narrative structure. This is the case for Stéphane Braunschweig: his *Misanthrope* in no way claims to have found the truth of Alceste's story, but does have enough coherence to reveal the characters' contradictions.[39] This is unfortunately not always the case in adaptations of classic works. It is as if the game consists of laying a false trail. In Brecht's *Im Dickdicht der Städte* (In the Jungle of Cities), Castorf drags things out.[40] The actors invent gag after gag to attract attention at all costs. A guitarist plays live, while an actor draws on the ground. Each actor has their chance to do a number. Instead of bothering to tell the story, which is already quite messy in Brecht's original, there is a series of effects, of mini-shocks underlining the live presence, as if live perception were deemed more important than the desire to tell or to signify. Without the guidance of a well-crafted dramaturgy, the mise en scène quickly becomes a series of gratuitous effects, repetitive background music, a springboard for virtuoso actors with tics and tricks. But who is it supposed to impress? Not only is the story unchanged, it is hardly even told at all.

Changing the plot

The plot is not modified either. Most stagings of the classics, at least in France, still use the complete text: the plot therefore hardly changes. Directors rarely change the order of the sequences, or propose another way of telling. What does however frequently change is the 'actualisation', the universe in which the action takes place.

Often the plot is only interrupted between the acts: thus, in Benoît Lambert's version of *Le Misanthrope*, Alceste's friends sing, dance and enjoy themselves. In these moments of time off, the linear plot receives an ironic addition that does not damage the logic of the story. We, indefatigable hermeneutes that we are, take this unexpected opportunity to breathe.

Changing the textuality

Textuality varies according to the different translations, which are adapted into contemporary language. Sometimes the translation is also a true adaptation. Theatre, more than any other genre, plays on the materiality and malleability of the dramatic text and of the stage. Archaic text becomes once again readable and current thanks to a new translation. The translator has the possibility of adapting it to the needs of a future staging. There are numerous translations that have been redone for a specific stage project.

Figure 11.4 Dans la jungle des villes, by Bertolt Brecht, directed by Frank Castorf.
© Patrice Pavis.

In his staging of *Andromak,* Luk Perceval, hoping to make the language accessible to all: 'broke every classical form from Shakespeare to Racine not forgetting the Dutch classics. We rewrote, really rewrote. And now it's the norm for us, and nobody understands why anybody would want to stage Racine in the 'classic-classic' style.'[41] This rewriting in a simplified Dutch version unfortunately destroys any sensitivity to the original text. But this does not result, however, in a verbal or physical freedom of expression: the actors are regrouped in a narrow altar, from which they are always in danger of falling and injuring themselves on the shards of glass on the ground below. The straitjacket of seventeenth-century court language and etiquette is thus transformed into a cruel game, a theatre of risk and cruelty, where the bodies risk death. Words kill, not so much 'indirectly' – as in old-fashioned classical dramaturgy – but by way of the body and of desire.

Racine is subjected to a rejuvenation treatment the minute he is translated into contemporary language – Dutch in this case – which is certainly smoothed out compared with the French alexandrines, but is also adapted to the semantics of today's listeners and spectators. This process of translation and adaptation is basically characteristic of mise en scène as a way of reworking (reviving, recycling) a language and a history. Sometimes the acting and the directing are sufficient, sometimes it is necessary to make an incision in the flesh of the writing the better to save the whole sick body and regenerate it for a brief moment. It is obviously more tricky to change texts in their original language. Sometimes obscure passages are omitted, or even slightly rewritten. The German *Regisseur* Michael Thalheimer reduces classical plays by condensing them and reducing them to their core: his *Emilia Galotti* (by Lessing) is reduced to a quasi-musical score, which the actors execute according to a new rhythmic pattern, usually delivering the lines at top speed. Such a process of condensation does not mind making numerous cuts and changing the ending! This process allows the director to 'avoid all superfluity onstage': 'thus I focus attention on the nucleus of the play, which I consider essential',[42] he claims. Notions of 'faithfulness' obviously vary depending on which side of the Rhine you find yourself.

Changing the system of characters

The golden age of acting exercises, proposed by Vitez or Brook in the 1970s, is long gone. We hardly ever witness endless switching of roles or announcements like 'I'm playing x or y'. Mesguich, a pupil of Vitez in the 1970s, is one of the sole directors still to practise, albeit in moderation, the doubling-up of some characters, as in his production of *Andromaque* at the Comédie Française (2002). The mistress and the handmaid sometimes function as the double of one another. Rarer still, but very impressive, is the splitting of the performer into actor and dancer, as in Montet and Fisbach's *Bérénice*.[43]

A character can be split into an infinite number of figures, becoming a single element in a chorus, losing thus its individual and psychological dimension. Opera lends itself particularly well to such chorus effects. Marthaler, in Mozart's *Les Noces de Figaro*, and Barry Kosky in *Der Fliegende Holländer*,[44] did not hesitate to give the chorus a certain banal anonymity. In both cases, the effect is heightened as the performers enter in single file. All are dressed in the same impersonal costume.

Changing the conventions and the figuration

Mise en scène is no longer reluctant to mix and to oppose conventions proper to different genres: naturalism and symbolism, realism and theatricality. The acting style often varies considerably from that of the original production. In Ibsen's *Brand*, directed by Braunschweig, a character in a mountaineer's outfit walks on an inclined floor, which is white and far removed from even the smallest mountain. We quickly forget this hiatus, this incompatibility, the better to concentrate on the text and the characterisation.

The figuration of the stage world often proceeds more by metonymy than by metaphor, as if it were easier and more provocative to signal a reality with a stage detail than to figure it mimetically or symbolically.

Changing the paradigm: performance for mise en scène

Changes in the acting conventions sometimes even equal a change of priority: the rapidity and virtuosity of performance get the upper hand on the precision and the depth of mise en scène. It becomes necessary to discuss Declan Donnellan's production of Shakespeare. In *Cymbeline*, Donnellan succeeds in making the play and the plot understandable. Thanks to the lively acting, the quick changes of character and situations by way of conventions, to the coordination of word and gesture, the plot proceeds without any difficulty; the codes of the performance are made apparent. Irony and humour faced with the implausibility of the Shakespearean 'script' are not reduced to clumsy parody or a profound discourse claiming to explain away all the contradictions, as it would be in the case of a Brechtian or 'continental' 1960s staging. We owe the performance to the acting, in every sense of the term. The visual beauty and clarity of the groupings, the harmonious movements of the groups and their blocking, the mastery of language and the lightness of the delivery, the vivaciousness of the characters' exchanges, all of these are to the credit of the actors, who have been directed without this becoming apparent (and thus very effectively).

This is an art of drawing in space, of clarifying the relationships between characters by way of parallelism and references to today (for instance, with costume) which nonetheless does not seek to transpose or historicise the story in the manner of a 'continental' mise en scène. Such a corporeality unburdens a very sinuous plot: it sets the text in motion, it synchronises word and movement. The motivations and emotions are highlighted, rather than spread out or held back, without psychologisation or didacticism. The impression of perpetual motion and energy, coming from the actors onstage, emerges from the rhythms and impulses of Shakespeare's language, which is relayed, channelled and organised. The actor is capable – thanks to a perception of the objective, of the actor's internal 'target'[45] – of directing everything: emotions, desires, movements, the dynamics of the spoken text.

Changing cultural context

Every classical production implies a cultural transposition, if only because of gaps of a temporal or geographical nature. The question of interculturality in the theatre[46] has been articulated around questions on the staging of universal classical works, especially stagings by Brook and Mnouchkine in the 1970s and 1980s. Since the fall of the Berlin Wall (in 1989) the debate on multiculturalism has shifted to a North/South opposition. It is sometimes absorbed into – or twisted by – the question of religious fundamentalism, which discourages the most well-intentioned artists. The turn of the century does know how to negotiate the intercultural turn. Experimental theatre – leaving to one side international showbiz – is suspicious of cultural hybridity, for fear not that it might épater le bourgeois, but rather that it might shock the sensibilities of local fundamentalists or the wardens of political correctness.

Fortunately, miracles still happen – some productions dodge or transcend such polico-cultural baseness. Philippe Adrien's *Phèdre* is one example. The staging invents a new way of reconciling different cultural demands by placing them at the service of the interpretation of the play. It is nevertheless not an intercultural mise en scène in the 1970s sense, since even the black actors (who mainly come from Martinique) do not seek to reference any African acting technique. Indeed, the play cannot be located in any given geographical context: Aurélie Dalmat's Phèdre is as Asian as she is African: the Antillais, white, mixed race and black actors are here not bound to any determined geographical context. And yet the production is not entirely 'colour blind' either: the spectator is allowed to be grabbed and marvelled by the beauty and strangeness of the different bodies and skin-tones. Racine's imaginary, which is 'both fantastical and archaic', adapts well to the 'complex mix of influences and characteristics – African, Caribbean, Indian – specific to the Antilles',[47] a mix that would perhaps be alien to ancient Greece, or the court of Louis XIV, but not to Antiquity as a whole, with its 'labyrinthine', 'Amazonian', 'Neptunian', 'Creto-Minotaurian' imaginary.

The power of this production comes from the actors, and notably from their impeccable delivery of the alexandrines. This diction is the necessary form in order that the story holds together and in order that the characters retain their identities. There are no mistakes and no hesitations in Phèdre's delivery. She appears in a succession of striking items of headwear, with each change of hat corresponding to a new phase in the evolution of the character and the story. The

Figure 11.5 Phèdre by Racine, directed by Philippe Adrien.
© Antonia Bozzi.

sensuality of Phèdre can finally be sensed: she is indeed a mature woman, and not a child like Dominique Blanc's interpretation of the role. This Phèdre is 'experienced', whereas little Hippolyte is still wet behind the ears: the little stick he uses as a sword hides a weapon that is not much of a deterrent. With his stag's horns, Thésée seems somewhat primitive, or shamanic, but he is pitiful too; a patriarch gone wrong, he is completely ridiculous. Théramène perfectly controls diction and rhythm, especially in the final speech: he reestablishes order. This casting and interpretation are rooted in very coherent dramaturgical analysis.

No pedant is present to tell us how to reread the play, in the manner of Mauron, Barthes or Goldmann, doubtless only because we have assimilated their conclusions, and they are obvious. Refusing a new or global reading from above, and ground-breaking hermeneutical discoveries, Philippe Adrien and company return to the essential: to show and share passion. We find pleasure in hearing a tragic story carried by bodies from today, beyond cultural differences. Suddenly, a line reminds us that intercultural theatre is still to come or still to come back.

A few signs of the times

All of these changes, as tiny they might be, lead eventually to a new zeitgeist. At the risk of seeing this sublime spirit coming to life as a banal identikit picture, a few rapid remarks might be in order.

Cases of deconstruction are fairly rare, at least in France where the weight of the past remains palpable. Who, apart from the Théâtre du Radeau, is practising deconstruction on France's stages? A few groups that are regularly invited to perform, such as the *Volksbühne* of Castorf and Pollesch, New York's the Wooster Group, the theatre of Arpád Schilling, and the theatre of Jürgen Gosch.

And yet we should still distinguish between deconstruction and provocation: Castorf and Gosch engage more in a demystification and desacralisation than in a true deconstruction in the Derridean definition.[48] Their shows and their performances (in the performance-art sense) reconnect with the Viennese actionism of the 1960s (Otto Mühl, Hermann Nitsch and so on).

Text is frequently desacralised. Jürgen Gosch's desacralisation is as banal as it is anal. In his staging of Macbeth,[49] Gosch even managed to shock young German theatregoers, which says something of the amplitude of his provocation. The play is performed in an excellent and faithful German translation by Angela Schanelec. The actors of the Düsseldorf Stadttheater – seven men played all the roles – have impeccable vocal technique, a sense of space and impressive timing. They know how to shout and to murmur, to inhabit their role and take their distance, to follow the gestural score and improvise. Thanks to them, the work maintains a humid freshness. Arriving in modern dress, it takes them little time to stand on the tables and take off their clothes, then to fight in a mire of fake blood and excrement, generously poured from plastic bottles onto the bodies and the ground. The poor taste, the crudity or even cruelty, but also the comedy, the lightness and the theatricality are at the very heart of this act of violence. They leave the spectator if not pensive then at least amazed by this unprecedented marriage of the horrible and the playful. This nudity, more excremental than artistic, parodied and 'prettified' by purely theatrical means, seems rather healthy. It leads to a collective release for the actors as well as the audience. It also shows all the difference between the true violence of the story and of the characters in *Macbeth*, with the violence of football fans and patriots singing the American national anthem.

At other moments, the physical expenditure is not merely parodied; it is literal, like a potlatch[50] or a performance offered to us by the actors: for example the one-on-one final fight between Macbeth and Macduff. Unlike Castorf's shows, Gosch gives us the keys and the references to follow a story that he respects in all its continuity and complexity. The dramatic thread, unlike that of Castorf's shows, is readable, albeit thin, repetitive and liquid. There is a (b)analisation of the work, since everything happens in the same run-down style, in the same violent and sordid atmosphere. Everything is banal, because everything is the same in a horror conceived as obvious: everything is anal also, because the story can be reduced to a sadistic-anal problem.

According to Freud, anality is a sexual activity based on the function of defecation. In the sadistic-anal phase, the subject is submitted to a destructive and regressive tendency, especially in thoughts. The actors of this *Macbeth* have the visible and infantile pleasure of spraying themselves with red liquid, of defecating as a group, then of rolling around in their excrement, of defying the disapproving gaze of the audience and of decent society. At the same time, this provocation is purely playful and theatrical: we see the actors pouring the liquid and fecal matter, and they all have fun like big disobedient babies.

Let us attempt the following general hypothesis: there might be two traditions and two types of performance, wet and dry. In wet theatre, the actor gets wet feet, literally and figuratively, taking risks, breaking a sweat, externally and internally, producing an excess of energy that leads to an overflow of bodily fluid, of residue, of detritus and of filth produced onstage. This style is very current on the contemporary German stage, whatever is being performed, classical or modern. On the other hand, dry theatre (for example classical French tragedy which is 'represented' and not 'performed' or 'acted out' on most French stages) stays dry, linked to the word alone, to pure language: the symbolic replaces the literal, the cerebral neutralises the visceral, dry convention takes the place of realities. The actors of this *Macbeth* get their feet wet in every sense of the word: they dirty the few clothes they have, exposing their skin. They endlessly take great physical risks: they run the risk of falling on the stage or even slipping off it, into the obscene, of stumbling on a text or subtext that is difficult to read, or on the frightened and disapproving looks of the audience, distracted from the essential. But does it make sense, in the essential sense?

These two traditions and stage practices rarely appear in their pure form. By getting dry, a performance loses its radical nature, but it gains clarity and rationality: it becomes more readable. Thus, this *Macbeth* 'dries up' as soon as it acquires any abstraction, as soon as we lend it the slightest interpretation. It becomes almost bloodless, and

Figure 11.6 Macbeth, directed by Jürgen Gosch. © Patrice Pavis.

dries up, as soon as we understand things, as soon as we seek to define its power mechanisms. Conversely, an explanation that is too dry, too intellectual and cerebral quickly tires the spectator. It demands a concrete figuring, it requires a touch of madness, a dose of disorder, a stream of water to wet the stage and incite the actors to revel in a sense of delicious provocation and the spectators to accompany them with their thoughts.

(B)anal desacralisation of the great texts means that nothing is safe from water damage, from the pleasures of anal regression, from the imperious need to rub up against everything that is wet and dirty, from the anal, banal but normal, phase.

Syncretism of interpretations always heralds the greatest successes. Here are two examples from an infinite supply: *Le jeu de l'amour et du hasard*, directed by Jacques Kraemer, and Ariane Mnouchkine's *Tartuffe*.

In *Le jeu de l'amour et du hasard*, Kraemer maintains the illusion of a classic in costume, with the gestural and verbal elegance of his actresses, but he also produces a strong contemporaneity effect. Thus the first scene sees Sylvia and her servant sleeping under the same sheet, fighting over it while discussing the virtues of marriage. The bodies, the gestures, the freedom of speech are contemporary. We immediately identify with the scene; we walk straight in, unfettered, into this charming imaginary universe. Then, when Lisette finishes dressing

Figure 11.7 Macbeth, directed by Jürgen Gosch. © Patrice Pavis.

her mistress, the tone changes, according to the well-known principle that the clothes make the man (or the woman): we discover the social relationships of the period. The play no longer needs to be actualised, and social and historical distance come back with a vengeance. Throughout the performance, Kraemer unfolds every possible stage interpretation, and finds every way of touching the spectator.

In *Tartuffe*, Ariane Mnouchkine combines several acting methods. She recontextualises the play by locating it in a Muslim country, where fundamentalism threatens families and society. This leads her to a political analysis of Islamism, and the religious and economic grip of the phenomenon. By confronting, as in Molière, the family controlled by Tartuffe and the society invaded by false devotees, confronting the intimate and the political, she offers an overall explanation; she enriches the different levels of interpretation. The acting constantly changes in terms of register and genre: farce, political play, historical play, psychological comedy. Mnouchkine necessarily addresses the intercultural question by way of the widened thematic content of the play and by confronting actors coming from very different places. To this she adds a method and a touch that is 'very Théâtre du Soleil': direct address to the audience and a frontal form of acting, the physical expression of all the emotions is conveyed by the text and embodied by the actors. Thus the mise en scène reconciles different perspectives on the play. This syncretism of perspectives leads in reality to a natural synthesis of debates in existence since the 1960s, not without sometimes risking taking us back to the notorious debate on fidelity to the text: proof that philological debate still occupies the minds of the postmoderns and the postdramatics alike.

The debate on faithfulness resurfaces from time to time, taking different names, of course – for example the distinction made by Didier Plassard between 'stagings with a view to restitution' and 'stagings with a view to projection'.[51] This distinction should not be confused with the 'break between directors who see text as text, and those who see it as material'.[52] This latter distinction, made by Braunschweig, seems indeed to characterise two types of practice and to correspond to a real difference between two productions, which deserve a specific and distinct theoretical treatment.[53]

For stagings of classics, precisely defined as a dramatic text considered intangible or even sacred, the 'author-ity' of the play, implicit reference to an author and author's text, remains the most common position. Only extreme (and indeed fascinating) experimental productions, like those produced by Robert Wilson, Romeo Castellucci, François Tanguy and Frank Castorf conceive of the text as pure sonic material, and do not take on the task of 'staging' it. Such scattered material does not suffice to envisage a totality, or to construct a fiction or story. Nevertheless, there are clearly no rules, or clear limits between a text transmitted onto a stage and a material used musically, without recourse to the meaning. Whatever the real, theoretical and practical difficulties of distinguishing between text and material, it is still possible to judge whether a particular agency – a director, an actor, a scenographer and so on – was in charge of the shift from page to stage (or whether such an agency sought to use one to shed light on the other). The point is to find out how the written, and then staged, work is interpreted. The findings of the humanities since the 1960s remain at our disposal, even if we no longer believe in the possibility or the benefit of exhausting a text and offering a definitive interpretation. Refusing any explanation, refusing every theory, is not really a sign of maturity, and thus the discussion must go on.

As for the distinction between restitution and projection, it is unclear how such criteria should be established: how can we know what the text actually contains; how can we know what is 'restituted' by way of mise en scène and what is 'projected' onto the text from the outside, by the artist in charge of staging the text? Can we differentiate so cleanly? To do so would presuppose that we can know what is to be restituted from the text, and what constitutes the integrant and essential part. But who is up to the task? To differentiate would also presuppose, on the other hand, that we have no right to look at the text to be staged from an exterior, 'unpredictable' point of view. But whether the (contemporary or classical) play is staged by a director or simply interpreted by a reader, there is always necessarily an outside gaze, which updates it, makes it exist – a gaze full of all kinds of projections. And thus we must concede that restitution and projection go hand in hand. It remains to show how, but is that not precisely the art of mise en scène?

General conclusions

- The mise en scène of classical plays went through its great classical period between 1950 and 1980. Such practices of interpreting canonical texts must be preserved as experiments that can still serve a purpose. They are constantly recycled and often without correct referencing.
- The cultural politics that inform these great manoeuvres is barely decipherable, varying from country to country and from context to context. We should therefore beware of hasty generalisations. For many theatres, programming a classic remains a guarantee of commercial success, avoiding risk. Such programming choices no longer even need to invoke the benefits of popular education. Stuck between an incomprehensible political landscape and an anonymous cultural industry, it will often lead to work that is poor, lacking any radical substance or even relevance. No surprise there, then!
- Nevertheless, and contrary to alarmist prognostics, might we not anticipate at some point a new era inaugurating an ecology of the classics? Instead of looking for the solution to a text (a golden opportunity), the stage increasingly sees the classics as renewable energy, part of sustainable development. Thanks to the possibilities of storage and conservation, each new staging is in for the long haul, a long-term process. Each staging extracts from the play that which is important for that moment alone; it is limited to one or two new insights. Recent attempts at *Le Misanthrope* by Lassalle, Braunschweig, Loyon, Lambert and Hergenröder are characteristic of this patient work, wherein each staging does not cancel out the previous ones, but deepens our knowledge about the play.
- Anyone who saw all of these productions, these concretisations of a single work, would understand that it is inexhaustible and renewable; only on the condition, however, that we do not

completely exhaust it, that we do not make it say everything and say nothing, or leave it with nothing (left) to say to future generations. Arpád Schilling's *Hamlet*, from the land of Attila the Hun, is perhaps the epitome of this kind of over-exploitation.

- Faced with open provocation, we should not ask ourselves if a particular case is overstated, scandalous, disgusting or immoral. Rather (and prosaically), we should ask whether a new energy is being released, or if the possibility and the pleasures of any other reading are being irretrievably destroyed. Intuitively and without available proof, we might suggest that Castorf, in a nihilistic fashion, destroys our will to know, while Gosch's naked men, enthusiastically rolling around in excrement, help us put our finger on the will to power and appetite for power (and this is not without worth).

- We remain in search of an analysis and a dramaturgical reading of the play that can be translated in terms of staging. It is the least we can do. Nevertheless, the current tendency of stage figuration tends towards a limitation of the visual and explanatory excess of the years from the 1960s and 1980s, and thus towards the disappearance of the dramaturgical view. The performance no longer seeks to illustrate the text by way of visual excess (supposed to fix it in a precise and figurative context). It is content to set a few reference points for the text, to provide a few indications and acting conventions. In this way it is subject to the influence of contemporary writing and its spartan acting. 'The project of writing is not separate from that of staging, acting, etc. – mise en scène does not illustrate the text, it gives it its urgency, it makes it live by lending it a voice and some muscles.'[54]

- The mistrust between the great means of the stage grows: there are no more metaphors or images that globally signify a location or a mental landscape, there is no more arrangement allowing for a collective political alienation, there is no longer any purely rhetorical use of the stage.

- The challenge is altogether different: to access a better knowledge of the stage practice of the past. Not in order to discover the right solution for today's staging, but the better to understand how this 'textual flower', the only remaining trace we have, opened up in the soil of an extinct theatrical practice. We thus seek to read this work within its time and according to its style, knowing that we must be 'inventive', because we were not there. And, at the same time, we imagine a new stage practice, so as to see the play in a new light.

- This historical work obliges us to return to, to test, and to develop methods of textual analysis, taking note of everything that was learned in the last thirty years. This even leads us to return to the methodological questions that the postmodern and the postdramatic claimed to have overcome. This means that we should not jump the gun, or burn our bridges, but patiently go back to analysis and knowledge of the text. Few are prepared for this humble and thankless task. Literary or theatrical theory should not be on the defensive faced with performance studies, nor should it be inhibited faced with this imperialist domain, but rather it should be conscious of its necessity and of the key role it has to play.

- Should the gauntlet not be thrown down to postmodernism and the postdramatic, asking what these labels hide, and also reveal? The challenge is to observe and to describe the deconstruction of the text or production. In actually seeking out in concrete terms what follows postmodernism, or what comes after drama and theatre, the spell of the 'post' (of the eternal present, endless youth, which fascinates but also imprisons) might be broken. Presentism will not last forever. The postdramatic is surely just a passing moment.

- Whatever the labels, the important thing is to work out what they – more or less voluntarily – describe, what they hide under the slick and easy terms 'deconstruction' and 'provocation'.

- Such terms participate in the debate on forms of culture in the postmodern world. Since the 1980s, the culturalist conception has dominated the discussion. Everything was a question of rehabilitating undervalued cultures, marginal texts, little-known practices and less academic styles. The impact of culturalism on theatre has been appreciable. It has appeared in the levelling of readings, the interchangeability of interpretations, and finally in the disappearance of original or provocative offerings. Since this culturalist democratisation, it has become very difficult for young directors to get back in the ring, to get over the progressive stage, the degradation of the artistic into the cultural, of the cultural into the sociocultural. But does the reconciliation of mise en scène and the art of the classics not demand a return to form? Only a genius could say if the view from the top is worth the climb.

The range of different works, of perspectives, of artists, and especially of spectators makes it difficult – if not impossible – to establish precise categories of mise en scène.

Even if we limit ourselves to seven shows seen in Avignon in 2006, chosen almost at random, according to inexpressible or unjustifiable expectations and tastes, the body of work demonstrates an infinite number of properties, functions and facets that would put off even the most quibbling of analysts.

We had expected, that summer, merely to extract seven principles, seven functions of mise en scène, seven among others: harmony, recontextualisation, settling, assemblage, crossing, framing, silence. Seven ways of showing and saying the real.*

Seven, like the seven wonders of the world or the seven days of the week.

But on the seventh day, we were overtaken by doubt and a silence fell: what if no theory of mise en scène could be created? What if this was nothing more than a cluster of particular instances, of isolated examples, without links, without logic, without a future; what if we could not make head nor tail of it? What if it was merely a formless representation, an indescribable empirical object, an unspeakable experience, a dull art form refusing all theoretical reflection?

And what if everything we said was nothing more than pure fiction, in theatre as in life? What if theatre was pushing us into a corner?

In theatre as in life, this would be a risk worth running.

* See our article *Théâtre/Public*, no. 183, pp. 65–74.

12 Staging calamity

Mise en scène and performance at Avignon 2005

The effect produced

The notion of the effect produced (*Wirkung* in German) has seen little use in theatre theory and yet is very useful if one seeks to examine how theatre acts upon society, the audience, or on the spectator. It should be defined in opposition to the notion of reception, that is the way in which society, the audience, or the spectator reacts to the dramatic text or its performance. These two notions: the effect produced, and reception (which are not always differentiated in common usage) lead us to understand how theatre influences us and how in turn we influence theatre.

In the 1960s and 1970s, German aesthetic theory contrasted *Wirkungsästhetik* (aesthetics of the effect produced) to *Rezeptionsästhetik* (aesthetics of reception) and it was a question of knowing if, in order to analyse texts, one should take into account the mechanisms of production, or rather focus on the act of reading and of reception. The aesthetics of reception filled a gap: audiences' lack of knowledge and their horizons of expectation, something that the study of authors and of their writing techniques had often overlooked. Today, we acknowledge that the production and reception of a literary or theatre work must both be addressed, and we know that the production of effects must not be separated from the way in which these effects are received by the reader or spectator.

The notion of effect has a long classical tradition behind it. The effect produced is more readily observed on the spectator than on the reader, and it is in this regard that classical theatre takes an interest in the notion, as if to check whether theatre is effective: "let us observe in a comedy only the effect it has upon us" suggests Molière (*La Critique de l'école des femmes*, sc. 6). Racine, too, underlines that that the effect of his theatre is universal and lasting: "I have recognised with pleasure, by way of the effect produced upon our theatre by all that I have imitated from Homer or Euripides, that common sense and reason were the same in every century" (Preface to *Iphigénie*).

Whether it be a question of comedy or tragedy, of the Greeks or the French, of the audience of the 17th Century or of the 21st Century, theatre produces effects that are distinct from those produced by the other arts. The performance is necessarily 'live'; it brings together, if only for a short moment, everything onstage (the actor, the text spoken, 'stage effects') and the spectator, in a unique and unrepeatable event. For the duration of this event, there is even a communication and a motion of to and fro between the stage and the auditorium, the effect produced is also sensitive, by way of feedback, to the actors' performance.

'Good' or 'bad' reception/reaction rebound into the performance, facilitating or hindering it. A history of the influence of audiences or societies on dramatic texts, performances, and productions remains to be written. And what is mise en scène if not a mechanism (one that became indispensable in the late 19th Century) to adapt the work shown to the specific audience intended to be its recipients, and thus a recognition of the role of the receiver in the creation of stage performance?

In order to imagine this history of effects produced (by theatre upon the audience and by the audience upon the theatre), one must begin by specifying what exactly effects the spectator: theatre in general? The play that is read? The performance ? The style of the mise en scène? It is also appropriate to distinguish the effect produced according to the type of receiver as well as the mode of reception, and particularly its duration.

At whatever level the text or the performance are approached, it is clear that the effect they produce upon the reader or spectator depend as much on the object itself (its configuration) as on the receiver (its identity). The notion of effect produced operates as a mediation between production and reception. To determine the effect produced by a performance requires both that the manner in which it was produced be established and that the expectation according to which it is received and understood be imagined. If we only take the example of the mise en scène, there are two ways in which this can be approached: to describe the tasks and working process of the director, or instead to reconstitute the role of the spectator within it in terms of expectation and the concrete situation. Production and reception are intimately linked and are interdependent: production anticipates its effects on the spectator and imagines that what will be understood of the received object reconstitutes the project, and even the intentions, of the staging. Thus, to stage a play is as much about implementing a material and its development in the hands of the actors and other artists as it is about taking heed of the changing view of the spectators according to their customs, expectations, their new situation. Being aware of the effect produced thus prevents us from focusing on only one of the two sides of the theatre event - production/reception - from reintroducing a dualistic model by applying the communication grid (transmitter/receiver) on the theatre work.

Therefore, we clearly see that to stage is to generate and maintain the interest of the spectator, to instil in the spectator the desire to see and to understand, without which nothing can be achieved. There exists, however, no universal theory of effects, nor any infallible recipes for reaching the spectator. This is because the important thing is not the intrinsic value of the signs and the effects of any particular 'stage language' (music, space, design, language, etc.), but rather the combinations, proper to each staging (and even to each 'stage' in the performance) - all of the materials. Only a 'militant' and political aesthetics, like Brecht's, for example, is keen to calculate the respective effects of each of these languages. Thus, Brecht advised the worker in charge of making the set (*Bühnenbauer*) to set up a 'chart of possible effects' and suggested that he mark, for each scene in each play, the quantum of effect (*Wirkungsquanten*), for example, "social markers, historical markers, alienation effects, aesthetic effects, poetic effects, technical innovations, effects of tradition, destruction of illusion, exhibition value". This construction-worker's checklist for the stage seems mechanical and difficult to test, but it at least measures the power of different effects and outlines their range.

Thus the effects of theatre are countless. But to measure these effects produced upon the spectator is not easy, since there exists no clear, or final typology of effects. Might we not instead, and not without recourse to metaphor, imagine what "internal staging" the spectator creates once "affected by the staging": how does the mise en scène embed itself, carve itself, sculpt itself within the spectators? Cognitive psychology might perhaps help us to see how the stage configuration gets lodged into the imagination and the body of the spectator as a 'negative figure' of the perceived or hallucinated figure coming from the stage. The spectator perceives it and feels it like a re-play, like an interior mime, specifically a mime of the actors' moves on the stage. The spectator is able to comprehend an entirety, an imaginary network that the staging has endeavoured to set up. The spectators are aware, with an embodied awareness, that the performance, in the process of the mise en scène, always leaves traces within them - be it by way of a sensation, an aesthetic pleasure, a figure or an overall score. This effect upon the spectators provides the certainty that everything is organised around them, without being entirely explainable or communicable.

The director always asks: how should I ensure that something emerges for a spectator, "my fellow, my brother" (Baudelaire), so that my art has an effect upon them?

Even before the fifty-ninth Avignon Festival began, if anyone heeded the press or listened to the festival regulars, one thing seemed clear: there would be no more theatre, either classical or contemporary. Mise en scène would give way to performance art, and all the productions would be struck with the same despair, blighted by all the calamities of the world. Calamity, in all its forms from destruction to catastrophe, offered the only theme common to all the productions I saw at Avignon 2005. This tendency reveals an obsession and a profound discontent that we should take seriously: but is this civilization and its discontents, or culture and its calamities? Things have escalated since Freud, but we should be on guard against catastrophism, a fascination with unhappiness. So let us instead content ourselves with recounting the week and seeing how it might have taught us to face unhappiness and to work for the theatre.

On paper, and perhaps in the minds of the festival directors, Hortense Archambault and Vincent Baudrier, and of the guest artistic director, Jan Fabre, the festival was a golden opportunity to bring together 'artists of the stage' who, 'by way of their creations, question our human identity spiritually and as animals', 'examining our relationship with our bodies and with our fantasies, our relationship with beauty, but also with violence, things which sometimes coexist in us'.[1]

We should check this proposition by analysing eight productions seen in the festival's first week. 'Calamity' is a sufficiently general leitmotif to allow us to make comparisons. If catastrophe is a punctual and irreversible phenomenon, calamity is a more lasting, or even permanent, state: a scourge affecting crops, an ecological disaster hitting a region, a misfortune or collapse affecting a people. Whether it is a natural disaster or a human-made one, calamity brings about a long-lasting state of apathy for many artists. Their works nonetheless often show a will to overcome the dead end brought about by calamity and to seek a fictional and aesthetic way out of the crisis. As always, artists' responses are individual, and it is thus more valuable to analyse their achievements than their discourses – their commentaries or what we assume to be the intentions that accompany and sometimes even precede them.

Once the theme of calamity had been identified (and it would have been difficult to miss it!), it became necessary to ask how different productions treat and represent this theme. We make a distinction between two kinds of representation, mise en scène and performance art: mise en scène, meaning theatre as we have known it since the end of the nineteenth century; and performance, as it has been practised since the 1960s. If none of these eight productions can be called performance art in the strictest sense, each contains moments of performativity in which the present moment, risk, uncertainty or chance prevent any fictional representation of an event. Despite this mixing of representational modes, the distinction endures. We must simply grasp their unfailing alliance. Everything hinges on the question of presence and representation of meaning. According to Alain Badiou, theatre is 'the perception of the instant as an instant of thought'.[2] Is performance art not, then, the perception of theatre as a thought of the instant?

The audience obviously does not ask itself whether it is attending a mise en scène or participating in performance art. The spectator setting foot in Avignon suspects that things will not be easy, that simple mimetic representations of the world cannot be hoped for, and that they must 'go with the flow'. Nothing surprises or shocks the audience: what is a naked body, or a snake hanging over a well-trained dog, compared with a kamikaze who kills scores of bystanders? The audience has become used to media representations of the worst calamities or feels protected by an imaginary bubble, not believing – if only in order to go on living – that bombs and catastrophes could one day befall them, like a calamity, a real calamity.

L'histoire des larmes

'May our bodies weep / to prevent a catastrophe' is the claim of the Knight of Despair in *L'histoire des larmes,* Jan Fabre's production, which opened the festival a few days before the reprise of *Je suis sang.*[3] This leitmotif of the production also offers a key to most of the official festival shows.

Most of the Avignon productions required the free expression of a sympathetic, rather than heroic, body pushed to its extremes in order to save humanity from the calamity in which it finds itself. The body without language – dance more than dramatic art – appears, at first sight, capable of meeting this requirement. But in order to represent and show calamity, the responses vary from artist to artist. There are basically two solutions: mise en scène and performance art. Mise en scène requires dramatic fiction, representation; performance art presents a live, unrepeatable, real, not fictive, action. The examples I have chosen vacillate between these two theoretical poles, making any distinction problematic.

L'histoire des larmes is above all a choreographic piece, a production organised as movement in space. In the Cour d'Honneur of the Palais des Papes, Fabre brought together percussionists, dancers and actors. There are three actors, playing the Knight of Despair, the Dog (Diogenes the Cynical) and the Rock, and all have the power of speech. The Knight operates at centre stage; the Dog runs from one side to the other; the Rock, '*obscenam in mulierem*', speaks from a window in the facade, almost offstage – ob-scene, meaning in front of the Latin *scaena*, so on the edge of the playing space. They take the floor regularly for fairly long monologues, but the show does not hinge on this spoken dramaturgy.

The composition incorporates the vast expanses of the Cour d'Honneur and the facade, the trajectory of the groups and objects, and the temporal unfolding of the musical score (renaissance harp, percussion and voice). With an admirable architectural and pictorial sense, Fabre gives us one scene after another each in a different style, from an individual routine to a ballet for six or eight dancers, to simultaneous and coordinated actions. As in a Hieronymus Bosch painting (think of his *Last Judgment* at the Alte Pinacothek in Munich), elements are juxtaposed with a certain autonomy, but the viewer is in a position to perceive a figure of the whole all the more easily, since the huge percussion instruments and the musical compositions of Eric Sleichim create an auditory continuum and make the spatiotemporal composition, the symmetry of the motifs, more noticeable.

We fleetingly notice occasional references to Bosch's grotesque figures climbing immense cliff faces. They are monstrous forms, such as eiderdowns with feet criss-crossing the stage. At times an image surfaces in the production: for instance, glass blown on long sticks. The glass vessels the dancers lie on are both concrete and abstract – that is to say, allegorical – manifestations of human tears. The auditory, pictorial and choreographic composition, and the appearance and development of visual motifs, all have their own logic; they are not subject to the text. Indeed, the verbal utterances seem more like foreign bodies in the overall composition, especially those of the Knight, spoken with a slight accent and a certain distance, as if split from the image and the visual and auditory event. There is no fixed, frozen or global image, as in a Wagnerian *Gesamtkunstwerk*, but rather moments of explosion, flashes of light, fleeting references to medieval painting. Never does the closed system of mise en scène, coherent in relation to a dramaturgical conception or a philosophy, come into play. This production has nothing of the 'histoire des larmes' seen by Roland Barthes:

> In which societies, in which periods, have we wept? Since when is it that men (and not women) no longer cry? ... Perhaps 'weeping' is too crude; perhaps we must not refer all tears to one and the same signification.[4]

Fabre does not consider tears in a cultural history of emotion. He sees them simply as a watery secretion, alongside sweat, urine and to a lesser extent semen, these 'golden tears [which] compose love songs and symphonies of joy', as the Knight so poetically puts it.[5]

But where does this Knight come from? From the wandering knights of our time, artists? And what philosophy is he advocating? He has some very fixed ideas about bodily fluids, particularly tears: 'The crying body / can bring about / a magical transformation of the world', he says.[6] This magical thinking is impregnated with ideal-ism – as he points out, 'Thought is a heritage of the soul.'[31] Often declamatory, explicit and talkative, the Knight is concerned about the drying out of human beings, but his message remains obscure. Do the tears take us back to the tragic nature of existence or to the biological necessity of hydrating body and mind? Faced with such a dubious philosophy, and given the beauty and power of the images, we might be tempted to disregard the words in favour of bathing in the sensuality of the visual and auditory. Far from being text-based theatre, this heterogeneous production is made up of choreographic and musical fragments arising from improvisation and reworked by Fabre.

Moments of performance art occur whenever an action is repeated or prolonged in an improvisation. Ironic counterpoints are always a possibility – for example, the stage rain at the end in the style of *Singin' in the Rain*, right after a lament about things drying out.

Je suis sang

In *Je suis sang*, we find the same principles of composition, in particular in the coordination of the stage actions and the very didactic final text. This production, which originally premiered in 2003, deals with blood (as its title would suggest), a subject of vital importance for medieval thought and desperately neglected in our times. The final litany, 'Je suis sang, sanguis sum', is taken up by a chorus of dancers, when a red liquid, more like wine than blood, is sprinkled, taking us back to a Dionysian ritual and to a vitality that the Renaissance and the evolution of civilisation have supposedly repressed. This call for a society that no longer oppresses such instincts is strangely reminiscent of the birth of tragedy according to Nietzsche.

Je suis sang finds a balance between the harmony of forms and the turbulent violence of blood. Here too, are the Dionysian and Apollonian forces, 'both of these artistic drives are required to unfold their energies in strict, reciprocal proportion, according to the law of eternal justice'.[32] What threatens humanity with annihilation would therefore be the death of instinct, the taming of the body, the anaemia caused by the civilising process of modern times. But is it a cause or a consequence? What the spectator perceives is just as much about violence, castration and bloodshed. Calamity is preprogrammed ('the blue planet will become red'), parodied ('the tango of the butchers of the La Villette slaughterhouse'), aestheticised, and all of this along with the realistic representation of violence: stumps oozing blood, severed genitals, women dancing with their hands tied behind their backs, tortured bodies emptied of blood. Once again, the text shocks by way of its directness and naïveté: 'I like my impotence', 'jouissance beyond jouissance', 'I am a wounded, uninterested man.'

Fortunately, the stage event always takes the upper hand over such textual moments. The constant production of new images, visual shocks, the overflowing imagination of the images, and the virtuosity and energy of the dancers give new impetus to the production. There is nothing perverse or decadent in this picture of destruction and reconstruction, only an overflowing vital energy that refuses to be channelled into veins, into words, or into stage space, and that flows abundantly while the blood inscribes itself onto the black of the stage and the white of the wedding gowns. Calamity, be it an absence of water or of blood, is never the final state of things, because everybody fights against it. When speech makes an appearance, as direct as it may be, it also becomes an impetus for reaction and the surpassing of self.

Dieu et les esprits vivants

Dieu et les esprits vivants, written and directed by Jan Decorte, is a disconcerting experience. The story is scarcely comprehensible, and the silent presence of Decorte, as a monk/soldier, in no way enlightening. Even if, as the programme states, 'this is writing, not biography', and if 'the way of writing has nothing to do with automatic writing, it's more of a writing directed in all directions', the reader instinctively searches for meaning, for a narrative direction. As Decorte further explains:

> *Dieu et les esprits vivants* encompasses a great deal of subjects: good and evil, language, the world and so much more, but it is probably above all a text about murder. It's a kind of anatomy, philology, or encyclopaedia of murder. Something sends this man named Blood-Wolf-Devil into a mad rage, mad with rage to the point of killing.[9]

While calamity is anonymous, murder is personal, provided we understand the motives; in this case we don't even know if it has even been committed. This situation would not be hopeless if the stage action caught the attention in such a way as to transport the spectator into a dream world. Yet this spectator merely witnesses, for the first twenty minutes, the actor washing his entire body from head to toe. Throughout this unending introit, the spectator waits for a real beginning, the start of the fiction. But the washing has no other function than to test the patience of the audience, provoking anger or boredom. The only remaining option is to see this long episode as a provocation, a moment of performance art intended to make the spectators reflect on their expectations, limits and impatience. The only thing preventing us from definitively rejecting the piece is Arno's haunting music, providing an uncanny basso continuo. Likewise, the audience appreciates the dance solo by the great choreographer Anne Teresa de Keersmaeker, who appears, without dramaturgical justification, for a virtuosic impromptu number done in a 1980s style. The washing, music and dance number are autonomous moments of performance art within a production that finds it hard to get off the ground or create an illusion of a possible world.

In the same way, the tour de force of Sigrid Vinks, who speaks the text, finally earns our attention: the strangeness of her words, her slightly foreign accent, the relationship of entranced confidence she shares with the audience, her way of leaning forward, showing the palms of her hands – all of this creates an intimacy and a tension which owe nothing to textual fiction. It is a performance art effect, as unexpected in a murder story as it is in a traditional staging. This performance would surely seem lean compared with what has been left aside: the untapped beauty of the space, the inanity of the text, the provocation that wears itself (and us) out, the monotony of the hopping of the monk. It's a total disaster, and makes one miss even Fabre's obsessions.

B.#03 Berlin

The question of calamity, as opposed to tragic catastrophe, has always been at the heart of the work of the Societas Raffaello Sanzio, the company run by Claudia and Romeo Castellucci and Chiara Guidi. Since 2002, they have produced eleven episodes of the *Tragedia Endogonidia*, a tragedy destined to grow by fission, that has already given birth to a dozen offspring in various European cities. *B.#03 Berlin*, shown at Avignon's municipal theatre, is, according to the programme:

> an Episode that tells the parable of the life and death of a woman who has known motherhood, crime and the confusion between the power of life and the power of death. Her anonymity is confused with that of the audience, while her lack of speech, her weakness before the law and her helpless pain constitute the essential conditions for this tragedy, which also includes the 'role' of the spectator by way of a metaphor of stalls inhabited by rabbits.

Who could understand such a muddled text? The important thing is the production! Reading these commentaries or Castellucci's theoretical musings will only confuse the well-meaning spectator. This is even more the case since the Castelluccis define tragedy in terms that might better describe calamity: anonymity, the absence of speech, the confusion between life and death. It is obvious in any case that it is no longer a question of Greek tragedy, but of an 'inhuman' tragedy yet to come, which is precisely the object of their theatrical research. 'I feel', says Romeo, 'that this will be a cold, transparent, clean and unnamed tragedy. I feel that nobody will realise they are faced with a tragedy and that will be the best proof of its effectiveness.'[10]

If we use only the images shown onstage in *B.#03 Berlin*, we observe a series of tableaux in constant development, figures made foggy by the gauze (or plastic) curtain separating stage from auditorium. There is always, in the literal as well as figurative sense, a screen between us and the action. We never have access to a clear perception of the objects and the bodies; they are represented by silhouettes, shadows, forms or phantoms. Only a King Kong, whether the famous gorilla or the brown Berliner bear, comes to the foreground, in his traditional outfit, to move rabbit corpses around with a fork, an image we know well from the concentration camps. Behind the curtain, which becomes more or less translucent depending on the lighting, we can make out scenes of torture or of the intertwined bodies of lovers, and it is not easy to differentiate the two. Crime, vengeance and the massacre of the innocents are clearly out there, but we are refused access. Reality escapes us, as if it were all a mirage. Here, calamity is the impossibility of reaching the real, to see only its shadows, not to – or not yet to – perceive the tragic (as Castellucci rightly states), no longer to possess the instruments necessary for judging and accepting fate. We hope for the tragic, in order at least to know with whom we are dealing, but we only run into calamity, a Medusa's head.

For the Castelluccis, to stage is to propose a series of anthropomorphic figures in constant transformation, without a final destination. To describe and interpret them, we could draw on Panovsky's definition of the work as a formal object and bearer of conventional meaning, and finally as symbol and symptom of the mental attitudes of a time. For example, we might look at an object resembling a pillar, a tomb or perhaps the stone tablet of the Law of Moses. We first identify it as a form that could be toppled; next we think of the familiar form of the tablets of law that a furious Moses smashes before the Israelites; then we watch as a little girl appears, in a moment of calm, to put some order back into this place of calamity, replacing the tablet without thinking. Law is restored, and this image becomes a distillation of the conception of Judeo-Christian cosmology.

This iconographic interpretation allows us to understand how the figures, objects and human beings transform themselves and escape from both their creators and their spectators without ever reaching a final conclusion. At every stage, we must work out exactly where in the Castelluccis' narrative we are and what human figures are emerging. The enigma is never solved; instead it drives the mise en scène, 'a figure that arrives in a flash[;] no sooner has it appeared ... than it disappears. It brings together something that is simultaneously both obvious and enormously complex.'[11]

The theatre of images needs the iron fist of the director, who must stick to the action's through-line and who cannot allow the slightest dip in energy, lest the spectator awaken from the daydream. Castellucci and Guidi manage to do this well, provided that the spectator tolerates the slow changes, the lengthy blurring of figures and the narrative uncertainty. They know at exactly which moments the image must coagulate into a possible meaning before going on its way. They know how to play on the progression of stage images: for example, after the long shaping of a blurry, uncertain, and dreamlike grey image, suddenly a rainbow descends from the flies, marking a contrast and altering the narrative rhythm. At other times, the directors contrast the blurred image with realistic sounds from the score. The sudden use of external elements is not necessarily without opportunism: the quotations in German ('show yourself', 'cross the bridge', 'come here', 'closer', 'eat my ashes', 'eat my metal', 'drink my water') are entirely without justification except as a reminder that the play, funded by the city of Berlin, makes reference to Germany (to its flag, the white Berliner bear, and in inexhaustible allusions, the death camps). The mise en scène is not entirely faithful to its idea of keeping the enigma alive; it ends up telling a story and moreover ending on a note of innocence and hope. Within a chorus of celestial voices, the young girl appears, a sort of Alice in Wonderland, lifting up the tablet of laws, peering through a translucent curtain, looking for a way out, in short bringing a last-minute note of childlike innocence as the curtain drops to the sound of soothing music.

Unlike previous Castellucci productions such as the *Oresteia* and *Genesi*, the stage here does not contain any disruptive element: no animals, no wailing baby, no unpredictable element imported from the world of performance art to threaten visual and aesthetic harmony. Without putting the iconography, so tightly controlled by the mise en scène, in danger, the production – cold and calculated, and beautiful in a glacial way – becomes irreproachable: could we criticize a dream for being too vague, banal or subjective? Would we reproach a director's vision for being too personal, indecipherable or untranslatable? This theatre of images is the culmination of the theatre of art and Western mise en scène. Its score is as beautiful, but also as fragile, as a spider's web.

It remains to be seen whether this production corresponds to this 'cold, transparent, clean and unnamed tragedy', to which we have given the name calamity, in contrast with Greek classical tragedy. Calamity is precisely the unnamed, as yet unimaginable and perhaps unnameable. The Castelluccis approach it through figures struggling with the material to attain a certain figurative and mimetic representation.

When this happens, it either brings us to King Kong, the production's herald of calamity; or to the little girl and the return of innocence. We are left either frightened or surprised, like the rabbits in the stalls.

Anathème

With *Anathème*, the Jacques Delcuvellerie Groupov offers quite another way of addressing calamity. It is the anathema that the God of the Old Testament casts on the peoples that do not do his will: massacres, mass executions, floods and plagues. Yet the anathema, in biblical Greek, is a cursed object as well as a curse. It is at once total condemnation (excommunication for Christians) and the person or people cursed by God. This production is made up of readings by a group of six of extracts from the Hebrew Bible, the Old Testament, recounting the massacres, genocides and collective executions following the divine anathema. For an hour and a half, the Avignon audience is faced with a classical painting depicting an idyllic landscape. Stage left, we hear the readers in their raised platform numbering the destructions, while stage right three singers pick up on certain words as part of a musical composition by Garrett List and Jean-Pierre Urbano. The spectator, or rather the listener, sees only the painting, the light from the music stands, and so must concentrate on hearing the Bible in all its stylistic splendour and shameless cruelty. The diction is not consistent: it is very carefully and discreetly delivered by the women but is dramatic and bombastic when delivered by the men. The audience has trouble concentrating during this unending oratorio; many leave the theatre, having run out of energy and reached the end of their tethers.

The reading nonetheless continues for almost another hour while fifteen people appear onstage one by one. They come from the rear stage via a bridge. Surprised and defiant, each eyes the audience, then undresses and – as part of the same ritual – calmly removes jewels, personal items and clothing, before entering a square of light where all the arrivals remain, seated or standing, until the ceremony's end. We have the impression that these are 'real' people, not professional actors, who have come in from the street or from the audience. They do not play any role or character but rather take their places and wait while studying the audience. However, this act of undressing is not gratuitous; it obtains meaning when linked with the litany of anathemas. We read it as the illustration of the massacre of the innocents, like the final gathering before the Shoah, the gas chambers. In this sense, the stage action of undressing, real or fictional, not only has a direct and gripping impact on the audience but also conveys a very strong message about the violence of religion, the killing frenzy of the supreme being, and the close link between monotheism and genocide. The protest juxtaposes a terrifying (mostly) harmoniously spoken and sung narrative with a mute action, worthy of a happening or a sit-in. This juxtaposition, however, cannot last forever. The reading of the Bible, to which we grow accustomed (and tire of), ends up being little more than background noise – or a mechanical listing of violent acts – and has trouble competing with the presence of naked bodies onstage. These bodies are not aesthetically pleasing nudes; they are the bodies of people of all ages, of all body types, with various types of 'look'. This public display cannot be easy, even if unease is the artists' desired effect. It also has the effect of performance art, as the performers, in the eyes of the majority of the spectators, are not in the elsewhere and before of a fiction, but in the here and now of a real action. Within the theatrical structure (the institution, the stage, the narrative), there are always a few authentic events. Here, nakedness, hearing the Bible, the symbolic violence, and the allusions to extreme situations, as in Bruno Bettelheim's definition, are all traces of real performances addressed to spectators as individuals.

Unfortunately, the remarkably radical 'reality' borrowed from performance art is not backed up by the mise en scène. The space, the Cloître des Carmes, is poorly used; there is a total absence of dramaturgy; the repeated actions are tiresome; the only new action, the construction of a wall, is artificial and superfluous. A Heiner Müller quotation – 'I told you before not to come back, when you're dead, you're dead' – is borrowed from *Bildbeschreibung* (description of a landscape), where it refers to a dead woman brought back from hell but not back to life. Out of context, the line now refers to God, who is also asked not to come back, corresponding to the idea of a return of the religious following the predicted death of God. However, the construction of the small wall seems somewhat childish, particularly because of the animal masks. Thus as soon as radical performance art makes the slightest concession to theatre, the results are unconvincing. Of these eight festival productions, this piece treats calamity in the most radical way. The question is whether performance art can make do without a single illustration via mise en scène and ignore an audience's capabilities and needs to such a great extent.

Puur

With *Puur*, a choreographed piece by Wim Vandekeybus at the Boulbon quarry, calamity is visible in a film showing violent and bloody action. Onstage the dancers do not show this violence mimetically but stylise and aestheticise it. With such explicit film images of violence, it would be easy to become distracted by the themes, but it is better to analyse the physical actions of the dancers, their sequences of gestures and interactions. These danced actions do not produce a clearly decipherable story or message. Vandekeybus sees dance as 'emotions of the flesh onstage' and claims we need a 'state for dance since the state is more important than the content'. We can seek such things as calamity and violence in these emotions and states. Vandekeybus's aesthetic is not unlike Raymond Williams's notion of the 'structure of feeling': the 'continuity of experience from a particular work, through its particular form, until its recognition as a general form, and the relationship of this general form to a given era'. Calamity, in this sense, serves as both a formal and an ideological structure. Calamity is not merely the direct expression of violence and of a story, but a metaphor for a general state of the world.

In *Puur* this state, this 'structure of feeling', evolves throughout, stretching from birth to death. The film has the task of locating the story, alluding to events that will then be enacted, performed, in the playing area. It shows the birth of a child and the painful paradox this brings his mother: 'Now that I have you I can only lose you.' Birth is a severing: 'He had to be freed, millimetre by millimetre, from my flesh, made from my flesh. . . . He had to be hacked free, chipped millimetre by millimetre, sundered from me.'[12] This image of block-by-block separation is appropriate in a place of digging, the quarry where the live audience has gathered and onto which the film is projected; here the dancer must now cut a few blocks of dance, finding in a duet the heart-rending creation of the other. Here, at the end of the show, we hear the sound of a rock fall, as if the artistic creation has definitively detached itself from inert matter and each spectator will be leaving with a piece.

The relationship between the stage and film is neither a mirror image nor a dialogue between the recorded and the live. The gap widens between film and the concentrated abstraction of 'contact dance'. The two modes stand in total opposition: by digging in the quarry, by closing itself up in representation of the massacre, the film calls on blood, water, violence and hysteria. By removing the stones thrown at the beginning of the play from the theatrical stage, by pushing them to the edge of the playing area making a border, a wall to guard from the barbarian wilderness, the dance creates an aesthetic universe, a smooth and shiny surface suited to choreographic movement. Thus even cruel actions (hitting yourself, impaling another person on a stake, quartering them, tying them down with rope) are stylised, refined representations of violence. This piece must be enjoyed 'puur', like a glass of whiskey, without ice or water diluting its strength. For example, when the dancers throw sticks from one side of the stage to the other while in motion, it requires a great deal of skill, but unlike the bricks from the first Vandekeybus show, which were thrown and caught in the air, these sticks have protective rubber on both ends. The risk here is no greater than with other dance companies. Is it a question of our having developed a tolerance, as with dangerous performance art? We become accustomed to the danger such moves represent. The blows delivered to ourselves or others are fake, the trajectories perfectly drawn.

Resisting the temptation to give verbal explanation (the way that Jan Fabre does), the choreography never slips into performance art. Rather than offering a necessarily disappointing representation of a calamity, or a powerful but tiring description of plagues, Puur finds a pure form, which holds up and builds upon the addition of very beautiful poems by P. F. Thomèse and the never-illustrative music of David Eugene Edwards and Fausto Romitelli. I cannot stress enough the importance and quality of the musical compositions used in these productions.

Mue

In the long odyssey through the calamities of Avignon, *Mue*, performed at the Château de Saumane in deepest Provence, offers a quiet moment, the perfect counterexample to the prevailing obsession with despair. *Mue* presents a founding myth to understand not so much the nature of man as man's place in the universe.

Mue. Première Mélopée is billed as a 'sonic and poetic Wara for nine voices, one electronic voice, and a percussionist, and a sound installation' in the programme's strange wording. Jean Lambert-wild, the director, and Jean-Luc Therminarias, the composer, following a stay with the Xavantes on the Rio das Mortes native peoples reserve, in the Brazilian Mato Grosso, called on five Xavantes to reconstruct, with four French actors, a Wara or open space where the men of the council of elders gather every day in a circle at daybreak and sunset. The four members of the cooperative and the five Xavantes stand in a circle on the central mound, their backs to the audience, each in front of a microphone. The spectators sit around this mound on seats placed directly on the sandy ground and listen to the words spoken by the chorus and the narrator, who walks around the exterior circle. What they hear is described as 'a speech by Serebura, a dream by Waëhipo

Figure 12.1 Mue. Première mélopée, directed by Jean Lambert-wild.
© Jean Lambert-wild.
We might imagine, in the Amazonian rainforest, a group of natives, assembled to discuss the day just ended or the one to come. We cannot hear what they are saying, neither the voice nor the meaning. We cannot know how to represent their life. We only imagine the calamities they have survived. Let us remember this group of natives seen that summer on the esplanade of a château in the Provence night, jumbled with French actors and musicians. We heard only their voices, received fragments from their lives, from their way of speaking and relating, backs turned on the world and those who had come to hear them. Is there nothing left to represent? True or false? But there is! The world is there to be discovered inside each of us, to hear by lending ones ears. Is theatre the laboratory of the real? We will find out later.

junior and myths from the Xavante community of Etenhiritipa'. It would be futile to attempt to differentiate what comes from Serebura, Waëhipo or Lambert-wild's own re-creation, since everything becomes deliberately mixed: word and dream, myth and poetry. The origin of the words and the dreams, and the source of the sounds, remains undetermined. There is much tact, much restraint, much elegance and much integrity in this thoughtful and sensitive intercultural collaboration, which avoids being voyeuristic or patronising.[13]

The resulting ceremony (can it really be called a 'show', or should we not rather call it a 'cultural performance'?) avoids the trap of 'exotic' ritual, artificially transported to this park under Provence skies for an enlightened audience open to the world's many cultures.

The spatial, musical and discursive structure renders obsolete any theoretical notions of authenticity, cultural identity, universality or cultural essentialism. We witness, instead, a quiet questioning of the intercultural theatre of the 1980s and 1990s – that of Brook, Mnouchkine and Barba. We do not get a transference of cultural bits and pieces or a reconstitution of the culture of the other, nor do we get an apology for cultural universalities or a postmodern relativity of all cultures, much less the whiny discourse banning the quoting of any culture that does not belong to us and which is protected by laws governing communities, disguised as political correctness.

Far from seeking to reconstitute the authentic speech of the Indians, to display scraps of dance or ritual, *Mue*'s mise en scène unapologetically employs the latest sound technology and uses Therminarias's remarkable talents as composer. The voices, each one different in texture and emotion, are brought to the fore, in the sometimes centred and sometimes peripheral space created by the speakers. These voices disorient the audience. We are no longer able to distinguish original and primary speech; instead, we must treat voice and music as speech in motion, constantly changing its origin. The Wara becomes a decentred centre, giving impetus to poetic reflection. Each person's voice breaks, as if they were adolescents. We become something else while remaining ourselves. We change our voice and our voice changes us. Our voice breaking also signals a change in our mental and political attitude toward other cultures, abandoning our concepts and words:

> here's what the A'Uwé Uptabi taught me,
> these men of truth from Etênhiritipa,
> to slip into all the contained faraway places of my dreams
> to find the form to share them
> to free myself from my words and to say,
> the dawn of the change
> which will no longer belong to me.

These words are penned by Lambert-wild, but they convey everyone's dream. This dawn of change has nothing of the '*grand soir*', the evening before the revolution, when universal humanist values will make a discreet comeback. Such a return after abandonment corresponds to the phase Philippe Descola describes in contemporary ethnology. In his studies of the Jivaros Amazonian people, Descola insists both on learning about cultural diversity and on critiquing extreme culturalist positions that:

end up saying that everything is a product of social life and cultural constraints. ... Anthropology, for a very long time, had as its object of study the understanding of human nature in all its diversity. The accumulation of ethnographic data meant that we lost sight that our fundamental objective is indeed the understanding of a single human nature, bringing solutions to some of our problems. Our world places great emphasis on the discontinuity between human and nonhuman (in a sense a moral discontinuity) and on material continuity. In societies like that in which the Jivaros live, the emphasis is – on the other hand – placed on moral continuity and material discontinuity.[14]

Without denying obvious cultural differences, Lambert-wild insists on a similar vision of a single human nature. He brings together different voices, people, texts and styles, but the staging, endless translations and changes of identity counterbalance this cultivated diversity with deliberately blurred boundaries: who is speaking, and to whom? Towards the end of the evening, the external commentator, the 'electronic voice', declares his intentions: 'I'm going to tell you how the world was made. Here I am, as our forebears told.' He concludes the Xavante narrative like an anthropologist well versed in Lévi-Strauss: 'This is the way myth speaks. ... The myth I'm speaking of maintains a living tradition. ... You are similar to us. ... you also come from our forbearers. ... I ask you to respect us. ... I don't want you to treat us like animals any more. ... You may leave. Forget we ever existed.' The calamity already happened five centuries ago: the only thing that matters today is to limit the damage and learn to live together.

It is surprising to hear a white narrator speak this way, even when rechristened as an electronic voice: the representative of an invisible chorus or of the European audience speaks for the native people, giving European humanist discourse and using concepts from Western anthropology. But if we look more closely, this discourse actually tries to transcend the usual divisions. In sociological terms, we might well be tempted to point out the huge economic difference between the Xavantes and the citizens of Belfort, between the international coproduction (about which the programme contains fifteen lines of text) and the fragile community of the natives. Lambert-wild builds upon poetry and dream to justify this convergence, and his work tests these principles. Institutional support must have been vital for this expensive enterprise; certainly the production's politics remain at a preliminary stage (with a neoliberal dead end that leaves open inevitable questions around ownership and the division of labour). But no other performance at the Avignon festival so renewed the art of directing or asked burning questions with such energy.

To Conclude with *The Biography Remix*

The Biography Remix, eighth and the final production I saw that week, is a retrospective of the life and performances of Marina Abramović, directed by Abramović's colleague and old friend Michael Laub. There is no ambiguity in the event: it is not for the general public, but rather is a very clear and well-devised presentation of a genre little known at Avignon, making use of historical examples and performance works from the performer's past.

This remixed biography, which is a sort of work in progress for Abramović as it recaps her (already) long career, is probably a key to understanding the other productions, to evaluate without prejudice the changing relationship between mise en scène and performance art. This remix too offers an occasion to contemplate the notion of calamity, as opposed to the risk or danger courted by the performer. In a way, the (often female) performer plays the role of a calamity, in the second meaning of the word: not the natural plague, but the person who causes constant problems in addition to being the victim of these self-inflicted problems, a 'Calamity Jane'. Is the performer not a calamity for herself, someone who endlessly creates problems and troubles? If she excels at creating her own unhappiness, she can also undo it with brilliance, sometimes with humour, and can triumph despite the trials and tribulations. She has nothing of the natural calamity, which by definition remains in place for as long as possible and leaves humans little chance to avoid or neutralise it.

We sense that this production has found its balance and its positive pedagogical strength. Laub designs it as a chronology by displaying two lines of scrolling text (in French and English) with key dates in Abramović's life as well as dates of her main works. Laub's exterior eye is not critical – that is not his job – but he likes to give humorous points of reference. He opts for a double presentation: video extracts play on a screen covering the stage opening and live events start the minute the screen is raised, giving the impression that the stage reality comes out of the screen. Thus he sets up simultaneous actions and serial repetitions, conveying a real aesthetic quality. When performed by five groups, the famous slapping duel becomes a beautiful rhythmic moment, losing its original violence in the ensemble effect: it sounds like several ping-pong games taking place in the same immense hall.

Figure 12.2 Marina Abramović in *The Biography Remix*, directed by Michael Laub.
© Patrice Pavis.

In the first sequence Abramović, hanging from the wall, welcomes the audience, holding two snakes in her hands, while two huge placid hounds come onstage and gnaw on a bone, just underneath the snakes. Disturbing growls come from the loudspeakers; an Italian prima donna talks into a microphone, then a megaphone. Fear is soon replaced with admiration for the composition, humour and visual beauty.

The entire production shares this quality of a smoothly run mise en scène that, without excluding performance art, nonetheless keeps its risks at a distance, putting them in perspective, offering us a sample conceptual version perfect for a Master's thesis. Laub's remix eliminates the risk – or at least minimises it and reduces its impact. Protected by distance, the spectators slowly get to know Abramović, grow to like her, learn of her painful path, leave aside their prejudices about the smoke and mirrors of art, the frivolity of the theatre, and discover presence and silence. When Abramović finally sits down before them wearing a formal grey suit, looking them in the eye, and enjoying a spell of silence and stillness, there is a moment of universal relief; it is a mutual state of anagnorisis, deep empathy, a meeting. Then suddenly there is a ripple of applause, like a warm fire nobody expected any more, in this rather sombre festival line-up.

Figure 12.3 Marina Abramović in *The Biography Remix*, directed by Michael Laub.
© Patrice Pavis.

The snakes move. Are they dangerous? Yes, since we do not dare take them on! And because they might fall on the dogs. This is thus performance art: non-repeatable, risky, unpredictable, irritating. But, as for the Christ-like pose, the halo of light, the beauty of the lighting and of the singer's voice, the ironic relationship between the elements onstage – these bring us back to the unspeakable joys of theatrical relations. Must one choose performance or mise en scène? *Mise en perf* or performise?

Figure 12.4 Marina Abramović in *The Biography Remix*, directed by Michael Laub. © Patrice Pavis.

The face is masked, with bodily 'imperfections' (as they would seem according to current norms) exposed; she is guided onstage by her teacher and mentor, becoming an aesthetic object telling a story. Well, almost, but we cannot forget the human being, and thus its suffering. We never quite manage to see the world simply in terms of beauty and fiction. Behind all the theatre, we discern someone as real as we are. Performance tests our capacity to react and to protest as a human being: and yet we do not dare to do it. We take refuge behind theatre.

Final remarks

Tragic catastrophe, which is sudden and punctual, has been supplanted by foreseeable and enduring calamity. Many productions, and spectators, today seem afflicted with a deep and long-lasting depression, with a black vision of history. Calamity, in these Avignon productions, is more a metaphor or allegory than a tangible reality, a plague sent by God or the forces of evil. It is present as an endemic evil, a situation offering no way out, a social or religious disaster that will linger on and against which we are defenceless. We have seen how the productions make numerous references to religious fundamentalism (*Dieu et les esprits vivants, Anathème, Puur*), to hatred of women and bodies, to the Holocaust, to genocide (*Mue*), and to the inquisition (*Je suis sang*). All of this, of course, invokes either historical realities or current events. In these renderings of the world as a grey and calamitous landscape, there is no trace of the grotesque comic, of Homeric laughter, or of a rejoicing body. But there is nothing explicitly tragic either, since, despite the anathema, condemnation and imprecation, we find no God to blaspheme against, nor any transcendence to rage against, or destiny to oppose.

With no new comedy and no renewal of the tragic, the situation is clearly desperate – almost like a drama! The spectator's catharsis is no longer possible, since there is no functioning identification with a hero or acceptance of transcendence. Catharsis is based on fear and pity; calamity on angst and disinterest ('compassion fatigue', or apathy in the face of the suffering of others, with implications for performance that Guillermo Gómez-Peña has written about). Calamity is a drama of irreversible degradation inflicted by a God more blinded than hidden. Unlike catastrophe (which affects particular individuals by consciously making them disappear, laying its cards on the table), calamity affects the anonymous masses, without apparent reason or with an absurd reason, refusing to show any cards at all. Unnameable calamity thrives in the spiritual void, as bodies disappear and body and mind split. Although linked with all civilisations since time immemorial, calamity today feeds on the death of ideologies, on the absence of any political analysis that might lead directly to action, on the renunciation of critical thinking. Calamitous thinking – of the end of history, of postmodern relativism, of the well-fed and right-thinking – displaces the natural plague onto social life, placing us in the axis of evil, threatening us with divine punishment just at the moment when faith has been lost.

Calamity – a weapon of mass destruction, universal depression, indescribable panic – lets the audience believe that everything around them is rotten, destroyed, condemned. This dehistoricised way of thinking is found with nuances and variations in these Avignon productions. It is, in general, more defeatist than nihilistic, more provocative than subversive. Violence, the most frequent and obvious sign of calamity, is ubiquitous, but as Denis Guénoun has written:

> the idea that violence should in itself have the value of revolt or provocation appears to be one of the founding presuppositions of contemporary representational ideology … violence no longer has any critical value and from now on it is violence itself that must be the subject of criticism.[15]

But violence is certainly not the subject of criticism in all eight of these works. Each shows it in an extremely different way; to see that this is so, we need only observe calamity's effect on the bodies of the actors, dancers and performers. For Jan Fabre, the performers' bodies are naturally valiant and naked and in no way anaemic, despite his concerns. His is a dancing, rejoicing, tortured body, subject to despair (the Knight), to wandering (Diogenes), to tears (the Rock), but still ready for new conquests. Calamity is, perhaps paradoxically, what the process of civilisation (according to Norbert Elias) does to the vital instincts. But should we not fear new calamity with the arrival of a superman given over to warlike instincts and thirst for blood? Jan Decorte's insipid character Sangloupdiable (Blood-Wolf-Devil) becomes 'mad with rage to the point of killing', as the programme says, but we only ever see him naked or dressed as a monk, sword in hand, a body at times untied and at times tied to his partner with a thick rope, suitable for hanging someone.

The bodies of *B.#03 Berlin* are vague outlines, silent and malleable figures, phantoms and fantasies in constant evolution. They are the blurry images that we today make of the tragic body: tortured, though it is impossible to grasp the victims. But precisely who are they? We remember only King Kong and the anonymous rabbits he unloads with a fork. Apart from this struggle between two figures, the body eludes us, fainting undecided between coup de théâtre and calamity.

The naked bodies of *Anathème* are both present and insistent, something rarely achieved on stage. Beyond evoking those who have been sacrificed, they refer only to themselves, as in performance art. This ambiguity transforms a boring but disturbing show into an unending sit-in. In *Puur*, the battered bodies in the film, and later the gassed and disinfected bodies from the ballet, engage in almost acrobatic contact. Their lifting, throwing, balancing, and duelling are active and decisive responses to violence, not an acceptance.

In the Wara in Provence, we particularly notice the participants' voices, as if an entire struggle for survival had taken refuge in ancestral speech and in a close-sounding voice amplified with the aid of a microphone. Therefore the survivor's fragile body forms an alliance with people of goodwill, using sound technology to collect and preserve words. Elsewhere still, Marina Abramović's body faces all dangers – snakes, slaps, exhausting journeys, and all kinds of trials and tribulations – but avoids catastrophe, refuses enslavement, and ends up facing the audience, calmly sitting before it, all suffering forgotten, turning its back on all the calamities of the world. Jean Lambert-wild received visitors in his bed at the edge of the castle; Marina Abramović takes her leave of the audience in a moment of universal calm. Have we moved from calamity to calm?

Overwhelmed by so many universal misfortunes, exhausted by recurring calamities, I tried, in my room at Saint-Joseph, in good company and well looked after by the CEMEA, to get to sleep. But under my window I heard Jean-François Sivadier's actors performing *La Mort de Danton*. 'What?' I asked myself, 'more of the awful fatalism of history?' More of this 'revolution that devours its own children?' Later that night they performed Brecht's *Galileo*. Galileo too was defeated by the Church's obscurantism, but for the time being, in this scene at the beginning of the play, I see him explaining the workings of the world to his pupil. It is illuminating, light and inspiring. Then it turns – it is that simple! With a few boards, a backdrop, and clear gestures fitted to the actions, a miracle occurs: the world is reborn, and with it the theatre. We need only to follow the trajectory of the stars and the actors' gestures, to put simple words into orbit onstage, to rely on the audience's lively imagination – captive but alert – to see and construct a world both based on our own and transforming it. Could hope triumph over calamity? Before falling into a doubtful sleep, a warning from Raymond Williams comes to me: 'It is in making hope practical, rather than despair convincing, that the ways to peace can be entered.'[16]

Where is mise en scène at?
And where are we at as an audience?
We had imagined mise en scène as the tuning of the performance by the various artists, for our benefit. It is also a negotiation between them and us. The artists are happy to give us something, but only if we join in.

So we do join in, but only to a certain degree. After all, it is not enough to do as the current theoretical fashion encourages, to bear everything on our frail shoulders, our hyperactive brains, our troubled hearts. To begin with, the work must be analysed, the performance object must be appreciated, evaluated and described, its forms and forces must be discovered, and we must not imagine that we are creators in our own right.

Of course, we might well like to be creators. But surely we are at least an assembly of theatre spectators, a community of reflection and of emotion, configured to receive, appreciate and understand theatre?

Everything depends on how certain thorny questions will be answered, and how certain tight knots will be undone.

What ails mise en scène is not incurable, but is merely a childhood illness, weakening it significantly. Money is scarce, interest wanes, desire dims, the community leaves the game, sending us back to the hills.

Directors (who are troubled as well as being troublemakers) are in an endless dialogue with their doubles: actors, authors, dramaturgs, choreographers and so on. There, too, past agreements are being renegotiated.

The old question of the (old) couple, text/performance, returns. The eternal debate on the faithfulness of the director to the play comes back like the return of the repressed.

13 Conclusions
Where is mise en scène going?

What is mise en scène? It is theatre put in its place, in its proper place, theatre made accessible to a given audience at a given moment. The terms of this accessibility remain to be seen! This book's journey was itself the staging of a few spectacles: gems, brief encounters – mostly good ones. It took us across very varied experiences, and into very contrasting regions. And yet it was one of the many paths that criss-cross stage productions of the last few years; it was a path that very quickly disappeared into the forest, a Heideggerian *Holzweg*, a path that leads nowhere.

But no compass can get us out of the woods. Even Hansel's trail of breadcrumbs might offer a better way to get home safely. We have certainly tried to make short stops along the way at high points of theatre production from the last few years, but we were aware that the rules of the game would escape us, that mise en scène would take previously unseen shapes and identities, and that burying the hatchet (definitively classifying theatre materials) would remain forever impossible.

What have we nevertheless managed to bring back from this perilous voyage? There is the intuition that mise en scène is a good ruse for speaking about the theatre and that the term is not as trite and old-fashioned as is sometimes suggested. Mise en scène is not only the proper place for researching forms and stage experimentation, it is also, or at least can be, a place where the human link is repaired. It is the final utopia of a collective experience and deliverance, since theatre, as the current director of the Berliner Ensemble, Claus Peymann, suggests:

> takes hold of the spectators and makes them live a communal experience, which is in certain cases a communal deliverance: a catharsis that, in the space of a utopian second, transforms everybody concerned into fundamentally good people .... [Such

people] all aspire to this sacred second, during which a 'deathly hush' spreads across the auditorium. ... Each time, theatre offers an image of man well beyond his clichés.[1]

Does this second of human sharing permit us to go from despair to utopia, to turn Jean-Claude Lallias's perspective around? Lallias claims that 'to the utopia of unifying audiences in an assembly of sharing, there corresponds a micro laboratory pulverisation of a fragmented society, which is losing identity and perhaps common destiny'. There are, then, two utopias: the utopia of unifying the audience, and the utopia of responding to the alienating fragmentation of the theatre and the world.

Nobody still expects that art or theatre will save humanity. But who, at this beginning of the millennium, does not need this 'sacred second?' After the era (which is today somewhat idealised) of theatre at the service of the public (or public-service theatre) after 1945 – and following Vitez's dream of a theatre that would be 'elitist for all' in the slightly demagogical 1980s – are we not today in the cynical and disillusioned era of 'egalitarian theatre for me'? Yet another reason to hope for some oxygen!

This is what we have attempted here in quenching our thirst at a few springs in the life of the theatre of our time. At each stop, in each chapter, we have had to modify the method of analysis, not due to a taste for eclecticism, but in order to adapt the theory to the diversity of the object. Was this perhaps a means, a deliberate will to resist the postmodern and postdramatic rejection of any systematic theory? So what path did we take, and why was it such a winding one?

A winding path

- At the frontiers of mise en scène, but also inside it, the theatre of voice, the theatre of *mise en jeu* and of rehearsed reading appeared to us as 'mise en scène all the same', but which would benefit nonetheless from being described in terms of performative actions. This discovery opened the way to a confrontation of mise en scène and performance (Chapter 2).
- This confrontation was sustained, systematised (Chapter 3), tested by analyses and methodologically generalised as an alternative to mise en scène semiology and the phenomenology of performance.
- Scenography afforded us the opportunity to compare the merits of functionalist description and the phenomenology of perception, that of the scenographer as much as that of the spectator (Chapter 4).

- Even the *mise en jeu* of contemporary texts, despite our being sceptical about analysis, represented a challenge to theory, which had to refine and extend its methods into practices in the course of being invented (Chapter 5).

- The *non-European performance*, in this case, a Korean one, was for mise en scène (originally a European notion) the main intercultural stumbling block, even if the Korean artists frequently claim Western acting 'methods' and directing as their own (Chapters 6 and 7). The absence of major intercultural productions in Europe is symptomatic of the crisis of intercultural or multitheatre, and at the very moment when politicians and social workers are working hard to convince artists of the benefits of multicultural society and cultural exchange. A cultural challenge is made to artists, one to which they cannot rise, since they lack both the means and the desire.

- The entrance onto the stage of audiovisual media has pushed theatre into a corner, obliging the theatre and the audience to show more tolerance and flexibility, instead of staying on the defensive. It is here that theatre risks losing its soul, but also might regenerate, diversify and update itself, instead of wasting away, essentialising itself, 'Grotowskifying' itself (that is, reducing itself to a more and more pure ethereal essence). Such a methodological challenge has reached its peak, thanks to the diversity of the media involved. A meeting of different types of analysis, with methods from the visual arts and technology, can only be beneficial. All these perspectives converge in the notion of intermediality, and mise en scène seems more and more like 'tuning'. But tuning is not the same as 'ruling', nor indeed is it the settling of scores (chapter 8).

- This tuning,[2] either semiological or performative, sets things into play, throws things into crisis, and deconstructs the insights of dramaturgy, of media theory, and of phenomenology (Chapter 9). Such deconstruction is also that of the frontier between types of theatre practice: text-based theatre, scenographic writing, the staging of classics, theatre of images, multimedia performance. The distinction adopted in the present study is more pedagogical than it is characteristic of the probable future of productions.

- All of these mediatic and discursive effects have repercussions on the body of the actor, a question which should be approached with tact. A model of multiple identities, which borrows significantly from gender theory, has replaced the expressionistic and semiological model of the 1960s (Chapter 10).

- Classical plays are the terrain where these parameters and methods of analysis can best be tested. Their staging reveals their true novelty, their finality and their way of proceeding. Mise en scène oscillates between legibility and illegibility, illegibility often being a gauge of the postmodern or the postdramatic (Chapter 11).
- All of these hypotheses have been tested one more time in several productions at the Avignon festival (Chapter 12). Despite distinguishing, for practical reasons, between all of these types of production, an examination of the 'cross-breeding', the way that each type influences the others, is proposed. Analyses of the different performances readily reveal this.

A contrasting state of affairs: the 1990s

Given the diversity of stage practice, which has been given ample attention on these pages, the following remarks will necessarily be rapid and general, perhaps useful also in order to gain awareness of the evolution of the art of mise en scène in its entirety. This evolution can be attributed to two sets of variables, extratheatrical (sociological) and theatrical (aesthetic), factors that are tightly entwined and are distinguished only for the sake of clarity.

Sociological factors

These factors are crucial since they deal with social life as a whole, offering no possibility of escape for the artists. The effects of globalisation and the privatisation of the economy made themselves felt in the creative process. A significant number of independent artists or groups disappeared, simply because they could not meet their budget or receive the grant that would make an artistic project viable. It is estimated that around 15 per cent of subsidy was returned to banks in the form of charges. At the level of large institutions, the necessity of mounting national and – increasingly – international co-productions led to a standardisation of aesthetic norms, to a simplification of the problems addressed. Mise en scène and money: this is something that the theory of dramatic criticism often leaves to one side, because of a lack of knowledge and information, and because of a legitimate concern not to mix aesthetic choices and 'big money'. Money nonetheless had a clear impact on the final results.[3] Only a few aspects will be mentioned, for the record and as a suggestion for future research, drawing on the excellent study by Pierre-Etienne Heymann.

The end of the welfare state, or of the state as a simple provider of money, the near-disappearance in the former Eastern Bloc and the strong reduction in Western Europe of state subsidy and of local funding had serious repercussions for theatre production. With this disappearance came the fear that the *théâtre d'art*, as understood by Paul Fort at the end of the nineteenth century and as practised in the national theatres of Eastern and Central Europe until the end of the 1980s, might be gone forever, for want of economic means as much as of any strong political and national hegemonic will.

Heymann shows how the public theatre in France, and also elsewhere, depended increasingly on sponsorship, and privatised ever more domains of theatrical activity, while opening up to the market economy by way of ambitious co-productions. Globalisation attracted:

> multinational money invested to produce luxury events, mounted by star directors (like Robert Wilson, Peter Sellars, Robert Lepage, Luca Ronconi and Luc Bondy). Artistic research was pre-financed, preprogrammed and calibrated to the expectations of the audience of half a dozen prestigious international events.[4]

The privatisation of public theatre, the misappropriation of public subsidy towards the private sector, and the rehabilitation and promotion of boulevard theatre were accompanied by a:

> *boulevardisation* of certain performances – all in the name, of course, of the spectator's enjoyment: the abuse of the text without any concern for a point of view, the imposition of gags and gratuitous jokes no matter what the play; shameless ham acting by star actors.[5]

Heymann's observation is damning, not only for theatre's financial situation, but also for the aesthetics of mise en scène:

> Extravagant, anecdotal and conceptual art are the most visible faces of neoliberal public theatre: its conformist face, all about displaying money; the populist face, masked with charitable intentions; and the modernist, with its discreet taste for provocation, which validates the spirituality of the 'creative artist' and the self-satisfaction of the consumer initiated into the mysteries of the avant-garde.[6]

The financing of the theatrical enterprise is at once what saved it from extinction and what did it damage from which it cannot always recover, at least in terms of aesthetics. Theatre depended more and more on the laws of the market and on the economic conditions of the time. Theatre institutions, which artists could not hope to escape, constitute an enormous stock exchange of artistes, with their market value floated and their talent quantified. They made projections on career plans, they turned to industrial espionage to discover these talented young people, to place them where their visibility would be greatest.

These sociological factors of change were aggravated further by the evolution of theatrical forms, upon which this study has mainly focused. A short addition, on the subject of writing and scenography, will demonstrate their importance.

Theatrical factors

Over the last ten or fifteen years of the twentieth century, dramatic writing changed fundamentally. Mise en scène has needed to invent new acting methods, which are simpler and more sophisticated at the same time. That the stage and acting might change as the result of a shift in writing is nonetheless not a new development. Vitez perceived a law in the evolution of theatre since Claudel and Chekhov:

> At first, nobody knew how to perform Claudel, nor Chekhov, but having to perform the impossible is what transforms the stage and the acting; thus the dramatic poet is at the heart of formal changes in the theatre; his solitude, his inexperience, even his irresponsibility, are valuable to us. What's the point of having seasoned authors predicting the lighting effects and the rake of the stage? The poet knows nothing, predicts nothing, it's the artists' turn to play.[7]

The mise en scène is no longer fragmented, but is in miniature: it potentially sometimes contains the whole, it is centred on the actor, who is rigorously directed, it does not rest upon a scenographic or decorative overproduction. It finds a coherent way to 'execute' the text, scrupulously following its score. Thus, for instance, a style of acting had to be invented in order to perform Koltès or Vinaver, or any of the authors who do not insist on a given acting style, especially a psychological one. From Stanislavski to Grotowski, acting possesses a wide range of possibilities. For an acting style that does not imitate psychological behaviour, we must moreover find a previously unknown way of 'opening' the text or the action, a way of deconstructing them, of commentating on them rather than illustrating them.

On the other hand, research on space and the relationship between stage and auditorium appears to have not made much progress since the scenographic revolutions of the historical avant-garde or the 1960s avant-garde. Most spatial possibilities have been tested, and sometimes exhausted. Scenography always returns to the frontal relationship of days gone by, even to the old Italianate stage.

By way of homage to Barthes' famous article on 'The diseases of costume',[8] we can consider such a disease in terms of the whole of mise en scène, without claiming to know, let alone have any remedy. These 'diseases' are more symptoms of recent artistic mutations than incurable or fatal illnesses.

The diseases of mise en scène

*   When mise en scène is a *style*, a trade mark, a recurring label no matter who the writers and productions may be, it is little more than stylistic exercise, a hallmark. Colleagues also imitate each other: in Germany, for instance, Laurent Chétouane takes up the famous slowness and stillness of Claude Régy, applying it to every author's work. Once the novelty has worn off, the slowness and stillness soon become a tiresome oratorio.

*   Young directors on the verge of institutional recognition sometimes feel obliged to impose their particular stamp, to attract attention to some detail or device called for by the institution. Such a particularity will sometimes be requested, and will sometimes become the object of tacit reproach. An acute attack of 'youthism' marks the contemporary landscape, especially in Germany. The *Intendanten* (artistic directors) ravenously seek out young people, especially women, and offer them little stage jobs, in the hope that one day they will become the next Peter Stein.[33]

*   In its early days, mise en scène had the function of transferring the meaning of the text to the stage, of using the performance as a means of explaining the play. To clarify, or to make apparent the meaning of the play, is not a suspicious or even useless undertaking, but nor is it the ultimate aim of theatre work.[10] Legibility is of course only possible against a background of illegibility. One ceaselessly turns into the other, and vice versa! A compromise must be attempted. It is not the aim of art to be either totally legible or totally illegible. As regards mise en scène, we might say: 'it must be visible, but discreetly so, as is fitting for the "discreet charm of the *bonne régie*"'! It need not hide, it takes responsibility for its choices or its hypotheses, but it gains nothing in directly giving away its

strategy, since the spectator quickly loses interest in what is already understood. Adorno remarked of works of art, 'The afterlife of artworks, their reception as an aspect of their own history, transpires between a do-not-let-yourself-be-understood and a wanting-to-be-understood; this tension is the atmosphere inhabited by art.'[11]

- A *decorativist temptation* emerges from the desire to receive attention for the luxuriousness of the materials (sets and costumes). The artist, required to provide accounts to the grant-giving public authorities and tempted to please the widest audience at the same time, tends to put on quite a show. The scenography, the onstage media, and the publicity that surrounds the show are the means of this visual overproduction, of this search for a set-laden aesthetic: 'The development of the cultural sector definitely produced nouveaux riches: the rise in public funding did not primarily help actors and writers, but massively increased scenographic and technical means.'[12]

- *Conceptual art* is the opposite temptation; it aims to reduce as far as possible the sensuality of theatre, its ecumenical perception, as Barthes put it, to call on the spectator's abstract reasoning and the stage conventions. The current staging of contemporary texts is often conceptual, and not just for economic reasons (in every sense of the word),[13] but due to a sort of postmodern or postdramatic terrorism. Deconstruction, when it does not fall into the same trap, is particularly able to denounce this contemporary obsession for the dismantling of concepts and representations.

- The festivalisation of productions leads to a certain standardisation, a fear of experimentation. Productions are conceived in view of a festival, Avignon (the main festival or the *off*) in particular, where they will be broken in, bought and eventually distributed. This is a concentrated and effective, economical and profitable way to produce standardised shows, forgotten no sooner than they are presented, and which must leave room for the next festival, like films that only last for a few days, books that disappear from the shelves within a month, kisses taken back as quickly as they are given and so on.

- A new division of labour stems from the mutation of the politico-sociocultural context, at least for *Centres dramatiques nationaux*. Indeed, theatre production needs new specialisations: sound engineers, specialists in computer-controlled light or (live or recorded) video and so on. These highly technical specialisations impose themselves on the director. Without necessarily controlling them, the director is supposed to include them in his work.

- Hence, new professional identities keep appearing. Occasional collaborators are involved in specific tasks, often very complex ones (such as lighting, sound and choreography). The production ends up being stamped with a label corresponding to each collaborator: we get space x, light y and gestural language z. These fashionable signatures are like Post-its, which are not always integrated in the overall aesthetic of the production. Conversely, the invention of new and experimental tasks for mise en scène, like for example the reappraisal of the role of the dramaturg or the direction of actors, is often curbed by lazy habits in the production process or by the tough laws of productivity.

- What results for the major types of mise en scène is standardisation, which is accentuated by a double bind: on the one hand an insistence on out-and-out artistic originality at any price, which imposes unheard of and striking work: on the other hand a formatting of demand emanating from increasingly specialised groups of aficionados with very precise expectations. The public splits into a set of closed groups who are no longer interested in a single type of performance. The spectator quickly specialises in a single genre: it is a sad state of monogamy!

- Along with the ghettoisation of audiences, the autonomisation of stage practices, and theatre's recourse to other independent forms, we can also observe a certain suspicion towards the other arts. Distinct from what happened in the 1970s when – thanks to the *Festival d'automne* in Paris being opened up to the American avant-garde – painting, visual arts, dance, performance art and theatre were joyfully combined; the last twenty years of the twentieth century did not (contrary to declarations made) abolish the frontiers between the different arts. And yet there exists a tradition of crossover, ever since dance-theatre (Pina Bausch or Maguy Marin), street performance and *nouveau cirque*, which in each case were events that approached contemporary art, as opposed to strictly theatrical mise en scène.

- It is very fortunate that despite this purism, some artists are not afraid to go 'off limits'. Jacques Rebotier, musician and poet, creates shows by mixing the principles of different arts: 'To tackle an art with the tools of another stimulates invention. Every art is fractal and refers to the others.'[14] Valère Novarina confronts his painting and his poetic creation within the stage event. François Lazaro creates human-sized marionettes that are operated by actors playing contemporary authors such as Daniel Lemahieu. Alain Lecuq offers a 'theatre of paper', where a story by novelist

Mohammed Kacimi bends to the subtleties of the handling of surfaces, objects and the bodies of the actor-narrator-storyteller.

• The resignation of public service and of the subsidised theatre, the withdrawal of the state, appears, in France, as a politics of demagogy. There is a great temptation now to subsidise only spectacular shows: shows loaded with audiovisual media, laser beams, hip-hop right in the heart of the play, as in Büchner's *Woyzeck* staged by Ostermeier for the 2004 Avignon festival.[15] To this end, the classics are an ideal prey: the argument can be readily simplified, superficially modernised, adapted to the tastes of a young audience, directly transmitted, by way of the local authorities, from the producer to the consumer, from the decision maker to the decoder. Theatres and artists are little more than cogs in the machine. We have finally got rid of directors, they have become mere garden gnomes, used by the bosses of the République to span the world, transmit their lies and count the beans.

The *mise en cause* of mise en scène

• We often hear of the death of the director, after the so-called death of the author in the 1960s. But is the director dead, or merely transformed and in a state of crisis? And is the crisis faced by the director a sign of imminent demise? Nothing is certain. For a long time now the 'director of the stage' (to borrow the Spanish term) has ceased to be the uncontested master of the domain. The director has become a limited company, a discontinuous postmodern subject whose powers are lost and dispersed (but who still receives the dividends).

Mise en scène as a semiological sign-system, overseen by a single pair of eyes, has died out. The classical ambition of figures like Copeau, Craig and even Strehler, who dreamed of replacing the auteur-dramatist with the auteur-stage director, and who would remain faithful to this to the end, has, ever since the turning point of the 1970s, shattered upon impact with the postmodern reality of the stage and the world. Such was the moment of deconstruction, which, inspired by Derrida, 'dismantled' semiology as well as mise en scène, accusing it – rightly – of being a closed system that masked the dynamics of acting and representation; it is in that same moment that Barthes moved from 'the fashion system' to 'the pleasure of the text'.

To his credit, it was Bernard Dort who (in 1988) warned against the risks of closed theory and closed performance. His critique concerns the conception of the show as a *Gesamtkunstwerk* (Wagner) or as stage writing (Craig): 'A critique of Wagner and of Craig becomes necessary. And with it a new definition of theatrical representation which sees it not as a static piecing-together of signs or a meta-text, but rather as a dynamic process that takes place in time and is effectively produced by the actor.'[16] It could not be any clearer. In the manner of Vitez, he describes mise en scène as an autonomous production of meaning and not as a translation or an illustration of the prexisting text: 'Today, we can observe a progressive emancipation of the elements of representation and see in this a shift in structure: the rejection of an organic unity prescribed a priori, and the recognition of the theatrical event as a signifying polyphony, involving the spectator.'[17] Twenty years after this evaluation, it is clear that Dort's diagnosis was correct. The director, as new postmodern neo-subject, can no longer look down from a position on high.

- But this loss is not so much a personal failure as a sign of the times. The failure – if this notion has any relevance in art – instead concerns a few theatrical attempts to create a school and to be the founder of a system. No director would risk founding his entire work on a *Gesamtkunstwerk*. Nonetheless, the fad for total audiovisual spectacle is far from over. Thus the shows of Romeo and Claudia Castellucci appear to be animated images from which sounds, or even shreds of sentences, can emerge. Hence their obvious organicity and the equality of the signs and the materials, all of which constitutes the very opposite of theatre staging a text or even of a proposition for action or event. In his *Tragedia Endogonidia* (2002–07), Castellucci is not aiming to produce images that leave the spectator voiceless, but on the contrary to offer images that will be torn down from the inside, by way of the irruption of voice or a reality effect, or the irruption of the irrational or the unconscious. The Castelluccis' creations refer to the painting of Raphael, to the:

    > opposition, conflict between the eurhythmic order, the perfection of forms, the geometric beauty of the canvasses on the one hand, and on the other the rupture of this order by the dazzling evidence that calls vision into question by propelling it towards dark and unexpected places.[18]

Brook's research to find a universal language of theatre, an art for everybody, does not lead to a universal production and reading of signs, but at best, and as Vitez notes,[19] to a 'translinguistic', sonic, visual and gestural Esperanto that creates the illusion of general understanding beyond specific languages and cultures. This illusion manifests itself either as a universalising idealisation of cultures (this is the essentialism with which Brook has frequently, and sometimes unjustly, been charged), or as an undifferentiated eulogy to difference, leading sometimes to sectarian communitarianism. The crisis of the intercultural, its incapacity to situate cultures both in their local specificity and in their universal humanity, does not make any easier the task of multicultural artists.

The postmodern neo-subject does not fare much better in the domain of political theatre, as no audience wants a lecture. Brechtian epic theatre, with its sharp edge, is supposed to touch the audience at the heart of its interests, to highlight contradictions and nail down the gestus of the characters. But for fear of being too direct or too painful, the neo-director softens the dramaturgical analysis, staying in the realm of the general or the ambiguous.

There are hardly any 'Brechtian' directors left, nor is there much overtly political theatre. This does not mean, however, that the social preoccupations of theatre have entirely gone away. Hence Mnouchkine, after the 1980s (a series of Shakespeare plays) and 1990s (a series of Greek tragedies), has returned to a theatre that is more anchored in the everyday, with productions of *Le dernier caravansérail* (*Odyssées*) (2003) and *Les éphémères* (2006). The collective creation of short texts by the actors – fragments of life which are literally carried onstage on a wheeled platform – as well as the way in which the realities of immigration or of collective and individual histories are evoked no longer owes much to Brecht's immense socio-critical frescoes. The words, like the gestures, are always allusive; the political discourse is implicit, almost subjective. It would seem that Mnouchkine's former vision as creator and director has given way to a thousand impressions that are ephemeral but precise, coming from the actors, who embody the nobodies of history (*sans papiers*, immigrants torn from their origins), and who are also the witnesses of these fugitive instants worthy of Cartier-Bresson. Thus Mnouchkine's staging loses its external, overseeing, centralising eyes in favour of little notes on the ephemeral and the loss of origin. The stage work must be compared to a mosaic, and no director can stick the fragments together. Amidst this profusion of materials, the director is the person with the courage to cut and to clarify.

• This critique (*mise en cause*) of the powers of theatre performance without any clear perspective, reflecting the world in which we live. Finding itself in a damaged landscape, performance has trouble finding its way; there is much to be repaired and also prepared for in a future that seems far from rosy.

The main thing that needs repair is in fact not broken, but works only too well – communication, as in mass media and ready-made messages. Theatre precisely questions the pretension of communicating everything, the tyranny of information and of surveillance. As we understand it today, mise en scène need not be clear, readable or self-explanatory. Its role is not to mediate transmitter and receiver, author and audience, to 'smooth things out'. Instead of simplifying and explicating, it remains deliberately opaque. After the clarity of Brechtianism, it instead favours ambiguity and vagueness. This has been apparent in very unorthodox and rather 'aestheticising' (as post-'68 militants used to say) productions. Brecht's *La Mère* (The Mother), staged in 1995 by Jacques Delcuvellerie, gave the eponymous figure a sensitivity and brought ambiguity to the motivations of the play's characters. In his *Cercle de craie caucasien* (The Caucasian Chalk Circle), Benno Besson, as in all of his Brechtian productions, emphasised the rough, poetic and sexual nature of the objects and costumes, and the humanity, the irresistible goodness of the principal character. In *L'exception et la règle* (The Exception and the Rule), directed by Alain Ollivier (2002), *Les Fusils de la Mère Carrar* (Señora Carrar's Rifles), staged by Antoine Caubet (2006), and in *Homme=Homme* (Man Equals Man), revisited by Emmanuel Demarcy-Mota (2007), we see an identical tendency: not the reduction of the play to slogans, but the reintroduction of a poetic dimension if only by short-circuiting or unsettling grand political messages, to produce a stage materiality that does not translate into univocal signifieds.

Every mise en scène oscillates between construction and deconstruction. When the structure of the play – which was once closed, coherent and narrative – breaks down, opens up and becomes what we (since the 1970s) call a 'text' (in the semiotic sense, and as opposed to a 'work'), it becomes difficult to read and to perform this text 'in one piece', in a univocal way. Mise en scène has the specific mission of finding a compromise between opening the semiotic 'text' and its own natural tendency to explain, justify and interpret the work performed in a univocal and conclusive manner. Conversely, for a coherent play with a predictable structure, using classical language and with an explicit story, the actor and the director reintroduce some 'text': that is, some 'play' within the structures. They create a semantic ambiguity and recover the pleasure of the enigma and of complexity:

Barthes's 'pleasure of the text'. When dramatic works become open texts without a clear story or when directors 'never [give] the impression of seeing the story for what it is in their shows',[20] the mise en scène often sets itself the task of 'repairing' this story, or at least of substituting another organising structure.

The repairs also include compensating for the absence of cultural references through staging. This is one of the principal functions of mise en scène, in particular when the play belongs to another cultural area from that of the audience and when, as discreetly as possible, missing references and keys that are indispensable to the reading need to be provided. Aid is provided for the spectators without their necessarily being aware of it, and sometimes against their will. This spectator is thus consciously manipulated. Such manipulation is the work of ideology and of the unconscious. Mise en scène is always unconscious ideological filling-in.

Directing and its doubles: doubling the director

Contemporary mise en scène, as we see, is in dire need of repair. What was already its original function has become more and more necessary as humans have become distanced from a well-ordered world and as the disorganisation of the senses has itself come up for repair. But is repairing perhaps too normative an activity? And do we still repair things at all? Do we not just discard anything that does not meet our norms?

There is a tendency, and doubtless a real necessity, to believe that mise en scène only pertains to the classics, or perhaps to text-based theatre, repertory theatre, art theatre and that 'you are only a director when directing classics'.[21] This is why we should complement (and not replace) the notion of mise en scène with the Anglo-American notion of performance. The notion of performance, or even that of 'production', considers theatrical performance as the accomplishment of an action, and not as 'stage writing' (Planchon's écriture scénique), to transpose, illustrate and double the text.

Once mise en scène sees itself as performance (suggesting live and ephemeral activities and tasks) it becomes diversified and enriched. It must resolve its inherent contradiction: on the one hand, it was born of, and feeds on, the division of labour, which necessitates new collaborators; on the other hand, it only makes sense if it succeeds in globally seizing the spirit of the performance with some degree of coherence. The director is host to an uncomfortable tension, and must divide into various roles while remaining very much the director. The director's collaborators (and the director alone, if working solo) acquire new functions. This can be seen in the examples chosen for this volume, and I shall attempt to create a profile of the real and virtual doubles of the director.

The actor

None of the director's doubles demonstrates such duplicity as the actor in contemporary mise en scène or performance. The actor, who should often instead be called a performer, is present in all these practices. The actor is not only a mimetic double of the realistic or naturalist character, but also frequently an open and empty figure, non-psychological and therefore non-mimetical, a 'face carrier' (as Marivaux put it), which, in contemporary writing, serves as a support for the discourse without necessarily representing a real being. When the actor is also the dramaturg, the actor is obviously one body with what is said or shown, becoming organically present to the words and to the actions, and to the director if the director persists in wanting to guide and control. The actor deconstructs a means of representation (as in the work of Claude Régy) or an imposed identity (like Guillermo Gómez-Peña), or a certain distance is found (as for Marina Abramović), further separating the actor from the fate of a character. Such an actor's director, then, is in a position to decentre the actor, to 'work with the actor on not being preoccupied'.[22] The relationship with the text has changed: the director no longer needs to be 'preoccupied with knowing what is underneath'.[23]

In all of these configurations, the actor has become a full partner of the director: a double who is 'preoccupied' not with the self any more, but with the place occupied in the show and in the overall functioning of the mise en scène. The best example is Daniel Mesguich. His actors are not psychological entities, but rather figures that take positions and oppositions in the space, on the chessboard of the stage. In his productions of Marivaux and Racine, the effects of doubling (mistress and servant, queen and handmaid) reinforce this mirror impression. We are confronted with two interchangeable personae: one refers to the other and they are reversible. As such, Mesguich wants to show that a character is always a construction and that classical dramaturgy often operates with doubles, dialogism and a split personality.

The author

The relationship between the director and the author has often been one of conflict, the latter feeling exploited by the former. But, after the 1980s, after the 'money years' or the 'society of the spectacle' (as defined by Debord), and with the renewal of dramatic writing in the 1990s, the author now needs the director even more than the actor, not so much in order to be performed but rather in order to help to test and unfold the possible meanings of the text. The relationship 'profits' both parties. Thus, authors no longer feel the need to stage their own play (running the risk of staying too timorous and too much a prisoner of their own texts) in order to avoid any betrayal, or to state the 'correct' point of view. The author gladly hands the text over to an actor who will be capable of unfurling it, unfolding it, as if to better reveal it to the author and the spectator.

The dramaturg

The dramaturg, in the German sense (literary advisor), is hardly ever used by French directors. If it remains an essential piece of the theatrical machine in Germany and in Scandinavia, it has never taken hold in France or the Iberian peninsula. Perhaps this is because its essential and indispensable function has been absorbed by mise en scène. After years of rereading the classics, dramaturgy has become too heavy a science, preventing a direct relationship with the text, masking the delicate nervous system of the text with the ballast of cultural references and political analysis, crushing the subtle and fragile work of the contemporary theatre actor. After the Brechtian wave in Western Europe, the French theatre establishment did not retain the dramaturgy that was central to this wave, as it no longer saw the necessity or the relevance of Brechtian and Marxist critical analysis. 'What use would I have for a dramaturg?' Antoine Vitez once asked, and not without provocation. Many contemporary artists, from Braunschweig to Cantarella, avoid excessive 'table work' and any analysis that determines a priori the staging choices of a future mise en scène.

On the other hand, dramatic analysis, whether or not it is done by the dramaturg, is something from which the performance might benefit, not just in terms of clarifying the ideological stakes, but also in order that the story is well told and its conflicts clearly outlined. This is what happened with Alain Ollivier's production of Brecht's pedagogical play *L'exception et la règle* (*The Exception and the Rule*). How can we transpose this classic about man's exploitation of man, the violence of the merchant towards the 'coolie', to our own times? In not taking sufficiently into account the contemporary spectator and the new forms of exploitation, which are less direct and are more effective, and by not attempting more visible and original formal work, Ollivier missed the opportunity to 'update' the play, to extract its current relevance. In the absence of dramaturgical analysis, of the kind offered by a professional (namely the dramaturg) or by a director dotting all the 'i's, the mise en scène seemed to step back from political and historical interpretation of the work. The task was never easy for Vitez's former actor, since how can you get away from the didactic heaviness of Brechtianism without falling into an 'invisible' dramaturgy, which quickly becomes insipid and anaemic? How can you transform a story that is itself a transposition of a theoretical schema that poorly renders the complexity of the world?

In a German context, one that cannot escape the influence of Brecht and which remains marked by the national institution of the *Dramaturg*, it is worthwhile examining how this figure is used in different ways in contemporary practice. We need only study the dramaturg as conceived by Thomas Ostermeier and Frank Castorf. In directing *Woyzeck* (2004, Avignon) and *Nora* (2002), Ostermeier called on a dramaturg (who is also a recognised author, associated with the Schaubühne): Marius von Mayenburg. The latter did a conscientious and precise work of analysis and of transposition, although the pertinence of his choices is far from obvious. Thus *Woyzeck* was transposed into our contemporary world, taking place on the margins of a huge metropolis in Eastern Europe, in a sewer, where all the trafficking takes place. In a certain sense, the production was too faithful to Büchner's play. It never stopped reiterating the same ideas: the violence of the world, the degradation of man, the suffering of the poor. But what was revolutionary in Büchner's era – the emergence of a sub-proletariat in a world that seeks to crush it – seems banal today. It is precisely mise en scène that should comment on and explain this state of affairs.

In another context, British theatre, it seems that the function of dramaturgical analysis is taken care of in devised work. An example is the working method of Simon McBurney, who does not mount a text that is fixed and decided in advance, but rather works with the actors and designers, and elaborates the score step by step, seeking textual material according to the needs of the story and the acting. The continental notion of mise en scène does not correspond to the reality of this practice of devised theatre, even if the director obviously takes the final decisions. The role of McBurney remains crucial due to his capacity 'for creating images that defamiliarize and redirect the geometry of conventional, received attention to reality, and etch themselves into our imagination'.[24] Thus there is an opposition between the rigidity and precision of dramaturgical analysis and the flexibility of a new kind of stage writing. Many other examples could be located in Europe of this type of practice, as with the work of Els Joglars or Comedians in Spain.

The director of actors

The distilled nature of new dramatic writing, the mistrust of the lavishness of scenography and spectacle, the intimidation caused by the technical aspect of stage machinery: all of these things reinforce a desire for simplicity and a move back to basics for the director, as well as a move toward the work of the actor. This reduction of mise en scène to the direction of actors stems from a very poor mode of production. To make a virtue of necessity, the director of actors is now only interested in acting, with the basic idea that they must give birth in the rehearsals to the actor, who is then provoked, trapped, mistreated and martyred. Hence actors and directors often drift into a pathological relationship. Most of the time, fortunately, everything goes in the right direction: the direction of the actors, in rehearsals or within the performance, establishes itself through a contrast and a difference within the mise en scène. Mise en scène is therefore conceived as the visible, the visual, the superfluous, the blocking, the choice of costumes and objects. The direction of actors is supposed to be the foundation of the theatrical relationship, to reproduce the human link between the actor and the organiser, between the creature and God the father. We are reminded of Cocteau's phrase about directors as midwives who think they are the father!

Criticism sometimes (rarely) distinguishes the two functions: the direction of actors and mise en scène. Sometimes we reproach a director for creating a stage set that imprisons the actors in the stage machinery, preventing them from 'breathing'. Scenographers-turned-directors and directors with a background in visual arts are often accused of this.

The particular attention that today we rightly place on the direction of actors should nonetheless not eliminate the function of mise en scène and all that it does or has implied historically or currently. The director certainly plays a fundamental role in the discovery and interpretation of the text and stage actions, but does not eliminate the more global function of mise en scène, for the simple reason that direction is part of the final production. If the direction of actors animates, irrigates and illuminates the mise en scène, the acting, however subtle and central it may be, only takes its meaning in the entire stage production. Therefore the *metteur en scène* cannot be reduced to the role of director of actors, and even less to that of the casting director, marketing director or director of communications.

Many contemporary directors have still chosen to concentrate first and foremost on the direction of actors, giving scenography and stage representation a secondary role, or one that is merged into the acting. The space and the world of the stage are recreated by the moves and the rhythmic management of time. In his stagings of *Twelfth Night*, *Cymbeline* and *Andromaque*, Declan Donnellan places the actor at the centre of the process, in order to avoid basing the work on a preconceived conception of the staging: 'One of the aims of Cheek by Jowl is to reexamine the classic texts of world theatre and to investigate them in a fresh and unsentimental way, eschewing directorial concepts to focus on the actor and on the actor's art.'[25]

The aesthete of theatrical forms

Fearing that their art is drifting towards casting and management, fearing the loss of all aesthetic, dramaturgical, ideological and political control, certain directors call on *théâtre d'art* and the heritage of Vitez. They reinforce the elements that give a show its aesthetic, artistic and artificial character: theatricality, and respect for conventions and forms. Their actors describe beautiful and clear choreographic figures with honed and precise movements; their way of speaking is deliberately rhetorical, musical, stylised and formalised (think of artists such as Jean-Marie Villégier, Daniel Mesguich, Robert Cantarella). The 'overacting' that results from this is not necessarily a mark of ham acting, but rather of the movement from simple acting to choreographic, heightened acting.

Many directors seek this choreographic, heightened, theatricalised acting. The emphasis on form does not necessarily seek to make the performance seem false. Often in fact, the theatricality goes hand in hand with a search for authenticity and for psychological precision. Patrice Chéreau, from the start of his career, under the influence in particular of Giorgio Strehler, is a good example of this aesthetic vision of the real. In Chéreau's productions, taking place against the often monumental scenography of his regular designer Richard Peduzzi, he seeks the image, the attitude, the lighting effect or the recorded sound that, thanks to their formal perfection, will aestheticise even the most sordid reality (as is the case in the plays of Koltès), and will provide a shiny surface, a perfect form, an uncanny atmosphere, a refined and sombre environment. In his staging of *Phèdre* (2004), Chéreau brings together highly psychological acting and a formal declamation of the alexandrine verse. Avoiding rhetorical and melodic tirades, the actors encourage identification with their characters.

According to the training and vocal habits of the actors, a very wide palette of ways of speaking and identifying with a role is obtained. All have in common an unusual mixture of authenticity and artificiality.

The silent musician

The term and the notion of mise en scène (in the modern sense, since the end of the nineteenth century) were invented for theatrical practice based on the text, and in particular on the literary text that pre-existed the performance. Is mise en scène still a legitimate notion for a theatre that works with things other than a text, in particular with images-without-text, with 'huge spaces of silence, so in fact virtual images?'[26] Should we not find another word, and thus another theory, for a mise en scène that does not represent an already-written text but which works with silence and non-verbal signs, be they visual or musical? Can we, should we, continue to speak of mise en scène in general, as if its principles had not been systematised in the nineteenth century? The notion of mise en scène is elastic, but is also irreplaceable if conceived as a mechanism of tuning and auto-regulation, not only for the stage, but for the world and the relationship between the stage and the world.

The director is sometimes comparable with a conductor, but also with a composer, since a director establishes and enforces a rhythm for an entire score. From Meyerhold to Marthaler, many artists have seen their role as that of a musician. Whatever the theme or the argument, Marthaler treats the words of the actors like polyphonic voices or instruments in an orchestration. In *Die Stunde Null* (1996) and in *Seemannslieder* (2004), the actor-orator-singers have unexpected encounters where they suddenly sing in chorus, something they do rather well, and with a dry sense of humour. What results is a singing chorus, seeking not to give a verbal or visual message, but to enjoy a nice time together, as if music, however parodic it may be, might offer an opportunity (or indeed an illusion?) of togetherness, of unison in the same universe, or of involvement in the same absurd and moving quest. Music plays the unexpected role of social cement; it gives the audience another vision of mise en scène, that of audio-vision. It tunes human relations as much as it tunes the performance.

The choreographer of silence

Is it the – real or metaphorical – choreographer who is best placed to execute this tuning? Theatre becomes dance when a game is established between elements of the performance without any need to go via language. This suggests that the choreographer is always present, especially when forgotten. Music set to a rhythm begins to dance, at least in the poetic sense that Corvin gives it:

> Theatre disintegrates or rather is metamorphosed: it becomes dance .... Dance does not mean choreography but specific time that, no longer depending on the necessity of exchange and dialogue, introduces play into dreams. Play, that is to say a rhythmical pulsation by which the director-author ... makes the text breathe.[27]

As it becomes dance and rhythmical play, mise en scène, such as the work of Wilson, Marthaler and Kantor, abandoned the too-obvious signified, in order to concentrate on mute and silent images: that is, on the signifier which, for as long as possible, refuses to be interpreted and turned into a sign. This mise en scène understood as pure dance brings us back to silence and to the spectator. It becomes the art of teasing out the unsaid, or even the unspeakable, as one of the voices of silence. It is not (or no longer) the art of expressing something, of perceiving the message and the noise, when we go from the textual to the visual. Rather, it is the art of bringing out silence for a spectator waiting for meaning. Mise en scène is the *mise en vue* of silence.

All of the director's doubles – actor, author, dramaturg, director of actors, choreographer and musician – far from relativising the importance of mise en scène, actually reinforce it, making it an essential concept in theatrical organisation. We should not give up on this notion and on this method, even if, in some respects, the conception of theatre work as performance and as production might be better equipped to illuminate the unpredictable relationship of art to the real, the effect produced on the spectator, the importance at times of detuning rather than tuning the performance, and the possibility of theatre encroaching on the world. Tuning and detuning, discipline and dissolution, regulation and deregulation: our heart wavers between two possibilities, as does the heart of mise en scène. Identities change so fast that it makes us dizzy.

Thus mise en scène might be in a state of constant crisis; it might even be the art of creating and solving problems at the same time. It is therefore not disappearing, only looking for new forms and strategies. Mise en scène is not only a matter of fine tuning, of 'adjustment' or 'regulation'; it is a survival kit not only for texts but also for new ways of looking at art and at reality. The debate of mise en scène versus performance has been very useful in going beyond the sterile opposition of mise en scène as mimesis versus performance as performative action.

Europe has, for the last thirty to fifty years, been a field of these eternal and pointless struggles, but it is no longer the space where all contradictions are resolved. Mise en scène happens elsewhere. It might seem like a good idea, but it still has to be invented, and must be immediately globalised and relativised. In Asia, the Americas and Africa, mise en scène is renewed and challenged by all these new 'performises' (a monstrous mixture of 'perf-' and 'mise', of acting and shaping).

Europe might be an inbox for the world's theatrical practices, but the box is empty, like a resonant drum, or a vessel ready to be filled with all the e-mails of the world, with all the sound and fury.

From the spectator to the theatrical assembly

Theory fatigue and spectator fatigue

It is notable that current criticism and theory tend only to be interested in the spectator's perception, sensation and subjective evaluation. Everything has moved miraculously from production to reception. Instead of examining, as was done in the past, the constitution of the performance, the narrative structure of the story, the conflict between the characters or the power relations between the components of the production, the perspective has moved toward the field of tension between the stage and the spectator. Hence the current interest in phenomenology. Every single theory or critical reflection, in dance or in performance, invokes it or uses it, and usually appropriately.

How can this sudden and unilateral infatuation with the reception side and with phenomenology be explained? There are a few simple reasons for it. The spectator has trouble grasping the structure of the work as production. Production no longer emanates from a unified and identifiable community. The spectator is a bit tired of theory, or else intimidated by deconstruction. Artists encourage the spectator to wander.[28] Former semiologists might very well say that the production/ reception circuit is too centred on a mechanistic semiology of communication.[29] It has become difficult to draw a clear line between the theatre and the world, between the production and the reception of works. The forceful development of individualism encourages (so as to avoid saying it forces) everyone to play and to 'enjoy' on their own and in their place, to propose their own hermeneutic journey, to try deconstruction, far from the production/reception circuit of Mukařovsky.[30] Simple good sense should demand that we also take into account the semiological organisation of the producers of the work, to confront them with the spectator's perceptions and experiences.

Already long ago, Bert States[31] invited us to avoid a separation of semiology and phenomenology, to join them the better to grasp the functioning of the performance. Is an equilibrium between production and reception, between semiology and phenomenology, not necessary?

The re-emergence of a damaged audience

This equilibrium is all the more essential since the spectator feels helpless amidst a rather perplexed audience. The spectator would like to be integrated into a collective 'we', which would somehow be reassuring. 'We' has become guilty ('I ought to understand something'), distrustful ('this performance is making fun of me'), challenging ('nothing is resolved'), suspicious ('I used to be a sovereign subject, have I now become a consumer?'), restless ('they are trying to get rid of me'), bad-tempered ('I can't let go') and worried ('What if I let go?').

The damaged world around us wants to damage us as well: to harm us, to swallow us, to stop us from getting away. 'Every man is an abyss': Büchner puts these words in Woyzeck's mouth. And yet we still aim for the top. As postmodern observers, are we not caught between bottom and top, serious and derisory, nonsense and sense, yin and yang?[32] We endlessly ask ourselves, tilt or *satori*? Bingo or *tao*? Con or *koan*?[33]

The helpless community and the disassembled assembly

The answer to these existential questions is slow in coming. No sense of community will ever come to our aid. The '*sans cible*' (those who are goalless, or sensitive) have thought a great deal about the theatrical assembly. Obviously such an assembly no longer has much in common with that of the Greeks, where the 'living together' of the community helped to ensure that 'violence was controlled by reason and discourse'.[34] What real or symbolic violence could be controlled by the fragmented and specific audience of today's theatre? Helpless, atomised and thwarted, the audience has trouble judging the complex and open works, having lost every criterion of judgement. This free, but fragmented and disseminated subject is faced with an embarrassment of riches and cannot make a choice. It does not close up on itself, nor take a new form based on any common value. But, as Marie-José Mondzain asks, how can we 'maintain ourselves when sharing the world'? According to Mondzain:

> nobody can ever flatter themselves with knowing what the other sees or feels faced with the spectacle of the world, and nevertheless

a community cannot maintain itself when sharing the world unless it gives itself the means to make networks of signs that circulate between bodies and produce a political sociality of emotions.[35]

In order to reconstitute these 'networks of signs' between bodies, it is necessary to describe the stage where such bodies move around as much as the spectators who receive them. This obliges us, appropriately enough, to avoid neglecting the description of the performance by bringing everything back to the 'feeling' of the spectator alone. Even a conscientious surveyor at times finds the way and finds the spectator's heart, thus causing a 'silent seismic shift': 'Certain performances are like a time-delayed bomb: they only explode when we have stopped being suspicious.'[36]

On faithfulness: or the difficult life of the couple that is text–performance

We have always considered mise en scène as a category in itself; it is the inheritor of a long Western tradition from literature and text-based theatre, but is open to many other practices. We might have approached it as a subcategory of cultural performances, as the twentieth-century string quartet that, according to Richard Schechner, the theatrical avant-garde has become. But did we perhaps not sufficiently decentre the eurocentric and text-centric position? Whatever system of classification has been employed, we have taken pains to widen out to the maximum the scope of performances, without making judgements in advance about their limits or, even more so, about their value or originality.

The couple that is text–performance

One Western obsession never ceases to torment: the relationship of text to performance, the 'faithfulness' or otherwise of a mise en scène to its text, or of the theatre to its double. What hierarchy can be established? How does theatre practice effect change within this infernal couple and does it still need them? Is this opposition relevant in other cultural contexts than that of Western theatre, and how does it vary across history?

The debate remains open, and it is not our intention here to add to the confusion. The old question whether theatre is literature or an autonomous art has not commanded interest for some time. Throughout history it has sometimes been one, and sometimes the other. Plays, literary works and dramas are still being written, but a performance does not need a textual origin, aid or trace in order to exist. The most important thing in fact is to identify the status of the text in the performance: is it received as a source of meaning to be meditated upon by a spectator or listener, or is it to be treated as musical material, more audible than understandable? But artists themselves need not decide this in any definitive or univocal way. Indeed, the director often cultivates doubt: actors carry the text, they pronounce it, but they often do so as if they do not understand it and as if it was not their problem any more. And on the other hand, spectators are sometimes obsessed with deciphering the text, while the important thing lies elsewhere, in the image, for example. No law can impose on us what we desire to perceive.[37]

Stéphane Braunschweig makes another distinction between 'theatre as text' and 'theatre as material'. In the first instance, the director presupposes that the text contains a coherence that must be recovered or established, since 'that thing was thought, wanted, if unconsciously, and it forms a whole: the whole of the author'.[38] This 'whole of the author' allows us to find the author 'at the source': that is, as the instance that helps us to reconstitute the play as a whole. It is thus possible to start from the totality of the text in order to analyse the text. In the second instance, we do not worry about reading bits of the text as a whole, but we assemble, we edit, we bind together these verbal and extra-verbal fragments within a show. Afterwards we grasp the logic of the director, the synthesis that has been made from these heterogeneous materials.[39]

This distinction between text and material is comparable with another opposition, which came about in the 1960s and became relevant in the 1970s, particularly in the Anglo-American world. Thus, as Chris Baugh has suggested, we can distinguish between directing a play and making a performance.[40] Either we push the existing text in a certain direction and according to its own logic, or we create a stage event in making a new object, which owes nothing to any textual source. 'Directing a play' is therefore choosing a direction, an orientation, an interpretation, reducing the range of possibilities. It specifically means taking as a starting point the text's givens as unalterable, to the letter. This is what Jürgen Gosch did with his *Macbeth*: he followed the order of the scenes and saw violence as offering a coherent reading despite the scatology.

This fabrication of the event can even lead to textual production. From acting indications given, the performers improvise words that will then be re-transcribed. This is what Chris Balme, in the working process of Robert Lepage, calls '*ein szenisches Schreiben*', 'a stage writing':

What comes about during rehearsals are stage events and texts. These texts are sometimes fixed as writing during the process of rehearsal. Often, movements or images precede textual choices. In such a context we could talk about stage writing, where the aim is not to create a ready text without stitching, or to deconstruct that text as a foreign object. The text is a necessary product of the work of staging and is continually being altered.[41]

The stage and the scene are thus at the point of origin of textual production. This text is a verbalisation of stage actions: it varies according to stage improvisations and is only fixed at a given, arbitrary moment. It is not the source of the dramatic situation, but rather its consequence, its moving trace. Mise en scène is not the execution of the text, but its discovery.[42]

Fateful faithfulness

Whatever the status of the text, be it at the very source of mise en scène or in the final results of stage work, it is worth distinguishing two radically different ways of treating the 'play'. Everything depends on whether the accent is placed on the literary text, on dramatic art, or on the stage event, the acting and the stage considered in themselves. Stephen Bottoms notes that:

There remains a primary divide in theatrically-oriented studies – the divide between those who address performance through a focus on the language and literatures on which it is often based, and those who see the performance event itself as the key concern, and text as simply supportive of it.[43]

Things have cleared up in recent years and we seem to be enjoying an appropriate status quo between the texto-centrists and the sceno-centrists. Neither is trying to prove that the other is wrong, and theatre-goers and theatre-makers often appreciate both kinds of show and both kinds of operation (to direct a play/to make a performance). There is thus a clarification of the possibilities and the positions. Nonetheless, theories of interpretation and of mise en scène sometimes come back to the old argument about fidelity. Faithfulness: such is the illusion that we have of reading, interpreting and performing the play following the author's intentions, as if there existed a correct reading, a reading that reveals a verifiable truth in the play or the interpreted work. It seems that at whatever historical moment, in whatever culture, common sense – and society with it – holds on to an idea of a truth of the text, inscribed in it, unchallengeable, inalienable, and so to an idea of a necessary and possible faithful interpretation. This faithfulness argument has always been a subject of discussion; it was considered right and incontestable, at least until the moment when, with the simultaneous invention of mise en scène and psychoanalysis (at the same time, the end of the nineteenth century, and according to the same epistemological break), we came to question the very possibility of being faithful (to a text, to a word, to a person). Directors, at least, started to question faithful reading and saw their work as an inevitable and productive betrayal regarding the so-called truth of the text, which according to them never existed and had neither meaning nor appeal. But the dogma of fidelity has thick skin; it reappears regularly in theory, even where theory thought it had finished with it, and with the norms of faithful reading.

Three examples of the resurgence of faithfulness

* Didier Plassard, in his remarkable 'typology of the staging of classics', suggests distinguishing between:

> two major types of choice, stagings with a restitutive aim and those with a projective aim. By restitutive stagings we refer to those that are centred on an immanent reading of the text; it is a labour of understanding the work, usually taken at the moment of its historical emergence …. Projective stagings, on the other hand, are those that use the work to produce a commentary that goes beyond the work's own limits, bearing on more general objects, be they historical questions (for instance contemporary society, or that of Louis XIV), philosophical questions, psychoanalytical questions, or others.[44]

Plassard's examples are rather convincing and we can readily recognise these two 'types of choice'. Our objection is rather of a theoretical nature, and is a question of principle: can a classic be read in an immanent way, and without projecting all that we know today (thanks to philosophy, psychology, sociology and so on)? We surely always read through such filters (we can no longer function without them)? And, on the other hand, what is the point of reading a classic according to our 'contemporary preoccupations' if we lose sight of the vision of long ago and of historical forms? Are we not in danger of creating an object that may well be of our time, but which no longer has much to do with the original? Is it still a classical play that we are staging? Are we directing a play or making a performance? We can surely agree that the art of mise en scène is precisely the art of compromise between these two types of aim, between an immanent structural analysis and a hermeneutical relationship built with a new audience. The notions of 'restitution' and 'projection' cannot be categorically opposed; they call for a compromise and a transaction, and it will be the task of the director to lead the negotiations. The restitution/projection couple is in danger of straying towards the fidelity/infidelity couple whose epistemological and conjugal problems are well known. Or, to be more positive, restitution requires projection and projection requires restitution. In order to be faithful, we must be unfaithful!

• A comparable debate seems to occupy recent theories of mise en scène: it is expressed in different terms, perhaps, but according to the same scheme of thought. The question still revolves around what the director brings from outside, or around the manner of restitution of what the text supposedly contained before, when the director set off looking for it. Bruno Tackels takes up this alternative, which I have just criticised:

> There remain two distinct attitudes of mise en scène confronted with the chosen text. Either the director says: I am going to try to tell you what the text wanted to say. Or he answers: I am going to try to tell you what I want to tell you, by exploiting in the best way possible what the text wanted to say. In each case the politics are radically different.[45]

In fact, the first attitude has become rare. Who would still claim to be able to say what the text wanted to say? The second attitude, despite looking like the compromise so praised above, remains an ambiguous solution and is doubly problematic: do directors know from the start what they want to say, and do they really know what the text means to say? This seems doubtful, at least in contemporary practice. We have witnessed in fact many experiments that do not take any absolute certainty as a starting point, but instead invent a framework of enunciation, and effect a tuning and adjustment to draw unexpected solutions out from the text, which only acting and staging can invent. Such artists do not wonder what the text or what they themselves wanted to say. Why, indeed, would they take that into account in any case, given that they often consider that they themselves work with materials, and can be considered creators in their own right, authors of the performance, sceno-centrists who are more or less aware or conscious of this fact? The argument for the necessity of fidelity (or, amounting to the same thing, of inevitable infidelity) is never far away. It goes hand in hand with an implicit conception of mise en scène qua a superfluous and harmful additive, a useless supplement. The return of the philological and logocentric conception is never far away either. For instance, in the introduction to *Théâtre aujourd'hui*, by Jean-Claude Lallias,[46] we find forms – sometimes quoted and sometimes taken up by the author (it is not always easy to tell the difference) – which betray a possible slippage of the conception of mise en scène towards a theory that advocates pedagogical justification and fidelity. According to Lallias, mise en scène is a contingent and personal 'translation':

> Even if traditions exist in the West, an art theatre can better be defined in terms of its innovations of staging, i.e. by the creation of a unique work and a work of stage translation which is knowingly contingent and personal. Hence the essential role of the director.[47]

Lallias rightly points to the emergence of the director in a Western context, but he perhaps 'essentialises' the director's function in limiting it to that of 'stage translation' (a very improper term). In evoking 'stage translation' he is probably implying that any 'worthwhile'[48] mise en scène is the translation of a text or a personal idea. He also emphasises the potentiality of the text, stating that it is the task of dramaturgy to sort this out: 'Perhaps one must first of all learn to describe what potentiality the text brings by way of an open, patient and informed reading. This is the role of dramaturgy.'[49] The implicit typology of the tasks of mise en scène goes back to the usual opposition in critical discourse of the director as tyrant v. the director as servant of the text: 'So, in the hierarchy of the theatre, the image of the omnipotent director contrasts with the idea of the pedagogical facilitator of a collective undertaking (which very often goes beyond the stage object), or with that of the modest servant who disappears in the face of the work'.[50]

It is hard to say how the author evaluates this hierarchy, or whether he brings the extreme differences of this typology to bear in order to complain about them or to celebrate them. In any case, this polarity can be a cause for concern, since it depends upon a normative evaluation of the work of the director who is torn between creative omnipotence and pedagogical humbleness. This normative and pedagogical vision of mise en scène is very common, and it can also be found within a quite different polarity that is just as contestable, the polarity that, 'confronted with texts, will oppose work that renders opaque, concentrates, creates a 'multitude of references – both intertextual and inter-scenic – with the dream of transparency, readability and a homogeneity of signs'.[51] Once again in the theoretical doxa, this fateful opposition between a 'degree zero of mise en scène' and a plethora, made redundant due to an excess of extra-textural and extra-scenic references, comes to light. This opposition is just as problematic as that which distinguishes visual productions and 'those that rarefy the signs, tend towards a bare stage and privilege listening, the sonic and the vibrating body of speech'.[52] This false opposition between the plethoric vision and immaterial listening is a resurgence of the Western dualistic conception, dividing the external vision bound to the represented body and the internal word bound to the naked voice. Thus these great supposed oppositions are merely dualistic metaphysical constructions, which are implicitly based on the dogma of a faithful word as opposed to an uncontrollable corporeal visuality.

It is not enough to say, as Lallias does, that truth lies between these extremes; we must also attempt a theory that describes particular cases and explains the functioning of existing shows by way of different criteria and different couples than those traditionally used, such as power/modesty, opacity/transparency, present-day/archaeology, writing/architecture, natural/theatrical, baroque vision/word neutrally spoken, archaism/media. This is what I have tried to do here in seeking to overcome these false oppositions by way of a few allusions to diverse recent experiences of theatre practice. Visual, media-based, intercultural, deconstructionist and gestural experiences in the contemporary theatre world are necessary challenges to theatre and to its theorisation. They share the possibility of displacing the supposed binaries of stage production, of forcing us to rethink the tuning mechanism that underlines the creation of this aesthetic object called 'mise en scène'.

The historic relativism of this dualism

Such a rethink is, however, by no means easy: the spectator, like the reader, remains subject to logocentric premises regulating the relationship of this fateful and very Western couple, text–performance. We find it difficult to escape from logocentrism, to imagine that the text is not always and necessarily at the origin of meaning, to imagine that it is not always illustrated and incarnated in the acting or the staging. This is why Derrida's deconstructionist position might be helpful in rethinking these delicate relationships. It is also very helpful in dealing with non-verbal or non-word-centred work, such as intercultural, media-based and gestural theatre. How, then, can we continue to think about, or 'unthink' and overcome, these binaries: text/stage (page/stage), readable/unreadable, readable/visible? The situation is clear, and it is an impasse. We have put aside the norms of the 1950s regarding the cursed couple of text and/or performance, fidelity and/or betrayal. We have ceased to see the performance as a semiotics emanating from the text. But have we come any further, in particular in theorising a 'post'-theatre: postmodern, postdramatic, post-post? And are we jumping out of the frying pan and into the fire when we refuse theoretical explanations en masse, or put off until tomorrow's 'post' what could be done today?

A simple and helpful measure might be to historicise and localise this debate between text and performance and to desist in treating it as an atemporal logical problem. The break with the philological thread for theatre people came towards the middle of the 1960s, when authoritarian structures were questioned and the body was placed at the centre of attention, when psychoanalysis and literary theory were on the verge of reversing the subject. All of this suffices to reverse the direction of the text/stage relationship, to privilege spectacular performances, to marginalise dramatic literature. Contextual and geographical variations relativise or modify these changes. Germany in the 1960s, with its rebellious youth discovering the ill effects of blind obedience, brutally rejected daddy's *Regietheater*, and before long it put its great classics through the mincer, to a degree that would have worried even Brecht. The United Kingdom, being more sober, resisted the dictatorial cult of personality and confirmed the importance of acting and the actor. It delegated to actors or participants of the work the task of devising, of collectively creating the show, step by step from the research of the themes to the establishment of the score, without recourse to the central perspective of a patented and labelled director. In the 1990s, in France, the text/stage relationship continued to evolve: the separation described by Braunschweig between text to be staged and material to be mixed became accepted, all the more as the former 'directator' assumed a low profile, renouncing the easy effects of spectacular mise en scène, and yielding to the delights of directing actors, taking inspiration from performance art and site-specific performance.

In contemporary practice it is nonetheless not easy to distinguish clearly the staging of text and staging as show, as an autonomous art. Often the artist has not consciously decided if it is one or the other, and the spectator will, to an even greater extent, be caught between the two ways of seeing. There are obviously no rules for telling them apart. Thus Gosch's *Macbeth*, which could shock and seem cut off from the play, ends up revealing itself to be a reading of the text. And, the other way around, the classics mounted by Castorf are more stage events than readings of a literary work, as the spectator (at least in my case) does not manage to make the link with the source text.

'Switching roles'

An unexpected consequence is that confusion about roles, and huge confusion about genres, reigns. Long ago, from Craig, with his praise of the director, from Artaud, and beyond from the generation of the 'directators', directors ended up mistaking themselves for the authors of the show, to the point of giving the real author leave to go. Then, in the 1960s and 1970s, annoyed with dramatic literature, authors mistook themselves for directors, and proceeded to stage their own texts, seeing them as mere scripts for performance, something which had all of a sudden become the supreme ideal. Since the 1990s the opposite has happened: authors give free reign to the director, to allow them to explore the possibilities of the text. This dramatic text is not 'incomplete' because it is an orphan of the stage, but rather 'full' because it is open to being used by actors and spectators alike.

Island or peninsula?

As Michel Vinaver has shown, in the twentieth century theatre has 'constituted itself as an island'.[53] It has separated from literature, and even from culture, to realise Craig's prophecy: 'when he will have mastered the uses of actions, words, line, colour, and rhythm, then he may become an artist. Then we shall no longer need the assistance of the playwright – for our art will then be self-reliant.'[54] This newly independent mise en scène, rejecting dramatic literature would, according to Vinaver, be the reason for the formation of this island, and would lead to the suppression of the duality of text and performance and the promotion of shows that force 'admiration because of the harmony that distinguishes them'.[55]

This radical position dates from 1988, when Vinaver's article was written. We must also bear in mind the extraordinary growth of dramatic writing in the 1990s, in France and in Europe, a shift due in part to Vinaver himself.[56] His island became a peninsula. Until the 1980s, at least in France, theatre was actually rather stage-based and cut off from literature. Texts were buried within shows or reduced to the status of scripts or librettos, or else made into a montage of linguistic material. A welcome result of this was that work on classical plays profited from a singular interest, and was a conduit for the interpretative energy of the directors, subjecting the classics to a 'catalytic' process:

> There exists the great universal repertoire, the classics, through which the director can express himself intimately, making of them a personal and contemporary work, provided there is catalytic process, to make elements of the present react by use of old substances, or to reactivate the past through an injection of today's materials.[57]

The chemical reactions of the classics could hardly be better described. It is up to theorists and artists to decide what exactly they would like to reactivate from the past and according to what vision of the present. The intertwining of the reactivation of the past and of this vision leads to an interpretation that is original and unique every time, to an intimate director's signature.

This conviction remains at the heart of the creative act, an act that tends to escape any control and any theoretical pretension. Such a conclusion might sound very worrying, but it is surely the case that it is not the theoretician's role to clarify the intimate and unconscious choices of artists.

Reconsidering the text–stage couple

The old question of the text–stage couple arises again. The eternal debate on whether the director is faithful comes back like the return of the repressed. Other couples, other ruses (more modern ones) intervene in order to disguise the old line about the necessity of fidelity to the interpreted text – an illusory fidelity, a right-thinking fidelity. But can we escape normative thinking? Are we not ourselves – as spectators, actors, directors – always after-the-(f)act, in the act of reading, interpreting, using language, and staging the word? And can we, or should we, escape the desire to reconstitute the whole of the author by way of the coherence guaranteed by an author and a textual structure? The desire for coherence, for verification, validation and fidelity, runs very deep.

The desire to create another theatre, one that is less logocentric and more eccentric, runs just as deep. Sometimes, in fact, the text fails to show up or there is nothing audible, readable or relevant about it.

It has then become sonic material, a sound without a sense, a signifier without a signified. Thus the stage event, the physical action and the performance are all that counts. We respect them as visual or musical works, an attempt to escape the word, and sometimes the meaning as well. And (by the miracle of meaning), this materialisation of the situation of enunciation, of the material in the time–action of the stage, sometimes manages to provoke the text, the dogma, the immobile, making it fly off the handle, giving rise to unexpected vibrations and unpredictable connotations.

It is, however, not so easy to mix and liquidate the text: like living tissue, a hydra or seaweed, it regenerates at the slightest touch, the moment there is a listener, but it potentially remains a symbolic system, a textual hydra whose tentacles grow back before your very eyes. The text–stage couple remains a very good barometer for judging mise en scène. A barometer should not, however, prescribe the weather! It would be preferable if it malfunctioned all the time, or was subject to permanent adjustment: checking and fine-tuning, but also a systematic and anarchic detuning of the senses.

'Mise en scène' is an untranslatable French term, enjoying all the ambiguity of an oxymoron. If the emphasis is placed on 'mise', on transference, on the passage of a material (be it textual or not) onto the stage, we remain in the logic of stage representation, whatever we do to escape 'the fate of representation' (as Derrida put it). If the emphasis is on 'scène', we lend the term a weight, an existence and an autonomy that owes nothing to what came before, be it textual, narrative or thematic. Fortunately we never actually know which of the figures we are dealing with at any particular time. And deep down, we do not want to know. We can only observe the historical slippage of 'mise' towards 'scène', of mise en scène towards performance.

On the horizon we see a new figure: '*mise en perf*', or '*performise*'. This is perhaps only a mirage. Even if the figure never materialises, it at least encourages us to go forward, to take the necessary steps, rather than staying perfectly in tune. We can thus avoid the old simplifications, and the old faithful philanthropic philology.

We will end up envisaging this *mise en perf/performise* as a new hybrid species in the inexhaustible reservoir of 'cultural performances'. It is a vivacious and voracious species, just like the textual hydra of the past. It is inexhaustible, because it is fictional.

It is high time that we thus recover the fictional, ludic, artistic and poetic dimension of the theatre, whatever its current identities may be.

It is time to return *in extremis* to the old text–performance couple, which is constantly challenged by both textual practice and stage practice. The prevailing current, at the beginning of the millennium, actually displaces certainties and undoes the unions of the past. Thanks to this, we seem to be abandoning essentialist research on the specificity of the dramatic text and of theatricality. And a clear distinction between text and mise en scène now only holds in the staging of classics, where the director cannot claim to be ignorant of the existence of a play when it is not only published and recognised, but also carries a tradition of readings. Even with contemporary texts, it is often the case that the published text takes previous productions into account. It becomes like a transcript. It becomes harder and harder to distinguish the text from the show. The evolution of dramatic writing, as well as that of mise en scène, tends towards convergence. Certain directors and authors no longer distinguish between the two practices, for example François Tanguy and the Théâtre du Radeau, or Joel Pommerat, for whom 'directing and writing will increasingly merge'.[58]

Paradoxically, today, the coming together of the text and the stage is borne out in the use of classics. There is a tendency to treat the text, even the classical text, by way of 'showing', 'quoting' and 'displaying' it in a sort of sonic and graphic installation. It is thus no longer a question of interpretation, or illustration, but of exposing the text like sonic material, of finding a device that allows the audience to walk around it. Think of one Hungarian *Hamlet* (directed by Árpád Schilling at Bobigny in 2007): the performers know very well that they will not be understood in Paris. The language is quoted in the subtitles, not as the speech of a character but as a series of texts borrowed from other authors. The performers speak it without seeming to let it affect them. They hold it at a distance and do not show what they think, or make any interpretation. The main concern is not saying the words, but rather seeing how they take their place and are exposed.

This Hungarian *Hamlet* helps us to grasp recent attempts at deconstructing the text–performance split, notably thanks to the theory of performativity and 'genetic' criticism of text and mise en scène. As Jean-Marie Thomasseau and Almuth Grésillon point out:

> genetic analysis, if it seeks to comprehend the creative processes of theatre, can be maintained only by convenience and concern for the cleanness of the parse between text and stage. At the same time, we must remember that the truth of theatre does not reside in the autonomous functioning of two separate mechanisms, but in the movement that links them and gives life to the work to be done. Everything is played out, in reality, in this no man's land

between the text and the stage, in this complex and fragile shift between the space of the page and the space of the stage, in a continuous and reversible to and fro between the readable, the speakable, and the visible.'[59]

To show this shift, this to and fro, we will call on a performative theory of the text. In this way, not only is performance (stage representation) a performative act, the text itself is also a performance, a production by way of an act of reading. The dramatic text, in fact like any fictional text and any real text accepting ambiguity, actually remains apparently the same but its reading changes every time, individually as well as collectively. We never step into the same river twice, nor dip into the same text. The dramatic text, just like performance, is only made up of a performative action: reading and especially a new mise en scène.

We will note that it is not only the text that is treated as a performative action and as a performance, but inversely so is the stage, the performance which, under the control of the director, can become centred and readable as a text, 'author-ised' by a 'maître (master) en scène' directing it. Hence this continual coming and going: text is 'performised', performance is 'textualised'.

Mise en scène, as it has been defined here, is the act of tuning and detuning, the compromise and the negotiation between opposing acts. It is as much about tuning-detuning the text by way of a stage enunciation, it is about trying the words on (in the sense that we 'try on' clothing): a detuning-tuning of the stage by way of the adjustment of the textuality, of the implicit discursiveness.

In the examples of classics located or dislocated by inventive teams of people, we saw that text and performance no longer function as antitheses, but as a couple in the process of losing its identity; each half of the couple hopes only to become the other (the classic situation in which lovers find themselves!). It is not, however, a question of fusion. The example of a *Hamlet* in Hungarian showed us that it is more a question of an installation, of a juxtaposition of scraps of text and stage actions.

This principle of installation, of juxtaposition, the desire not to explain, but only to cite, to add something without a word being spoken, certainly explains the fortunes of postmodernism and postdramatics. These notions seek only to allude to what comes after without tackling what or why. It is as if history was frozen, and as if we were no longer capable of chancing an overall theory of theatrical production today; as if after the dialectics of Marxism and Brechtianism

Figure 13.1 Hamlet, directed by Árpád Schilling. © Patrice Pavis.

we were no longer capable of grasping 'progress', or even the progress of our understanding of the world; as if there were no dialectics left, only 'supplements' of the 'post', because we can no longer manage to think of what will follow, what will progress, and less still think about progress itself. We have entered a 'Post-it' society: we write a reminder about what we (might) do tomorrow, later, in the lazy perspective of the postmodern. As for the postdramatic, it confuses the textual – nothing else after the dramatic (thus after the Brechtian epic) – and the staging – no more 'centred' mise en scène, be it centred on a text or on a privileged meaning. This category of the postdramatic is in this way far from being applied to all current textual and stage production. Moreover, when an author like Sarah Kane declares: 'Just a word on a page and there is the drama',[60] the catch-all category is questioned and we are more returned to the neo- or the pre-dramatic than the postdramatic.

But who exactly are we, and more importantly, where are we at?

Where are we going?

Where *is* mise en scène going? This is a question that today is somewhat unfashionable or has lost some of its relevance, as if knowing 'what use is theatre?' was an idealist leftover from the Enlightenment. So, we are not asking where theatre is going, but, more modestly, asking in what way the tool of mise en scène can help us to grasp this perpetually working, moving, fusioning art. 'The dramatic work is an enigma that theatre must resolve. This sometimes takes a long time.'[61] We will not say any different here: dramatic text is a problem that mise en scène must solve by tuning it.

Having reached a certain perfection, a diversity and a complexity, mise en scène is also experiencing a serious identity crisis. It is at pains to remain an aesthetic notion, since metaphors on all sides pull it towards other domains than the stage and fiction, to apply itself indistinctly to visual arts, performing arts and social reality, to the world seen as show business (more business than show). It is ceaselessly summoned to identify itself among cultural performances that claim to have the same status, among performance practices that touch the cultures of the entire world. Instead of feeling merely tolerated and suspended in many performing arts, performance studies or cultural studies departments, it must reconquer its aesthetic and fictional place inside all such cultural practices. Many stage artists sense that their art is being downgraded to the cultural, then to the sociocultural, then finally to the social.

Taking a narrow perspective, the view apparent when universities are charged with the crazy task of studying theatre matters, we notice that the gap is widening: the drift from theatre studies to performance studies to cultural studies becomes more and more accentuated. At the same time, this epistemological rivalry is an opportunity for theatre: if, that is, it is capable of assimilating these methods from other cultural practices as much as being assimilated by them. Thus research on the media, on interculturalism, or on new writing, far from weakening or watering down the performance and the representation, provokes it, forcing spectators to reconsider their modes of perception.

This is why mise en scène is doing rather well, despite the rivalry of notions (such as theatricality, spectacle, performance, or more recently chorality) claiming to overtake it or push us past it. It is doing so well, in fact, that it sometimes finds itself setting up a new tradition, not some stuck tradition, but a tradition in the process of being consolidated. The history of Western mise en scène offers a rich assortment of acting methods, textbook examples, signature methods and a few recognisable styles. Experienced artists like Peter Brook, Eugenio Barba and Ariane Mnouchkine have established a knowhow that could have become a model, had they not taken the care to challenge it constantly. In the manner of Noh or Pansori masters, our

Western masters could almost leave their actors to sort out the details, take care of the practicalities, and draw the rough lines of a style that belongs to them alone.

Despite these sketches of tradition, mise en scène, the anti-traditional tradition of the West, has not become a conservatoire of forms and methods. It is not limited to the *théâtre d'art*, even if this remains its flagship. *Théâtre d'art*, for some time, has ceased to be the directors' only aspiration; it is sometimes their pet hate, but often also their desire and their secret garden, their forbidden fruit. But in this secret garden, beyond the first circle of the initiated, the unconditional, will they still meet an audience to validate their choices? Or will they find only a dissolved assembly? And how can we know?

Whatever the frantic whirl of metaphors and definitions, mise en scène bravely stands astride the twentieth century; in terms of representation, theatricality, performance, intercultural communication, performance practice, deconstruction or performise, it maintains itself where it is able to adapt itself and undertake the necessary tuning in order to be transmitted from the world of art to that of the public assembly.

Perhaps it maintains itself because we, one evening's random spectators, or artists committed for a lifetime, agree to be transformed by it, like the metamorphosis that Copeau's director must face: 'When the director is confronted with dramatic work, his role is not to ask "What will I do with this?", but to say "What will this do to me?"'[62]

The work transforms us, and we transform the work in allowing ourselves to be traversed by it, putting ourselves in danger, taking the risk – for the work and for us – of the anamorphosis of uncertainty, the loss of identity, the old trace and the new path.

Who would not feel lost and orphaned at the start or the end of such a journey? But let us nevertheless risk this voyage without return, let us even chance a bet on the future, an act of faith and of love! Despite fanaticism, presentism, catastrophism and all the post-isms, all hope is not lost: spleen will dissipate, pain will lessen, and art will flower once again.

Glossary

Rather than listing terms of classical drama, many of which are already defined elsewhere,[1] this glossary is a collection of contemporary notions 'at work' in turn-of-the-millennium theatre practice. Some other terms are defined in the main body of the book and so do not feature in this glossary. Using the index, readers can readily find definitions for such terms.

Acting (acting style)   the way in which the acting is part of an aesthetics, determined by its relationship with the real, for instance realistic, naturalistic, impressionistic, expressionistic, epic, postmodern.

Address   not only the way in which a character might address the audience, but the way in which the performance as a whole approaches the auditorium, as if there were no separation, no fourth wall.

Alienation effect   or more precisely, 'distanciation effect' (*Verfremdungseffekt*). This Brechtian term describes the process that consists of rendering strange – and thus open to critique – that which is too familiar. This takes place by way of artistic procedures that betray the usual ways of representing, and then perceiving, an object. Other forms of alienation, such as **deconstruction** and **dissemination**, which are less political than Brecht's forms, are commonplace in contemporary productions.

Art (théâtre d')   this was the name of Paul Fort's symbolist theatre, founded in 1890, and refers to a style and conception of staging that rejects commercial concerns in favour of an elaborate and exacting art form.

Author-ity   that which the author of a text or of a staging, as master of meaning, is able to control and lead: for example this is the case in a very 'directed' staging, focused on staging choices.

Body art   an art form that takes the human body as its object, interrogating and provoking it, testing its limits and its most extreme possibilities of expressiveness.

Chorality   the performance's possibility of treating the stage as a group of united and distinct elements, bringing together the different elements that comprise the mise en scène. Choruses are not only vocal and musical; they bring together all elements of the stage work. It is not a question of recovering some forgotten rite, or a disappeared community, but of leading and exposing the spectators' own community.

Chronotope   Mikhail Bakhtin's term for 'the intrinsic connectedness of temporal and spatial relationships'.[2] Mise en scène often seeks this connectedness, in order to produce an effect of integration and metaphorisation of the stage materials.

Collective creation   work that is not exclusively controlled by a director, but with many choices left to the artists, and particularly the actors. When we emphasise the collective and progressive conception of the elaboration of a project as a whole, we can use the term devised theatre.

Corporality   the sum of the physical qualities of the actor's body, notably appearance, and the materiality of the physiological body and the action that it performs.

Decentring   a staging is decentred when it is no longer constructed according to any stable or identifiable meaning-making. The director and meanings are no longer stable or central elements, they have lost their hegemony along with every other philosophical, political, or artistic authority.

Deconstruction   a term from Jacques Derrida describing a process consisting of undoing a hegemonic system, showing its contradictions, its many possible readings, and its shifting interpretations.

Devised theatre   an English term that is difficult to translate into French. It refers to a working method that constructs the production step by step, without a predetermined scheme imposed by an authoritarian director. All the tasks: writing, choice of space and place of staging, acting, soundtrack and so on are approached simultaneously and without a hierarchy of values.

Différance   a term from Jacques Derrida (sometimes conveyed as 'differance' in English). Différance is the fact of differing or deferring meaning, leaving it for later, until it becomes clear that it can never be reached.

Directing actors   the work taking place throughout rehearsals relating to the – harmonious or conflicting – relationship between the director and the actors discovering their characters or tasks. This is the very heart of mise en scène.

Dissemination   a term from Jacques Derrida. The impossibility of locating and of reifying the meaning in a text or artwork, beyond our need for coherence and of centralisation of meaning. Meaning does not reside in the text, but in its performance, its disappearance and construction/deconstruction in all possible contexts.

Effect produced   what the performance induces in the spectator in terms of emotions and reactions, the way in which the spectator is affected. Today, it sometimes seems easier to describe such effects than to interpret the work that provokes them.

Ethnoscenology   the study of organised human spectacular behaviours and practices in different cultures.[3] Ethnoscenology goes beyond the study of Western theatre to consider performance practices from the entire world, in particular those that relate to rites, ceremonies and cultural performances, seeking to avoid projecting any Eurocentric vision.

Expectations   what the audience is ready to receive, the limit created by the spectators' knowledge and previous experiences.

Figure   a term used to avoid the term character, which might be considered too psychological and too mimetic. The figure is a structural entity that concentrates or disperses figurative and abstract elements at the same time. The actor traces figures on the stage, which are almost choreographic, and these often constitute the most pertinent structure available in order to see and follow meaning.

Genetic   genetic criticism examines the genesis of a play, which is necessarily mobile and unfinished, until it is performed. It is concerned with the work of mise en scène, particularly the manner in which staging choices reassess the reading of the dramatic text.

Gestus   Brecht's term for the social quality of characters' gestures, wherein are revealed relationships of power or of class.

Hermeneutics   a method of interpretation of texts and images, it is 'the totality of the learning and skills that enable one to make the signs speak and to discover their meaning'.[4] Stagings impose a hermeneutics of texts and of stage practices with a view to their production (genetics), their reception in wider or narrower frames, the author's perspectives, of the work and finally of the spectator. Thus mise en scène is a hermeneutic tuning of meaning, negotiated between the work given, the director and the actors interpreting it, and the specific audience that receives it.

Installation   a display of objects, animated images, visual artworks. The visitor moves around these at will and following no specific path. Theatre also sometimes 'installs' itself, becoming a kinetic art, with site-specific performance, land art, presenting the text by 'hooking' it onto the space, the place, and attempting to explain and embody it.

Intercultural (theatre)   a theatre that, in terms of its themes as much as its style of acting and staging, calls upon elements that, at least originally, come from different cultures.

Kinesthesia   the perception, by the spectator, of movement, particularly that of the dancer or actor. The staging and acting take into account the spectators' reactions. These spectators perceive, but also involuntarily transmit, their reactions.

Koan   a Japanese word for a question meant to provoke thought. In the Zen philosophy, a koan is a question posed by a master to a pupil, a question that cannot receive a response according to traditional logic, but which nevertheless causes a sudden moment of awareness or illumination (satori). Example: the sound of one hand clapping.

Kut   a shamanic ceremony in Korea conducted by a *mudang* (a female shaman) in which a community is present and participates and with elements of spectacle.

Live   acting produced before an audience, or transmitted live by way of audiovisual media.

Mise en espace (blocking)   spatial choices when reading the play and an attempt to translate these into the actors' positions and moves.

Mise en jeu ('setting in motion', or 'playing')   the first stage of work with the actors, at the start of the rehearsal process, consisting of having the actors speak and perform.

Mise en piste ('taking the space')   the organisation of a circus show according to the artistes and their actions in the space–time.

Mise en place   the placing of characters, the establishment of their respective positions in the space, the system of the actors' entrances and exits.

Mise en vision   Barba's term.[5] Having made the story understandable, having put things in place and into time (determined the blocking and rhythm), the mise en vision consists of 'removing all that is not necessary, that is simply cutting', as with the editing of a film.

Mise en voix   reading aloud of the play by the actors for the director, not only in order to find intonations, but to create vocal gestures, their stylisation, and their effects on the spectator.

Multimedia (theatre)   a show using one or more forms of available media, for example cinema, video, projections, computers.

Mudang   a Korean shaman, generally a woman, undertaking the ritual of *kut*.

Pansori a Korean form of narrative poem, sung and spoken by a single performer accompanied by a percussionist.

Performative and performativity the performative verb accomplishes an action in its very enunciation. For example: 'I ordain you …' Just as gender is constituted by the normativised repetition of behaviours more or less imposed by society, the performance is a repetition and an accomplishment of actions planned by the mise en scène according to a series of conventions.

Performer the artist who, instead of playing a character, as an actor would, appears as an individual person, creating a virtuoso and unrepeatable performance.

Phenomenology a philosophical method, literally the 'science of phenomena', seeking, by way of descriptions of things, to discover the structures of consciousness. Just as mise en scène is the abstract part of the performance (that we do not see but which organises the whole production), phenomenology constitutes the meaning of the phenomenon and refers the phenomenon to the act of consciousness that is directed at it.

Political theatre if this seems to have disappeared since the 1980s and 1990s, this is because it is less visible and less straightforwardly militant, and because it is more concerned with resistance than with revolution, with performativity rather than with the ideological message.

Polyphony 'A unitary conception of the theatre, be it founded on the text or on the stage, is in the process of disappearing. It progressively is giving way to the idea of a polyphony, or even to a competition between the family of arts that make up the entity that is theatre.'[6]

Postdramatic A term from Richard Schechner, taken up by Hans Thies Lehmann.[7] This theatre is not a new and unified genre, a notion of a whole, but beyond drama and theatre, a tendency of the practice to challenge mimetic action, story, character, dramatic conflict, and psychological acting in the Stanislavskian tradition.

Presentation and representation since Aristotle, theatre is considered the mimetic representation of an action. By contrast, since the performance art of the 1950s, the actor is instead engaged in a presentation of the self as an private person and not as a character: the actor exhibits a persona, a person with its mask, and is a performer rather than an actor representing a character.

Self-directing the way in which an actor, away from the gaze of the director and without the director's help, takes decisions regarding the acting or the strategy. For Michael Chekhov, the psychological gesture can play this role, since it 'helps and leads you like an invisible director, friend and guide who never fails to inspire you when you need inspiration most.'[8]

Short form   a reading of a few minutes, a short theatre performance, piece of music or film, video. These short forms, like haiku, are a flash of light, and are created as a reaction against the complete or explicit work.

Silence   the absence of speech, of noise, but also of movement or of meaning. Silence is …

Soundscape   playing on landscape, this refers to the organisation of sounds, music, recordings, forming a whole, a composition that enters the space thanks to the possibility of producing sound sources in the landscape of the stage or the auditorium.

Stage management   not to be confused with mise en scène, which is the artistic organisation of the production.

Stage writing (écriture scénique)   a term primarily in use in the 1960s and 1970s. The use by a director of stage or scenographic means to create an autonomous work, not dependent on a text or on 'dramatic writing'.

Street arts   performances taking place in the street or in public spaces, the term is not limited to theatre (street theatre), but encompasses dance, performance art, and the visual arts.

Theatre of gesture   a synonym of physical theatre. This is a way of performing that is essentially based on the actor's body, at the expense of the text, psychology, repertoire, and even the overall central notion of mise en scène.

Visual arts   installations, projections and media art, and performance works in a museum often join theatre as such within the category of visual arts.

Notes

Foreword

1 Pascal Charvet, 'Foreword', in Jean-Claude Lallias (ed.), *L'ère de la mise en scène, Théâtre d'aujourd'hui*, no. 10, Paris, Centre National de Documentation Pédagogique, 2005, p. 3. Particularly valuable are the responses of eighteen directors to this questionnaire.

2 Patrice Pavis, *Analyzing Performance*, Ann Arbor, Mich., 2003.

3 Patrice Pavis, *Le Théâtre contemporain. Analyse des textes de Sarraute à Vinaver*, Armand Colin, 2002.

1 Where did mise en scène come from?

1 Bernard Dort, 'Condition sociologique de la mise en scène théâtrale' in *Théâtre réel*, Paris, Editions du Seuil, 1971.

2 Ibid. p. 51.

3 See, on nineteenth-century mise en scène, the work of Jean-Marie Thomasseau, notably in Michel Corvin, *Dictionnaire encyclopédique du théâtre*, Paris, Bordas, vol. 2, p. 612. See also, 'Le Théâtre et la mise en scène au xixe siècle', in Patrick Berthier and Michel Jarrety (eds), *Histoire littéraire de la France*, Paris, PUF, 2006.

4 Roxane Martin, *La Féerie romantique sur les scènes parisiennes (1791–1864)*, Paris Honoré Champion, 2007.

5 The term 'mise en scène' applied to practices before the nineteenth century is anachronistic and can be misleading. To translate Aristotle's term *mimesis* as 'mise en scène' is audacious at the very least: 'the effect [fright and pity] by means of performance has nothing to do with art: it is a matter of mise en scène' (Aristotle, *La poétique*, 50b17, trans. R. Dupont-Roc and J. Lallot, Paris, Editions du Seuil, 1980).

6 See Sophie Proust, *La Direction d'acteurs dans la mise en scène théâtrale contemporaine*, Montpelier, L'Entretemps, 2006.

7 Jacqueline Razgonnikoff:

> If one examines the documents, one realises that, since the seventeenth century, from the raw text intended to be staged, different possibilities emerge, that through history, actors did not systematically reproduce the same patterns, and that 'tradition', so often invoked, can be evolution or revolution. The acting, the decor and costumes, the

music, and the props, all the details of a production bear witness to the will, conscious or not, to reach a conclusion that is the performance. The convergence of these details constitutes the embryo of a 'mise en scène' which, so as to not be 'interior' in Antoine's sense of the word, is no less the reflection of a conception and of a subjective attitude which, faced with a text, renews themselves, cancels themselves out, or complete one another as time goes on.

(*Journal des Trois Théâtres*, no. 18, January, 2006, p. 30)

8   Jean-Loup Rivière, *Comment est la nuit? Essai sur l'amour du théâtre*, Paris, L'Arche, 2002, p. 90.

9   Polly Irvin, *Directing for the Stage*, Mies, RotoVision Stagecraft, 2003, p. 170.

10   Thomas Postlewait, 'Mise-en-scène', in *The Oxford Encyclopedia of Theatre and Performance*, Oxford, Oxford University Press, 2003, p. 863.

11   Emile Zola, Le Naturalisme au théâtre, in *Oeuvres Complètes*, Paris, Cercle du livre précieux, vol. XI, [1881] 1968, p. 357.

12   Ibid. p. 358.

13   Ibid. p. 366.

14   Ibid. p. 339.

15   Ibid.

16   André Antoine, 'Causerie sur la mise en scène', *La Revue de Paris*, March–April 1903.

17   Ibid. p. 602.

18   Ibid. p. 603.

19   Ibid. p. 602.

20   Ibid. p. 603.

21   Ibid. p. 610.

22   Jean Vilar, *De la tradition théâtrale*, Paris, L'Arche, 1955, p. 17. *Tréteaux* are the boards of the stage, as in the expression 'to tread the boards'. Vilar is referring to traditions of unembellished, popular theatre that would usually be performed in the open air.

23   Stéphane Mallarmé, 'Crayonné au théâtre', Paris, Gallimard, [1887] 1945, p. 235.

24   Maeterlinck, *La Jeune Belgique*, 1890.

25   Aurélien Lugné-Poe, quoted in Jean-Pierre Sarrazac, 'Reconstruire le réel ou suggérer le réel', in Jacqueline de Jomaron (ed.), *Le Théâtre en France*, Paris, Armand Colin, 1992, p. 725.

26   Pierre Quillard, 'De l'inutilité absolue de la mise en scène exacte', *Revue d'art dramatique*, 1 May 1891, p. 15.

27   Ibid. p. 17.

28   Guido Hiss, *Synthetische Visionen. Theater als Gesamtkunstwerk von 1800 bis 2000*, Munich, Epodium Verlag, 2005.

29   Adolphe Appia, 'Acteur, espace, lumière, peinture', *Théâtre populaire*, no. 5, 1954, p. 8.

30   According to David Bradby and David Williams, *Directors' Theatre*, London, Macmillan, 1988, p. 3.

31   Edward Gordon Craig, *On the Art of the Theatre*, London: Theatre Arts Books/Heinemann, 1956, pp. 180–1.

32   See Michel Vinaver, 'L'île', *Théâtre en Europe*, no. 18, September 1988; see quotation in Chapter 13.

33 Jacques Copeau, *Notes sur le métier d'acteur*, Paris, Michel Brient, 1955, pp. 4–7.

34 Jacques Copeau, *Appels. Registres I*, Paris, Gallimard, 1974, p. 29.

35 Antonin Artaud, *Theatre and its Double*, New York, Grove Press, 1958, p. 60.

36 Ibid. p. 106.

37 Ibid. p. 106.

38 Ibid. p. 107.

39 Ibid. p. 73.

40 Bertolt Brecht, 'Questions sur le travail du metteur en scène', in *Ecrits sur le théâtre*, Paris, Gallimard, 2000, p. 783.

41 Jean Vilar, *De la tradition théâtrale*, Paris, Gallimard, 1955, p. 71.

42 Beyond American or British performance studies, the term 'mise en scène' is used in a partly metaphorical way in two recent works: Joseph Früchtl and Jörg Zimmermann (eds), *Asthetik der Inszenierung*, Frankfurt, Suhrkamp, 2001; and *Mises en scène du monde: Colloque international de Rennes*, Besançon, Les Solitaires intempestifs, 2005.

43 Edward Braun, *The Director and the Stage, From Naturalism to Grotowski*, London, Methuen, 1982, p. 202.

44 See David Bradby, in collaboration with Annabel Poincheval, *Le Théâtre en France de 1968 à 2000*, Paris, Honoré Champion, 2007.

2 On the frontiers of mise en scène

1 Marshall McLuhan, *The Gutenberg Galaxy*, London, Routledge, 1962, p. 250.

2 Denis Podalydès, 'Le spectacle de la lecture', *Littérature*, no. 138, June 2005, p. 68.

3 Cited in Marie-Claire Pasquier, 'Claude Régy: garder le secret du livre', *L'Art du théâtre*, no. 6, 1987, p. 62.

4 Jacques Copeau, *Registres*, Paris, Gallimard, 1974, vol. 1, p. 59.

5 Pasquier, op. cit., p. 23

6 Marguerite Duras, *L'Arc*, no. 98, 1985, p. 65. Cited in Joseph Danan, *Le Théâtre de la pensée*, Rouen, Editions Médianes, 1985, p. 300.

7 Staging by Phillip Zarrilli, Singapore, Summer 2004. This performance of Water Station is available on DVD.

8 Avignon festival, cour du Lycée Saint-Joseph, 2001.

9 Albert Thibaudet, 'Physiologie de la critique: Conférences au Vieux-Colombier de 1922'. Physiologie de la critique, *Nouvelle Revue critique*, 1930, pp. 23–4.

10 Bernard Dort, *Théâtre réel*, Paris, Seuil, 1971, p. 47.

11 Ibid. p. 47.

12 Bernard Dort 'Trois façons d'en parler' [*Le Monde*, 1982], in Thomas Ferenzi and Chantal Meyer-Plantureux, *Un siècle de critique dramatique. De Fransisque Sarcey à Bertrand Poirot-Delpech*, Paris, Editions Complèxe, 2003, pp. 139–43.

13 *Le Monde*, 1982. Text reproduced in Chantal Meyer-Plantureux, *Un siècle de critique dramatique*, Paris, Complexe, 2003, p. 142.

14 Georges Banu, *Théâtre/Public*, no. 50, 1983. Text reproduced in Meyer-Plantureux, op. cit., p. 146.

15 Henning Rischbieter, comments in *Theater heute*.

16 Banu, *Théâtre/Public*, no. 50, p. 149.
17 We are no longer faced with a choice of criticism either wishing to speak
    of the staging (as a system), or of mentioning the actors' performance.
    Theatre critic Jean-Pierre Léonardini puts it thus:
    > I am absolutely convinced that not speaking of the actors in my own
    > work is a blind spot. I think that in our current situation, the concept
    > of mise en scène should be defended as much as that, in our articles,
    > of critical perspective. But to speak of that, and not of the actor, I
    > amputate a secondary construction from my work.
    ('La critique en question', *Théâtre/Public*, no. 18, 1977, p. 19)
18 Yves Michaud, *L'Art à l'état gazeux. Essai sur le triomphe de esthétique*, Paris,
    Stock, 2003, p. 100.
19 Georges Banu, cited in Meyer-Plantureux, op. cit., p. 150: 'The body of the
    critic is not only her own, but is also that of the generation to which she
    belongs.'
20 M. Shevtsova and S. Mitter (eds), *Fifty Key Theatre Directors*, London and
    New York, Routledge, 2005.
21 Comments by Antoine Vitez, on taking over at the Théâtre national de
    Chaillot.
22 Christian Rist, *Rimbaud/Illuminations. Fragments scéniques improvisés*.
    Théâtre d'Antony, 20 January 2005.
23 See Chapter 3.
24 Ludovic Janvier, 'Le spectacle de la lecture', *Littérature*, no. 138, June 2005,
    p. 66.

3 The difference between mise en scène and performance

1 Andy Lavender, *Hamlet in Pieces: Shakespeare reworked by Peter Brook, Robert
    Lepage, Robert Wilson*, London, Nick Hern, 2001, p. 82.
 2 Jacques Copeau, *Appels*, Paris, Gallimard, 1974, p. 30.
 3 Jean Vilar, *De la tradition théâtrale*, Paris, Gallimard.
 4 According to Boireau, English theatre is particularly close to social reality:
    'As a mirror of ideologies which express themselves through it, and are
    elaborated by it, English theatre gets its strength from the surrounding
    space and it transforms itself, via a process of symbolization, into a machine
    to explore time' (Nicole Boireau, *Théâtre et société en Angleterre, des années
    1950 à nos jours*, Paris, PUF, p. 1).
 5 To use the title of Anne Ubersfeld's work, published in 1976.
 6 Simon Shepherd and Mick Wallis, *Drama/Theatre/Performance*, London,
    Routledge, 2004, p. 237.
 7 Boireau, op. cit., p. 235.
 8 Jacques Derrida, 'The theater of cruelty and the closure of representation',
    in *Writing and Difference*, trans. Alan Bass, London, Routledge, 1978.
 9 Boireau, op. cit., p. 235.
10 One of the only books on this question in France is written in English:
    Alec G. Hargreaves and Mark McKinney (eds), *Post-Colonial Cultures in
    France*, London, Routledge, 1997.
11 Phenomenology applied to theatre was theorised by Bert O. States as early
    as 1985, in his *Great Reckonings in Little Rooms: On the Phenomenology of
    Theatre* (Berkeley, Calif., University of California Press), and in the article

'The phenoenological attitude', in a very influential collection: Janelle Reinelt and Joseph Roach (eds), *Critical Theory and Performance*, Ann Arbor, Mich., University of Michigan Press, 1992. See also Les Essif, *The French Play: Exploring Theatre 'Re-creatively' with Foreign Students*, Calgary, University of Calgary Press, 2006.

12 Jon McKenzie, *Perform or Else. From Discipline to Performance*, London, Routledge, 2001, p. 18.

13 See Chapter 9.

14 Josette Féral, *Théâtralité, écriture et mise en scène*, Montreal, Hurtubise, 1985.

15 Clive Barker, 'Joan Littlewood', in Alison Hodge (ed.), *Twentieth Century Actor Training*, London, Routledge, 2000, pp. 124–5.

16 See Mihaly Csikszentmihalyi, *Vivre: La psychologie du bonheur*, Paris, Robert Laffont, 2004.

17 Jacques Derrida, *Sur parole: Instantanés philosophiques*, Paris, Editions de l'Aube, 1999, p. 53.

18 Stéphane Braunschweig, *Petites portes, grands paysages*, Arles, Actes Sud, 2007, p. 150.

19 Kirsten Hastrup, *A Passage to Anthropology*, London, Routledge, 1995.

20 On the question of 'density', see Patrice Pavis, *Analyzing Performance*, Ann Arbor, Mich., 2003.

21 Simon McBurney, *Mnemonic*, London, Methuen, p. 8.

22 Declan Donnellan, quoted in Gabriella Giannachi and Mary Luckhurst (eds), *On Directing: Interviews with Directors*, London, Faber & Faber, 1999, p. 19. See also Declan Donnellan, *The Actor and the Target*, London, Nick Hern, 2005.

23 Joan Rivière, 'Womanliness as masquerade', *International Journal of Psychoanalysis*, Vol. 10, 1929, pp. 303–13.

24 At Seong Arts Center, Seoul, November 2006.

25 Michel Vinaver, *Théâtre Complet*, vol. 1, Actes Sud et L'Aire, 1986, p. 25.

26 For Richard Schechner, 'showing doing' is the way of showing what is done, and is the object of performance studies.

27 Michel Vinaver, 'Présentation', in *Théâtre Complet*, vol. 1 p.41.

28 Ibid. p. 41.

29 We note that quotation marks protect these designations.

30 As Schechner has often pointed out.

31 An imaginary, but not apocryphal quotation.

32 Vinaver, 'Présentation', p. 41.

4 Tendencies in French scenography

1 This chapter developed from a lecture given at the conference 'L'Espace théâtrale', organised by Hyun-Sook Shin in Seoul in November 2003.

2 Luc Boucris, *L'Espace en scène*, Paris, Librairie Théâtrale, 1993, p. 9. For a vision of scenography in the United States, see Arnold Aronson, *Looking into the Abyss*, Ann Arbor, Mich., University of Michigan Press, 2005.

3 Daniel Jeanneteau, 'Notes de travail', *Revue de l'esthétique*, no. 26, 1994, p. 20.

4 Jean-Marie Pradier, *La scène et la fabrique des corps*, Bordeaux, Presses universitaires de Bordeaux, 1997, p. 18.

5 Nicola Sabbattini, *Pratique pour fabriquer scènes et machines de théâtre*, Neuchâtel, Ides et Calendes, 1942.
6 André Diot, 'Les comédiens', *Actualité de la scénographie*, no. 100, 1999, p. 37.
7 Pierre Quillard, 'De l'inutilité absolue de la mise en scène', *Revue d'art dramatique*, 1 May 1891, p. 17.
8 Éric Vigner, 'L'architecture au théâtre' *Actualité de la scénographie*, no. 100, 1999, p. 56.
9 Daniel Jeanneteau, 'Quelques notes sur le vide', www.remue.net, 2000.
10 Claude Régy, 'Entre non-désir de vivre et non-désir de mourir', *Théâtre*, Oct.–Nov. 2002, p. 14.
11 Daniel Jeanneteau, 'Entretien avec Georges Banu', *Nouvelle revue française*, 1999, p. 15.
12 Ibid. p. 170.
13 Valentin Fabre and Jean Perrottet, 'La position du spectateur', *Actualité de la scénographie*, no. 100, 1999, p. 6.
14 Yannis Kokkos, 'Entretien', *Opus*, no. 84, 1982.
15 Jean Chollet and Marcel Freydefond, *Les Lieux scéniques en France*, Paris, Editions Actualité de la scénographie, 1996.
16 Joël Hourbeigt, 'Le rapport salle-scène', *Actualité de la scénographie*, no. 100, 1999, p. 14.

5 The *mise en jeu* of contemporary texts

1 Bernard-Marie Koltès, *In the Solitude of Cotton Fields*, trans. Jeffrey Wainwright, London, Methuen, 2001, p. 41.
2 Emmanuel Darley, *Théâtre Ouvert, Programme of the 1999–2000* season, p. 17.
3 Jean-Marc Lanteri, 'Les écritures théâtrales en Grande-Bretagne (1980–2000)', in *Ecritures contemporaines 5: Dramaturgies britanniques (1980–2000)*, Paris, Minard, 2002, p. 5.
4 Bernard-Marie Koltès, *Combat de nègre et de chiens*, Paris, Ed. de Minuit, 1983; *Black Battles with Dogs*, trans. David Bradby and Maria M. Delgado, Methuen, 1997.
5 Marie NDiaye, *Papa doit manger*, Paris, Editions du Minuit, 2003.
6 Ibid. p. 95.
7 Ibid. pp. 65–7.
8 See www.theatre-contemporain.net/spectacles/Papa-doit-manger/ensavoirplus/idcontent/9440
9 Catherine Anne, *Le Bonheur du vent*, Paris, Actes Sud-Papiers, 2003.
10 Ibid. p. 29.
11 Catherine Anne, press pack, Théâtre de l'Est Parisien, 2004, p. 5.
12 Catherine Anne, *Le Bonheur du vent*, Paris, Actes Sud-Papiers, 2003, p. 29.
13 Ibid. p. 30.
14 Michel Corvin, 'Mise en scène et silence', *Revue d'esthétique*, no. 26, 1994, p. 126.
15 Noëlle Renaude, *A tous ceux qui*, Paris, Editions théâtrales, 1994.
16 Press pack for the production, Avignon, 2005.
17 Renaude, op. cit., p. 13.
18 Pierre Bourdieu and Loïc Wacquant, *Réponses*, Paris, Ed. du Seuil, 1992.
19 Ibid. p. 101.

20 Production mounted in Cork, 3 September 2005, and then at the Théâtre Ouvert in January 2006.

21 Michel Vinaver, quoted in 'A brûle-pourpoint: Rencontre avec Michel Vinaver', *Du Théâtre*, special issue no. 15, Paris, Centre national de documentation pédagogique, November 2003, p. 10.

22 Michel Vinaver, *Le Compte-rendu d'Avignon*, Arles, Actes Sud, 1987.

23 Ibid. p. 36.

24 Ibid. p. 55.

25 Eugène Durif, season programme, Théâtre Ouvert, Paris, 1999–2000.

26 See the special edition of *Contemporary Theatre Review*, 'The director as cultural critic', vol. 13, August 2003.

27 'Entremetteur' Robert Cantarella, 'La main-d'oeuvre', *Revue d'esthétique*, no. 26, 1994, p. 191.

28 'Mettre en scène le théâtre contemporain', *Trois pièces contemporaines*, reading led by Françoise Spiess, Paris, Gallimard, 2002, p. 147.

29 Heiner Müller, *Gesammelte Irrtümer*, Frankfurt, Verlag der Autoren, 1986, p. 156.

6 The intercultural trap

1 Carolina Ponce de Leon, in Henry Bial, *The Performance Studies Reader*, London, Routledge, 2004, p. 295.

2 Guillermo Gómez-Peña, *Dangerous Border Crossers*, London, Routledge, 2000, p. 210.

3 Gómez-Peña in Bial, op. cit., p. 295.

4 Ibid. p. 298.

5 Ibid. p. 298.

6 Dennis Kennedy (ed.), *The Oxford Encyclopedia of Theatre and Performance*, Oxford University Press, 2003, p. 1141.

7 A. E. Green, 'Ritual', in Martin Banham (ed.), *The Cambridge Guide to World Theatre*, Cambridge, Cambridge University Press, 1988, p. 829.

8 Anthony Hozier, in Colin Chambers (ed.), *The Continuum Companion to Twentieth Century Theatre*, 2002, p. 649.

9 Pierre Smith, 'Rite', in Pierre Bonte and Michel Izard (eds), *Dictionnaire de l'ethnologie et de l'anthropologie*, Paris, PUF, 1991, p. 630.

10 Green, op. cit., p. 829.

11 Christian Wulf, *Penser les pratiques sociales comme rituel: Ethnologie et genèse de communautés*, Paris; L'Harmattan, 2004, p. 13.

12 Mary Douglas, *Natural Symbols*, London, Routledge, 1996, p. 72.

13 Roger Bartra, *Blood, Ink, and Culture*, Durham, N.C., Duke University Press, 2002, pp. 46–7.

14 Patrice Pavis (ed.), *The Intercultural Performance Reader*, London, Routledge, 1996, pp. 3–4.

15 Gómez-Peña, in Henry Bial, op. cit., p. 297.

16 Klauss-Peter Köpping, 'Ritual and theatre' in Kennedy, op. cit., p. 1139.

17 Heiner Müller, *Rotwelch*, Berlin, Merve, 1982, p. 141.

7 Theatre in another culture

1 See the dossier on Korean theatre in *Théâtre/Public*, no. 175, Oct.–Dec. 2004, pp. 35–62.
2 This chapter borrows from an article published in *Culture Coréenne*, no. 70, August 2005, and parts of my foreword to Cathy Rapin and Im Hye-Gyông's book, *Théâtre coréen d'hier et d'aujourd'hui*, Paris, Les Editions de l'Amandier, 2006. This latter book constitutes the best introduction to modern and contemporary Korean theatre.

8 Media on the stage

1 Frédéric Barbier and Catherine Lavenir, *Histoires des médias*, Paris: Armand Colin, 1996, 5.
2 Jean-Marie Pradier, *La scène et la fabrique des corps: ethnoscénologie du spectacle vivant en Occident*, Bordeaux, Presses Universitaires de Bordeaux, 1997.
3 N. Katherine Hayles, *How We Became Posthuman: Virtual Bodies in Cybernetics, Literature, and Informatics*, Chicago, Ill., University of Chicago Press, 1999.
4 Hans Thies Lehmann, *Postdramatic Theatre*, trans. Karen-Jürs Munby, London, Routledge, 2006.
5 Régis Debray, Introduction à la médiologie, Paris: Presses Universitaires de France, 2000, p. 220.
6 On the notion of a 'soundscape', see Christopher Baugh, *Theatre, Performance and Technology: The Development of Scenography in the Twentieth Century*, Basingstoke, Palgrave Macmillan, 2005.
7 On this subject, see Baugh, op. cit., pp. 203–19, and Guido Hiss, *Synthetische Visionen: Theater als Gesamtkunstwerk von 1800 bis 2000*, Munich, Epodium Verlag, 2005.
8 Dominique Pitoiset, 'Un autre rapport d'échelle', in *Les écrans sur la scène*, ed. Béatrice Picon-Vallin, Lausanne, L'Age d'homme, 1998, pp. 322–4.
9 For a few others, see Picon-Vallin, op. cit.
10 See Denis Bablet, *Svoboda*, Lausanne, L'Age d'homme, 1970. See also Jacques Polieri, *Scenography and Technology*, Paris: Bibliothèque Nationale de France, 2004.
11 See Markus Moninger, Shakespeare inszeniert (Tübingen: Niemeyer, 1996).
12 Frédéric Maurin, 'Scène, mensonges et vidéo,' *Théâtre/Public*, 127, 1996, 41. This issue of the journal, edited by Maurin, is devoted to theatre and technology.
13 Stéphane Braunschweig, 'L'enfer d'un monde virtuel', *Théâtre/Public*, 127, 1996, p. 57.
14 Jean-François Peyret, 'Texte, scène et video', in Picon-Vallin, op. cit., p. 284.
15 Robert Lepage, 'Du theatre d'ombres aux technologies contemporaines', in Picon-Vallin, op. cit., p. 330.
16 Braunschweig, op. cit., p. 57.
17 Peyret, op cit., p. 289.
18 Markus Moninger, 'Vom Media-match zum Media-crossing', in Christopher Balme and Markus Moninger (eds), *Crossing Media: Theater—Film—Fotografie—Neue Medien*, Munich, Epodium Verlag, 2004, p. 7.

19 Christopher Balme, 'Theater zwischen den Medien: Perpektiven theaerwissenschaftlicher Intermedialitäsforschung', in Balme and Moninger, op. cit., pp. 13–31.
20 Philip Auslander, *Liveness: Performance in a Mediatized Culture*, London: Routledge, 1999, p. 2.
21 Balme, op cit., p. 29.
22 Auslander, op cit., p. 158.
23 Ibid. p. 51.
24 Ibid.
25 Peggy Phelan, *Unmarked: The Politics of Performance*, London: Routledge, 1993.
26 Matthew Causey, 'Media and performance', in Dennis Kennedy (ed.), *The Oxford Encyclopaedia of Theatre and Performance*, Oxford, Oxford University Press, 2003, p. 8.
26 See also his book *Theatre and Performance: From Simulation to Embeddedness*, London, Routledge, 2006.
27 According to Jay Bolter and Richard Grusin, 'A medium is that which remediates. It is that which appropriates the techniques, forms, and social significance of other media and attempts to rival or refashion them in the name of the real' (*Remediation: Understanding New Media*, Cambridge, Mass.: MIT Press, 2000, p. 65).
28 Moninger, op. cit., p. 10.
29 Bernhard Wadenfels, *Phänomenologie der Aufmerksamkeit*, Stuttgart: Suhrkamp, 2004, p. 206.
30 Marie-José Mondzain, *Le commerce des regards*, Paris: Ed. du Seuil, 2003, p. 180.
31 Choreography by José Montalvo and Dominique Hervieu, Paris, Chaillot, 1997. There is a video, produced by Arte, 2004.
32 Thomas Oberender, 'Mehr jetzt auf der Bühne', *Theater heute*, 4, 2004, p. 23.
33 Ibid.
34 Barthes's title, 'Comment représenter l'antique?' is translated in English as 'Putting on the Greeks', in Roland Barthes, *Critical Essays*, trans. Richard Howard, Evanston, Ill., Northwestern University Press, 1972, pp. 59–66. Original in *Essais critiques*, Paris: Seuil, 1964, pp. 71–9.
35 Carole Talon-Hugon, 'Passion', in Michela Marzano (ed.), *Dictionnaire du corps*, Paris, Presses Universitaires de France, 2007, p. 686.
36 Roland Barthes, 'Encore le corps', in *Oeuvres complètes*, vol. 3, Paris: Seuil, 1995, p. 913. First published in *Critique*, 38, 1982.
37 Ibid. p. 914.
38 Le Brun.
39 Quoted in Maria Brewińska (ed.), *Bill Viola*, Warsaw, Zachęta Narodowa Galeria Sztuki, 2007, p. 90.
40 See Marie-José Mondzain, *L'assemblée théâtrale*, Paris, Editions de l'Amandier, 2002, pp. 39–69.
41 Marie-José Mondzain, 'Le temps et la visibilité', *Frictions*, 8, 2004, p. 19.

9 The deconstruction of postmodern mise en scène

1 Jacques Derrida, 'There is no one narcissism', 1986, trans. Elisabeth Weber, in *Points …: Interviews 1974–1994*, Stanford, Calif., Stanford University Press, 1995, pp. 211–12.

2 Jacques Derrida and Elisabeth Roudinesco, *For What Tomorrow ...: A Dialogue*, trans. Jeff Fort, Stanford, Calif., Stanford University Press, 2004, p. 198 no. 2.

3 Antoine Vitez, *Ecrits sur le théâtre*, vol. 2, Paris, POL, 1996, p. 29.

4 Ibid. p. 30: 'Intimidation by our classics has the strange consequence that we deny them the quality of classics, believing instead that they are modern, ever young, like ourselves in fact.'

5 Carmelo Bene et Gilles Deleuze, *Superpositions*, Paris, Minuit, 1979, p. 120.

6 On baroque gesture, see Ian Caddy's website, http://www.baroquegestures.com

7 Antoine Vitez, *Ecrits sur le théâtre*, vol. 2, Paris: POL, 1995, p. 273.

8 Ibid. p. 265.

9 Specifically, I am referring to Patrice Chéreau's 1992 staging of *Dans la solitude des champs de coton*.

10 *Différance* is Derrida's term for the action of deferring meaning, and is spelled with an a to differentiate it from *différence*.

11 Derrida and Roudinesco, op. cit., p. 21.

12 Jacques Derrida, *The Archeology of the Frivolous: Reading Condillac*, trans. John P. Leavey, Lincoln, Neb., University of Nebraska Press, 1987.

13 François Tanguy, 'Le théâtre comme expérience', *La Terrasse*, December 2005, p. 11.

14 Ibid. p. 11.

15 Jacques Derrida, 'Structure, sign, and play', in *Writing and Difference*, trans. Alan Bass, London, Routledge, 1978, p. 290.

16 Claude Régy, *Programme du spectacle au Théâtre de la Colline*, 2006.

17 Valérie Dréville, 'Interview', *Bulletin du Centre national de Normandie de Caen*, March–April 2006.

18 Derrida and Elisabeth Roudinesco, op. cit., p. 21.

19 Régy, op. cit., 2006.

20 Ibid.

21 Jacques Derrida, 'Structure, sign, and play' in *Writing and Difference*, trans. Alan Bass, London, Routledge, 1978, pp. 369–70.

22 Jacques Derrida (1978) *Writing and Difference*, London, Routledge, p. 316.

23 Alain Françon, *La Représentation*, Paris, Editions de l'Amandier, 2004, p. 85. In this remarkable volume, Marie-José Mondzain and Myriam Revault d'Allones suggest that 'perlaboration' might be translated as *Perainein*, an Aristotelian word that 'designates both the act of limiting that which has no limits and the act of terminating a movement that leads to its own completion. This is precisely what is in question in the process of symbolisation that Freud tries to achieve in the work of analysis. Perlaboration (or 'working-through') was the term chosen by Freud's translators for the German word *durcharbeiten*.'

24 Sarah Kane, *4.48 Psychosis*, in *Complete Plays*, London, Methuen, 2001.

25 Ibid. p. 229.

26 Ibid. p. 213.

27 Ibid. p. 245.

28 Ibid. p. 245.

29 Ibid. p. 213.

30 Ibid. p. 223.

31 Antoine Vitez, *Ecrits sur le théâtre*, vol 3, Paris, POL, 1996, p. 273.

32 Alain Françon, in Marie-José Mondzain (ed.), *L'Assemblée théâtrale*, Paris, Editions de l'Amandier, 2002, p. 76.
33 Bernard Dort, *La Représentation émancipée*, Arles, Actes Sud, 1988.
34 Jacques Derrida, *Rogues: Two Essays on Reason*, Stanford, Calif., Stanford University Press, 2005, p. 175.

10 Physical theatre and the dramaturgy of the actor

1 On physical theatre, see Dymphna Callery, *Through the Body*, London, Nick Hern, 2001.
2 Jacques Lecoq, *Theatre of Gesture and Movement*, trans. Joel Anderson, David Bradby, Luke Kernaghan and Dick McCaw, London, Routledge, 2006. In the chapter 'An actor's view of a theatre of movement', Alain Gautré includes in the 'theatre of gesture and movement' artists like the Footsbarn Theatre, Théâtre de Complicité, Kantor, Jérôme Deschamps and Mummenschantz.
3 Thomas Leabhart, 'Physical theatre', in Dennis Kennedy (ed.), *The Oxford Encyclopedia of Theatre and Performance*, Oxford University Press, 2003, p. 1031.
4 Louis Aragon, Linda Moses, Jean-Paul Lavergne and George Ashley, 'An open letter to Andre Breton on Robert Wilson's "Deafman Glance"', *Performing Arts Journal*, Vol. 1, No. 1, Spring 1976, pp. 3–7, p. 6.
5 Eugenio Barba and Nicola Savarese, *A Dictionary of Theatre Anthropology: The Secret Art of the Performer*, London and New York, Routledge, 1991, p. 17.
6 Jacques Lecoq, *Theatre of Gesture and Movement*, London, Routledge, 2006, p. 129.
7 Iben Nagel Rasmussen, 'La dramaturgie du personnage', *Degrés*, nos. 97-98-99, in Patrice Pavis (ed.), *La Dramaturgie de l'actrice*, 1999, p. 19.
8 Iben Nagel Rasmussen, 'Interview', in Erik Exe Christoffersen, *The Actor's Way*, London, Routledge, 1993, p. 101.
9 'La dramaturgie du personnage', p. 22.
10 Simon Shepherd and Mick Wallis, *Drama/Theatre/Performance*, London, Routledge, 2004, p. 210.
11 Beckerman, quoted in Shepherd and Wallis, op. cit., p. 210; see Bernard Beckerman, *Dynamics of Drama*, New York, Drama Book Specialists, 1979, p. 151.
12 Bertolt Brecht, 'Song of a loving woman', in *Poems 1913–1956*, trans. Willet *et al.*, 1979, p. 430.
13 Macha Makaeïeff, *Inventaire d'un spectacle*, Arles, Actes Sud, 2000, p. 11. Makaeïeff refers to her work as a 'poetics of disaster'.
14 'Whether it is a question of another's body or my own, I have no means of knowing the human body other than that of living it, which means taking up on my own account the drama which is being played out in it, and losing myself in it. I am my body, at least wholly to the extent that I possess experience, and yet at the same time my body is as it were a 'natural' subject, a provisional sketch of my total being. Thus experience of one's own body runs counter to the reflective procedure which detaches subject and object from each other, and which gives us only the thought about the body, or the body as an idea, and not the experience of the body or the body in reality' (Maurice Merleau-Ponty, *Phenomenology of Perception*, trans. Colin Smith, Routledge, London, 2002, p. 231).

15 For this example and the following ones, see William A. Ewing, *Le siècle du corps*, Paris, Ed. De la Martinière, 2000 (pp.72–3 for this quote).

16 Carolee Schneeman, quoted in William A. Ewing (ed.), *The Century of the Body*, London: Thames & Hudson, 2000, p. 130. The square brackets are Ewing's.

17 'Orlan', in Paul Allain and Jen Harvie, *The Routledge Companion to Theatre and Performance*, London, Routledge, 2006, pp. 58–9.

18 'Photo', in Jean-Jacques Courtine (ed.), *Histoires du corps: Les mutations du regard*, vol. 3, Paris, Éditions du Seuil, 2006, plate 14, p. 415.

19 Directed by Michel Liard at the Fol Ordinaire theatre, Avignon; July 2000, at the Théâtre du Grenier in Toulouse. With Florence Dannhofer, Karin Madrid, Yves Arcaix, and Dominique Delavigne. On Michel Liard's poetics see his posthumous book *Parole écrite, parole scénique*, Nantes, Ed. Joca Seria, 2006, with a foreword by Patrice Pavis.

20 Antonin Artaud, *Theatre and its Double*, New York, Grove Press, 1958, p. 84.

21 Ibid. p. 38.

22 See in particular Chôgyam Trungpa, *Mandala: Un chaos ordonné*, Paris, Ed. du Seuil, 1994, pp. 41–52.

23 Gilles Deleuze and Félix Guattari, *What is Philosophy?*, New York, Columbia University Press, 1994, p. 164.

24 Roland Barthes, 'Dire Racine', in *Sur Racine* (1963), *Oeuvres complètes*, vol. I, Paris, Ed. du Seuil, 1993, pp. 883–1103; *On Racine*, trans. Richard Howard, New York, Hill and Wang, 1964.

25 'Devising', Allain and Harvie, op. cit., p.145.

26 See Rebecca Schneider, *The Explicit Body in Performance*, London, Routledge, 1997.

27 1991 colour print in Ewing, *The Century of the Body*, p. 199. The strength and the ambiguity of the photograph reside in the gaze to the camera and in the impossibility of knowing whether the provocation is an erotic invitation or a critique of the classical representation of the Japanese geisha.

28 *La Kabuki Club Girl*, in *Ethno-Techno* in *Los Video Graffiti*, vol. 1, La Pocha Nostra, 2004.

29 Simon Shepherd and Mick Wallis, *Drama/Theatre/Performance*, London, Routledge, 2004, pp. 145–6.

11 The splendour and the misery of interpreting the classics

1 Anne-Françoise Benhamou, *Outre scène*, journal of the Théâtre Nationale de Strasbourg, no. 5, May 2005, p. 4.

2 Antoine Vitez, 'Notes pour Le Précepteur de Lenz', *Ecrits sur le théâtre*, Paris, POL, vol. 2, 1995, p. 243.

3 These reflections are based on the article 'Classicism' by Florence Dumora-Mabille, in Paul Aron, Denis Saint-Jacques and Alain Viala (eds), *Le Dictionnaire du Littéraire*, Paris, PUF, 2002, p. 96.

4 Italo Calvino, *Why Read the Classics*, London: Penguin Classics, 2009, p. 3.

5 Didier Plassard, 'Esquisse d'une typologie de la mise en scène des classiques', *Littératures classiques*, 48, p. 252.

6 Antoine Vitez: 'The intimidation resulting from our classics has the strange consequence of us refusing them the status of classics in order to

think them modern, ever young, just like us, in fact' (*Ecrits sur le théâtre*, Paris, POL, vol. 3, 1996, p. 30).

7 Régis Debray, *Sur le pont d'Avignon*, Paris, Flammarion, 2005, p. 37.

8 Patrice Pavis, 'Du texte à la mise en scène: l'histoire traversée', *Kodikas/Code*, vol. 7, no. 1/2, 1984, pp. 24–41. These reflections were developed alongside a thesis on the stage interpretations of Marivaux in the 1970s: *Marivaux à l'épreuve de la scène*, Paris, Publications de la Sorbonne, 1986.

9 Antoine Vitez, 'A propos d'Electre', *Les Lettres françaises*, no. 1125, March 1966.

10 For the reconstitution of baroque opera, see the work of Ian Caddy: http://www.baroquegestures.com/

11 Vitez, 'A propos de Richard II' in *Ecrits sur le théâtre*, Paris, POL, 1995, vol. 2, p. 130.

12 Bertolt Brecht, 'Entretien sur les classiques', in *Ecrits sur le théâtre*, Paris, Gallimard, 2000, p. 160.

13 Programme, Comédie Française.

14 The signifying practice is a semiotic notion of the 1960s, particularly that of Roland Barthes: 'To interpret a text is not to give it a (more or less justified, more or less free) meaning, but on the contrary to appreciate what plural constitutes it' (*S/Z*, trans. Richard Miller, New York, Hill & Wang, 1974, p. 5).

15 Peter Brook, *Travail Théâtral*, no. 18, 1975, p. 87.

16 *La Contestation et la mise en pièces de la plus illustre des tragédies française, 'Le Cid' de Pierre Corneille, suivie d'une 'cruelle' mise à mort de l'auteur dramatique et d'une distribution gracieuse de diverses conserves culturelles.*

17 Benhamou, op. cit., p. 31.

18 Jean-François Sivadier, 'L'acteur au rendez-vous de l'instant et du passé', *Outre scène*, no. 5, May 2005, p. 35.

19 See page 000.

20 Benhamou, op. cit., p. 58. Reprinted in Stéphane Braunschweig, *Petites portes grands paysages*, Arles, Actes Sud, 2007, p. 290.

21 Braunschweig, op. cit., p. 57, p. 289 s.

22 Programme, Sceaux, Théâtre des Gémeaux.

23 Performance at the Théâtre de la Cité Universitaire, February 2001.

24 Frédéri Fisbach, notes in the press pack.

25 Benoît Lambert, 'Note liminaire sur les classiques', press pack, Théâtre de Malakoff, January 2007.

26 'Sur un départ' by Saint-Amant [1594–1661]. A rough translation: 'Must I prepare for that fateful day/ When despite my loyal ardour/ Destiny constrains me, shaming love away,/ To betray my lover, thus to abandon her?/ Alas, I cannot obey,/ And yet I must away.'

27 Plassard, op. cit., p. 248.

28 For a more complete analysis of the production, see Patrice Pavis, 'Woyzeck à la cour d'honneur', *Théâtre/Public*, October 2004; see also the analysis of *Dans la jungle des villes*, directed by Castorf.

29 Antoine Vitez, 'Britannicus', 1981, in *Ecrits sur le théâtre*, Paris, POL, vol. 3, 1996, p. 216.

30 Georges Forestier, 'Quelques mots sur le spectacle', programme for *Mithridate*, Théâtre de la Sapience, May 1999.

31 See Eugène Green, *La parole baroque: Essai*, Paris, Desclée de Brower, 2001.

32 Note by Frank Castorf in the programme, 2007.

33 *Regietheater* ('directors' theatre') is in Germany the theatre which carries the brand and the signature of a director. See David Bradby and David Williams, *Directors' Theatre*, London, Macmillan, 1988.

34 Plassard, op. cit., p. 252.

35 But, as early as 1976, Antoine Vitez was suspicious of poorly executed expression corporelle: '*L'Age d'or*, Théâtre du Soleil. A very patchy performance ... But if the performance was in the circus, its inadequacies would appear to all. Here, however, moving the audience around several times gives the impression of a no-fuss dinner and hides the weaknesses of the actors' text. It's only a party, let's not ask too much.' (*Ecrits sur le théâtre*, vol. 3, p. 32.).

36 See Chapter x.

37 Staged at the Théâtre de la porte Saint-Martin, February 2007.

38 At the Comédie Française, 2000.

39 See the excellent analysis of the play by Stéphane Braunschweig in 'Quelques mots sur Le Misanthrope, à mi-chemin des répétitions', in op. cit., pp. 145–50. A DVD of the production, produced by the Théâtre national de Strasbourg, is available.

40 At MC93 Bobigny, February 2007.

41 Luk Perceval, 'La contradiction, c'est la poésie de la vie', *Outre scène*, no. 5, May 2005, p. 66.

42 Michael Thalheimer, 'Sans passé, nous sommes incapables de vivre l'ici et maintenant', *Outre scène*, no. 5, May 2005, p. 25.

43 Thalheimer, op. cit.

44 Produced at the Essen Opera, May 2006.

45 Declan Donnellan, *The Actor and the Target*, London, Nick Hern, 2005.

46 See, for example, Dennis Kennedy (ed.), *Foreign Shakespeare*, Cambridge, Cambridge University Press.

47 Programme notes by Philippe Adrian, Théâtre de la Tempête, September 2006.

48 See Chapter 9.

49 Mounted at the Düsseldorf Stadttheater, May 2006. Presented at the MC93 in Bobigny in March 2007.

50 A potlach is a gift or a destruction addressed to the donee, who is thus obliged to respond with an equivalent offering.

51 Didier Plassard, op. cit., pp. 250–2. See Chapter 13 for three examples of resurgence.

52 Anne-Françoise Benhamou, 'Entretien avec Stéphane Braunschweig', *Outre scène*, no. 5, 2005, p. 57. Reproduced in Braunschweig, op. cit., p. 289.

53 Ibid. p, 57.

54 David Bradby with Annabel Poincheval, *Le Théâtre en France de 1968 à 2000*, Paris, Honoré Champion, 2007, p. 600.

12 Staging calamity

1 Avignon Festival programme, p. 1.

2 Alain Badiou, 'Rhapsody for the Theatre: A Short Philosophical Treatise', trans. Bruno Bosteels, Theatre *Survey*, 49:2 (November 2008), p. 229.

3 Jan Fabre, *L'histoire des larmes*, Paris: L'Arche, 2005.

4 Roland Barthes, *A Lover's Discourse: Fragments*, trans. Richard Howard, London, Penguin, 1990, pp. 180–1.
5 Jan Fabre, op. cit., pp. 35–6.
6 Ibid. p. 32.
7 Ibid. p. 39.
8 Friedrich Nietzsche, *The Birth of Tragedy*, trans. Ronald Speirs, Cambridge, Cambridge University Press, p. 116.
9 Jan Decorte, festival programme, 2005.
10 Working materials, read at Avignon, 13 July 2005.
11 Claudia Castellucci, festival programme, 2005.
12 P. F. Thomèse.
13 On the conception of intercultural theatre today, see Patrice Pavis, 'Intercultural theatre today (2010)', *Forum Modernes Theater*, 2011.
14 Philippe Descola, 'Les Jivaros d'Amazonie et nous', *Le Nouvel Observateur*, 14–20 July 2005, p. 71. See also Philippe Descola, *Par-delà nature et culture*, Paris, Gallimard, 2005.
15 Denis Guénoun, 'Dispositions critiques', *Alternatives théâtrales*, Nos. 85–6, 2005, p. 107.
16 Raymond Williams, *Towards 2000*, London, Chatto and Windus, 1983, p. 240.

13 Conclusions

1 Claus Peymann in *De Groene Amsterdamer*, 21 April 1999.
2 This 'tuning' of the performance cannot be overemphasised. Director Alain Françon sees it as the function of representation: 'Tuning seems to me to be what defines the performance, more than the space itself or any sign. It requires a series of precise choices. These choices must be practised at each moment, since the tuning is necessarily continual. To direct is to understand the gap constituted by the performance and to see that this gap is not a fixed point but a continual tuning' (*La Représentation*, Paris, Ed. de l'Amandier, 2004, p. 74). According to the philosopher of the visible, Marie-José Mondzain, 'if it is the case that the science of phenomena is an uninterrupted tuning of saying on seeing and of seeing on saying, to control their mutual overlap, then art – poetic and theatrical art – on the contrary, consists of rendering the detuning of the visible and the speakable to the senses by giving a finely tuned form to detuning itself' (ibid.).
3 This aspect has been neglected, with at least three exceptions: Robert Abirached, *Le Théâtre et le Prince: Un système fatigué, 1993–2004*, Arles, Actes Sud, 2005. Pierre-Etienne Heymann, *Regards sur les mutations du théâtre public (1968–1998)*, Paris, L'Harmattan, 2000. See also numerous articles by Philippe Henry in the journal *Théâtre/Public*, as well as his forthcoming monograph.
4 Heymann, op. cit., p. 130.
5 Ibid. p. 141.
6 Ibid. p. 146.
7 Antoine Vitez, 'Éditorial', *L'Art du théâtre* , no. 1, Spring 1985, p. 8.
8 Roland Barthes, 'The diseases of costume', in *Critical Essays*, Evanston, Ill., Northwestern University Press, 1972, pp. 41–50.
9 See the special edition of *Theater der Welt: Radikal jung. Regisseure*, no. 25, 2005.

10 Referring to an amicable polemic debate with Jean-Pierre Han, in *Théâtre d'aujourd'hui*, no. 10, p. 165.

11 Theodor W. Adorno, Gretel Adorno, Rolf Tiedemann and Robert Hullot-Kentor, *Aesthetic Theory*, trans. Robert Hullot-Kentor, London, Continuum, 2004, p. 384.

12 Bruno Tackels, *Des écrans sur la scène*, Lausanne, L'Age d'homme, 1998, p. 126.

13 See Chapter 5.

14 Jacques Rebotier, 'Cocasseries et consonances', *Mouvement*, no. 21, p. 71.

15 See Patrice Pavis, 'Woyzeck à la cour d'honneur', *Théâtre/Public*, no. 175, October 2004.

16 Bernard Dort, *La Représentation émancipée*, Arles, Actes Sud, 1988, pp. 177–8.

17 Ibid. p. 178.

18 Romeo Castellucci, 'Remonter aux sources inhumaines du théâtre', *Europe*, no. 873–4, 202 ('Artaud'), p. 176.

19 Antoine Vitez, *Écrits sur le théâtre*, Paris, POL, vol. 2, 1995, p. 428.

20 Bruno Tackels, 'Le "jeune théâtre" de demain', *Revue d'esthétique*, no. 26, 1994, p. 90.

21 Roger Planchon, 'Lecture des classiques', *Pratiques*, no. 15–16, 1977, p. 53.

22 Robert Cantarella, *in* Marie-José Mondzain, *L'Assemblée théâtrale*, Paris, Éditions de l'Amandier, 2002, p. 63.

23 Ibid. p. 65.

24 David Williams, 'Simon McBurney' in M. Shevtsova and S. Mitter (eds), *Fifty Key Theatre Directors*, London and New York, Routledge, 2005, p. 250.

25 Donnellan, quoted in Giannachi and Mary Luckhurst (eds), *On Directing: Interviews with Directors*, London, Faber & Faber, 1999, p. 19.

26 Corman quoted in Michel Corvin, 'Mise en scène et silence', *Revue d'esthétique*, no. 26, 1994, p. 126.

27 Michel Corvin, 'Mise en scène et silence', *Revue d'esthétique*, no. 26, 1994, p. 125.

28 For example, Claude Régy: 'There are no doubt things that are shared, but there are also personal wanderings. Also, I almost think that the most important part of a work is the wandering of the reader or the spectator' (in Marie-José Mondzain, *L'Assemblée théâtrale*, Paris, Editions de l'Amandier, 2002, p. 123.

29 For example Erika Fischer-Lichte in *Asthetik des Performativen*, Frankfurt am Main, Suhrkamp, 2004, in particular p. 29.

30 See Patrice Pavis, *Vers une théorie de la pratique théâtrale*, Lille, Septentrion, 2007, pp. 337–430.

31 In Bert States, *Great Reckonings in Little Room*, Berkeley, Calif., University of California Press, 1985.

32 'What animates Chinese thought is the fact that these opposing forces (yin and yang), non fusional, irreducible one to the other and entering into relation only because there is a void. That is to say, breath, void, speech, what we call tao which means a path or to march, to move' (in Mondzain, op. cit., p. 94).

33 *Koan* is the logical impossibility of thinking a proposition or producing an image, for example the sound of one hand clapping.

34 Myriam Revault d'Allones, in Mondzain, *L'Assemblée théâtrale*, op. cit., p. 10. See also Marie-Madelein Mervaut-Roux, *L'Assise du théâtre*, Paris, CNRS, 1998 et Figurations du spectateur, Paris, L'Harmattan, 2006.

35 Marie-José Mondzain, *Le Commerce des regards*, Paris, Ed. du Seuil, 2003, p. 180.

36 Sylviane Dupuis, *A qui sert le théâtre?* Geneva, Ed. Zoé, 1998, pp. 8 and 22.

37 Thus in Robert Wilson's staging of *Fables de La Fontaine* we do not find a rereading of the fables, and less still a dramaturgical plot for each fable. The stage image, its logic and its visual evolution, are the only thing that counts, enhanced by the fact that the textual detail, the textuality is not always accessible. This is the case for two reasons: acoustic (we cannot hear everything) and hermeneutic (the contemporary auditor sometimes struggles to understand certain passages in the *Fables*, since the language has evolved a great deal.

38 Stéphane Braunschweig, *Petites portes, grands paysages*, Arles, Actes Sud, 2007, p. 290.

39 *Le Misanthrope*, staged by Lassalle, Braunschweig or Lambert is legible as a system that may be open and enigmatic, but which each time proposes a way of globally conceiving of the motivations and the 'destiny' of the character.

40 Christopher Baugh, *Theatre, Performance, and Technology*, London, Palgrave, 2005, p. 17: 'The "making of a performance" has become a significantly different activity from that of "directing a play" and has required new practices, new technologies and a new stagecraft.'

41 Christopher Balme, 'Robert Lepage und die Zukunft des Theaters in Medienzeitalter' in Erika Fischer-Lichte, Doris Kolesch and Christel Weiler (eds), *Transformationen: Theater der Neunziger Jahre, Theater der Zeit*, 1999, p. 142.

42 Writing about text in Noh theatre, Antoine Vitez states,
> The text is full of gaps, incomplete, incomprehensible, a scribble that must be deciphered. To show that a text is never anything other than that: incomplete, obscure, it is not clear to whom it is addressed. Mise-en-scène (and acting) not as an execution of what is known but as research. In other words, research does not (will not) precede mise-en-scène. Mise-en-scène is research: we set out to discover.
> (From Antoine Vitez, 'Qu'aurais-je fait d'un dramaturge')
> (interview with Emile Copfermann), *Théâtre/Public*, no. 67, Théâtre de Gennevilliers, 1986, pp. 59–60.

43 Stephen Bottoms, presentation at 'Performing Literatures', University of Leeds, June 2007.

44 Didier Plassard, 'Esquisse d'une typologie de la mise en scène des classiques', *Littératures classiques*, 48.

45 Bruno Tackels, *Fragment d'un théâtre amoureux*, Besançon, Les Solitaires Intempestifs, 2001, p. 119.

46 Jean-Claude Lallias, 'Les tensions fécondes entre le texte et la scène', *Théâtre aujourd'hui*, 10, 2005, Paris, Centre National de Documentation Pédagogique, p. 4.

47 Lallias suggests that this process of translation is necessary for 'any mise en scène of worth.' Ibid. p. 4.

48 Ibid. p. 4.

49 Ibid. p. 5.

50 note needed.

51 Ibid. p. 5.

52 Ibid.

53 Michel Vinaver, 'L'île', *Théâtre en Europe*, 18, September 1988.

54 Edward Gordon Craig, *On the Art of the Theatre*, London: Theatre Arts Books/Heinemann Educational Books, 1956, p. 148. This text is quoted in Vinaver, 'L'île', p. 21.
55 Vinaver, op. cit., p. 21.
56 See Vinaver's report for the Ministry of Culture: Michel Vinaver, Le Compte rendu d'Avignon, Arles: Actes Sud, 1987.
57 Vinaver, op. cit., p. 21.
58 Joel Pommerat, 'Vers l'autre langue', *Théâtre/Public*, 184, 2007.
59 Jean-Marie Thomasseau and Almuth Grésillon, 'Scènes de genèses théâtrales', *Genesis*, no. 26/05, Paris, J.-M. Place et Imec, 2005, p. 21.
60 Sarah Kane, *4.48 Psychosis*, in *Complete Plays*, London, Methuen Drama, 2001, p. 213.
61 Antoine Vitez, 'L'Art du théâtre', *L'Art du théâtre*, no. 1, Spring 1985, p. 8.
62 Jacques Copeau, extract from a lecture at the Vieux-Colombier, Lyon, 21 December 1920. Cited in *Appels*, Paris, Gallimard, 1974, p. 194.

Glossary

1 For example, in Patrice Pavis, *Le Théâtre contemporain. Analyse des textes de Sarraute à Vinaver*, Armand Colin, 2002.
2 Mikhail Bakhtin, 'Forms of time and of the chronotope in the novel', in *The Dialogic Imagination*, Austin, Tex., University of Texas Press.
3 Jean-Marie Pradier, *La Scène et la fabrique des corps: Ethnoscénologie du spectacle vivant en Occident (v e siècle av. J.-C. – xviii e siècle)*, Bordeaux, Presses universitaires de Bordeaux, 1997.
4 Michel Foucault, *The Order of Things*, London, Routledge, 2002, p. 33.
5 Josette Féral (ed.), *Mise en scène et jeu de l'acteur. Entretiens*, Morlanweltz, Éditions Lansman, 1997–1998 (2 vols).
6 Bernard Dort, 'Le texte et la scène : pour une nouvelle alliance', *Encyclopædia universalis*, Symposium, 1984, p. 241.
7 Hans-Thies Lehmann, *Postdramatic Theatre*, London, Routledge, 2006.
8 Michael Chekhov, *To the Actor*, London, Routledge, 2002, p. 74.

Bibliography

Abirached, Robert, *Le Théâtre et le Prince: Un système fatigué, 1993–2004*, Arles, Actes Sud, 2005.

Adorno, Theodor W., Adorno, Gretel, Tiedemann, Rolf and Hullot-Kentor, Robert, *Aesthetic Theory*, trans. Robert Hullot-Kentor, London, Continuum, 2004.

Allain, Paul and Harvie, Jen, *The Routledge Companion to Theatre and Performance*, London, Routledge, 2006.

Anne, Catherine, *Le Bonheur du vent*, Paris, Actes Sud-Papiers, 2003.

Aristotle, *La poétique*, trans. R. Dupont-Roc and J. Lallot, Paris, Editions du Seuil, 1980.

Aron, Paul, Saint-Jacques, Denis and Viala Alain (eds), *Le Dictionnaire du Littéraire*, Paris, PUF, 2002.

Aronson, Arnold, *Looking into the Abyss*, Ann Arbor, Mich., University of Michigan Press, 2005.

Artaud, Antonin, *Theatre and its Double*, New York, Grove Press, 1958.

Auslander, Philip, *Liveness: Performance in a Mediatized Culture*, London: Routledge, 1999.

Bablet, Denis, *Revolutions of Stage Design in the Twentieth Century*, New York: Leon Amiel, 1976.

——, *Svoboda*, Lausanne, L'Age d'homme, 1970.

Badiou, Alain, 'Rhapsody for the Theatre: A Short Philosophical Treatise', trans. Bruno Bosteels, *Theatre Survey*, vol. 49, no. 2 (November 2008).

Bakhtin, Mikhail, *The Dialogic Imagination*, Austin, Tex., University of Texas Press, 1982.

Balme, Christopher and Moninger, Markus (eds), *Crossing Media: Theater—Film—Fotografie—Neue Medien*, Munich, Epodium Verlag, 2004.

Banham, Martin (ed.), *The Cambridge Guide to World Theatre*, Cambridge, Cambridge University Press, 1988.

Barba, Eugenio and Savarese, Nicola, *A Dictionary of Theatre Anthropology: The Secret Art of the Performer*, London and New York, Routledge, 1991.

Barbier, Frédéric and Lavenir, Catherine, *Histoires des médias*, Paris, Armand Colin, 1996.

Barthes, Roland, *Oeuvres complètes*, vol. 3, Paris, Seuil, 1995.

————, *A Lover's Discourse: Fragments*, trans. Richard Howard, London, Penguin, 1990.

————, *S/Z*, trans. Richard Miller, New York, Hill & Wang, 1974.

————, *Critical Essays*, trans. Richard Howard, Evanston, Ill., Northwestern University Press, 1972.

————, *On Racine*, trans. Richard Howard, New York, Hill & Wang, 1964.

Bartra, Roger, *Blood, Ink, and Culture*, Durham, N.C., Duke University Press, 2002.

Baugh, Christopher, *Theatre, Performance and Technology: The Development of Scenography in the Twentieth Century*, Basingstoke, Palgrave Macmillan, 2005.

Beckerman, Bernard, *Dynamics of Drama*, New York, Drama Book Specialists, 1979.

Bene, Carmelo and Deleuze, Gilles, *Superpositions*, Paris, Minuit, 1979.

Berthier, Patrick and Jarrety, Michel (eds), *Histoire littéraire de la France*, Paris, PUF, 2006.

Bial, Henry, *The Performance Studies Reader*, London, Routledge, 2004.

Boireau, Nicole, *Théâtre et société en Angleterre, des années 1950 à nos jours*, Paris, PUF.

Bolter, Jay and Grusin, Richard, *Remediation: Understanding New Media*, Cambridge, Mass.: MIT Press, 2000.

Bonte, Pierre and Izard, Michel (eds), *Dictionnaire de l'ethnologie et de l'anthropologie*, Paris, PUF, 1991.

Boucris, Luc, *L'Espace en scène*, Paris, Librairie Théâtrale, 1993.

Bourdieu, Pierre and Wacquant, Loïc, *Réponses*, Paris, Ed. du Seuil, 1992.

Bradby, David, with Poincheval, Annabel, *Le Théâtre en France de 1968 à 2000*, Paris, Honoré Champion, 2007.

———— and Williams, David, *Directors' Theatre*, London, Macmillan, 1988.

Braun, Edward, *The Director and the Stage, From Naturalism to Grotowski*, London, Methuen, 1982.

Braunschweig, Stéphane, *Petites portes, grands paysages*, Arles, Actes Sud, 2007.

Brecht. Bertolt, *Ecrits sur le théâtre*, Paris, Gallimard, 2000.

————, *Poems 1913–1956*, trans. Willet *et al.*, 1979.

Brewińska, Maria (ed.), *Bill Viola*, Warsaw, Zachęta Narodowa Galeria Sztuki, 2007.

Caddy, Ian, www.baroquegestures.com

Callery, Dymphna, *Through the Body*, London, Nick Hern, 2001.

Calvino, Italo, *Why Read the Classics*, London: Penguin Classics, 2009.

Causey, Matthew, *Theatre and Performance: From Simulation to Embeddedness*, London, Routledge, 2006.

Chambers, Colin (ed.), *The Continuum Companion to Twentieth Century Theatre*, London, Continuum, 2002.

Chekhov, Michael, *To the Actor*, London, Routledge, 2002.

Christoffersen, Erik Exe, *The Actor's Way*, London, Routledge, 1993.

Collective, *La Représentation*, Paris, Editions de l'Amandier, 2004.

Copeau, Jacques, *Appels. Registres I*, Paris, Gallimard, 1974.

————, *Notes sur le métier d'acteur*, Paris, Michel Brient, 1955.

Corvin, Michel, *Dictionnaire encyclopédique du théâtre*, Paris, Bordas, 2008.

Courtine, Jean-Jacques (ed.), *Histoires du corps: Les mutations du regard*, vol. 3, Paris, Editions du Seuil, 2006.

Craig, Edward Gordon, *On the Art of the Theatre*, London: Theatre Arts Books/ Heinemann, 1956.

Csikszentmihalyi, Mihaly, *Vivre: La psychologie du bonheur*, Paris, Robert Laffont, 2004.

Danan, Joseph, *Le Théâtre de la pensée*, Rouen, Editions Médianes, 1985.

Debray, Régis, *Sur le pont d'Avignon*, Paris, Flammarion, 2005.

——, *Introduction à la médiologie*, Paris, Presses Universitaires de France, 2000.

Deleuze, Gilles and Guattari, Félix, *What is Philosophy?* New York, Columbia University Press, 1994.

Derrida, Jacques, *Rogues: Two Essays on Reason*, Stanford, Calif., Stanford University Press, 2005.

——, *Sur parole: Instantanés philosophiques*, Paris, Editions de l'Aube, 1999.

——, *Points ...: Interviews 1974–1994*, trans. Elisabeth Weber, Stanford, Calif., Stanford University Press, 1995.

——, *The Archeology of the Frivolous: Reading Condillac*, trans. John P. Leavey, Lincoln, Neb., University of Nebraska Press, 1987.

——, *Writing and Difference*, trans. Alan Bass, London, Routledge, 1978.

—— and Roudinesco, Elisabeth, *For What Tomorrow ...: A Dialogue*, trans. Jeff Fort, Stanford, Calif., Stanford University Press, 2004.

Descola, Philippe, *Par-delà nature et culture*, Paris, Gallimard, 2005.

Donnellan, Declan, *The Actor and the Target*, London, Nick Hern, 2005.

Dort, Bernard, *La Représentation émancipée*, Arles, Actes Sud, 1988.

——, 'Le texte et la scène : pour une nouvelle alliance', *Encyclopædia universalis*, Symposium, 1984.

Dort, Bernard, *Théâtre réel*, Paris, Seuil, 1971.

Douglas, Mary, *Natural Symbols*, London, Routledge, 1996.

Dupuis, Sylviane, *A qui sert le théâtre?* Geneva, Ed. Zoé, 1998.

Essif, Les, *The French Play: Exploring Theatre 'Re-creatively' with Foreign Students*, Calgary, Canada, University of Calgary Press, 2006.

Ewing, William A. (ed.), *The Century of the Body*, London: Thames and Hudson, 2000.

Fabre, Jan, *L'histoire des larmes*, Paris: L'Arche, 2005.

Féral, Josette (ed.), *Mise en scène et jeu de l'acteur. Entretiens*, Morlanweltz, Éditions Lansman, 1997–8 (2 vols).

Féral, Josette, *Théâtralité, écriture et mise en scène*, Montreal, Hurtubise, 1985.

Ferenzi, Thomas and Meyer-Plantureux, Chantal, *Un siècle de critique dramatique. De Fransisque Sarcey à Bertrand Poirot-Delpech*, Paris, Editions Complèxe, 2003.

Fischer-Lichte, Erika, *Asthetik des Performativen*, Frankfurt am Main, Suhrkamp, 2004.

——, Kolesch, Doris and Weiler Christel (eds), *Transformationen: Theater der Neunziger Jahre*, Theater der Zeit, 1999.

Foucault, Michel, *The Order of Things*, London, Routledge, 2002.

Früchtl, Joseph and Zimmermann, Jörg (eds), *Mises en scène du monde: Colloque international de Rennes*, Besançon, Les Solitaires intempestifs, 2005.

——, Jörg, *Asthetik der Inszenierung*, Frankfurt, Suhrkamp, 2001.

Giannachi, Gabriella and Luckhurst, Mary (eds), *On Directing: Interviews with Directors*, London, Faber & Faber, 1999.

Gómez-Peña, Guillermo, *Dangerous Border Crossers*, London, Routledge, 2000.

Green, Eugène, La parole baroque: Essai, Paris, Desclée de Brower, 2001.

Hargreaves, Alec G. and McKinney, Mark (eds), *Post-Colonial Cultures in France*, London, Routledge, 1997.

Hastrup, Kirsten, *A Passage to Anthropology*, London, Routledge, 1995.

Hayles, N. Katherine, *How We Became Posthuman: Virtual Bodies in Cybernetics, Literature, and Informatics*, Chicago, Ill., University of Chicago Press, 1999.

Heymann, Pierre-Etienne, *Regards sur les mutations du théâtre public (1968– 1998)*, Paris, L'Harmattan, 2000.

Hiss, Guido, *Synthetische Visionen. Theater als Gesamtkunstwerk von 1800 bis 2000*, Munich, Epodium Verlag, 2005.

Hodge, Alison (ed.), *Twentieth Century Actor Training*, London, Routledge, 2000.

Irvin, Polly, *Directing for the Stage*, Mies, RotoVision Stagecraft, 2003.

Jeanneteau, Daniel, 'Quelques notes sur le vide', www.remue.net, 2000.

Jomaron, Jacqueline de (ed.), *Le Théâtre en France*, Paris, Armand Colin, 1992.

Kane, Sarah, *4.48 Psychosis*, in *Complete Plays*, London, Methuen, 2001.

Kennedy, Dennis (ed.), *Foreign Shakespeare*, Cambridge, Cambridge University Press.

——, *The Oxford Encyclopedia of Theatre and Performance*, Oxford University Press, 2003.

Koltès, Bernard-Marie, *In the Solitude of Cotton Fields*, trans. Jeffrey Wainwright, London, Methuen, 2001.

——, *Combat de nègre et de chiens*, Paris, Ed. de Minuit, 1983.

——, *Black Battles with Dogs*, trans. David Bradby and Maria M. Delgado, Methuen, 1997.

Lallias, Jean-Claude (ed.) *L'ère de la mise en scène, Théâtre d'aujourd'hui*, no. 10, Paris, Centre National de Documentation Pédagogique, 2005.

Lanteri, Jean-Marc, *Ecritures contemporaines 5: Dramaturgies britanniques (1980–2000)*, Paris, Minard, 2002.

Lavender, Andy, *Hamlet in Pieces: Shakespeare reworked by Peter Brook, Robert Lepage, Robert Wilson*, London, Nick Hern, 2001.

Lecoq, Jacques, *Theatre of Gesture and Movement*, trans. Joel Anderson, David Bradby, Luke Kernaghan and Dick McCaw, London, Routledge, 2006.

Lehmann, Hans-Thies, *Postdramatic Theatre*, trans. Karen-Jürs Munby, London, Routledge, 2006.

Liard, Michel, *Parole écrite, parole scénique*, foreword by Patrice Pavis, Nantes, Ed. Joca Seria, 2006.

Makaeïeff, Macha, *Inventaire d'un spectacle*, Arles, Actes Sud, 2000.

Mallarmé, Stéphane, *Oeuvres Complètes*, ed. Henri Mondor and Georges Jean-Aubry, Paris, Gallimard, 1945.

Martin, Roxane, *La Féerie romantique sur les scènes parisiennes (1791–1864)*, Paris Honoré Champion, 2007.

Marzano, Michela (ed.), *Dictionnaire du corps*, Paris, Presses Universitaires de France, 2007.

McBurney, Simon, *Mnemonic*, London, Methuen, 2000.

McKenzie, Jon, *Perform or Else: From Discipline to Performance*, London, Routledge, 2001.

McLuhan, Marshall, *The Gutenberg Galaxy*, London, Routledge, 1962.

Merleau-Ponty, Maurice, *Phenomenology of Perception*, trans. Colin Smith, Routledge, London, 2002.

Mervaut-Roux, Marie-Madelein, *L'Assise du théâtre*, Paris, CNRS, 1998.

——, *Figurations du spectateur: Une réflexion par l'image sur le théâtre et sur sa théorie*, Paris, L'Harmattan, 2006.

Meyer-Plantureux, Chantal, *Un siècle de critique dramatique*, Paris, Complexe, 2003.

Michaud, Yves, *L'Art à l'état gazeux. Essai sur le triomphe de esthétique*, Paris, Stock, 2003.

Mondzain, Marie-José, *Le commerce des regards*, Paris: Ed. du Seuil, 2003.

——, *L'Assemblée théâtrale*, Paris, Éditions de l'Amandier, 2002.

Moninger, Markus, *Shakespeare inszeniert*, Tübingen, Niemeyer, 1996.

Müller, Heiner, *Gesammelte Irrtümer*, Frankfurt, Verlag der Autoren, 1986.

——, *Rotwelch*, Berlin, Merve, 1982.

NDiaye, Marie, *Papa doit manger*, Paris, Editions du Minuit, 2003.

Nietzsche, Friedrich, *The Birth of Tragedy*, trans. Ronald Speirs, Cambridge, Cambridge University Press, 1999.

Pavis, Patrice, *Vers une théorie de la pratique théâtrale*, Lille, Septentrion, 2007.

——, *Analyzing Performance: Theater, Dance and Film*, Ann Arbor, Mich., University of Michigan Press, 2003.

——, *Le Théâtre contemporain. Analyse des textes de Sarraute à Vinaver*, Paris, Armand Colin, 2002.

—— (ed.), *The Intercultural Performance Reader*, London, Routledge, 1996.

——, *Marivaux à l'épreuve de la scène*, Paris, Publications de la Sorbonne, 1986.

Phelan, Peggy, *Unmarked: The Politics of Performance*, London: Routledge, 1993.

Picon-Vallin, Béatrice (ed.), *Les écrans sur la scène*, Lausanne, L'Age d'homme, 1998.

Polieri, Jacques, *Scenography and Technology*, Paris: Bibliothèque Nationale de France, 2004.

Pradier, Jean-Marie, *La Scène et la fabrique des corps: Ethnoscénologie du spectacle vivant en Occident (v e siècle av. J.-C. – xviii e siècle)*, Bordeaux, Presses universitaires de Bordeaux, 1997.

Proust, Sophie, *La Direction d'acteurs dans la mise en scène théâtrale contemporaine*, Montpelier, L'Entretemps, 2006.

Rapin, Cathy and Hye-Gyông, Im, *Théâtre coréen d'hier et d'aujourd'hui*, Paris, Les Editions de l'Amandier, 2006.

Reinelt, Janelle and Roach, Joseph (eds), *Critical Theory and Performance*, Ann Arbor, Mich., University of Michigan Press, 1992.

Renaude, Noëlle, *A tous ceux qui*, Paris, Editions théâtrales, 1994.

Rivière, Jean-Loup, *Comment est la nuit? Essai sur l'amour du théâtre*, Paris, L'Arche, 2002.

Sabbattini, Nicola, *Pratique pour fabriquer scènes et machines de théâtre*, Neuchâtel, Ides et Calendes, 1942.

Schneider, Rebecca, *The Explicit Body in Performance*, London, Routledge, 1997.

Shepherd, Simon and Wallis, Mick, *Drama/Theatre/Performance*, London, Routledge, 2004.

Shevtsova, Maria and Mitter, Shomit (eds), *Fifty Key Theatre Directors*, London and New York, Routledge, 2005.

Spiess, Françoise (ed.), *'Mettre en scène le théâtre contemporain', Trois pièces contemporaines*, Paris, Gallimard, 2002.

States, Bert O., *Great Reckonings in Little Rooms: On the Phenomenology of Theatre*, Berkeley, Calif., University of California Press, 1985.

Szondi, Peter, *Theory of the Modern Drama*, Cambridge, Polity Press, 1987.

Tackels, Bruno, *Fragment d'un théâtre amoureux*, Besançon, Les Solitaires Intempestifs, 2001.

Trungpa, Chôgyam, *Mandala: Un chaos ordonné*, Paris, Ed. du Seuil, 1994.

Ubersfeld, Anne, *Reading Theatre*, Toronto, Canada, University of Toronto Press, 1999.

Vilar, Jean, *De la tradition théâtrale*, Paris, L'Arche, 1955.

Vinaver, Michel, *Le Compte-rendu d'Avignon*, Arles, Actes Sud, 1987.

——, *Théâtre Complet*, vol. 1, Actes Sud et L'Aire, 1986.

Vitez, Antoine, *Ecrits sur le théâtre*, vol 3, Paris, POL, 1996.

——, *Écrits sur le théâtre*, Paris, POL, vol. 2, 1995.

Wadenfels, Bernhard, *Phänomenologie der Aufmerksamkeit*, Stuttgart: Suhrkamp, 2004.

Williams, Raymond, *Towards 2000*, London, Chatto & Windus, 1983.

Wulf, Christian, *Penser les pratiques sociales comme rituel: Ethnologie et genèse de communautés*, Paris; L'Harmattan.

Zola, Emile, *Oeuvres Complètes*, Paris, Cercle du livre précieux, 1968.

Key texts

Banu, Georges, *Les Cités du théâtre d'art de Stanislavski à Strehler*, Paris, Éditions théâtrales, 2000.

Biet, Christian and Triau, Christophe, *Qu'est-ce que le théâtre?* Paris, Gallimard, 2006.

Bradby, David and Delgado, Maria M. (eds), *The Paris Jigsaw*, Manchester, Manchester University Press, 2002.

Bradby, David and Sparks, Annie, *Mise en scène: French Theatre Now*, London, Methuen, 1997.

Bradby, David, with Poincheval Annabel, *Le Théâtre en France de 1968 à 2000*, Paris, Honoré Champion, 2007.

Carlson, Marvin, *Performance. A Critical Introduction*, London and New York, Routledge, 2004.

Christie, Judie, Gough, Richard and Watt, David (eds), *A Performance Cosmology*, London and New York, Routledge, 2006.

Colloque International de Rennes (collective), *Mises en scène du monde*, Besançon, Les Solitaires intempestifs, 2005.

Corvin, Michel (ed.), *Dictionnaire encyclopédique du théâtre*, Paris, Bordas, 2008.

Debray, Régis, *Sur le pont d'Avignon*, Paris, Flammarion, 2005.

Delgado, Maria M. and Heritage, Paul (eds), *In Contact with the Gods? Directors Talk Theatre*, Manchester University Press, 1996.

—— and Svich, Caridad (eds), *Theatre in Crisis? Performance Manifestos for a New Century*, Manchester, Manchester University Press, 2002.

Évrard Franck, *Le Théâtre français du xxe siècle*, Paris, Ellipses, 1995.

Féral, Josette (ed.), *Mise en scène et jeu de l'acteur. Entretiens*, Morlanweltz, Éd. Jeu – Éd. Lansman, 1997–8 (2 vols).

Früchtl, Joseph and Zimmermann, Jörg (eds), *Ästhetik der Inszenierung*, Frankfurt am Main, Suhrkamp, 2001.

Helbo, André, *Le Théâtre: texte ou spectacle vivant?* Paris, Klincksiek, 2007.

Heymann, Pierre-Étienne, *Regards sur les mutations du théâtre public (1968–1998)*, Paris, L'Harmattan, 2000.

Irvin, Polly, *Directing for the Stage*, Mies, RotoVision Stagecraft, 2003.

Lallias, Jean-Claude (ed.), *Théâtre aujourd'hui*, no. 10, Centre national de documentation pédagogique, 2005.

Lehmann, Hans-Thies, *Postdramatic Theatre*, trans. Karen-Jürs Munby, London, Routledge, 2006.

Lista, Giovanni, *La Scène moderne. Encyclopédie mondiale des arts du spectacle dans la seconde moitié du xxe siècle*, Arles, Actes Sud, 1997.

Mitter, Shomit and Shevtsova, Mariaeds (eds), *Fifty Key Theatre Directors*, London, Routledge, 2005.

Outre Scène, no. 5, 'Dialogue avec les classiques', May 2005; no. 6, 'Pourquoi êtes-vous metteur en scène?', May 2005; no. 9, 'Metteuses en scène, le théâtre a-t-il un genre?', May 2007.

Pavis, Patrice, *Analyzing Performance*, Ann Arbor, Mich., University of Michigan Press, 2003.

——, *Dictionary of the Theatre: Terms, Concepts and Analysis*, trans. Shantz, Christine, Toronto, Canada, Toronto University Press, 2002.

——, *Vers une théorie de la pratique théâtrale*, Lille, Presses universitaires du Septentrion, 2007.

Proust, Sophie, *La Direction d'acteurs dans la mise en scène théâtrale contemporaine*, Paris, L'Entretemps, 2006.

Registres, no. 6, 'La Formation du metteur en scène,' 2001.

Rivière, Jean-Loup, *Comment est la nuit? Essai sur l'amour du théâtre*, Paris, L'Arche, 2002.

Saison Maryvonne, *Les Théâtres du réel. Pratiques de la représentation dans le théâtre contemporain*, Paris, L'Harmattan, 1998.

Svich, Caridad (ed.), *Trans-Global Readings*, Manchester, Manchester University Press, 2003.

Tackels, Bruno, *Fragments d'un théâtre amoureux,* Besançon, Les Solitaires intempestifs, 2001.

Thomasseau, Jean-Marie (ed.), *Le Théâtre au plus près,* Saint-Denis, Presses universitaires de Vincennes, 2005.

Key journals

Alternatives théâtrales
Études théâtrales
Performance Research
Théâtre/Public
Theatre Forum
Contemporary Theatre Review

Other journals cited

Actualité de la scénographie
L'Art du théâtre
Culture Coréenne
Degrés
Du Théâtre
Europe
Forum Modernes Theater
Frictions
International Journal of Psychoanalysis
La Jeune Belgique
Journal des Trois Théâtres
Kodikas/Code
Les Lettres françaises
Littérature
Littératures classiques
Mouvement
Nouvelle Revue critique
Opus
Outre scène
Performing Arts Journal
Pratiques
Revue d'art dramatique
Revue d'esthétique
La Revue de Paris
La Terrasse
Théâtre aujourd'hui
Theater heute
Theater der Welt
Théâtre

Théâtre en Europe
Théâtre populaire
Travail Théâtral

Name Index

Note: page references in *italics* indicate illustrations

Subject Index